NGOs
and Governance
in the Arab World

NGOs
and Governance
in the Arab World

Edited by

Sarah Ben Néfissa
Nabil Abd al-Fattah
Sari Hanafi
Carlos Milani

The American University in Cairo Press
Cairo   New York

This book is the result of a conference organized in Cairo in March 2000
by the Management of Social Transformation (MOST) program of
UNESCO, the Institut de Recherche pour le Développement (IRD),
the Centre Etudes et de Documentation Economiques, Juridiques et
Sociales (CEDEJ), and the Al Ahram Center for Political and Strategic Studies.

Copyright © 2005 by
The American University in Cairo Press
113 Sharia Kasr el Aini, Cairo, Egypt
420 Fifth Avenue, New York, NY 10018
www.aucpress.com

All rights reserved. No part of this publication may be reproduced, stored in a retrieval
system, or transmitted in any form or by any means, electronic, mechanical, photocopying,
recording, or otherwise, without the prior written permission of the publisher.

Dar el Kutub No. 17416/04
ISBN 977 424 904 6

Designed by AUC Press Design Center
Printed in Egypt

Contents

About the Contributors — vii

List of Abbreviations — viii

Introduction
NGOs and Governance in the Arab World: A Question
of Democracy — 1
Sarah Ben Néfissa

Part I. Globalization and Governance: Situating Arab NGOs

1. Non-Governmental Organizations in Global Governance — 19
   Carlos Milani

2. Insiders and Outsiders: NGOs in International Relations — 39
   Pierre-Jean Roca

3. Civil Versus Political Culture in NGOs — 55
   Muhammad Al-Sayyid Sa'id

4. Promoting Democracy and Governance in the Arab World:
   Strategic Choices for Donors — 69
   Guilain Denoeux

Part II. NGOs of the Arab World: Between the Democracy Question and the Social Question

5. From Inertia to Movement: A Study of the Conflict over the
   NGO Law in Egypt — 101
   Viviane Fouad, Nadia Ref'at, and Samir Murcos

6. Hegemony and Counter-hegemony in Egypt: Advocacy NGOs,
   Civil Society, and the State — 123
   Nicola Pratt

7. Islamic NGOs and the Development of Democracy in Egypt — 151
   Abd al-Ghaffar Shukr

8. NGOs and the Reform of the Egyptian Health System:
   Realistic Prospects for Governance or Pipe Dream — 167
   Sylvia Chiffoleau

9.	New NGOs and Democratic Governance in Palestine: A Pioneering Model for the Arab World? *Dina Craissati*	181
10.	NGOs and Civil Society in Palestine: A Comparative Analysis of Four Organizations *Salma Aown Shawa*	209
11.	Agency and Ideology in Community Services: Islamic NGOs in a Southern Suburb of Beirut *Mona Fawaz*	229
12.	The Poverty Alleviation System and the Role of Associations in Yemen *Blandine Destremeau*	257
13.	NGOs in a Country Without a Government: Islamic Movements and Aspirations to Replace the State in War-torn Somalia *Marc-Antoine Pérouse de Montclos*	291
14.	Civil Associations, Social Movements, and Political Participation in Lebanon in the 1990s *Karam Karam*	311
15.	Donors, International NGOs, and Palestine NGOs: Funding Issues and Globalized Elite Formation *Sari Hanafi*	337
16.	Conclusion Arab NGOs: Advocacy and the 'Globalized' Debate on Democracy in the Arab World *Nabil Abd al-Fattah and Sarah Ben Néfissa*	361
	Bibliography	367

About the Contributors

Nabil Abd al-Fattah Lawyer and co-director of the al-Ahram Center for Political and Strategic Studies, Cairo.
Sarah Ben Néfissa Researcher at the Institut de Recherche pour le Développement (IRD), Cairo; affiliated with the Centre d'Etudes et de Documentation Economiques, Juridiques et Sociales (CEDEJ), Cairo.
Sylvia Chiffoleau Researcher at the Centre National de la Recherche Scientifique (CNRS), Paris, and the French Institute of the Near East, Syria.
Dina Craissati Project manager at the Canadian International Development Research Center (IDRC), Cairo.
Guilain Denoeux Professor of political science at Colby College, Waterville, Maine.
Blandine Destremeau Researcher at the Centre National de la Recherche Scientifique (CNRS) and the Institut du Développement Economique et Social (IEDES), Paris.
Mona Fawaz PhD, Massachusetts Institute of Technology, Cambridge, Massachusetts.
Viviane Fouad, **Nadia Refʿat**, **Samir Murcos** Researchers at the Center for Study and Consultation, al-Fustat, Cairo.
Sari Hanafi Sociologist and director of the Palestinian Refugee and Diaspora Center, Ramallah.
Karam Karam PhD, Institut d'Etudes Politiques, Aix en Provence; researcher at the Centre d'Etudes et de Recherches sur le Moyen-Orient Contemporain (CERMOC), Beirut.
Carlos Milani Political scientist and socioeconomist at the Federal University of Bahia, Brazil.
Marc Antoine Pérouse de Montclos Researcher at the Institut de Recherche pour le Développement (IRD), Paris.
Nicola Pratt PhD in political science, University of Exeter.
Pierre-Jean Roca Director of the Institut de Formation et d'Appui aux Initiatives de Développement (IFAID), Bordeaux
Muhammad Al-Sayyid Saʿid Deputy director of the al-Ahram Center for Strategic and Political Studies, Cairo.
Salma Aown Shawa PhD, London of School of Economics.
Abd al-Ghaffar Shukr Researcher at the Center for Arab Studies, Cairo.

List of Abbreviations

AF	Agri Friends
AIDA	Association of International Development Agencies
AIDS	Aquired Immune Deficiency Syndrome
AMR	Approach to the Mobilization of Resources
ANERA	American Near East Refugee Agency
AWSA	Arab Women's Solidarity Association
BTUTP	Bureau Technique d'Urbanisme et des Travaux Publics
CAPMAS	Central Agency for Public Mobilization and Statistics
CDA	Community Development Associations
CIHRS	Cairo Institute for Human Rights Studies
DDM	Data for Decision Making
DFLP	Democratic Front for the Liberation of Palestine
DIS	Democratic Institutions Support
DoP	Declaration of Principles
EC	European Commission
ECHO	European Commission for Humanitarian Operations
EOHR	Egyptian Organization for Human Rights
EPI	Expanded Program on Immunization
ERSAP	Economic Reform and Structural Adjustment Program
ESCWA	Economic and Social Commission for West Asia
FAO	Food and Agricultural Organization
HDIP	Health Development Information and Policy Institute
HF	Health Friends
HSC	Health Services Council
ICPD	International Conference on Population and Development
IDA	International Documentary Associations
IFLO	Islamic Front for the Liberation of Oromia
IGOS	Inter-Governmental Organizations
ILO	International Labour Organization
INGOs	International Non-Governmental Organizations
INTRAC	International NGO Training and Research Centre
GDP	Gross Domestic Product
GFETU	General Federation of Egyptian Trade Unions
GNP	Gross National Product
GOT	Government of Tunisia
GOVs	Governmental Organizations
GPC	General People's Congress
HIV	Human Immunodeficiency Virus
LADE	Lebanese Association for Democratic Elections
LDC	Least Developed Countries
LDNGOs	Least Developed NGOs
LTDH	Tunisian League of Human Rights
MCF	Mother and Child Friends
MOHP	Egyptian Ministry of Health and Population
MoPD	Ministry of Planning and Development
NAPPE	National Action Plan for Poverty Eradication

List of Abbreviations

NCSSN	National Committee for Social Safety Nets
NDI	National Democratic Institute for International Affairs
NGO	Non-Governmental Organization
NPAEGP	National Poverty Alleviation and Employment Generation Program
NSM	New Social Movement
OECD	Organization of Economic Cooperation and Development
OLF	Oromo Liberation Front
OMDH	Moroccan Organization for Human Rights
ONLF	Ogaden National Liberation Front
OPEC	Organization of Petroleum Exporting Countries
PDRY	People's Democratic Republic of Yemen
PFLP	Popular Front for the Liberation of Palestine
PHR	Partnership for Health Reform
PIMS	Poverty Information Monitoring Systems
PLC	Palestinian Legislative Council
PLO	Palestine Liberation Organization
PNA	Palestinian National Authority
PNGO	Palestinian NGO Network
PPP	Palestinian People's Party
PRIP	Policy Research Institute Palestine
PVOs	Private Voluntary Organizations
RCM	Rally for Civil Marriage
RF	Rehab Friends
RME	Rally for the Municipal Elections
SAP	Structural Adjustment Program
SME	Small and Medium-sized Enterprise
SNM	Somali National Movement
SPO	Structure of Political Opportunity
SSDF	Somali Salvation Democratic Front
UGTT	Union Générale des Travailleurs Tunisien
UHCC	Union of Health Care Council
UHWC	Union of Health Worker's Council
UNCDF	United Nations Capital Development Fund
UNCED	United Nations Conference on Environment and Development
UNCHS/HABITAT	United Nations Human Settlements Programme
UNCTAD	United Nations Conference on Trade and Development
UNDP	United Nations Development Programme
UNESCO	United Nations Educational Social and Cultural Organization
UNICEF	United Nations Children's Fund
UNIDO	United Nations Industrial Development Organization
UNOPS	United Nations Office for Project Services
UNRWA	United Nations Relief and Works Agency
UPMRC	Union of Palestinian Medical Relief Council
USAID	United States Agency of International Development
USSR	Union of Soviet Socialist Republics
WFP	World Food Program
WHO	World Health Organization
WSLF	Western Somali Liberation Front
WTO	World Trade Organization
YAR	Yemeni Arab Republic
YSP	Yemeni Socialist Party

Introduction: NGOs and Governance in the Arab World: A Question of Democracy

Sarah Ben Néfissa

The relationship between non-governmental organizations (henceforth NGOs) and governance in the Arab world raises three substantial questions: Are Arab NGO's contributing to the democratization process? Consequently, do these NGOs create trial arenas for citizen participation and/or new alternative forums to promote and define the 'common welfare'?

Are Arab NGOs contributing to building and animating genuine civil societies? As such, they should be capable of standing as a 'counterweight' or a 'mediator' between transitional communities and the old, inflexible and authoritarian public authorities. The entrenched habits of governmental institutions stop them from responding and taking action to alleviate poverty and unemployment, enhance intellectual and political freedom, and protect the interests of different sectors.

Do Arab NGOs demonstrate superior capabilities and respect in terms of 'good governance' in comparison to the public authorities? Are the NGOs better equipped because of their flexibility, size, and transparency to tackle and undertake effective measures toward collective, local, and national problems—which remain undetected or are simply ignored by the public authorities? In other words, can we understand Arab NGOs per se as a model for good democratic, financial, and administrative governance?[1]

The introduction will be built and developed around these three questions, which will be further explored throughout the successive chapters. This book was collectively written after the conference 'NGOs and

Governance in the Arab Countries,' which took place in Cairo in March 2000 and was co-organized by UNESCO, the Al-Ahram Center for Political and Strategic Studies, and the Centre d'Etudes et de Documentation Economiques, Juridiques et Sociales (CEDEJ).

While the rich and varied content of the papers presented take them beyond the three fundamental questions tackled in the introduction. However, it is essential to dig into the core of the issue, which is as normative as it is scientific. It raises the question of whether Arab NGOs represent positive entities for their communities or whether their contribution to the development and democratization process has been overestimated.

Although the authors present divergent opinions on the matter, they all remain objective so as to prove that the ideological, scientific, and political efforts dedicated to these Arab NGOs over the last decade outweigh the NGOs' standards and capabilities. Does the 'para-administrative' nature of the majority of Arab NGOs entail that the Arab communities live without any inclusive participative dynamic? Or is it just a question of the NGOs' incapability of taking them into consideration, or furthermore, not acknowledging them?

What are the root causes of such a phenomenon? Within the globalization era and with the emergence of the 'new social question,' the countries of the North are currently facing a crisis with regards to their dominant democratic model. We can, therefore, wonder if the Arab countries are learning anything from this crisis and how it affects their democratization process.

Are new citizenship formats spawned by globalization, overriding the so-called 'classical' ones? Should the democratization process of the Arab world not start from the top down? Should we not start by democratizing the political system of the Arab countries in order to foster a genuine growth of their civil societies and a rehabilitation of the different forms of social and political participation?

An Objective Perspective on Arab NGOs:
Between Advocacy and Service

For the purpose of analysis, Arab NGOs can be divided between two poles. On one hand, the NGOs that seek to assist the communities and on the other hand, NGOs dedicated to social mobilization on different topics and that are working to modify the present social order by positioning themselves as venues for critics and propositions.

While this division is only an analytical one, as Guilain Denoeux demonstrates in his chapter, "Promoting Democracy and Governance in the Arab World: Strategic Choices for Donors," more and more NGOs can be divided in terms of these two axes. The service-oriented and charitable NGOs remain active and dynamic due to two factors: the reduction of the state redistribution capacities and the collapse of state instruments following severe crisis situations such as civil wars or liberation conflicts. These NGOs are pioneers in the field of social services and health care. They target and help either the pauperized urban middle classes, as in Egypt, or a whole population, in the case of Palestine. These organizations also face a rationalization and modernization of their financing and management systems. Despite their experience, their contribution to public and social policies remains minimal.

In Egypt for example, the participation of these NGOs in the global health reform project—launched by the Egyptian government and the World Bank—is barely existent. Moreover, they reproduce some of the errors committed by the public authorities instead of correcting them. For example, the concentration of health care services in urban areas, which sets the focus on curative rather than preventive trends, and the tendency to regroup specialists rather than general practitioners.

As Blandine Destremeau notes with respect to the relative power of these organizations in Yemen, the associations dedicated to poverty alleviation are highly financially dependent on international donors and remain constrained by the restrictive state political regime ("The Poverty Alleviation System and the Role of Associations in Yemen"). Consequently, these NGOs are merely sub-contractors and cannot coin their own visions as to how to approach and alleviate poverty. On the contrary, as demonstrated by Dina Craissati, Palestinian organizations working on similar issues are not as constrained and have more freedom ("New NGOs and Democratic Governance in Palestine: A Pioneering Model for the Arab World"). As a result, the characteristics of the action plans of the 'new social movements,' such as 'the politics of senses' and 'the politics of influence' can be found in the Palestinian organizations' action plans. This is how these organizations can offer alternative values and visions to health policies, which otherwise would remain hierarchical, centralized, and traditional. These new values advocate for new relationships between the practitioners, the nurses, the assistants, the patients and the communities being served.

However, this situation has been possible because of the absence of a state. The creation of the Palestinian Authority has modified this framework with an abusive interventionist policy. This is confirmed by Salma Aown Shawa's analysis on Palestine ("NGOs and Civil Society in Palestine: A Comparative Analysis of Four Organizations"). She highlights how the financial donors like the Palestinian Authority, have tried to depoliticize Palestinian NGOs and stop them from taking active action in the definition of 'public policies.' In his essay, Sari Hanafi tackles the relationship between donors and Palestinian NGOs. His studies verify the existence of an interaction between these two actors, as well as some measure of autonomy for the Palestianian NGOs with respect to donors' agendas.

The Arab NGOs with religious referencesæIslamic or Christianæare well known for being the leaders of the service-oriented NGOs in the world. The Islamic NGOs are more under the spotlight recently because of their connection to Islamist trends. The critique directed at these NGOs, with regards to the democratic question, can be broken down to the negative vision of Abd al-Ghaffar Shukr ("Islamic NGOs and the Development of Democracy in Egypt") and the positive one of Mona Fawaz ("Agency and Ideology in Community Services: Islamic NGOs in a Southern Suburb of Beirut"). Abd al-Ghaffar Shukr investigates more than twenty Egyptian, Islamic associations, and despite their social impact, he does not consider them to be valid venues for democratic experiments because they have very few members. Moreover, he notes, their democratic qualities can be called into question based on the fact that they count more on their paid staff than their volunteers, the decision-making power is within the hands of one or two people, and finally, the members clearly state that women should only take care of their households.

On the contrary, Mona Fawaz argues that the associations from South Lebanon related with Hizballah have developed action and intervention plans, which enable them to get closer to the targeted communities. These plans include: decentralized and flexible management within the organization, easy access to the populations, and an emphasis on volunteering, building trust, and maintaining cooperative relationships.

Nicola Pratt's chapter is the product of nearly twenty interviews with Egyptian advocacy organizations ("Hegemony and Counter-hegemony in Egypt: Advocacy NGOs, Civil Society, and the State"). As a result, she asserts that these organizations support an anti-hegemonic trend, quite different from the current official Egyptian political discourse. With regards to these

Introduction

practices, three Egyptian researchers, Viviane Fouad, Nadia Ref'at, and Samir Murcos, present their analysis of some Egyptian organizations that mobilized themselves in order to protest against the bill on associations proposed by the public authorities ("From Inertia to Movement: A Study of the Conflict over the NGO Law in Egypt"). They explain how Egyptian NGOs have passed from refusing any dialogue to a cooperative attitude toward public institutions. This shift started in the mid-nineties. The NGOs acted as lobbies, talking to the Ministry of Social Affairs, newspapers, and deputies of the People's Assembly with sensibilization campaigns regarding the problem about the law. They then switched from these campaigns to other more more tenacious ones (such as holding demonstrations). Even though the bill was passed, the NGOs pursued the case and started legal actions before the Constitutional High Court. The NGOs won and the bill was overruled (see 'Chronique politique égyptienne, 2002,' *Etudes et Documents du CEDEJ*, no. 8/9).

Karam Karam also stresses upon this similar action mode in his chapter on how Lebanon saw new forms of associations emerging in the mid-nineties ("Civil Associations, Social Movements, and Political Participation in Lebanon in the 1990s"). They started focusing on the neglected problems of the past and formed their action plans, taking into consideration the effects of globalization, such as the role of financial donor organizations. These NGOs stand out due to their internal management, which includes more horizontal than vertical relationships, smaller budgets, more volunteers than paid staff, members whose average age ranges from twenty to forty, and creation of a sense of community among the members. Finally, these organizations work on a project-to-project basis. These NGOs have proved their mobilization capacity and the power of their intervention in the public sphere. As a result of their actions, the date for the local elections, which were supposed to be delayed, was maintained as a result the committee created by the NGOs called the 'Gathering,' which also enabled the authorization of civil marriage as a possible alternative to religious marriages.

The conclusion, with regards to the influence of Arab NGOs on the democratization issue, seems quite mixed or at least unsatisfactory in comparison to the magical virtues the political and intellectual elites have believed civil societies to be made of over the last thirty years.[2] Such a conclusion comes with a positive note, reminding us all that civil societies, and in particular NGOs, cannot carry out the democratization process of the whole political and social system on their own. This was not the reason behind their initial creation. Even in the 'dominant' model of civil society—the western model—where civil society can exert pressure on the authorities by mobilizing the interested parties and opinions, the passage to democracy still entails a political society: it requires political parties, elections, and a political leadership.

Naturally western donors, especially the United States, have not omitted such a reality while trying to promote democracy in the Arab world. Guilain Denoeux emphasizes this reality in his chapter and argues that it echoes the conclusion of international donors with regards to the democratization process in the Arab region—that an exclusive focus on civil society is not the best solution and that the NGOs may promote unrealistic aspirations ("Promoting Democracy and Governance in the Arab World: Strategic Choices for Donors"). Denoeux claims that the existence of a strong and well-established civil society sector does not necessarily generate democracy. Moreover, in the Arab countries where some progress toward democracy has been observed, the process was initiated by the government and not as a result of pressure from civil society. Consequently, he asserts that it would be preferable to support the democratic reform of state institutions.

A second observation comes forward from this analysis of Arab NGOs. It highlights the difficulty in fostering and creating a democratic civil society within a social, family, educational, and religious system characterized by hierarchical and authoritarian values. This is one of the pessimistic observations and remarks made by Muhammad Al-Sayyid Saʻid with regards the connection between civil society and politics in the Arab world ("Civil Versus Political Culture in NGOs"). One of the four major structural defects of Arab civil societies is the lack of a political culture to foster peaceful conflict resolution. This defect generates numerous internal conflicts within the organizations themselves. As a result, they stall and become paralyzed, which consequently makes it easier for the state to exert influence while using these internal divisions to their advantage.

Some people argue that civil society involvement cannot exist in developing countries in general, because of the dominant social and political relationships within the Arab world and the existing infringements on private, social, and political freedoms. In these societies, they insist, the state is so present and powerful that no civil society could emerge genuinely and autonomously.

These arguments can be regarded as essentialist and extremist; furthermore it is difficult to believe in them since for quite some time political experts have been working on the social and political realities of developing countries and have proved that the vision of a state that totally absorbs society is wrong and unconvincing. This is simply because of the dynamics that characterize the global South and the states in developing countries.³ Applying René Otayek's analysis of African political realities to the Arab world, we see that on the one hand these societies have shown their ability for self-organization and for setting aside the state. On the other, the state itself is weak, as it lacks the ideological, political, administrative, and coercive resources to maintain and impose its hegemony.⁴ It is thus possible to acknowledge the existence of Arab civil societies, even if they lack the characteristics of a model civil society.

The 'Para-administrative' Nature of Most NGOs

'Civil society' is the self-organizational capacity of different social groups defending common interests. They organize themselves in order to protect and defend these interests before the public authorities or other groups promoting different ideas. Consequently, civil society is composed of numerous organizations, including NGOs and associations. In Europe for instance, trade unions were the first civil society organizations created. The difference between western organizations and Arab ones lies within the criteria of 'self-organization.' Most of the Arab NGOs are more or less linked to the states and their administrations. Luckily there are always exceptions to the rules, which, in this case, are the advocacy organizations. The latter have succeeded in reaching some of their substantial goals despite their lack of a social base. They have managed to keep the issue of human rights alive as a persistent debate on the political agenda, for example. However, these organizations cannot make up for the fact that the predominant nature of the Arab civil organizations remains linked to the state.

Researchers and observers cannot let themselves be fooled by the extreme visibility of these advocacy organizations if they want to fully understand the problems faced by the other, more dominant type of organizations. The advocacy organizations are the most studied and the most internationally active. They are easier to access and more noticeable. Moreover, they share the dominant discourse of the international community. Even the research papers presented in this book could not avoid the trap of paying these kinds of organizations a relatively great deal of attention.

Unfortunately, small neighborhood organizations specializing in social care and urban management and rural associations providing professional training are rarely covered in the following chapters. The reasons for this absence are many. First of all, these small organizations are difficult to access. Secondly, they are most of the time working in between the administrative organs of the state and are usually run by retired public officials, lawyers, or elected representatives—all of whom are affiliated with the party in power. The Moroccan NGOs dedicated to urban management are the typical example of such infrastructure. They are located in the poor or informal urban areas and are directed by the local elite: civil servants, military officers, and real estate agents. They are in charge of warning the people of possible demolitions ordered by the administration and are responsible for obtaining certain essential urban equipment (e.g., access to sanitation water). These are the characteristics of most Arab organizations (including trade unions, social clubs, and other organizations) and NGOs, which do not have an advocacy mission.

Occasionally some of these organizations become more autonomous and even start to have conflictual relationships with the public authorities; here, they are either supported by important social movements that represent the interests of numerous different social classes or they are run by influential political forces, such as the Islamists.[5] The networks of these Arab associations represent the biggest number and the most important associations in terms of social efficiency. They are 'satellites' of the state system both at the local and at the national level. They are the interface between the local population and the state administration. They are the mediators between the people's demands and the administration's offers. Consequently they are able to retain influence, despite the fact that their demands are atomized, personalized, and of a 'clientele' style. Contrary to these former organizations, advocacy organizations lack this social proximity. However, their efficiency is from another level.

The non-advocacy Arab NGOs perfectly know where their autonomy ends. Their relationship with the government can be described as a 'clientele' relationship, one which is much sought-after and has to be carefully maintained. In general, these NGOs rarely criticize the influence of the state or of the administration, as the latter are a valuable source of information and financial resources.

Advocacy NGOs, however, are run by middle class indivuals who can cultivate international relationships and raise funds from international donors. In reality, these organizations have no choice but to rely on external funding.[6] On one hand, the government distrusts them because of their activities and on the other hand, the people, mainly concerned for their material survival, have little faith in these NGOs. Moreover, the international funding only feeds the suspicions of both the government and people influenced by nationalist or Islamist ideologies. These advocacy NGOs have to face the difficulties of being both "inside and outside," as described by Pierre-Jean Roca. He considers that NGOs' references in developing countries are foremost constraints that their members also confront at the national and intra-national levels. Carlos Milani claims that NGOs at a transnational level acquire the right to act in the international public arena by producing new social demands and new requests to regulate the international system.

On the contrary, the other types of NGOs have to pass by the state and administrative infrastructures in order to access resources. It is clear that in certain countries (e.g., Tunisia, Egypt), it is state agents who run these organizations. Although some of these organizations have succeeded in gaining more autonomy, they still look to the state for support for a variety of reasons. The Egyptian regional leagues and the Moroccan urban planning associations are typical examples of this phenomenon. The Egyptian leagues regroup all the citizens from the same region or same village who resettled in the large cities of Cairo or Alexandria. These leagues represent one of the main categories of associations in Egypt. The aim of such organizations is to provide a minimal amount of basic support to its members; funerals, for example, are one of its main services. They are funded by members and by the community leaders—generally important traders or businessmen seeking people's votes. The example of the Moroccan urban organization highlights the fact that the real estate agents are ultimately protecting their own interests and the value of their informal properties by avoiding their possible destruction.

The service-oriented NGOs, which provide services to everyone in their environment and not only to their members, sometimes find ways to self-finance themselves by offering paid services. This was the case of the Egyptian Islamist Medical NGOs, which price their services according to the public and private sector tariffs. Moreover, in Egypt, for instance, NGOs manage to attract funds from both the private sector and the Gulf countries. However, this situation mainly applies to the Islamist NGOs, which have at their disposition large networks of businessmen affiliated with the Gulf region, and receive support from international Islamist associations scattered across the globe (Bellion 2004).

However, in general, as the private sector is closely linked to the state apparatus, the NGOs have difficulties in self-financing. The private sector of these countries only offers financial support to the organizations that are in favor with the established regimes and the clearly socially efficient NGOs. The transition to a more liberal economy favored the emergence of new businessmen, who now form the base of a new political and social contract in the Arab world. They therefore represent civil society as Muhammad Al-Sayyid Sa'id emphasizes in his paper, "Civil Versus Political Culture in NGOs." The public authorities support these associations and close their eyes to instances of fraud. In return, these organizations help the state administration tackle social problems and finance charities. They also sometimes help in the building of schools and infrastructure. This is how many candidates to the Egyptian parliament are simultaneously businessmen and directors of, or contributors to, NGOs.

These latest developments demonstrate how Arab NGOs, in general, are affiliated with both the communities and the public authorities. However, besides their close relationship with the local and national public authorities, their nature can be best described in terms of being 'para-public'—that is, under state influence—rather than being a genuine part of 'civil society.' They can either be seen to represent additional tools for public intervention, or privileged forums for mediation between the social and state orders. They can be compared to a channel of communication between the administration and society, an area where social and political recognition emerge and serves as an electoral base.

Despite this administrative reality of NGOs, Arab societies are neither under the influence of the state. On the contrary, they have shown an exceptional sense for survival and self-organization within a dire context informed by poverty, unemployment, misery, civil wars, and liberation. The realities of the Lebanese and the Palestinian civil societies confirm this statement. It is not surprising that the researchers, who questioned the link between the new social movements and the civil society sector, only had collapsing state institutions—or collapsed states themselves—as field study material. It is, in particular, the authoritarian tone of Arab public authorities, which prevents the institutionalized development of social movements. Even this is only in cases where these social movements actually exist, as the public authorities, it seems, would rather let them express themselves sporadically, and keep them atomized, disorganized, and in a state of anarchy. This is exactly what happened during the major social crises of the eighties and nineties in Egypt: hunger strikes, the mutiny of security forces, railway workers' strikes, and peasant movements protesting the real estate bill allowing landlords to change the leases.

As the different social classes are not allowed to organize themselves as autonomous associations, the leading elite are unable to detect social problems in advance. With the constant abortion of all organized advocacy movements, the other forms of social movements remained only at an informal level. For instance, the frameworks to provide social solidarity, alleviate poverty, curb violence and maintain a sense of social unity, can only be approached within an informal context—that of the family, the ethnic or religious community, and the public places in villages. Indeed, despite the social discrepancies, the highest protection is guaranteed among these entities. Muhammad Al-Sayyid Sa'id can therefore assert that the main allegiance of the people in this region is to the community. It is within these groups that the Arab individual becomes a volunteer. However, it must be emphasized that this faithfulness has nothing to do with simply appreciation or a sense of selflessness. On the contrary, it is a rational attitude based on reciprocity.[7]

These numerous groups, which are far from being monolithic or static, have the tendency to attach themselves to the Arab administrative NGOs or to the service-oriented ones. These latter, whether they are religious or not, are appealing as they offer services and resources such as information, materials, and contacts to influential people. These NGOs have a strong relationship with their social environment. They also have at their disposition large networks of contacts—a common characteristic among leaders and association directors. Such organizations also encourage different forms of social participation such as conflict resolution and fund raising for the building of roads, bridges, other forms of infrastructure, mosques, and schools.

This is the most original but contradictory characteristic of most Arab NGOs and associations. Thus, what are called 'grass roots' organizations in the West, are, in the Arab world, in direct contact with public authorities and the central administration at every level—even the most local. It is within this framework that we should raise the question of democratization and the impact of the NGOs on such a process.

The Necessary Democratization of the Arab Countries

In order to solve problems within these societies, the first and immediate solution appears to be the reform of the state infrastructure. All these problems cannot be solved by NGOs alone. On the contrary, certain issues such as economic under-development, the lack of essential infrastructure, and the organization of justice and public security all require the reinforcement of the state. The state should be capable of having a 'macro' understanding of these problems as well as 'macro' solutions. This does not only apply to Arab countries and the developing world, but also to the North.[8] Moreover, as Arab NGOs cannot resolve these problems on their own, they certainly cannot build democracy by themselves. This is one of the main conclusions of the political experts who worked on civil societies in the developing countries. A tangible and efficient civil society can only exist if a tangible and efficient state exists. Otherwise, the state will not let its civil society bloom and flourish.[9] From this point of view, the study carried out by Marc-Antoine Pérouse de Montclos on war-torn Somalia, is significant—lacking a state, the Islamist movement tries to replace the state.

Before talking any further about the need to democratize the political system first followed by the lower classes of Arab societies, it is necessary to first tackle the question of what 'democratization' entails. There are three fundamental aspects to this logic, which, in a way, reverse the articulations of the conference in Cairo.

The first reason is linked to the perverse effect of the Arab civil societies on the democratization process, which started in the seventies. Arab civil societies shadowed this process instead of pushing it forward using different approaches. First, they became, willingly or not, a tool of the state's administration; second, they offered the ideal source for the regrouping of political officials—without passing through democratic procedures.[10] Finally, they replaced the different institutions that were supposed to represent the people. For instance, as representatives of local and national assemblies, they took over collapsing political parties accelerated their fall.

This does not relate to advocacy NGOs alone. Indeed, the typical Arab NGO—the para-administrative organization—the main focus of this introduction, is also affected by this phenomenon. Beyond the advocacy NGOs' capacity to make up for the central bureaucratic deficits by attracting foreign funds (helped in no small part by their label as an NGO), they also play a political role by enlarging the areas politically controlled by the ruling parties. Charitable organizations, for their part, provide services to the population which positively affect the people as they help to slow down the disintegration process of all the state's social responsibilities.

All these phenomena affect the democratization process of Arab societies. The citizens should have the right to demand greater transparency from their leaders; they should be able to freely vote for their political representatives and to be witness to a democratic rotation of the ruling elite. Instead, the slow rotation of the ruling elite keeps aging leaders in power. Moreover, as the generation of the seventies did not fulfill any role within the political arena, the ruling elite oriented themselves toward civil society organizations, leaving the countries with poor political role models.

While in Europe, the democratic election rituals attached to the state institutions have become insufficient,[11] the Arab systems, on the other hand can be compared to nineteenth-century Europe during the beginning of the universal ballot.[12] This is just a necessity. It will be wrong to think that Arab citizens are not ready for democracy or to vote freely for their leaders and representatives. The combined effect of education, urbanization, cultural accessibility, and development of the means of communication have transformed Arab society. Consequently, it is possible to assert that the public authorities have not kept pace with their societies on the path toward modernization.

The second reason to democratize is linked to the implications of the 'top down' democratization process affecting Arab societies. Civil society today, seems to just correspond to Arab NGOs, and while these NGOs might make up for what is called the 'official' civil society of the Arab world, they are a far cry from the real demands of civil society. These Arab NGOs have managed to obtain the administrative authorization to exist and function. It is not surprising that in most Arab countries, the laws related to associations and NGOs carries substantial political weight and is the reason for the mobilization of advocacy NGOs. It is an essential issue to consider; what type of organizations and what kind of occupation and activities would the Arab citizens freely chose? The first measure would be to alleviate the state's and the administration's influence on the civil sector by switching the process of 'authorization' to a matter of mere 'declaration'[13] in order for NGOs and associations to exist. This reform would enable the state to exercise control following and not prior to the creation of such organizations. The control, nevertheless, remains necessary to avoid problems and mismanagement.

Judicial reform could spread a positive image of civil society within the Arab populace, instead of the current biased picture they have, which is further tainted by the administrative selecting process, i.e., the state authorization for an NGO to exist. However, such a reform process could have further substantial implications, which explains why the Arab states remain reluctant to minimize their control over the civil sector. Indeed, such a twist could minimize or totally break the 'clientele' relationship between the public authorities and NGOs. This reform would therefore help Arab civil society to explore its diversity and not rely only on the state administration. This would be a crucial step as it would question the nature of the Arab 'para-administrative' NGO, open it up to grass roots participation and develop it to its full potential. Once they are capable of interacting with their social environment, Arab NGOs and associations will be revealed as alternatives and experimental venues for the definition and promotion of the common welfare. This relationship between the NGOs and the social sectors, could also correct the defects of their internal systems, such as their democratic deficit. The gap between the advocacy NGOs and the service-oriented ones could also be reduced by such reform. Despite the administrative pressures, a new generation of NGOs is emerging nowadays. They are a mix of the two other models: service and advocacy organizations.

The NGOs fighting for womens rights are one example of this new category. They use certain services such as judicial services to protect the lives of certain categories of women. These NGOs adapt their speeches and practices to the social realities they come across and are, therefore, fostering certain forms of 'citizen mobilization.' This has been made possible because of the forms of actions that NGOs are taking and the connections they establish with different social categories of society.

We can also refer to another type of generation of NGOs which are animated by Islamist movements. They are also closely linked to different social sectors, which have enabled these NGOs to be innovative in terms of 'citizen practices.'[14]

European countries are seeking to experience and rehabilitate the diverse forms of what 'citizenship' can entail and no longer restrict it to a mere political activity—voting rights. Consequently, we can wonder why we in the Arab world cannot approach the different forms of pre-existing grass roots social and political participation in the Arab and developing countries with a positive perspective.[15]

Certain researchers,[16] who have worked on the democratization process in Latin America and certain countries in Africa, point toward this conclusion. These research papers demonstrate how these phenomena, hastily called 'clientele' relationships or 'communitarianism' are not necessarily in opposition to democratic principles and 'political modernity.' The conclusions based on field analysis and close scrutiny of these phenomena, highlight how they can be vectors for political and social democratization and create internal processes for a democratic transition. However, these case studies only concern countries where the state institutions have opened the path to democracy and proposed a genuine political choice. The articles composing this book are grouped into two parts. The first part is titled "Globalization and Governance: Situating Arab NGOs." It tackles the common problems faced by Arab NGOs internally and externally. The second part is called "NGOs of the Arab World: Between the Democracy Question and the Social Question." This part gathers articles which are case studies on specific countries such as Egypt, Palestine, Lebanon, Yemen, and Somalia.

Notes

1. For a critical analysis on the term 'governance,' see our own text: "NGOs, Governance and Development in the Arab World: Discussion Papers," Management of Social Transformations (MOST–UNESCO), 2000, (46): 1–32. This text constituted the preliminary work for the conference, which is the topic of this introduction.
2. The term 'civil society' entered in the vernacular in the Arab world in the eighties. The political and intellectual elites embraced the concept with eagerness almost immediately. For political leaders, the existence of civil society organizations favors a certain international recognition on the democratic level (without running any risk of authorizing political organizations, such as political parties, which directly affect their power. It also releases some built-up tensions within the opposing groups. The service-oriented organizations release the state from certain social demands, which it cannot fulfill. For the political opponents, investing in the civil organizations enables them to assume certain political roles, which would normally be impossible using the traditional political career road.
3. Read on this matter: René Otayek, *Identity and Democracy in a Global World*. (Paris, Sciences Po Press, 2000).
4. Ibid.
5. This is the case for certain trade unions as the General Union of Tunisian Workers, which opposed the regime of Bourguiba in the 1970s, or the Egyptian al-Jam'iya al-Shar'iya, which proves this statement. The Muslim Brotherhood succeeded in conquering this powerful charitable organization and in obtaining the autonomy from the Egyptian government by gaining support from the local chiefs and important personalities. In reality these movements have a short life span because they are quickly repressed by the Arab public authorities. This is what happened to the Union Générale des Travailleurs Tunisiens (UGTT) in Tunisia in the 1970s, the human right league in Tunisia in the 1990s, the Islamist-controlled trade unions in Egypt in the 1980s and 1990s, and to the al-Jam'iya al-Shar'iya around the same period.
6. A typical example of this phenomenon was presented during the debate on the law on associations in Egypt. At that time when Egypt was supposed to host the World Conference on Population and Development, the advocacy NGOs exerted pressure on the Egyptian regime. It had previously questioned and changed certain clauses

of this law, which authorized civil servants to take part in the administrative meetings of the associations under their control. These organizations, for a matter of fact, need these civil servants for their contacts, and information regarding the resources they control.

7. See Sarah Ben Néfissa, "Asabiats and Elections: Are the Egyptians Democrats?" in J.N. Ferrié and J-C Sanctucci, ed., *The Democratization Process in Northern Africa*. (Paris: CNRS-editions, 2005).
8. Robert Castel, *The Transformation of the Social Question*, Paris: Folio-essais, Gallimard, 1999.
9. Otayek René, *Identity and Democracy in a Global World*.
10. The most striking example of this phenomenon is what happened in Tunisia after the political turnover on November 7, 1987. Most of the Tunisian executives of the civil society organizations of the 1970s and 1980s were nominated to influential political positions within the new political regime.
11. Pierre Rosenvallon, *The Unfinished Democracy: History of the People's Sovereignty in France*. (Paris Gallimard, 2000).
12. Sarah Ben Néfissa, "Processo de Democratizaçao no Egito, Eleiçoes legislativas de 2000 e relaçoes de força entre as diferentes tendências," in C. Milani, C. Arturi, and G. Solanis, eds., *Democracia e Governança Mundial. Que regulaçoes para o século XXI?* MOST–UNESCO, Editora da Universidade, Universidade Federal Do Rio Grande Sul, Porte Alegre, Brazil.
13. This entails that the initiators of an organization would only have to declare to the public authorities their creation, their official address, their activities, and their funding resources. Jérôme Bellion Jourdan, "Réseaux transnationaux de l'aide humanitaire islamique: les ONGs islamiques," in *ONG et gouvernance dans le monde arabe*. (Paris: Karthala et CEDEJ, 2004), 113–42.
14. Sarah Ben Néfissa, *Citizenship and Participation in Egypt: The Virtuous Action According to al-Jam'iya al-Shar'iya*, Maghreb-Machrek, 2000, m(167): 14–24.
15. Pierre Rosanvallon asserts that in the West, people are discontented with their form of democracy as they have witnessed a decline in the role of the state due to the effects of globalization. He is talking about 'the ordinary age of politics' and of 'a social need for a plural and especially close citizen participation' (social, economic, etc.). Pierre Rosenvallon, *The Unfinished Democracy: History of the People's Sovereignty in France*. (Paris: Gallimard, 2000), 401, 422.
16. Read on this matter the book edited by Jean-Louis Briquet and Frédéric Sawicki: *The Clientele Political System in Contemporary Societies* (Paris: Presse Universitaire de France, 1998).

Part One

Globalization and Governance: Situating Arab NGOs

Chapter One

Non-Governmental Organizations in Global Governance

Carlos Milani [1]

Academic works and other documents of a political nature produced by intergovernmental organizations on global governance often contain analytic and normative dimensions concerning the shape of the world systems and how it should be redesigned. In another article, we analyzed how the debate regarding global governance has been integrated in the programs of international agencies, with the aim of serving precise yet frequently unexpressed strategic objectives.[2] It is true that the advocates of corporate governance, as well as the first World Bank publications on the so-called good governance, never wanted to make of it a concept of the social sciences. Inspired from the literature on 'transnational companies' management'[3] and often paired with adjectives such as 'good' or 'democratic,' 'governance' as a strategic notion is, to some people, a complementary element to corporate world regulation. The reference to the fundamental questions on management and on citizen participation—without necessarily mentioning the direct role of the state—made 'governance' a relevant tool for world economic and financial experts.[4] As a result, the fundamental political dimension of governance (and of social relations) has been erased from the international debate.

Nevertheless, despite a potential mystification and the risks of manipulation related to the utilization of a recipe for 'good governance'—mainly prepared for less developed countries—the debate may yield critical interrogations as it leads back to analysis of the evolution of democracy in the different local contexts. This debate also engenders the reconsideration of the relation of power within a non-traditional political approach, where the non-governmental actors also play a role alongside the state.[5] From an empirical point of view, one must admit that contemporary societies (and the international system) are more complex than they used to be, as they are composed of more autonomous sub-systems, within which the roles of the actors are diversified. Societies are going through a crisis of their democratic models, particularly in terms of the representing chorus, the participation and the legitimacy of the actors. Despite the fact that the debate on governance is taking place within a context marked by the globalization process, and the difficulty caused by the ideological and historical origin of the term, it has the merit of re-opening discussions on public space (at the local and global levels). The rationality of procedures within this space—in terms of the definition of rules for international negotiations on the effect of international protectionism, for instance—is as important as the content itself, which could include the definition of the economic fields requiring protection from international competitiveness in the developed and developing countries.[6] The demands for 'another' global governance that were expressed during the First World Social Forum held in Porto Alegre, Brazil, in January 2001 (and its subsequent editions since then), reflect the emergence of new forms of citizens' allegiances and the need to integrate them within the difficult equation of democracy at the world level.[7]

From this context and at the transnational level, this chapter will develop the hypothesis that the non-state actors and NGOs in particular have acquired an international 'citizen personality,' which enables them to coin new social demands and make new calls for the regulation of the world system. These social demands, which mobilize the public opinion along with the political relationships between NGOs and other actors of the system (states, large companies, as well as other non-state actors such as trade unions and professional associations), have a direct impact on global governance and on the new attempts to build international institutions. What sort of institutional transformations, in terms of organizing the world system, can ensue from the rapid rise of these organizations? What will be the sort of cultural and socio-geographical variations of the NGO 'phenomenon'? Where do these new political relationships between NGOs and other non-state actors stand as the latter gains importance in the debate on global governance? This chapter does not claim to have definite answers to all these questions, and will probably raise more queries than provide answers.

From Economic Globalization to the Demands for 'Global Governance'

The present context within which the debate on governance is taking place is closely linked to globalization and its impact on the renewal of models for development on the national scale. Globalization, the latest form/avatar of economic colonization, marks a break in world regulation. It is not only confined to trade, but also includes a political and ideological dimension since the ideology of the "globalizers" present it as being a total, uniform, and homogenous phenomenon. Finally, its impact is unequal from the geographical and temporal point of view (Milani 2001).

Nevertheless, the processes of globalization radically change the traditional role of the non-state actors present on the world scene. The quantitative and qualitative increase of economic, cultural, commercial, and demographic fluxes leads to increasing the importance of the action of those new actors—particularly NGOs, multinational companies, different solidarity networks, criminal networks, and mafias. In other words, as they move from the level of associations to that of international NGOs, all the actors become more autonomous and more capable of defining and implementing strategies to circumvent the states and the intergovernmental organizations.

The present social, economic, and political transformations are, however, more profound. It is not only the appearance of new actors and the influence of the global economy on national economies. There are at least three changes that make the present stage of globalization different from the previous ones: the transformation of the political structure of the borders (considering borders as a space for regulation; the borders as the terra incognita which can take the shape of a market, of civil society, of a legislative body or an information highway); the change in the structures of the global economy; and the evolution of the time frame within which these changes are taking place. As James Roseneau said, the immediate events, the timely tendencies and the 'epochal' of Braudel (daily life, decades, centuries) correspond today to days/weeks, months/years and decades; to better understand the term "epochal" one should avoid being absorbed by the transient (Roseneau 1997).

This real "shift in the world and in time," to quote Michel Beaud, could be the result of an ever increasing substantial interposition between the reproduction of capitalism and the reproductions of humanity and the earth. Capitalism may no longer be enclosed within the two dimensions of its early days: the national and international dimensions; it is increasingly becoming multinational and global (Beaud 1997). At the economic, social, and political levels, the games of today are mainly set up with reference to the international. As Bertrand Badie pointed out, the present debate has to do mainly with the nature of the world in which we live; consequently, we are reaching the end of the analyses based exclusively on the dichotomy of national versus international.[8]

Obviously, it is not a linear, unidirectional process. Globalization reinforces this dynamic of fluxes and transnational actors. It is also fed by the transnational strategies of large firms, of major world NGOs, of networks linked to drug trafficking, and others. This system is more complex than it seems, because it is relying on intensive interactions among global players and the weakening behavior of traditional actors (mainly of a governmental and an intergovernmental nature). In fact, since the early eighties and particularly since the end of the cold war, globalization processes are provoking drastic changes in the concepts underlying the functioning of the international system, such as principles of territorial integrity and national sovereignty.

Types of Governance: The Origins of the Debate

In 1937, Ronald Coase published a short article titled "The Nature of the Firm" that did not give rise to important debates for almost thirty years.[9] In the 1970s, Olivier Williamson contributed to his rediscovery: institutional economy became a full-fledged branch of economics.[10] According to the analysis of Coase and Williamson, 'governance' refers to the means applied, in a given firm, to ensure efficient coordination in two areas: the internal protocols when the firm develops its networks and reshuffles its internal hierarchies; and the contracts and the application of norms when the firm opens up to sub-contractors. There is thereafter a replacement of the vertically integrated hierarchal firms that function within the limits of the national economies; they are being replaced by global organizations in a network. The term 'governance' has been imported from the world of enterprises. It used to describe coordination protocols, which were different from the ones applied to the global markets. It is only later that the term was used to describe local powers (Lorrain 1998).

Later on, in 1975, the theme of the 'governability' of democracies was the subject of a report by the Trilateral Commission. The central hypothesis of the report—prepared by Crozier, Huntington, and Watanuki—focused on the problems of governability in Western Europe, Japan, and the United States, which were based on the fracture between the increase of social demands and the shortage of the state's resources (lack of financial and human resources, as well as poor management skills). Changes became necessary both within the institutions and in citizens' behaviors.[11] Since then, in the 1980s and 1990s, the political debate concerning the state focused on its shortcomings related to its ruling functions associated with regulation, welfare, and social development.

Starting from the deficiencies of the state, political theories have recognized the fact that non-state actors are increasingly acquiring a legitimacy in order to defend and promote public interest. The state no longer has the sole prerogative to define the 'public good.' It is also a question of defining the public arena within which democracy takes place; a public arena made up of a network of complex interests and interactions among actors and among levels of political interventions. To what extent can the approach of 'governance' be useful for understanding the complexity of those networks, as well as the nature of the ties between micro and macro, local and global, and political theory and practice?

Academic literature on 'governance' defines it, more or less, as a complex decision-making process—which surpasses the government. The aspects often stressed in the above literature on 'governance' (see the 'Visions of Governance' table) concern the legitimacy of a public arena in the making; the distribution of power between the governors and the governed; the process of negotiation among social actors (procedures and practices, the management of interactions and interdependencies leading, or not, to alternative systems of regulation; the networking and coordinating mechanisms); and the decentralization of authority and the functions related to the act of governing.

At the end of the eighties, the term 'governance' became part of the World Bank's language. The stakes were high for the neo-liberal economists of the Bank who, at that time, had clearly prevailed over their Keynesian counterparts. It was a matter of declaring the institutional incompetence of the developing states as responsible for the failures witnessed, almost everywhere, in the sectoral structural reforms—deemed indispensable for the generalized opening of the markets. The whole issue would be legitimized by the renewed objective of alleviating poverty (Osmont 1998). That is how the use of a supposedly new term may be explained in terms of the necessity of intervening in the area of politics but doing so by making it technical, as Structural Adjustment Programs (SAPs) remained a priority. The reasons for the failure of the SAPs would therefore, not be linked to the nature of the relations between the Bretton Woods agencies and the administrations of

Southern countries. The reasons, furthermore, are not seen to lie within the ways the liberalization of trade and finance were developed at the world level, but rather, are because of the 'bad governance' prevailing in the developing countries. In the actual practice of international cooperation, this means that the administrations of the countries of the South must reform themselves to better respond to the demands of the Structural Adjustment Programs. As a result, a series of national programs for the state's reform (national 'good governance' programs) were designed in Africa, Asia, and Latin America.[12] Such programs often go hand in hand with policies for decentralization and training in the techniques of 'New Public Management.'

The Visions of Governance
1) Governance as a minimal state: based on the need to reduce public deficits, this use of governance refers to a new form of public intervention and to the market's role in the production of public services;
2) Corporate governance: stems from management theories and stresses the need for efficiency and accountability in the management of public property
3) Governance as 'New Public Management' (N.P.M.) favors management and the new institutional mechanisms in economy by introducing management methods and incentive measures used in the private sector.
4) Good governance: originally used by the World Bank to refer to its loan policies; it is a norm, which expects efficiency of public services, the privatization of state enterprises, budgetary rigor, and administrative decentralization.
5) Governance as a socio-cybernetic system: governance may be considered "as a pattern of structure that emerges in a sociopolitical system as a common result or outcome of the interacting intervention efforts of all involved actors" (Jan Kooiman). The key words of this definition are 'complexity,' 'the dynamics of networks,' and 'the diversity of the actors.' Thus, the political world would be marked by joint strategies: joint-management, joint regulation as well as public-private partnerships. J.N. Roseneau suggests, for example, that government has to do with "activities backed by formal authority," while governance has to do with "activities backed by shared goals."
6) Governance as a grouping of organized networks, that is, managing networks that are self-organizing. Since the state is one of the actors (no

longer the exclusive one) that plays a role in the world system, integrated and horizontal networks (NGOs, professional and scientific networks, the media) have developed their policies and have shaped the environment of the system (Rhodes).

Adapted from Rhodes 1996

Our analysis falls within the sixth of the aforementioned visions. It better covers both the multiplicity of actors present in the efforts of establishing a global governance (or the different segments of global governance) and the concept of regulating. Regulation is, in fact, a concept born from the theory of systems and refers to a group of explicit and implicit rules, which guides the behavior of the actors present on the political stage and maintains a minimum of order and integration. Regulation seems relevant for understanding contemporary international relations since it is a set of rules, processes, and interventions that lead to stabilizing a given system or allowing the latter to adapt to circumstances while maintaining the main characteristics of the system thus regulated.

Moreover, this sixth vision of governance enables us, to take into account the history of the analysis of the world system from a sociopolitical angle. Sociology, based on the notion of regulation, has traditionally favored a destructive analysis of world system; this means that world disorder and global conflicts would be at the center of any sociological analysis of international relations: studies would firstly underline factors related to the world system disorganization. Secondly, analyses drew attention to the normative disorder. Public international law cannot be applied and respected everywhere in the same way. Consequently, the breaches committed by the different international protagonists are rarely scrutinized and are not always submitted to any established rules of conduct, because, in the final analysis, international law still lacks supranational efficiency.

Attention was also drawn to the absence of a pragmatic approach with regards the actors and their aims, playing a role on the world scene. In the field of international relations, for example, sociology tries to highlight that power is not the only aim or objective of the different actors and that other players are as important as the states as far as the logic of concerted regulation by the market is concerned.

A fourth element of this sociological critique is the refusal to embrace the strategic and geo-political approach, since the issues of the end of the twentieth century do not allow us to consider international relations solely from the perspective of realistic values based on strategy and power. Hence, the criticism directed against traditional categories such as sovereignty, security, or the nation-state, which no longer correspond to the paradigms that have reshaped the present world order. In short, traditionally, sociology studied international relations in order to criticize and question the premises of the realist and functionalist schools of thoughts based on a historical time-frame of the post-1945 years, one that is no longer concomitant with the reality of present-day international relations.

Looking at world public arena on the basis of governance shifts Latin and European political sciences toward a new theoretical matrix founded on Anglo-Saxon paradigms: the theoretical foundations of the governance approach are anchored in the management of complex social systems. They were formalized by the works of David Easton and Richard Rose, *Can Government Go Bankrupt,*[13] who applied to the concept of governance systematic notions taken from the 'hard sciences' (cybernetics, for example) and from political sciences.

The management of complex systems presupposes that the political subsystems and the decision-makers adopt their decisions in response to demands and to needs—and according to their stock of resources. But how can we avoid conflicts within the analysis of power relations on the pretext of a better management of collective affairs?

Another important element behind the emergence of such new analyses of 'governance,' one that joins the criticism of the field of international relations addressed by sociology, is a certain detachment from the intergovernmental approaches. The failures of intergovernmental organizations in providing solutions to the problems of the citizens have triggered other demands to participate in the political process via the non-governmental channel. Such an opening allows us to conceive hybrid governances and to circumvent a Manichean debate either based on the firms and the markets or on the reinforcement of the state and the renewal of intergovernmental organizations. This Manichean debate also tends to reduce the economic to the dimension of trade and the political to the level of the state, without conceiving the possibility of a pluralism of the modes of participation in political (the associative sector, for example) and economic life (an economy of solidarity and ecological responsibility).

To what extent can global governance be considered the result of a series of compromises between the two poles (economic and political) of world regulation? Where would the non-governmental actors stand in the arrangements that are being made? Are we on the way to setting up systems of governance of a mixed composition within which private operators (large firms of experts for example) would modify national budgetary rules to comply with international norms? Would these private operators use their influence within the national governments to do so whenever facing a liquidity crisis? Would this be a hybrid governance, within which the state would entrust ecological NGOs with the responsibility of ascertaining that production methods respect environmental standards?

NGOS as Agents of Civil Society

Civil society is a unique term that encompasses a series of explicit and implicit meanings wherein interact notions that are not far apart, such as democracy, citizenship, political liberalism, the state, sovereignty, and human rights. The sociopolitical stakes linked to the notion of civil society are essential today (such as: Who are the agents of civil society? What legitimacy do they have and how representative are they? Is civil society homogenous and similar in different social and geographical contexts?). It is particularly important in the Arab region since the latter was affected by the interference of religious dogma and since the crisis of political representation has restarted the debate between individualism, communitarianism, and universalism, all of which are ill-defined.[14]

The term civil society hides inequalities: for instance, the difficulties of the civil society representatives to access the world sphere, because lobbying, dissemination, and preparation of information, for example, are not cheap. The term also hides the resistance of some older organizations, which are worried about the arrival of these 'new partners.'

Moreover, the semantic configuration of the term civil society seems to be highly controversial, changing, and contradictory. Civil society stands on a subtle and fragile dialectic between individualism and collectivity, the interests of the clan and state rationality, community relations of affection, and economic or scientific rationality. From a political and anthropological point of view, civil society can include religious organizations, professional organizations, producers, unions from the industrial private sector, small and medium enterprises, and small farmers. It has better chances for growth in a market economy context (political liberalism), but also when the power of the state is effective.

The dichotomy of state/civil society does not necessarily appear in the form of a zero-sum game; the result may be positive when the agents of civil society influence global policy for a better congruence between the policies adopted and the needs of certain sectors of society. In this context, those agents relieve the state of some of its responsibilities and may improve the administration or the implementation of the state's authority (Ghils 1995). A weak state can become stronger by allowing the development of a certain societal pluralism. Yet, from civil society's point of view, does this not risk it becoming a subcontracting agent that implements certain social policies?

This part of the chapter is confined to an analysis of a certain set of agents of civil society present on the world arena: non-governmental organizations. We claim, to begin with, that NGOs cannot be considered as the equivalent of world civil society. Often, NGOs want to maintain an exclusive representation of civil society; this entails a theoretical and empirical problem. Moreover, we differentiate NGOs considered 'vectors of globalization' from those that adapt themselves to globalization and finally from the ones that suffer from its effects (particularly grass roots organizations). Each one of them interacts with the others, thus it becomes essential to sort out these interactions, particularly through the alliances and conflicts they give rise to.[15]

There is one fundamental point here: in what form and within what structures can these associated actors play some sort of influential part in world governance? NGOs play a role on the international political system by circulating and exchanging information, by pressuring the political and bureaucratic institutions, and by supporting advocacy campaigns to raise public awareness. This was the case for instance with the NGOs' lobbying strategies to change the structures of the IMF, with "The Bretton Woods Project's"[16] campaigns, and with the 2000 Jubilee which became "Drop the Debt." Such functions carried out by NGOs have become even more important as technological globalization has given them access to new modes of political participation beyond the state's national borders.

In political theory, Nicholson proposes five models of social systems related to this subject (1994). The NGOs and associated actors' status could therefore be analyzed at the international level. First, there is the purely hierarchic type of system, within which a central authority interacts with all the other members of the social system. Second, a purely interactive type, within which every actor interacts with all the others—without any centralized control or any actor playing a leading part. Nicholson called the third model a "simple realistic," one marked by a bipolar and a satellite characteristic, with regards to all non-dominant actors. This system is similar to the international feudal system conceived by Johan Galtung[17] to represent the structures of the bipolar, Cold War system. The fourth type is the mixed realistic system, within which the relations between the dominant actors and their satellites are the same as in the simple realistic model, while relations among the dominant actors are purely interactive. It is both an interactive and dominant model. Finally, the last type of system is composed, on one hand, of the states, which remain the dominant actors and on the other by secondary actors such as intergovernmental organizations, NGOs, enterprises, and individuals. However, can the states control the infra-static currents developed by the actors under their jurisdiction and under their sovereignty? Are the dominant actors capable of any mediation in the interactions among the different entities?

In the fifth model described by Nicholson, transnational movements and companies, political and ethnic groupings, and individuals have more influence at the world level. Even though the states maintain their fundamental role in the area of security and control of the borders, transnational actors no longer have to necessarily obtain the authorization of state actors when they implement their strategies of solidarity and consultation.

This last model allows us to envisage at least two difficulties in the construction of 'world governance'—and the democratization process of this 'world governance' as well. First of all, it is just in this sort of interaction that "the paradox of participation" is to be found: the more that world society opens up to new members, the more difficult it becomes to anticipate, and consequently, to undertake an effective and just collective action. It is for that very same reason that the diversity of new actors reinforces the general uncertainty of the system and may lessen the importance of the influence of transnational actors.[18] Second, one may wonder whether NGO participation, particularly in the form of public demonstrations in the midst of the political decisions taken by international financial bodies, falls within the issue of the question of democracy or simply within a progressive contestation of the world system's modus operandi. For example, the attempts to foster a dialogue between the Davos Economic Forum and the Porto Alegre Social Forum, between the protests in Genoa, Quebec, and Nice and the financial bodies have failed so far. The dialogue is instead replaced by a logic of confrontation. The NGOs often consider the invitation of civil society representatives to large international meetings as an attempt to recuperate these people (Caramel 2001).

This model puts us before a central feature of the current global system: the emancipation of the individual and of the non-governmental networks is one of the most characteristic processes of contemporary international relations. In fact, community- and identity-based social relations have multiple loyalties and hamper state monopoly on legitimate violence and on the exclusive promotion of public good and national interest. In other words, as the monopoly on security services has been challenged, the state has lost a great part of its legitimacy. At least five reasons can be set forward for this development:

a) The traditional institutional and governmental means of regulation are being set aside (the crisis of intergovernmentalism and multilateralism being an example of this);
b) It has become difficult to only think in terms of national interests;
c) The number of dispossessed people[19] is gradually increasing;
d) The exclusive concept of state territoriality has been achieved (firms do not define their strategic plans in accordance to frontiers, but to their own interest);
e) The notion of 'common good' currently means a whole series of new goods and needs, which still remain inaccessible to the exclusive protection of public authorities (global water systems, climate change, biodiversity protection).

The emancipation under discussion here directly depends on the degree of the individual's awareness of his/her rights and duties; this varies according to the degree of education, information, training, and sense of civic duty of the population in different contexts. The seriousness of the problems that affect the daily life of local communities is also an important factor. In fact, the 'enlightened' middle classes play an important role, as social conflicts are no longer mainly confined to the purely economic demands of the workers as was the case during the early times of industrialization. These demands now extend to aspirations such as a better quality of life, a more adequate way of living, or a democratic system. In the early days of the industrial era, material conditions caused political dissatisfaction which prevailed among low-income groups. Today, it is among the more privileged groups that we find the sources of dissatisfaction and political protest regarding environmental protection. These social groups are more easily mobilized for a more direct participation in the decision-making process. They no longer manifest themselves as much on the traditional occasions of political life (mainly elections), but rather in the daily political process in order to influence the decisions that have a bearing on their lifestyle, their work, their leisure, their culture, and also on the foundations of economy.

Today, this degree of awareness corresponds to a higher level of education, which could lead to a wider distribution within the population of the capable desiring elite to have a direct impact on specific matters. Is this 'individual awareness' really genuine in the Middle East and North African (MENA) context? Can this emancipation be the springboard for a new type of associative movements? It goes along the ideological exhaustion of traditional parties and the necessity to assume that the same constraints manage the market economy and respond to the demands for a democratic political system. Moreover, how does one consider the personal status (family, ethnic, religious, tribal, professional, and confidential), particularly in the North African region and countries of the mashriq, where it defines the role and solidarity networks of the citizens (Mohamedou 1998)?

NGOs and Regulations of the Political System

In what way does the rise of NGOs change the possible regulations of the political system? Roughly speaking, we can point out three types of associative movements, while admitting their increasing heterogeneity: local associations, organizations and associations of producers of consumer goods, and national to international NGOs (who can carry out their activities in coordination with local NGOs).[20] Generally speaking, these associations have three kinds of objectives: performing basic services (to begin with, they cover emergency needs, but it becomes a continuing action in favor of development projects); organizing the community (for example, identifying local problems and their possible solutions); and lobbying and advocacy in support of the policies of governments and international organizations, or pushing for changes. Their legitimacy stems from the logic of propinquity to local communities and from their efficiency in providing social services. There is no rigid distinction between these forms of organization of civil society, as many groups can easily belong to one or the other category at the same time

Moreover, the NGOs' means of actions vary a lot. They can be informative campaigns (using fundamental research to denounce environmental degradation, for example), social demonstrations, normative actions (creation of norms and implementation of the regulations), and operational actions (project management and responsibility to implement social policies). They are all actions aimed at changing the behavior of the citizens, the public authorities, and the economic sectors. The communication aspect is basic to their strategy: Greenpeace and Amnesty International, for example, have already been qualified as communication multinationals. Consultation, advising, and elaborating on particular positions often take up most of their energy, and their expertise varies according to their chosen subject and method of organization.

The key question is whether the NGOs working for the micro-initiatives can represent a counterweight to the negative economic effects of the ongoing macro-programs? Some of the regional NGO are trying, nevertheless, to move on from providing services (a traditional step) to directly supporting self-development based on the decentralization of activities and on allowing for the local powers to take decisions.[21] These initiatives are increasingly grounded on endogenous principles for development. It entails tapping into the available local resources and mobilizing field players.

In the Middle Eastern countries in particular, we can wonder how the pressures from the bottom-up are genuine sources of social change (Bayat 2001). As an urban phenomenon, the NGOs and the Islamist associations faced an incredible development in the 1990s. This era coincides with the international financial donors' change of attitude, where they started considering these associations as partners in development projects.

First, in general, these grass roots local organizations start their institutional life without having a clearly defined legal structure. They are created with specific objectives (to fight for environmental problems typical of local communities, such as processing household waste water, cleaning up parks, improving access to drinking water, and so on), which does not stop them from receiving a wide range of claims from citizens or from other associations.

The collaboration between NGOs in the North and the local Southern ones, especially starting from the eighties, tended to evolve from a donor-beneficiary relation into a partnership based on common objectives. Donations from Northern NGOs (and from international financial lenders) continue to be vital to sustain the projects of the organizations of the North African Region and the mashriq. Some of those Northern organizations wield large budgets that constitute a source of basic financial resources for the NGOs in the South: the budgets of the U.S.-based National Wildlife Federation and of Nature Conservancy, for example, are of more than $100 million per year.[22]

In fact, most of the big NGOs of the Southern hemisphere are very dependent on those of the North. Seen from the South, such a 'partnership' is far from being considered the most egalitarian formula in the sharing of responsibilities. Obviously, a relation of partnership is more efficient when donor and beneficiary can share their point of view with regards to development duties and rights within the decision-making process. It appears that this relationship is rarely applied. The key question is to find out who defines the development priorities at the local level. The international financial lenders rarely guarantee long-term resources and the NGOs that emerge in the Arab world are often constrained by the administrative requirements imposed upon them. Yet, in practice, such conditions are not always respected. As in all relations of dependence, donor NGOs are often in a position to determine the basic conditions for the relationship to exist, and they can always restrict the freedom of the beneficiary organizations.

Over the last few years, governments themselves made use of Northern NGOs as channels to subsidize those of the South, which further complicated the existing relations. In 1993, according to UNDP data, the percentage of aid for development distributed through such channels to developing countries was of 19.4 percent of the total for Switzerland; 11.1 percent for the United States; 10.8 percent for Canada; 7 percent for the Netherlands; 6.6 percent for Belgium; 6.5 percent for Germany; 1.3 percent for the United Kingdom and 0.3 percent for France. Moreover, some of the NGOs in the North and in the South try to form groups so as to present a united front when facing the regional authorities and when addressing international organizations, particularly the United Nations.

However, with so many disparities, how can we create coalitions of NGOs coming from both the North and the South? How do we rethink new regulations for the world political system from the NGOs and associations' relationships? How do we pass from a confrontation (within the movements themselves, as well as externally with the financial and economic powers of globalization) to a more creative attitude?

Traditionally, the international scene was a stage for inter-state relations. In the present context, inter-state relationships are facing difficulties. The international institutions lack legitimacy; they are no longer the only ones to respond to the needs for transnational disputes resolution. That is why, in the early nineties, international and governmental organizations tried to appeal to civil society to take part in development programs and international conferences. Such a process may be considered as an attempt to democratize world governance. The problem lies within the 'why' and 'how' this calling for new participation is taking place. Does the democratization process not presuppose the democratization of the state itself first? It also raises the recurring question regarding the functioning mode of the international financial institutions such as the IMF and the World Bank (Smouts 1999). Is democratization no longer aiming at the peoples' right to emancipate themselves from their government in order to express their opinions, and demands with regards world affairs? How can we validate the democratic value system sustained by the NGOs at the world level? How are people represented in this framework?

Indeed, it is difficult to find both the framework and the relevant actors to establish the social compromises that are necessary for global regulation. Hence, the need to rethink 'governance' in terms of a democratically renewed public space. Bob Jessop[23] talks about the necessity to think of the regulation of 'world governance' as a pre-condition to its democratization. It would be a question of applying a 'meta-governance' to the different contexts, to the sectoral policies and to the scales of interventions.[24] It is true that the national framework is often inadequate by being either too wide or too narrow. The so-called "representatives of civil society" are sometimes self-appointed and therefore lack genuine legitimacy. NGOs can do remarkable work and they can set up the necessary mediations between the various levels of political action: local, national, international, and global. However, the links are still lacking and this prevents the dialogue among different actors from actually taking place (for example between NGO and trade unions).

To think over 'governance' critically is supposed to, at the least, assume that world regulation includes the full participation of non-state actors in the decision-making process. However, in the hypothesis of a social regulation of the world system, there would be, at least two wrong assumptions to avoid: first, that the intergovernmental world is fully regulated, determined, and well-organized; second, that only a necessarily explicit social rule would set up a global order. One should not demand of the hypothesis of the regulation (social) of the world order more than what one demands of the world inter-state organization. Is the world that is produced by international agreements, by the so-called intergovernmental order, entirely well-ordered and regulated? Are the conflicts produced within the international system always able to be settled of their own accord?

The above reservations introduce the wide variety of non-state actors presently participating in the efforts of consultation concerning the world issues (environment, drugs, and human rights, for example). Besides the variety, it is obvious that the notions of a world civil society and of a global public conscience are still embryonic and are used almost as metaphors. Nevertheless, they do constitute a crucial research track for our debates, that is, the transnational dimensions of relations and social transformations. In social science research, we are still using theoretical tools that date back to the nineteenth century and were relevant through the post-World War era: classes, the individual, the state, and development. These are all notions produced within a major entity, the nation—that is currently undergoing a crisis due to the transformations of the end of the twentieth century. The Brazilian political scientist Octavio Ianni affirmed in 1995 that we seem reluctant to admit that the object of social sciences has been quantitatively and qualitatively transformed.

Implicitly or explicitly, the debates still, quite often, revolve around the individual and society—which are analyzed within the relations, processes, and structures at the national level. The world (and global) dimensions of social reality still seem to offer an epistemological challenge to social sciences today.

Notes

1. Carlos Milani wrote this text when he was a program specialist within the Management of Social Transformations (MOST) Program at UNESCO (1995–2002). He is currently a professor and researcher in the Organizational Studies Department and the post-graduate program at the School of Administration of the Federal University of Bahia (Salvador, Brazil). He is the author of numerous articles and co-author of books about the various dimensions of globalization, market regulations, international democracy, and the World Social Forum, among them Democracia e governança mundial (UNESCO, 2002) and Expressions of International Contestation and Mechanisms of Democratic Control (ISSJ, 2004).
2. See Milani, 1999.
3. See, for example, the reports of the Chartered Institute of Public Finance and Accountability, including the one entitled "Corporate Governance," Englewood Cliffs, NJ: Prentice Hall: 6–7.
4. See the works of Guy Hermet (France). Hermet Guy. "Une crise de la théorie démocratique?" in C. Gobin, B. Rihoux, ed., La démocratie dans tous ses états. Systèmes politiques entre crise et renouveau. (Louvain-la-Neuve, Academia Bruylant, 2000), 139–49.
5. Admittedly, the term 'governance' is highly misused and its scientific use and critique can suffer from negative effects. However, we have not reached a point where a new terminology can be proposed. What appears as an essential task today is to work on the content (sociohistorically and contextually located) of the possible world governance frameworks.
6. See the various articles of Revue Internationale des Sciences Sociales 155 (1998), particularly the one by H. de Alcantra, "Du bon usage du concept de gouvernance," 109–18.

7. See C. de la Planète, "The powerful climb of World Civil Society" (a joint SOLA-GRAL/UNESCO/MOST Management of Social Transformations edition), 65, September 2001.
8. Statements recorded by Sandrine Tolotti, "When Globalization Makes the Difference," in an interview with Bertrand Badie and Jean F. Bayart, in Croissance 399 (December) 1996: 30–35.
9. R.H. Coase, "The Nature of the Firm, 1937," in O. Williamson and S. Winter S., eds., The Nature of the Firm. (New York: Oxford University Press, 1991), 18–33.
10. If we were to sum up the arguments of Coase and Williamson, transactions can be organized along two lines: the market or organizations (qualified by Williamson as being hierarchic). To be efficient, the market must respond to a condition of fragmentation, a fragmented form of organization. This complexity of exchanges is costly. Choices are governed by prices. The large, integrated firm imposes itself historically as a means of reducing the costs of transaction.
11. The era is characterized by the beginning of the crisis of the 'welfare state.' The theme of structural reforms of the relation between the state and the citizen was centered on the need for state machinery to withdraw from the economic scene. It is really important to ponder over the thematic choices of the Trilateral Commission, mainly at the start of its activities (it was created in 1973). See M. Crozier, S.P. Huntington, and J. Watanuki, The Crisis of Democracy, Report on the Governability of Democracies to the Trilateral Commission. (New York: New York University Press, 1975).
12. It is important to notice that the OECD countries are facing 'austerity policies' as well. However, it is curious to see that within the international cooperation, the projects to reform public administration impute to the state a renewed capacity for planning (national relationships, national programs, frameworks, etc.), while the plans themselves have been perceived as superficial and ineffective by the Bretton Woods agencies.
13. Can Government Go Bankrupt? with Guy Peters. (New York: Basic Books, 1978; London: Macmillan, 1979; Norwegian edition, 1979; Swedish edition, 1980).
14. It is interesting to highlight that in the Arab world several actors can use the normative Islamist system to reinforce their social legitimacy, whether they are religious nationalists, liberal modernists, radicals, or populists. Even so, they are creating new public spaces.
15. The grid of the proposed analysis includes the definition of the actor according to his/her activities in relation with his/her environment; but also according to the rhetoric adopted at the international level: that is how we consider the interests and options of the NGOs, by attempting to rapidly describe the principles that they regularly stand for. The research in only in process and this chapter is a preliminary phase to it.
16. The Bretton Woods Project works as a networker, information-provider, media informant, and watchdog to scrutinize and influence the World Bank and International Monetary Fund (IMF). Through briefings, reports and the bimonthly digest Bretton Woods Update, it monitors projects, policy reforms, and the overall management of the Bretton Woods institutions with special emphasis on environmental and social concerns (www.brettonwoodsproject.org/project/index.shtml). Drop the debt means erase the debts that developing countries owe

to international funding agencies and to developed countries. Jubilee 2000 (currently Jubilee Research) was a world-wide debt cancellation campaign, which provided up-to-date, accurate research, analyses, news and data on international debt and finance (http://www.jubilee2000uk.org/).
17. Johan Galtung, "Feudal systems, structural violence and the structural theory of revolutions," Proceedings of the IPRA Third Conference, Assen, Van Gorcum, 1971.
18. Such a situation may lead to frustration among the newcomers to the world society, as the latter thought they could have a larger degree of influence on international relations. The examples of the Gulf War and its ecological consequences, or disarmament and peace dividends have revealed the frustration felt by NGOs.
19. They refer to the term 'dispossessed' in the meaning as Bertrand Badie used and understood it, i.e., the abandonment of part of their citizenship.
20. National and international NGOs were created throughout the 1960s and 1970s, especially after the Stockholm Conference on the Human Environment (1972). Their origin is, however, very old and their roots can be traced back to the discovery of the Americas. After World War II, the first generation of the NGOs was created in Europe, mainly dedicated to the reconstruction of Europe, the construction of an Israeli State, and the partition of India.
21. Adapted from K. Verhagen, "Self-development, a challenge facing NGO." (Paris: L'Harmattan, U.C.I. Collection, 1991), 95.
22. The growing number of members of the "Nature Conservancy" shows the growth of ecological movements in the United States: in 1969, there were approximately eighteen thousand members and a staff of thirty; in 1992 there were six hundred thousand members and a staff of thirteen hundred. The data is taken from D. Snow, Inside the Environmental Movement: Meeting the Leadership Challenge. (Washington D.C.: Island Press, the Conservation Fund, 1992), 17.
23. Jessop, B., "The Rise of Governance and the Risks of Failure: The Case of Economic Development," International Social Science Journal, no. 155, 1998, 29–46.
24. Bob Jessop's article in The International Magazine of Social Sciences, 155.

Chapter Two

Insiders and Outsiders: NGOs in International Relations

Pierre-Jean Roca

NGOs are difficult to encompass as they already have a negative definition—non governmental—so to what do they belong? These peculiar institutions, the NGOs, will not be once again defined by the diversity of their functions, but will be part of an analysis by "levels of governance" especially in the international arena. However, they will not be confined to this area, because it is in the accumulation of levels that their intrinsic characteristics will appear.

I will first give a brief account of their increasing power, and then place them according to their relation with the power and decision-making centers in the world. Then, I will make a detailed analysis of their role and place in the international area. A new problematic issue emerges here: the paradoxes of how these NGOs gained their legitimization according to the geographical and/or cultural levels in which they were situated.

The Increasing Power of NGOs and Their Participation in Governance

It should be briefly pointed out that NGOs first emerged in the West, with the confluence of two trends. The first trend, the 'associationist,' developed itself along the pattern of a free grouping of individuals, who were defending either the common interests shared by the group members (as seen in syndicates or trade unions), or their common values, which were sometimes ethical but always collective. They wished to embody a particular pattern of behavior, for instance, the association of 'militants' in supporting the abolition of slavery. The second trend was the 'missionary' one. From the outset, this trend had an expansionist vision; whether it was a religious or secular mission, proselytism was the rule. The 'real' missionary wished to convert souls to his cause, whereas the 'developer' wished to rally the biggest number of men and women around the models of progress and success that were measured by western archetypes. It would be too simplistic to say that this 'gene' of penetration[1]—in the sense of the military strategy of penetrating enemy lines—leaves an indelible mark on the 'chromosomes map' of all NGOs and that nothing has changed since the 1950s. However, the conditions that led to the shaping of these particular social structures, known as NGOs, should not be hidden, especially if we wish to understand the consequences of such phenomenon on the international domain. To continue the metaphor we can say that the gene of proselytism has only receded, whereas its counterpart, building a 'bridge between cultures,' is today predominant and, as a result, more apparent in its impact. However, this does not mean that the former is no longer present.

We should point out that this activity, from the beginning, was marked by two characteristics: substitution of the functions generally assumed by public authorities (education, primary health care, and agricultural extension, for example) and amateurism, which was of course compensated by the undeniable convincing qualities of volunteerism and proximity. In the 1980s, conditions emerged that were to shape the present-day scene.

First, there was the great pressure of international organizations, on top of which you find the Bretton Woods institutions, which undervalued the state and praised the market. The notion of the 'state,' which used to represent 'controlled structures' has been condemned, bypassed, and at times, emptied of its substance. Moreover, the number of employees, especially in sub-Saharan Africa was greatly decreased. These professionals, formerly employed by the public departments for aid and cooperation, were thereafter free to be employed elsewhere.

Similarly, the professionalization of NGOs (especially those in the North) was encouraged by the growing unemployment rate (that puts competent specialists on the labor market), helping these NGOs to be taken seriously in the aid and cooperation fields.

The new division of the world (following the demise of the Soviet Union and fragmentation of the third world) and the crisis of the traditional regulating modes in the international sphere (the declining influence of United Nations institutions, for example) created new spaces between nation-states. Furthermore, there was a new type of conflict that was no longer managed by the usual figures—the diplomat and the soldier—on the inter-state scene. These were new frontiers that the NGOs were to set out and conquer.

All the conditions were, therefore, combined for the power of NGOs to reach its present state. It has four outstanding characteristics:

The NGOs have become lawful institutions and they are mushrooming. This abundance of NGOs leads to listing organizations of very different size, scope, modes of operation, objectives, and methods of funding under the same heading.

Furthermore, the evolution of the fields of intervention should be noted. In three decades we have moved from material achievements to institutional support, from collective community work to contractual action with great involvement in the real economy (for both the intervening parties and the beneficiaries), and from confinement to rural areas to global areas with a fresh consideration for the city.

Then, it should be emphasized that the trust placed in NGOs is not so much due to what they stand for or what they are, but due to what they allow people to avoid: it is a sweeping movement of the pendulum, that is moved by mistrust in the state, and which explains that everything for which the state is being blamed, is being transferred to the credit of NGOs, without taking anything else into consideration.

Finally, a number of social groups and organizations in the South (and also in the East) copied the matrix of NGOs. This 'southernization' is very interesting from the point of view concerning us here, as there is an international dissemination of the NGO model, and an attempt to accommodate it to different contexts. Just like, the hermit crab, who slips into a shell that is not his, many free groups of individuals call themselves NGOs. They thus acquire a social existence and an identity label that protects them (from the police for instance, or the authorities in general), and gives them recognition by other NGOs (especially those who come from other countries looking for partners).

Between what is generally called the 'state'[2] and the formal or informal market pole that is found in every society, a third sector now exists, called 'civil society.' Two things should be pointed out here. First this term has a long history in the ideas that illustrate political theory. We can say that political theories have in common the designation of 'civil society' as a type of spontaneous association that is opposed to the state, or at least differentiated from it. We can refer to Bryant's definition of it as an area between households and the State that offers possibilities of concerted action and social self-organization (Bryant 1993). Or we can also refer to the Percy B. Lehning definition. He claims that civil society occupies the area between the public sector and the private sector (Bernard and Lehning 1998). It is the 'civic' area that we occupy when we are neither involved in activities related to the public sphere (voting, payment of taxes) nor the market (work, production, purchase, consumption).

The second useful assertion to be made is that this approach is, to a great extent, adapted to societies of 'individuals-citizens,' who make up the western nation-states. It should be admitted that these approaches are difficult to apply as such to many countries in the Middle East and the South in general (and the East). Indeed the state is an "imported" concept according to Badie. He claims that the individuals are in multi-belonging systems that make their position vague according to our criteria. Moreover, their identities are increasingly multiple and mobile and allegiances are fluid. It would, therefore, be wise to speak in the plural and refer instead to 'civil societies.' The consequences of doing so are many in the area of international relations. However, at this stage, let us agree that using the term 'international civil society' without any reservation would either be to beg the question, by using a concept of western origin, or to advance a pure fantasy.

In whatever case, in every civil society, the NGOs play a big social and political role in structuring, representing and (re)distributing goods, services, and ideas. We should reconsider the political role of the NGOs, as it may be asked: Is their growing power correlated to a certain political retreat, or is it a sign of the emergence of real 'popular alternatives'?[3]

The question raised in this manner may be impossible to answer because, first of all, the question conceives politics as being a mere game of powers. Secondly, because it only projects politics on a one-dimensional level, where two groups of actors take over from one another: the political class (of which the government is the offshoot), or the population (from which the alternatives can come). To see the problem from the point of view of governance, and particularly its organizational levels, is suitable for organizations that are located under or above the state.

It is important to look at how governance is applied within different spheres underneath the state. Let us first discuss infra-national governance. This will shed light on the complexity of the implicit or explicit options available to NGOs. Indeed, the sites of political power have always been identified as poles—and we can even say the same of economic powers. The concept of the state, as implemented by the OECD[4] countries, can often be described by the words 'central power.' Using this central power, the paths of the NGOs remain, in fact outside of the archipelago of centers. NGOs are by nature decentralized. This absence of location perfectly corresponds with the non-governmental nature of these organisations. We can therefore distinguish two types of positions available to NGOs in relation to the 'centers,' and hence two ways of taking part in governance at the infra-national level. Until a time when these concepts are better defined, let us call these two positions: 'far-from-the-centers' and 'without-the-centers.'

The 'far-from-the-centers' NGOs voluntarily abandon the political arena as a result of their leaders and founders, who were not recognized as political actors by the centers, or after aborted political actions. Since these leaders failed to take control of the centers, they changed their focus by putting their efforts into social activities and improving the technical efficacy of relief NGOs, for instance, or into lobbying for universal issues such as human rights and the enviornment. The authorities see this declared political withdrawal from power—more apolitical than neutral—as a non-aggressive position. The NGOs' participation in infra-national governance is confined to negotiating with the authorities over areas of legitimacy, concrete achievements, and the right of expression that allows for the co-existence of all groups of actors.

The situation is altogether different for the 'without-the-centers' NGOs, that can be seen to adopt a different set of strategies. They go away from the 'centers' for a while—staying away from them so they can grow safely—so as to be able to return and compete on their own playground of influence. However, we should understand the forms of this competition: three main types can be identified. The first one consists of promoting innovation and experimentation at the social and economic levels. An example of this category can be found in the NGOs that promote women's rights or work in the arena of micro-credit. The second type bypasses the operational logic of the 'centers' and is typical of NGOs that go beyond national control by being attached to assistance, methods, and sometimes, even material goods from other countries. This is often the case with the network of 'ecological' societies that are well organized at the international level. The third type of NGO in this category tries to contest the 'centers.' In this case, the NGOs aim at changing the center and/or its law and/or its operation. The operational logic here corresponds to that of syndicates and trade unions and/or of their federations. Each of the three types of competition represented by the three different models for 'without-the-centers' NGOs, namely, innovation, keeping apart, and contesting the centers, puts pressure on the 'centers' in its own way. The legitimacy of the NGOs hinges on this condition. To be credible, to be 'visible,' especially to their 'social base' and the media, they should at least appear to be separate and at a sufficient distance from the 'center.' If possible, they should even be seen to be opposing them.

In the large western democracies, we could think that these trends are congruous to the rise of individualism (the responsibility and choice of the individual), which has, among other things, resulted in the the fragmentation of territorial and sectorial legitimacies. In many countries of the South, other causes produce similar results: both the 'weakness' of the state and its partial legitimacy provide leeway for many sorts of social systems. The successive shocks of colonization, de-colonization and modernity—of which the ultimate result is globalization, have produced and today continue to generate the same kind of fragmentation. They have created the conditions for a re-formation of groups of actors, through the appropriation of western forms, a real hijacking of structures, whose legitimacy has its roots elsewhere in the North. These groups serve particular objectives, which sometimes have cultural frameworks such as those represented by ethnic communities and religious groups. We can therefore speak of the 'Creolization' of the NGO mold.

To sum up, whether the NGOs are exercising their right to autonomy, resisting, or combining the two approaches, they are essential actors in governance at the infra-national level. They contribute to the definition and regulation of the public area. They take part in the mechanisms for the elaboration and control of its rules. This term does not refer to the "constituent law" but rather to "the forms of regularity" of life in society. At this point, it should be highlighted that the NGOs are not alone in confronting the state's government in the area in which they operate. The national public area contains other groups of actors, such as syndicates and trade unions, political parties, chambers of commerce, and associations. The situation is very different, however, at the supra-national and international levels.

Fortunes and Misfortunes of NGOs

Traditionally, the international area was primarily the stage of interstate relations: the two major figures were the diplomat and the soldier.[5] The missionary, whether in his religious or secular aspect (the technical co-operator), also crossed borders. This picture corresponds with the second geopolitical model of Levy, Durand, and Retaillé,[6] in which the exercise of power consists of territorial domination in a "field of forces." With the decline of the colonial empires, the powerful nations (the United States, the

British Empire, etc.) used aid and cooperation as tools to ensure the allegiance of countries in their respective zones of influence.

While the specter of the Cold War is fading away, and other fractures are opening up, especially in the economic realm, in both 'real' or 'armed' peaceful times, the merchants or businessmen are becoming the chief protagonists on the international theater. The model referred to, in the classification suggested by Levy, Durand, and Retaillé,[7] is that of a hierarchical network. It takes precedence over the former model (that has, nevertheless, not disappeared) according to the new slogan of the "Global Business Class": "Where conquest has failed, business can succeed."[8] In this model, the archipelago of "centers" controls the "peripheral areas" by organizing in a dissymmetrical way the financial flows, raw materials and manufactured goods, as well as information and "cultural products." The "centers" accumulate, while some parts of the "peripheral areas" try to become more integrated within the operation system of the "centers." On the other hand other peripheral areas face an increase in the inequalities. Inequalities remain and even increase. The structure of interstate aid and cooperation circuits is wonderfully suited to the geography of flows that is described above.

However, in the early 1990s, the two models started to lose their auspicious qualities. The latter model of the "field of forces" was doubly weakened when its universality was challenged by the fall of the Berlin Wall and furthermore when local conflicts erupted. These events were unthinkable during the Cold War. The concept of the hierarchical network, which was based on the power of the "centers," is increasingly allowing gaps to appear, not only in the "peripheral areas," but also in the 'central' places of regulation. Power and authority were increasingly well articulated, when public opinion was mobilized in support of environmental or humanitarian causes.

What is happening then in the domain of aid and cooperation? The withdrawal of the state as the main actor on the international arena has left a relative vacuum to be filled by other actors. The state was both replaced or disturbed 'from below' and outdone 'from above,' when the international institutions (in which the state still had a dominating role) started applying Structural Adjustment Programs (SAPs). According to the promoters of the SAPs, these two dynamic processes—from below the state and above the state—were not to collide with one another, since the collateral damages caused at the macro level are supposed to be compensated at the micro level. This is a condition frequently emphasized by international institutions when they help grass roots operators and other NGOs.

However, there is more to the matter. The implacable logic underlying the operation of the "centers," leads to the concept of aid becoming useless unless dictated by geopolitical interests. This is reflected in two movements, the first of which involves commercially interesting "peripheral areas" raising the slogan of "Trade not Aid."[9] The second movement aims at a global decrease in state-sponsored aid to countries whose future remains outside global interest—except as a potential nuisance as a source of emigration or instability, as some developing countries.

The international system, especially the one of the United Nations (UN), is going through a crisis. This crisis is characterized by the growing defiance of the United States with respect to the UN. As the U.S. has become a hegemonic power, it hardly needs the Security Council. The UN agencies, which are not under the U.S.'s control, have become a financial burden. Moreover, supporting these agencies is of no use to the Americans. The U.S. only considers one area to be worthy of consideration: the headquarters of the International Monetary Fund and the World Bank. There, U.S. domination is not taken for granted. It is considered cynical and distant and void of any political project. While a minority might view it as 'satanic,' the majority perceives it as 'strictly economics oriented.' Consequently, it carries neither a collective value nor meaning.

With international institutions lacking legitimacy, interstate regulations are going through difficult times. As a result of this failure to find full legitimacy, these institutions, in the early 1990s, tried to regain partial legitimacy by appealing to civil society. This was both consistent with their anti-state credo of that period and with what preceded this period—the era of 'human rights.' We should remember that it was on international ideological grounds, that this banner of human rights helped former U.S. President Jimmy Carter undermine the credit of the USSR beyond its borders, and strengthened the movement of dissidents there.

However, 'human rights' must also mean 'minority rights,' 'women's rights,' 'children's rights,' and those of the future generations. All these areas are hardly covered by international law, which only reflects and regulates relations between entities that were known and therefore recognized, when the law was first formulated. Such relations were first and foremost relations between states. The international system therefore needs to 'find' organizations that embody this mediation, which is both new and necessary, without jolting the sovereignty of the states too much.

NGOs can serve this purpose as they have internationally voiced their opinions and views for quite some time on behalf of groups of individuals who share a common vision of certain problems. This international exposure differentiates them from associations. Furthermore, NGOs serve the purposes of the international system even better since they are very much in need of international recognition. In other words, there is an agreement of aims related to legitimacy that suits all the actors involved. Some NGOs have paved the way because they examine files and formulate proposals in a very professional way. For their part, international officers accept them and even solicit their services, as they see a possibility to orchestrate them in the same way that they did with organizations for technical cooperation.

At this level of governance, above the states, there is a high risk that the daily concerns of the population may be forgotten and that decisions will be taken without much transparency. The NGOs are therefore required to diminish these risks. Firstly, they should bring to the system some form of replacement: their presumed proximity to field actors—the so-called "grass root" level,[10] their proliferation, and their presumably disinterested approach are all made to be the guarantees of a subsidiary operation. Secondly, we often think that the organizations uphold partnership and this principle entails the participation of everyone in the decision-making process, with an equivalent level of information for everyone.

All the typical conditions that existed at the beginning of the 1990s led to a generalization by mistaking the part for the whole. Without taking anything else into consideration, it was believed that civil society was represented at the important international gatherings. For example, NGOs were invited to Rio in 1992 for the United Nations Conference on Environment and Development (UNCED)—that was also called the 'Earth Summit.' NGOs were represented in the Vienna Conference in 1993 on human rights, the Women's Conference in Peking in 1995, the Summit on Social Development in Copenhagen also in 1995, and in Rome in 1997 at the World Food Summit. Not a single forum organized by the UN failed to call for the participation of 'international civil society'— which was immediately taken to imply NGOs. Even the World Trade Organization (WTO), which lacks transparency, accredited NGOs when it met in Seattle in November 1999. The tenth session of the United Nations Conference on Trade and Development (UNCTAD) followed suit a few weeks later in Bangkok in February 2000.

Faced with the negative results of internationalization in the form of globalization, such as the growth of inequality and the damage caused to the environment, the NGOs represent a minimal defense of many 'common interests.' This is why they are courted by the international institutions. The problem is that despite their outward principles of partnership and providing alternatives, they are, in reality, more concerned with procedural matters than the definition of common interests and collective objectives. At this level of governance, principles that regulate the management of public choices have been added to international law, which is based on mutual recognition of states' sovereignty. However, nothing has been said about the content of these principles.

Furthermore, a major question emerges when the condition of democracy is put forward at the same time as the call to resort to civil societies. Indeed, international aid is increasingly being distributed according to some criteria, especially starting with an appreciation of democratic practices and respect for human rights in the recipient countries. However, there appears to be some confusion between subsidiary and citizen 'participation'? Indeed the invitation to civil society to participate, which has often been summarily reflected in the NGOs' intervention in the process of governance, works well according to the principle of complementariness. Nonetheless, there is nothing to indicate that NGOs are representatives of the opinions of all citizens. So, what or who constitutes the social bases of the NGOs? What interests do they represent? What methods of regulation have they invented so as not to slip from the pattern of 'taking the floor on behalf of . . .' (which is one of their legitimate approaches) into 'taking the floor instead of . . .'? To further push the question, we can ask what consistency exists between the positions upheld by the NGOs in their speeches (to promote, for example, "a more democratic social life") and their manner of operating. What mandate have their representatives been given? Who controls this mandate and when should it be renewed? Through such questions that are rarely raised in the circles of the NGOs, we can see how the alleged proximity to the 'terrain' can serve as a smokescreen for the question of citizenship—which refers to the citizen participation and involvement in their community and civil society.

We should also examine concretely how governance is exercised at the supra-national level. That interstate actors should decide to make room for the NGOs is acceptable, however, that they should choose which NGOs should participate is quite a different matter. Three difficulties have emerged during the past years because of this kind of thinking. First, we have noticed a certain reproduction of North-South inequalities. Furthermore, the Least Developed Countries (LDC) suffer from a cruel lack of resources, which prevents them from taking part in international negotiations. Consequently, the Least Developed Non-Governmental Organizations (LDNGOs) also have no material means to travel to the main capitals, where the international negotiations are being held. Secondly, we should not overlook the fact that, when NGOs from poor countries succeed in mobilizing financial resources to take part not only in the summits, but also in the different preparatory meetings, they then lend their support to the powers that have invited them. These powers thus gain further legitimacy by inviting the poorest NGOs to their negotiating table, while obviously reserving the right to pick and choose between them.

The matter does not end here. Difficulties arise from the inability of NGO representatives to understand and investigate the files and follow agendas that are often very complex. Finally, it is becoming increasingly commonplace that chambers of commerce, professional syndicates, trade unions, and 'exporters' clubs' slip in to the ranks of accredited NGOs. For their part, international institutions often wonder and are at a loss when it comes to identifying the 'good' NGOs. At this level of governance, it is easier to choose as privileged speakers, individuals from the headquarters or from decentralized branches of the organizations that have already gained recognition within the field of aid and cooperation. There are two predominant criteria: size and continuity. The 'largest' NGOs are preferred by the international organizations, because they absorb quickly and well the sums allocated to them. Moreover, they are preferable to a myriad of small, perhaps well-intentioned NGOs, which would overburden international institutional allocation and control circuits to obtain an equivalent budget. As regards continuity, the criterion of 'life span' is often simplistically correlated with 'reliability.' Here again, mutual recognition of a category of actors by another may lead to the parties losing sight of the original objectives of the relationship, in return for a reciprocal sense of security in the negotiating game.

The last point to be made is about the role given to those NGOs allowed to play alongside the 'big institutions.' Do they have any say in the matter, in the elaboration of agendas and questions to be discussed? Are they consulted on fundamental issues? Can they contest or compete with these huge institutions?

The Shock of Legitimate Methods and Universal Messages

The 'non-governmental organization' form incorporates, with no doubt, a certain amount of modernity. Its actors are certainly 'modern' at least at the technological level, if we are to judge by their over-consumption of the Internet! Another obvious fact is that this form that was brought from the West, is spreading everywhere in the world (with the aforementioned nuances). This is even more paradoxical, as this type of organization turns its back on the attributes of domination and stands opposed to historical methods of conquest used by the West, which are military force and the market. What can we conclude from the fact that by adopting the NGO mold, these actors acquire the means to expand worldwide?

This question is echoed in the supra-national scene: on the one hand, the fragmentation of the legitimacy of state actors and the growing partial legitimacy of the newcomers—the NGOs—corresponds to the fact that a concrete level of governance is being formed along this "new scalar."[11] On the other hand, we can see that global commercial flows and cultural flows—the American soap opera "Dallas," was translated into many different 'national' versions, for example, and CNN is broadcast worldwide—are accompanied by many contradictory offers of 'meaning,' all of which are perfectly equivalent and can take all possible combinations, even the recomposition of old meanings into neo-traditional values.

Today, the expansion of the NGO model corresponds to the fact that NGOs have no single, agreed-upon, predominant meaning and, at the same time, have many juxtaposed meanings. How will the superimposition of roles be organized at the different levels of governance? How will the contradictions be resolved? What does the actual cacophony mean? Is it only transitional? The answer will not be identical, depending on whether we look in the direction of the West or the South.

At every scalar level, NGOs use methods to acquire legitimacy in order to create their own area of expression. Thus, western NGOs can play with their infra-national credibility both 'without-the-centers' and sometimes, against the 'centers,' when they are engaged in defending the ideas of a minority. At the same time, they also have international recognition as a result of accepting the interstate game. A leader of a peasant organization, affiliated to a big international NGO network, commenting after the failed WTO conference in December 1999, said: "In Seattle we were inside and outside." For these organizations there are hardly any contradictions, as their inclusion, albeit different, is into systems of actors, which do not have the same indicators of governance.[12]

The situation is not the same for many NGOs in the South. Their references, first and foremost, are the result of the constraints that are placed on their members at the national and sub-national levels. Thus, when it is a matter of drafting trade rules, while respecting some social norms, during international conferences, their position is only to advance the point of view that reflects the survival of their economies and respective countries. They thus oppose western and international NGOs that uphold social conditions. Instead, they argue that the latter are only defending structural inequalities and the domination of the rich countries that pays for the 'luxury' of making their people live under social and environmental norms.

The opinions expressed above and below the national level may well be very different. Islamic NGOs, for instance, provide assistance to relieve the most underprivileged through religious conviction and according to Muslim associative action, with a strict respect for the customs of the communities. At the same time, when they take part in international summits and multilateral negotiations, while they claim a certain specific nature, they do so with a watered down syntax where 'communitarianism' does not conflict with the dominant ideology of 'individualism.' While the dominance of the paradigm of 'individual' may not be universally admitted at these summits, it is seen as being more politically correct.

At every level of governance, an adapted discourse enables NGOs to survive, and to be actors who should be taken into account and be recognized as speakers. They may have several levels of discourse if the rules of the game are not the same at the different levels of the organizations.

What happens when different NGOs' messages, each having a universal aspiration, compete with each other? Indeed, if the previously discussed methods of gaining legitimacy are context-specific, the NGOs that base their concepts on 'universal' values (or the ones declared as such by those who formulate them) are in essence expansionist: in the globalization era, is there room for two or even three 'global' visions of the world?

Let's take the example of emergency medical NGOs: the ones of western origin have the "permanent and non-contingent right" to intervene in order to alleviate the suffering of any physically injured human being or one who is in danger of physical injury. There is an entire anthropological story in the background of such actions. This has its roots in the Universal Declaration of Human Rights, which includes women's and children's rights. However, there are some real contradictions in many NGOs that also uphold respect for local customs and habits, which are sometimes hardly compatible with 'universal' rights. At any rate, the NGOs have two different attitudes that are justified by two representations depending on when the action is taking place. In 'normal' times, the national NGOs act within their countries or their cultural areas of reference, by conforming to local customs. Whereas, in 'emergency' situations, the more operational NGOs, that is, the international ones, go beyond their borders and act according to rules that are based on the western vision of men, women, and children. This is especially true with regard to the predominant and the functionalist vision of the 'body' as a 'machine.' It's an image that insists on the physical body and not in the spirit. The body machine is the way western NGOs work as opposed to Islamist NGOs which focus on the spiritual aspects of any situation and which are not only preoccupied by relieving physical problems as western NGOs do.

As opposed to these western NGOs, the Islamic NGOs (for instance Islamic Relief) also have a vision of the human being that would wish to win over the hearts and minds of people. Competition or representativity of these NGOs are settled by the division of the territories. Islamic NGOs intervene where Islam is the main religion, while the European ones intervene everywhere, which ultimately makes them more legitimate at the 'international' level. The Islamic NGOs remain confined to a given cultural area.

There is a confrontation of two social ideals; one is a global social ideal that Laidi refers to as "the globalization of affects" (Laidi 1994), the other is the Islamist cultural identity, which creates another social ideal. This theory expresses that "most international events are experienced through emotion." The NGOs form a "theatrical" duet with the media. (To this duet should be added the ever-present figure of the "military."[13] They contribute to the formation of an emotional way of living together, which expresses the growing sentimental side of societies on the debris of politics.

Non-western NGOs are endowed with a universal 'meaning' and 'values,' but they are less legitimate in international relations, because they resist the westernization of the world. Will these non-western NGOs ever be able to play a leading role at the level of supra-national governance? Here too, the level of governance and the extent of the area it controls will settle this question in an empirical way.

Conclusion

NGOs are at the same time 'outsiders' and 'insiders.' Their arguments are paradoxical in relation to the infra-national level and with regards to the system of supra-national level. Accordingly, the NGOs are a good analytical indicator of the restructuring of these new spaces that exist today between the areas of the market and public policy.

The recognition of the NGOs by other groups of actors and by media observers, as well as their ways of becoming legitimate, indicate that a new political mediation is emerging. Indeed, they reflect new collective concepts that are being formed. Will a new world scene emerge, where common emotions are shared, while backstage business continues? Or can we think that gradually we will have some interaction between the quest for common interests and supra-national regulations?

The NGOs could carry a certain 'meaning' in this last alternative. However, before going any further, citizens need to exercise a real political pressure on NGOs so as to make them more representative and use them to express themselves.

Notes

1. Interference, which is always possible and sometimes necessary, is not, for the time being, the question, even if it is supported by a right of the same name. Interference, according to etymology is the movement of an object (right of interference) that proceeds from outside a society or country toward the interior.
2. Even if the institutions that form this state are in their daily operation far removed from the western nation-state, and even if, in the cultural area where this institutional form emerged—the West, there is a big gap between what is said and what is done in practice.
3. To paraphrase the title of the work: "Les ONG: instruments du neo-liberalisme ou alternatives populaires," Center Tri-continental de Louvain la Neuve, by L. Harmattan, 1998.
4. The Organization of Economic Cooperation and Development (OECD) consists of the countries of the West along with some of their allies. Its aim is to promote economic expansion. It is a multilateral organization that in 1960 evolved from the Organization for European Economic Cooperation (OEEC), which was founded in 1948 to contribute to the reconstruction of Europe and since then has continued to expand.
5. Raymon Aron, *Paix et guerre entre les nations.* (Paris: Calman Levy, 1962).
6. Jacques Levy, Marie-Françoise Durand, and Denis Retaillé, Le monde: Espace et Systèmes, 1st ed. (Paris: Presses de la Fondation Nationale de Sciences Politiques and Dalloz, 1992).
7. Ibid.
8. The quotation is in English in the text.
9. A good example of this process would be the inclusion of Mexico in North

America Free Trade Agreement (NAFTA). This is a dynamic process that points to future accords that have rightly been described as commercial accords, such as those being sought in the Euro-Mediterranean accords.
10. The words 'grass root level' are quoted in English in the French text of Levy et al.
11. In a hierarchical system that contains levels fitted together, the new scalar designates the scale for the social, political, and economic relations from the institutional and procedural point of view. Roca's explanation.
12. Sarah Ben Néfissa, "NGO, Governance and Development in the Arab World: Discussion Papers, Management of Social Transformation." (MOST/UNESCO), 2000, 46.
13. *Le masque de l'urgence, Courrier de la Planète*, 1995, No. 27.

Chapter Three

Civil Versus Political Culture in NGOs

Muhammad Al-Sayyid Sa'id

We can acknowledge that the expansion of civil society in most Arab countries in the twenty-first century is reassuring. We cannot, however, be entirely optimistic about the quality of the Arab society and its capacity to foster a significant development in civil and political life throughout the Arab world. The qualitative development of civil society in most Arab countries is rather unclear and locked within a chronic contradiction that is not easy to solve.

A View of Non-Governmental Organizations

The theory of civil society goes back to the time when efforts to limit the state's totalitarian and despotic regimes were being taken. This qualitative development of civil society seems, to a great extent, to depend on democratic transformation. It seems extremely difficult for civil society to evolve without establishing the foundations of a state based on law and institutions first. Moreover, fundamental civil and political rights are also to be recognized and protected, along with a minimum of economic and social rights, as foundational roots for civil society to grow.

In fact, all of the above require stopping the continuous dwindling of public freedoms in the Arab countries, which adopted a limited political pluralism in the 1980s. They wanted to impose a new orientation for the development of democratic practices.

By fundamental guarantees of civil and political rights, we do not mean a mere change of the laws and legislations that stifled civil society in a number of Arab countries during the 1950s and 1960s. The birth and growth of a higher quality of civil life requires more than just a new legislation. Nevertheless, a new piece of legislation is necessary in order for the organizations to free themselves from the bonds of the state.

In fact, the development of civil society in the Arab nations requires four basic elements: volunteerism, managerial skills, economic resources, and a culture of peaceful conflict-resolution.

Volunteering is the embodiment of a sense of civil duty. Undoubtedly, the culture of voluntary work is the dividing line between an independent civil society and a dependent one, between the existence and non-existence of a civil society. So far, the culture of voluntary civil service has not seen much development in the Arab civil society as compared to the community or social lifestyle of Arab countries. This lifestyle is characterized by its intimate links with basic loyalties to: tribe, family, local community, and perhaps, religious groups. Indeed, an Arab citizen willingly offers his services and money to serve the interests of his tribe, but he will rarely do the same to serve general public interests, defended by non-governmental organizations working at the national level.

Moreover, Arab civil society also suffers from a shortage of managerial skills, of people capable of building institutions and of developing their capabilities to achieve their goals, face problems, and seize opportunities. They should also know how to find the best ways of working with the public, gaining its confidence and doubling its demand for services. This shortage is not confined to the civil sector; it also applies to other sectors of Arab societies such as the governmental and economic sectors.

There are only a few institution builders with the required managerial skills who would join and devote their time and effort to the civil sector. Consequently, most civil society organizations, and particularly those based on voluntary work, revolve around one person, depend on that person's efforts and collapse if she/he leaves. Therefore, such organizations can be assimilated to the structure of a state as its decision-making process is based on one person only.

For civil organizations to fulfill their role, they need economic and financial resources, regardless of their degree of dependency on voluntary work. Finance alone may not establish organizations of any sort, but without any financial resources, such organizations will not last long and can rarely fulfill their objectives.

Here again, we can note the fragile economic foundations of civil society in the Arab countries. In the past, voluntary work and expenses used to depend on the waqf. When the state took control of the waqf institutions, membership fees remained the only economic basis for voluntary social services; these barely cover the costs to build the infrastructure of civil organizations. While the waqf only financed a very limited circle of charitable, educational, and religious activities, the greatly expanded needs of modern civil society, which now encompass most aspects of civil life and activities, are in great need of financial support.

Even when a reasonable financial and economic basis is provided, along with acceptable managerial skills and a degree of voluntarism to pump life into large or open-ended organizations, such non-governmental organizations may flourish for a while, but will eventually implode. Their implosion comes from the insuperable internal conflicts, which cannot be peacefully and calmly resolved or negotiated using conciliation and compromise.

If we were, for example, to take Egypt's experience we would note that nothing could be done to avoid the conflicts and earthshaking explosions that destroyed what had been built after years of hard work. At least the activities of organizations were delayed for a period of time, and they suffered loss of confidence for quite a while. Even the Bar Association in Egypt, which had been a bastion of nationalism and democratic movements in the 1970s, found itself, in the 1980s, victim to savage conflicts among all parties, who all displayed a surprising degree of violence and irresponsibility. Until today, the Bar Association has been in a lethargic state, which makes it an easy prey for the state to take over.

Scores of trade unions, political parties, and non-governmental organizations witnessed, and are still witnessing, similar conflicts and have not escaped the states' claws. There are no sports clubs or federations that can hold elections without the resort to some kind of weaponry. Hence, the peaceful solution of internal conflicts seems to have become the basic condition for the sustainability of non-governmental organizations.

For any organization to develop peacefully, it must have a clear legislative and democratic basis. Layers of laws restricting the simplest concepts of freedom cannot govern it—as they do now. Even the sports clubs do not escape the state's influence and its administrative maneuvers.

However, that is not the only problem. There is also the need for a democratic legislative reform. This reform entails logical and applicable rules to generate the handover of decision-making powers. Its acceptance in the social and collective conscience of the people would be a first step toward peaceful conflict resolution techniques.

How then, did civil society develop in some Arab countries? It did so, through roots and entities inherited from the period prior to the establishment of the autocratic state, in the 1950s and 1960s. At that time, such non-governmental entities were established by the aristocracy and by public figures and intellectuals, who had acquired a prestigious social status thanks to their efforts and ingenuity.

Yet, after the establishment of the autocratic state with all its structures and legislative frameworks, civil work became dependent on one of two elements: politics and money. The political actors, who previously worked within the state, were seduced by the idea of establishing non-governmental associations or organizations as a way of returning to the political arena, or of remaining therein with the support and under the control of the government and its supreme leadership. Non-governmental organizations, led by second-rank politicians, are widespread in the Arab world. These NGOs do play a real role, although the final purpose of these politicians is to partially remain on the political arena and access elections by drawing the attention of official leaders. Such a non-governmental organization serves this purpose by establishing a sphere of influence among the masses.

There is yet another formula for the NGO, which is to articulate an opposing view to the state's ideology. Such a formula could create either a substitute or a complementary actor to political parties. This matter has raised many polemics among those who question the need for such a formula or the danger it represents for the democratic development of existing parties.

Another gateway to civil, non-governmental work is through successful businessmen, both those who have no political interests other than acquiring a certain status among the masses, and those who do have a political 'agenda.' The latter want to mobilize a large number of supporters in order to win the local or national elections and thus acquire a high political position by establishing a non-governmental organization.

Finally, there is civil service in the true sense of the word, voluntary service at the level of the family, the tribe, the area, and the province. Such type of service draws more resources, which enable the tribe, the group, or the community to fulfill important roles such as, security, redistribution of income, political support, and solidarity.

These ways to create NGOs affect the quality of civil society in Egypt. The fastest growing area is that of charitable work supported by the efforts of the wealthy. It is immediately followed by organizations defending public interests, which rely on the skills of professional politicians from both the government as well as the opposition. The most developed are those enjoying a reasonable degree of consensus such as human rights and environmental organizations. On the contrary, trade unions are suffering from stagnation and almost absolute control by the state authority and by security mechanisms in particular. The role of trade unions is confined to simple charitable activities rather than conducting economic industrial negotiations, as is normally the case. Naturally, professional trade unions and associations are in a better position because they belong to the middle class, which is less subject to the state's hegemony. However, this professional constellation suffers from several ailments, foremost of which are the acute political conflicts that ultimately lead either to monopoly or to collapse.

As for the organizations of intellectuals, they are the least developed since they are the least financed and the most subjected to politicization. Not to mention the conflicts between generations, professional, and public opinion conflicts and the fact that intellectuals either despise or lack interest in managerial skills, which are the key to the development of all organizations, particularly organizations of civil society.

Nevertheless, another 'intermediate' type of organization exists. They have little interest in politics and are active in areas of public service such as charity, education, training, and the environment. Such organizations often depend on skills, developed within local realities or trained in 'middle range' government centers, without having developed pro- or anti-government political ambitions. These (non-politicized) leaders enjoy great popularity and their organizations are considered the most stable.

Thus, Arab civil society is entering the twenty-first century struggling to regain its balance and its strength. It is motivated to progress and is aware of the incapacities of the state to solve and take care of any situation. Yet, it is limited by a weak culture of voluntary service and a shortage of economic resources. Moreover, it may, at any moment, explode as a result of external factors, such as changes of governments, or as a result of internal factors such as conflict of ideas or struggle for position.

The Political Versus the Civil in NGOs

The relation between the civil and the political is worth a more profound and concentrated examination. It represents the essence of the problematic experienced by non-governmental organizations, and by society as a whole. This problematic has not been resolved yet and has a destructive impact on the social fabric of society.

This problematic may seem like a repetition of a notorious binary where the 'political' is the area of vertical relations with the central power as a basic dimension, whereas the 'civil' is the area of horizontal relations wherein all people are theoretically equal in the eyes of the law.

Such a myth is easily destroyed, since all human relations are, to one degree or another, governed by inequality. In Arabic, terms such as 'force' (al quwwa) or 'capacity' (al-qudra) are different from what is meant by the term 'power' or 'authority' (al-sulta). The latter is inherent in or derived from the state (whether through formal empowerment or without it).

All legal and political systems are familiar with the inequality of civil relations. Suffice it to mention marital relations, or the relation between a man and woman in general, within or outside the family, as a blatant example of such inequality. Civil relations are, in fact, steeped in inequality. This truth cannot be understood in isolation from power, in the true sense of the word, and its ties to the state. This does not imply a one-way relation from the state to civil relations, since the state is involved in consecrating relations of inequality in the civil area. The state may thus be defined as the authority maintaining and orchestrating relations of inequality at all levels, including at the family level. Yet, the state as a social phenomenon can rarely maintain its superiority over individuals and over their direct daily existential concerns.

The cases of totalitarian and tyrannical regimes, along with the example of the permanent dysfunctions of public authorities, show inequalities that differ from the normal discrepancies, which are often codified. This is the case of Egypt.

Let us start with a basic fact. We have a crystallized structure of a quasi-modern legal system, parts of which may go back to the 1860s, and which carefully administers civil life. So far, with respect to political life, its destruction, or at least its partial sabotage, has been achieved partly by resorting to exceptional legislation. As for civil life, however, it was given its due respect in the legislation, including in times of violent revolutionary upheavals. Even the nationalizations and confiscations of the 1960s did not disregard the principle of compensation as being a vital civil right. The judiciary dealt with civil cases with a large degree of independence and honesty, despite the instances of corruption and abuse that infiltrated the judiciary.

In brief, civil law suffered far less disturbance than other politically related legislation as a result of civil morals, which were deeply rooted in Egyptian society and which would have prevented even the worst of tyrants from resorting to the political isolation and destruction of civil society. Private life was respected, even for the most ferocious opponents of the regime. We need to recall that libel regarding the personal or sexual life of the opponents, was never part of the arsenal used by the regime during the July revolution, except in very exceptional instances.

Similar to the rest of modern civil legislation, Egyptian civil law is based on the principle of equality before the law, respect for privacy, and the right to dignity, as well as respect for personal and family life.

Nevertheless, we cannot disregard the fact that civil codification and the legislative structure as a whole have not, thus far, entirely succeeded in establishing the principle of equality in Egyptian society—not to mention the many cases where the principle of inequality is codified. The treatment meted out to the individuals in governmental and non-governmental institutions depends on the individual's social status, which, today, is derived from education, wealth, and family origin. Political posts also guarantee a social status derived from closeness to political power. It is not necessary for the individual to hold a political position at all times to enjoy this social rank. He only has to present himself, from time to time, as a candidate to fulfill one of these positions.

At the present moment, Egypt is witnessing an interesting contradiction, since power is extremely centralized in the hands of certain people and specific political posts. Moreover, there seems to be a case of quasi-collective political resignation and total dependence that stifles the sense of initiative within the government apparatus. On the other hand, power has never been as close to the people as it is today. It means that a large number of people are imperceptibly very close to the centers of power—and they can use the latter in a very personal manner to further their interests and settle their civil contradictions and their troubled relations with the state.

What we refer to today as a 'clientele relationship' is no longer a simple tool to help solve some problems and obtain some benefits such as a job. In the past, it was mostly used as part of extended family relations, mostly resorted to by people from the rural areas to bridge the large gap separating them from the capital. Today, it has almost become a lifestyle and, perhaps, the primary and only method for achieving anything. It is no longer confined to relations between family members. For example, today, a mechanic devotes part of his effort and time to provide his services, often free of charge, to persons occupying important positions in exchange for assistance, which may be essential in his life. Even simple country folk have come to realize that family ties are no longer the most important means of obtaining the support they may need when facing the powerful state apparatus.

City dwellers of almost all professions find one way or another to approach those who wield government authority. Some even believe that there is always a need for some sort of cronyism. Such relations have now become available without need for family ties or previous acquaintances among the concerned persons. The sources of influence have multiplied alongside the ones of prestige. Individuals with no higher education may use their relatives, who are high-ranking civil servants. Other people may use their wealth, which was either built by working abroad or by the economic liberalization policies of the 1970s. Finally, the less fortunate with none of these attributes, may resort to violence and force.

This surprising closeness to power and authority for such a large cross-section of society could have been conducive to greater democracy. However, the difference lies in the fact that the people get closer to the 'power,' due to its relative diffusion, but not the opposite. On the other hand, and this is my second main point, society may still be able to benefit from this phenomenon to achieve democracy. How can this be made possible?

The determining factor, behind the difference between the two cases, is the possibility or impossibility of imposing the law with impartiality. Democracy does not only require a wide sharing of power, but also a legal and honest organization of power-sharing arrangements. In the absence of the latter, widespread power leads to widespread arbitrariness, which, in turn, leads to a unique situation of negative balance, hence to widespread abuse of power at all levels. Thus, any opponents in a civil dispute, however ordinary, can resort to a more or less balanced source of support, e.g., mediations.

The above phenomenon is extending to NGOs, a world of many other important aspects. The relationship between the civil and the political in the field of NGOs is the main area wherein we may seek the reason for the failure of these organizations and the stagnation of civil society. We can therefore analyze the consequences of such a method of diffusing power.

First of all, the 'clientele' networks have been reinforced and consolidated. Many NGOs are the mere expression of such networks. The power within these organizations is centered in the hands of one influential person; the other nominal members are marginalized and their role is confined to voting at the elections for the executive board or the president.

Secondly, it is the absence of horizontal contact among the organizations, as they all depend on vertical contacts with the management or the government. As a result, this vertical relationship leads to an almost continuous absence of the concept of negotiation and compromise, or of establishing a certain balance. Consequently, NGOs can be easily manipulated by the management and by the government so that the latter may shirk their commitment or favor one organization at the expense of another. Moreover, such an absence weakens the organization's capability to mobilize people to rally around an agenda or a list of public concerns.

Finally, this tendency also strengthens a deep-rooted preference in Egyptian culture for solving problems via secret negotiations with the government. These methods are far removed from transparency and public debate.

Against such a background, there emerges a basic and cautious question concerning the possibility of building a civil society in the absence of a clear and properly democratic legislation. We cannot explain all the ailments of civil society, including its stagnation, as being the result of arbitrary use of power or a lack of democratic organization of the political field. Here we wish to stress the fact that there is serious doubt as to the possibility of building a civil society and of guaranteeing its healthy development, without putting a stop to legislative manipulation aimed at maintaining state and government control over NGOs and without allowing a revival of politics in a society where a correct political life has been stifled by the state.

Defining the Problem

The question as to the nature of the problem remains and the whole matter is fraught with ambiguity. It is not easy to understand the complex and often contradictory results of the state's long hegemony over the space allotted to what is known as non-governmental organizations.

It would have been natural for the civil and the political to merge without the one being entirely absorbed by the other. A fertile and serious political life is not conceivable without a civil society, composed of the organizations for public interests, charities, humanitarian activities, *awqaf*, and trade unions. The patterns of the relationship between the two fields vary in accordance with the historical traditions of each society. What can be affirmed is that each of them affects the other. A rich political life embodied in real political parties, usually enriches civic life and gives a strong impetus to civil society, thus activating party members who work in NGOs and increases their collective or individual participation. Similarly, the existence of a strong civil life and institutions of public benefit imbue society as a whole, particularly in a political sense, with a new energy. The presence of such active organizations promotes the necessary awareness of real options in the political field.

This inter-relationship extends to all levels of the social field. As far as the law is concerned, until 1952, Articles 55–68 of the Egyptian Civil Code allowed full freedom to establish private associations and institutions, to the extent that led some political parties to register themselves as civil associations (the Muslim Brotherhood, for example). At the same time, it created an unprecedented active public space, which allowed for creative and intellectual activity on the part of the Egyptian intellectual elite. During the pre-Nasser era, this development fostered a creative and intellectual ardor within the Egyptian elite. This creativity prospered in all fields: from theater, cinema, and music to political ideas. This elite had not been isolated despite the prevailing illiteracy. The middle-range intellectual groups played an active role, as they carried ideas and debates from the media and from the universities to the smallest of villages. In order words, civil society took a moral and abstract shape. It had a fundamental role, which can be compared to blood circulation in the human body, which links gastric activity to the brain.

Meanwhile, those villages had begun to be alive again for the first time, due to the rise of small and medium landowners. With regards the religious society, it rapidly acquired a relative strength within the neighborhoods, as portrayed in Naguib Mahfouz's novels, particularly in his Cairo Trilogy. The activity of civil associations came to crown all of this rich civil activity, which had benefited from the contributions of both traditional and modern structures. Such was the state of Egyptian society in 1952. But the 1952 Revolution not only put an end to political party activity, by imposing tight restrictions after having allowed multi-party formats, but also imposed the same restrictions on public civil services. This strict interference by the state to delineate the limits of public civil space gave rise to several patterns of relationships between the civil and the political, which can be summed up in three basic patterns or models:

I

The first pattern is based on the strict separation of the civil and the political. This became the major trend in Egyptian public life, and remains as such today as it was expressed by NGO activism. This pattern became independent of government control or direct daily interference by government agencies and institutions.

Fear of politics became the driving force behind the sustainability of such a model. Politics was viewed with suspicion, not only by ordinary citizens, but also by the civil leadership. The state welcomed this type of leadership, which tends to be highly cultured in a politically active society, leading some of them to adopt particular ideas or support certain parties. Others continue to maintain their intellectual and political independence and remain unaffiliated to any party; they are the ones who give political life in a democratic society the capacity to ensure rotation of power.

In a totalitarian society, civil leaders often establish a complex and mutual relationship with political authority. They draw closer to the state admitting they need its support to facilitate their activities. Whereas some of these civil organizations are satisfied with civil action alone, others do not mind allying themselves more closely with the state within the political spheres. In Egyptian society, only a limited space for public action was created, and this is mainly occupied by leaders who avoid and distrust politics.

This fear of politics by some civil leaders has several reasons, and primary among them is that direct or indirect sanctions have been applied on those who engage in political activity or have independent or opposing political ideas. This culture of fear led these civil leaders to avoid any deep political interests to be considered.

Leaders from this group are ready to collaborate and to submit to the state, despite the fact that they do not feel reassured by it. At the same time, these leaders refuse the proximity with the civil and political actions whose actors are independent or belong to the opposition. In general, they even refuse to listen to these actors and to take part in their activities. All occasions, however, become suitable to express their allegiance to the government and the state.

II

The second type of relationship of the civil to the political is highly widespread. It involves an outright condemnation of politics per se, which it blames for all the decadence that Egypt is facing, even within the civil field. This type emerged in reaction to political maneuvers, which revealed 'politics' to be devoid of any coherent behavior and lacking integrity and loyalty. Politics is also perceived as being an abusive practice, seeking individual interest and clientele relationships rather than the public interest.

The second type of leaders can be understood as the typical governmental political model, which has the best seat in the NGOs' theater. Its existence is due to different factors. The main one is the equation fostered by the July revolution. In honor of this political role, the state and its representatives, including its former retired ones, offer essential services to the citizens, who cannot adopt opposing and independent political views. The leading figures in this pattern are important persons in the July revolution's political hierarchy, such as members of the national or consultative councils, or high- and middle-ranking party members and members of local councils. Their official designation is that of 'popular leaders.' Since they cannot all be given political posts, a system of rotation allows the imposition of 'temporary retirement' on some of them until their turn comes around again. For instance, the direction of the service-oriented NGOs, has found a way of keeping all its 'potential leaders' by using them as political reserves to mobilize public opinion, especially during election times. NGOs, in this context, became a vast network of 'cronies' that could be manipulated in the interest of the state whenever necessary.

The above type is, in many ways, different from the first. They are usually professional politicians, who have occupied posts in the political organizations created by the state after the July revolution: the liberation authority, the socialist union, the nationalist party are some examples. This group also includes the businessmen, who maintained close relations with the state. The chiefs of big families and tribes throughout the country, former trade union leaders who gained popularity among the working class or professional associations and were subsequently chosen by the state to work in its political or representative institutions, are other types of professionals. Most of these leaders are well versed in general politics and modern culture, and they vie with each other to satisfy the higher-ranking political figures. Most of them have maintained solid organic relations with their local communities. Even though their popularity may have dwindled with time, they have acquired some basic political skills, which make them noticeably tolerant with independent political or cultural elements and actors from the opposition. Their unshakable loyalty to the regime provides them with an immunity which protects them from losing their positions. In all cases, their allegiance has been previously tested on many occasions. Consequently, they have acquired a certain degree of freedom with regards their actions. They are in contact with the other political and cultural elements and even offer them help, especially when it concerns the creation or the management of civil institutions, which are marginalized from the electoral debate.

In recent elections, it was noted that many of the candidates, who had maintained solid relations with the state sought the help of independent intellectual actors, who used to play cultural or civic roles in the local communities.

III

The third and last type of relationship describes the feeling of inferiority expressed by the civil sector in relation to the superiority of the political one. The latter is perceived as being the field of the powerful people, who are capable of handling and facing the consequences of a career with many risks. On the other hand, the civil workers fear that their activities may be eliminated very quickly if any doubt is raised as to their good intentions. This fear comes from the fact that they hardly have any protection. This attitude is based on a pragmatic, direct, and useful approach of civil society.

It takes into consideration the fact that since political activity that is seen to be disloyal attracts sanctions, and could involve playing with the people's destiny, it is a better option for the civil sector to remain outside political debate and conflict. This principle is based on a separation between political and civil life. This action derives from the will of devoted civil leaders to cleanse their sector from the degrading activities exercised in the political realm. However, this division remains partial, voluntary, and not total.

Organizations of this type have a political perspective—independent, ambiguous, or oppositional. This type provides, at present, a channel of contact between a vulnerable and troubled civic society on one hand, and a corrupt political society on the other. The expression 'political perspective' means several things. The apparent perspective is more important as it provides direct and immediate information with regards to the communication with others.

This perspective is the intellectual and political background of the leaders of these organizations, many of whom were Marxists or Nasserists or Islamists, and a few of whom were liberals, mostly from the Wafd Party. Many of them were active in the ranks of the opposition, at least in their youth; consequently they had been politically classified for security reasons, and thereby, not particularly popular with the state, even if they no longer continue with the same kind of activism.

Civic service has become a substitute for party/political action, which these leaders have stopped believing in. That is why, at a civic level, the situation of the leaders of NGOs is often characterized by political tension. They are often critical of their intellectual and political origins and even more so if they maintain social and friendly relations with their former partners. The situation is exacerbated since most of the latter consider them to be traitors to their former loyalties and beliefs.

Moreover, due to the strict positions adopted by the state apparatus toward these organizations, Marxists, Nasserists, and Islamists alike suffer from such tensions caused, on the one hand, by the state's rejection, and, on the other hand, because of pressure from their former comrades. However, not all of these activists have the same potential to communicate with others in public and political space. In general, the activists with a Marxist or Nasserist background found themselves isolated from the ones coming from an Islamist structure. While these undertaken by these activities efforts have been successful in Cairo and among the most eminent personalities, they have faced a total failure in the other regions and at the local levels.

The third type of activist also finds it very difficult to deal with the purely civil leaders (type I) and with the other pro-government political ones (type II). Strong tensions sometimes emerge during meetings. None of these types of organizations have demonstrated genuine capacities to communicate.

Chapter Four

Promoting Democracy and Governance in Arab Countries: Strategic Choices for Donors

*Guilain Denoeux**

This chapter explores some of the critical choices and trade-offs that confront a donor interested in promoting democracy and governance in the Arab world. The main basis of reference will be the United States Agency for International Development (USAID), and the focus will be on debates that have taken place either within that organization or regarding its approach to fostering democratic governance in 'less developed' and 'transitional' countries.

'Supply' Versus 'Demand' in U.S. Assistance Toward Democracy

Since assuming office in January 1993, the Clinton administration showed a far greater propensity than its immediate predecessors for democracy promotion programs that rely significantly on civil society-strengthening activities. This was a significant departure from the previous Reagan and Bush policies. Except in Eastern and Central Europe, where supporting civil society was seen as consistent with a strategy aimed at undermining communist regimes, both the Reagan and Bush administrations had shown a reluctance to rely on civil society's work to support reform efforts in countries engaged in a transition to democracy. The fear was that such attempts to build democracy "from the bottom-up" might destabilize fragile political experiments, backfire, and unleash forces hostile to democracy and/or to the United States (Carothers 1999a: 89). Consequently, the Reagan and Bush administrations had usually opted for 'top-down' democracy-building efforts that relied instead on the transformation of selected state institutions, so as to make these institutions more representative, accountable, and transparent.

The Clinton administration's greater emphasis on civil society can be described as a partial shift from 'supply-side' to 'demand-side' assistance strategies. 'Supply-side' strategies focus on increasing the 'quality of governance' or the 'quantity of democracy' that are 'supplied' by the state. Typically, they focus on enhancing the effectiveness, representative nature, transparency, and accountability of those governmental institutions, which largely determine the quality of governance and level of democracy in a country—from legislatures and judiciaries to local government councils and selected agencies within the executive bureaucracy. The rationale for giving priority to these institutions in the delivery of assistance is that it is through them that popular demands for participation, competition, and respect for the rule of law are usually satisfied and converted into public policy.

In contrast to the 'top-down' approach of supply-side strategies, 'demand-side' assistance packages aim to strengthen civil society in relation to the state, and increase its capacity to articulate demands for democracy and good governance. Support for NGOs usually occupies a privileged position in 'demand-side' assistance strategies. The arguments usually put forward to justify such an emphasis are typically taken from the following list of four claims, which one could describe as 'the supply-side paradigm':

1. Participation in voluntary associations fosters habits, values, attitudes, and skills conducive to democratic governance: efficacy (the belief that through involvement in public affairs one can make a difference in public life), social trust, habits of cooperation, and collaboration toward common goals, a sense of civic duty, and coalition-building and lobbying skills (Putnam 1993). By participating in these groups, individuals develop patterns of behavior and progressively internalize norms that will help conscious citizens become interested and engaged in public affairs. The assumption here is that there exists a close correlation between individuals' propensity to participate in associations and their tendency to be engaged in public life in general.

2. The denser and the more active the network of voluntary associations in which individuals take part, the greater this network can act as a counterweight to the state. This network can also restrain this latter state, act as a watchdog, or mobilize resistance to its abuses.

3. Dynamic advocacy groups are essential to placing on governments the kind of pressures required to nurture a political will to reform, and to force them to become more responsive to citizens' demands.
4. NGOs provide vital avenues through which citizens, usually disillusioned with traditional political parties, can become engaged in the public arena, articulate their demands, and focus the public's attention on the key problems facing the country.

Drawing on the background that has just been summarized, the author of this paper will proceed in two steps. He will identify the limitations and potential dangers of assistance strategies that rely exclusively or predominantly on nurturing demands. This section is not intended to deny the benefits that may result from civil society-strengthening programs, but to warn against the excessive expectations that may be placed in such programs, especially where the political system shows an insufficient capacity to respond to, and process, political demands. Evidence from several Arab countries will be used to suggest that 'supply-side' assistance strategies are often a necessary complement to 'demand-oriented' ones.

The paper will then concentrate on 'demand-side' strategies to highlight the choice that donors face between 'service' or 'development-oriented' NGOs, on one hand, and advocacy groups on the other. Since the mid-1990s, indeed, the Clinton administration's propensity for working with NGOs, in its democracy- and governance-building programs, has raised a debate among aid practitioners. The debate was on the respective advantages and drawbacks of two options: should we support grass roots, community-based associations engaged in humanitarian, welfare, or relief efforts instead of backing up NGOs, which press explicitly political demands in areas such as human rights, women's rights, minority rights, or greater respect for the rule of law? After summarizing the main arguments, which were raised on each side of this debate, the paper will suggest that it is progressively losing its relevance, as a new generation of NGOs is increasingly blurring the line between advocacy and service-oriented organizations. Thus, just as the strategies that mix 'supply-side' and 'demand-oriented' initiatives may be the most appropriate way for donors to enhance prospects for democracy and good governance, civil society assistance may also find particularly high returns in projects that pay special attention to both service-delivery NGOs, that have taken on advocacy roles, and advocacy NGOs, which also engage in activities of direct benefit to grass roots communities.

Limitations and Potential Dangers of Demand-Focused Strategies

The main problems associated with donor strategies that concentrate on increasing the demand for democracy and good governance can be summarized in seven core arguments, each of which is developed below. Of course, not all of these arguments apply to any given country, and each one of them may vary according to the political setting. Nonetheless, when taken as a whole, these arguments should give pause to enthusiasts of civil society-strengthening projects, especially in the political context currently prevailing in most of the Arab world.

The 'Beware of Civil Society Romanticism' Argument

USAID professionals—especially the younger generation that entered the foreign aid bureaucracy during the Clinton years—have frequently placed excessive expectations in the capacity of civil society to contribute to democratic development and good governance. Among the factors accounting for this phenomenon was the critical role that civil society had played in mobilizing resistance to authoritarian regimes in Latin America during the 1980s, as well as its contribution to the downfall of communist regimes in countries such as Poland and Czechoslovakia at the end of that same decade. These events led some observers to rush into assuming that civil society could perform similar democratizing functions in environments, which were, in fact, far less conducive to allowing civil society to play such a role (as for instance, is often the case in the Arab world).

With regards to the new enthusiasm for civil society projects, the professional and political backgrounds of many of those who assumed positions of responsibility at USAID after Bill Clinton's election in November 1992 were also very important. For instance, Brian Atwood, whom Clinton appointed as director in 1993, had worked previously for the National Democratic Institute for International Affairs (NDI), a democracy-promotion organization affiliated with the Democratic Party, and which in its overseas work has heavily emphasized civil society-strengthening projects. Historically as well, Democratic administrations have shown a far greater propensity to emphasize civil society projects than their Republican counterparts. Republicans have been more inclined to support democratization through the reform of state institutions. According to numerous aid professionals, young age, relative inexperience, and lack of regional expertise of many of those who were suddenly propelled into decision-making positions at USAID after Bill Clinton came into office also contributed to the frequently unrealistic hopes they placed in the democratizing potential of civil society.

Reacting against that trend, a growing number of analysts have recently warned us against what one of them refers to as "civil society romanticism" (Carothers 1999a: 248). Such observers note that what is called 'civil society' often includes groups that are not democratic, whether in the values they espouse and reflect or the objectives they support. In the Arab world, for instance, the strongest and most dynamic segment of civil society often consists of Islamist groups, whose commitment to a democratic order is at best questionable. One may exclude such groups from one's definition of 'civil society'—but, then, the argument linking civil society to democracy becomes circular: if only pro-democracy groups were included in civil society, the latter can easily be shown to be consistent with the growth of democracy (Foley and Edwards 1996: 51, ft. 19).

Even when one focuses exclusively on NGOs that describe their primary mission as being the promotion of democracy, it is often possible to question the extent to which such groups do, in fact, foster democratic values. Many of them are quite small. Their membership and audience are limited—and, consequently, so is their mobilization capacity and their potential impact on public policy. These associations may be driven less by the desire to push structural political reforms forward than by the personal ambitions of their leaders. They may be primarily instruments, through which ambitious activists seek to advance their careers. Their leaders may, in reality, only have very little contact with the constituencies they claim to represent.

Finally, a robust civil society does not always lead to democracy—in fact, the opposite can sometimes be true. For instance, in a thoughtful, well-researched, and provocative article, Sheri Berman highlights the powerful contribution that a vibrant civil society had on the collapse the Weimar Republic in Germany (Berman 1997). Berman shows that, in the 1920s and early 1930s, Germany featured an unusually rich association life. In fact, ever since the nineteenth century, German society had displayed a frenzy of association activity. Through the 1920s, and up to Hitler's rise to power in 1933, the number and activities of associations rose even more dramatically. Berman demonstrates that it was precisely that vigorous civil society that was mobilized by the Nazi Party (the NSDAP) in its rise to power. Association activists dissatisfied by the inability of governmental institutions and the traditional political parties to respond to their demands flocked to the NSDAP, enabling it to evolve into a dynamic and remarkably efficient political machine within a few years. For its part, the NSDAP, deliberately sought to recruit civil society activists, harnessing their skills and networks to expand its power base (see Berman: 420–21). As Berman claims: "Had German civil society been weaker, the Nazis would have never been able to gather so many citizens under their cause or eviscerate their opponents so swiftly" (402). Berman draws on Germany's experience to suggest, more generally, that (a) far from always strengthening liberal or democratic values, civil society may undermine such values, or be used by those who oppose them; and (b) while civil society does mobilize citizens for political participation, such participation may be directed at, and against, an existing democratic system. In short, the vigor of association life can be inversely related to the prospects for a stable, democratic order.

The 'Additional Demands Are Unnecessary' Argument

According to this line of thought, Arab countries already suffer from a surfeit of unmet demands for greater political participation and freedoms. Even where earlier democratization experiments have suffered setbacks—as in Algeria since 1992, Yemen since 1994, and Jordan since 1996—governments backtracking on reform nevertheless continue to be faced with strong domestic opposition and demands for greater political pluralism and better governance. In many cases, civil society has been highly active, and huge and energetic protests have been raised during numerous elections to professional syndicates, student unions, local and provincial councils, and national legislatures. In such contexts, the demand-oriented strategies may be superfluous as the population already defend and express their demands in favor for democracy and good governance. Civil society, in most cases, seems capable of responding on its own to both political openings and persistent authoritarianism by articulating demands for democracy and good governance, and pressing these requests on the state.

The 'Even Limited Increases in Supply Usually Generate Far Greater Increases in Demand' Argument

The democratization experiments that took place in the Arab world during the 1990s suggest that one of the most effective ways of stimulating the demand for democracy is, in fact, to increase its supply. Consequently, even in countries where donors aim to increase demand, supply-oriented assistance programs should be given special consideration. Certainly, throughout the 1990s, civil society in each Arab country responded almost instantaneously to the supply of new political opportunities. Indeed, the critical variable accounting for the dynamism of Arab civil society relies less on the donors' support than the willingness of established regimes to concede greater space for autonomous political action. Moreover, it has been proved that even a marginal increase of the freedom of maneuver available to groups and individuals tends to yield far greater positive results in association activity. This latter, in turn, generates new demands being placed on governments.

In other words, where Arab regimes have opened up the political system, civil society has moved very quickly to occupy the political space created by the retreating authoritarianism. In virtually all Arab countries where democratization made any headway, the process began as a government initiative and not as a result of pressures from civil society (Harik 1994: 48–50).

As Harik put it several years ago, "governments in Arab States have had more to do with creating and promoting civil society than civil society has had to do with democratizing governments" (56). The Arab world differs in this respect from the experiences of, say, the Philippines in the mid-1980s, or Poland and Czechoslovakia in the late 1980s. Proponents of civil society often invoke these cases because they were indeed instances in which mobilization by civil society played a key role in bringing down oppressive governments. But in the Arab world, political liberalization and democratization have not been initiated by dissidents and grass roots activists; instead, the latter took advantage of political openings promoted by the regimes, and used the political space provided by these openings to press for further democratization.

To find examples that fit the scenario, which has just been described, one needs only to think of Algeria, Morocco, and Yemen. In Algeria, it was not an organized civil society but the spontaneous rioting of October 1988 that prompted the state to initiate what soon became the Arab world's boldest democratization experiment. Within weeks of the promulgation of the new constitution in February 1989, hundreds of new political and cultural groups were formed, many of which became vehicles for the dissemination of ideas related to democracy, pluralism, the rule of law, and human rights. Berber associations began to agitate for greater cultural rights, while women's groups sought to mobilize opposition to the 1984 "Family Code." For their part, religious militants organized themselves to campaign for an 'Islamization' of society and politics. In each case, however, the surge in association activity was a product, not a cause, of liberalization.

Morocco, since the mid-1980s, provides further evidence that once constraints on autonomous association activity begin to be lifted, even if partially and progressively, voluntary associations tend to emerge very quickly. The spectacular development of civil society in the kingdom from the mid-1980s onward was largely a product of King Hassan's strategic decision to liberalize the economy and to engage the country in incremental, but nevertheless genuine, democratization processes. Indeed, the three main phases of civil society expansion reflect primarily the degree of autonomous political space conceded by the regime. That degree was itself shaped by the fiscal and political constraints, both domestic and international, under which the regime was operating at any given historical juncture. Thus, the first wave of NGO expansion involved primarily service-oriented and development associations in areas such as health and small-business creation. This process stemmed largely from the Structural Adjustment Program (SAP) adopted in 1983 and the concomitant withdrawal of the state from key economic and social sectors. As the state found itself increasingly unable to meet the social and economic needs of a growing population, it decided to grant greater latitude to social, welfare, and development associations. The new opportunities available to welfare and community-oriented NGOs, stemmed largely from a conscious decision by the state to rely on these groups to address development challenges. But, at first, these changes did not lead to a significant broadening of the action space available to associations with more explicit political agendas.

By the late 1980s, however, a new phase of association development began when the State showed greater tolerance toward advocacy groups, which were active in sensitive areas such as human rights and women's rights. This process reflected a continuing need to broaden political participation in a society that was becoming younger, and increasingly politicized and urban. It also became more open to outside influences and felt the effects exercised by democratization experiments in the region and elsewhere. It was also in the late 1980s, that King Hassan II realized that Morocco would have to change its international image if it wanted to secure access to international loans, foreign investment, and coveted trade agreements (especially the association agreement with the European Union). Thus, the quest for greater 'international respectability' prompted the regime to grant increased freedom of speech and association activity in human rights-related areas. It is of no coincidence that the Moroccan Organization for Human Rights (OMDH) was allowed to form in 1988, the same year that Morocco applied for membership in the European Economic Community. Women's groups, too, took advantage of a favorable domestic and international environment to press such controversial issues as the need to reform the moudawwana, Morocco's personal status code.[1]

Finally, the third wave of civil society expansion began in 1995–96, when a new breed of advocacy groups appeared that were explicitly devoted to the promotion of citizenship and the advancement of Morocco's democratic transition. The most visible and active associations or 'think tanks' include Alternatives, Maroc 2020, Transparency Maroc, and Afak. They all have taken advantage of the deepening of Morocco's political reform process and of the concomitant broadening of civic space to draw attention to issues ranging from corruption (Transparency Maroc) to the importance of civic values and personal responsibility (Afak). Their mottos are transparency and accountability. The values they seek to promote are those associated with citizenship; their goals are good governance, the rule of law, and the free exchange of ideas. Their choice consists of a partnership between government, the private sector, and civil society, in order to further the process of political and economic reform. The point to be emphasized here is that the nature of these associations, their relative maturity and degree of sophistication, as well as the spirit and objectives that animate them, reflect very closely the stage that Morocco has reached in its democratization process. What made these associations possible was not only the determination and dedication of their leaders and members, but also, the significant increase in the 'quantity of democracy' supplied by a regime that has presided over gradual, but continuous and sustained 'democratization from above.'

In short, Morocco's experience demonstrates that as states are forced to give up their former ambition to exercise tight control over society, and as they allow the formation of new 'zones of autonomy' for groups and individuals, NGOs and other civil society institutions quickly move to advance their goals and agendas. The greater the political space that is conceded, the greater the sensitivity of the areas invested in by civil society, and the more assertive NGOs are likely to be.

Yemen's brief but remarkable democratic experience, between 1990 and 1994, provides another illustration of a sharp rise in association activity being made possible by democratization processes from above. Indeed, Yemen's case proved that even in a country located on the edge of the Arabian Peninsula and often misleadingly summarized as 'conservative,' 'traditional,' and 'tribal,' civil society could respond very rapidly and with great dynamism to a political opening by the state. Shortly after the former Yemen Arab Republic (YAR) of the north merged with the People's Democratic Republic of Yemen (PDRY) of the south in May 1990, a new constitution, press law, and political parties law created a broadly permissive legal and political framework which, in turn, directly encouraged the formation of numerous voluntary societies. As leading analysts of Yemeni affairs noted "more independent political, charitable, social, and professional organizations were founded after 1990 than in the preceding eight decades" (Carapico 1998: 140). This flourishing of civil society, Carapico notes was the third and most significant of three periods of civic activism experienced by Yemen in the second half of the twentieth century.[2] All three, she notes, were the direct result of relatively weak and fragile governments, seeking to enhance their legitimacy and mobilize popular support, resources, and energies by lifting many of the barriers to association, assembly, and free speech, and, more generally, by broadening the political space available to groups and individuals.

Jordan provides further evidence of the close relationship between the supply of democracy by governments and the vigor of the demand for it by civil society. Nonetheless, whereas the examples analyzed so far showed sharp increases in civic activism following a lifting of restrictions on association autonomy and freedom of expression, Jordan points to what happens when a regime provides insufficient political space for civil society to perform its democratic role. Indeed, the legal framework which governs voluntary associations in Jordan, as well as the strict manner in which this framework is enforced, greatly limits the ability of voluntary associations to perform the kind of 'democracy-promotion' functions with which civil society is invested by its advocates. Law 33 of 1966, which regulates associations, prohibits them from engaging in political activity. Meanwhile, the political party law makes it illegal for parties to use the resources (assets, premises, and others) of voluntary associations. That law makes a clear distinction between political endeavors and cultural activities, reserving the former for political parties, the legislature, and the electoral process, while containing associations to the latter. To prevent any politicization of civil society, the state strictly enforces this separation between political activism and cultural pursuits. Women's groups, for instance, are legally forbidden to agitate for women's rights, and associations seen by the authorities as crossing the line into politics will suffer retribution. Since that line is always hard to define and quite subjective, the state enjoys great latitude to repress associations of which it does not approve (Wiktorowicz 1999:

609–10). In such an institutional context, it becomes very hard for civil society to defend basic rights and liberties, to contribute to the expansion of political space, to articulate a reform agenda, to expose governmental abuses, and to press for better governance.

Overall, therefore, evidence from Algeria, Morocco, Yemen, and Jordan would seem to suggest that persisting authoritarianism in the Arab world is not due to an inherent weakness of Arab civil society, but to the continued unwillingness of many Arab regimes to allow its autonomous development. Put differently, it is the supply of democracy that is usually lacking in the Arab world, not the demand for it. When political openings broaden space for autonomous association activity—as was the case in Algeria between 1989 and 1991, in Yemen from 1990 until 1994, and as has been the case in Morocco since the late 1980s—civil society flourishes. Although civil society typically does not bring about initial political liberalization, it usually takes advantage of it to attempt to transcend the legal and political constraints that regimes still seek to impose upon it. In light of such realities, donors wishing to accelerate the slow pace of democratization in the region should emphasize not only 'demand-creating' and 'demand-sustaining' associations, but also changes in the rules that govern political competition.

The 'Sustaining and/or Satisfaction of Demand Requires Effective State Institutions' Argument

No matter how vivid a given civil society is, it is unlikely to sustain its role as a vehicle for greater democracy and good governance unless it operates in an enabling environment, which requires effective state institutions. In Eastern Europe, civil society has made the greatest advances in countries where governments were relatively competent, and where the NGOs could operate within an operational institutional framework (as in Poland and Hungary). On the contrary, civil society has been stunted in countries characterized by the opposite situation, as in Romania (Carothers 1999b: 26). There are no reasons to believe that the Arab world differs from these previous examples.

Algeria provides the most dramatic illustration of this connection between state capacity and the sustainability of civil society dynamism. In Algeria, much of the civil society that had developed from 1989 through 1991 withered away after the January 1992 coup. This coup constricted significantly the political space available to associations that had not had enough time to develop long-lasting roots. This phenomenon, however also reflected, more generally, the post-1992 regime's inability to provide the minimum level of order, security, predictability, and consistent enforcement of rules, without which a healthy civil society cannot develop. Where political institutions are not strong enough to provide the basis for a legitimate and stable public order, civic activism is unlikely to flourish.

Though of course very different from Algeria, the case of Morocco also shows that civil society's ability to foster democracy and good governance remains constrained by the capacity of state institutions and by political leadership. Morocco today features perhaps the most dynamic civil society in the Arab world. That civil society includes numerous advocacy groups that enjoy great latitude to press for change even in sensitive areas. The political context in which it operates was made even more favorable by the formation of a government headed by former opposition leader 'Abd al-Rahman Yusifi in March 1998 and by the new King Muhammad VI in July 1999. That government features many individuals, who, either as ministers or in high-level positions within ministries, have long been active in civil society circles and/or have close personal relationships with association leaders. On numerous occasions, the Youssoufi government has expressed its eagerness to establish partnerships with civil society, and it has stressed, repeatedly, its belief in the vital contribution that civil society can make to political and economic development. Yet, since the spring of 1998, actual reform has lagged far behind what civil society activists were hoping for. This discrepancy between discourse and reality has not only created growing impatience and frustration with the government among NGO activists, but it is also raising the question of civil society's ability to help move forward a reform agenda in the absence of two critical conditions: capable and responsive state institutions, and a governmental team that displays the requisite level of cohesion and overall competence.

Clearly, the greatest obstacle thwarting Morocco's reform process today is not the absence of political will at the top. Neither is it the resistance of vested interests that would be threatened by change (although this also constitutes a problem). Instead, the government's capacity to deliver on its reform promises has been hindered by two sets of variables. The first consists of the very heterogeneous nature of the governmental coalition. Combined with the lack of experience of many of those who now occupy critical decision-making positions this factor has led to internal bickering and numerous delays in policy implementation. The second even more critical and daunting obstacle to reform has been the ineffective and archaic political structures and institutions inherited by the government. These include a bloated and sluggish bureaucracy; an increasingly fragmented party system featuring weak and discredited political parties that are caught in the past and largely cut off from society; a parliament that is still struggling to become more central and effective, especially in the wake of the creation of a new upper chamber; local government institutions that operate in a system that remains excessively centralized and does not yet provide enough opportunities and incentives for voluntary associations to contribute to the resolution of municipal problems; and a judiciary that is in the midst of a courageous reform effort, but which still has a long way to go before it meets adequate standards of efficiency and independence.

In such a context, no matter how dynamic and effective advocacy groups may be in mobilizing public pressure for reforms, the pace and extent of these reforms is unlikely to measure up to the country's pressing needs. More generally, one may argue that those Arab countries that are already engaged in a transition to democracy and in which governments have shown at least a minimum level of political will to reform, suffer less from insufficient political demands than from an excess of demands relative to the capacity of the political system to satisfy them. Faced with such situations, donors might be advised not to add to an already overabundant flow of demands, but to focus instead on enhancing the capacity of existing political institutions—political parties, judiciaries, executive bureaucracies, legislatures, and municipal government— to respond to these demands and convert them into public policy.

Indeed, one wonders whether some analysts often erroneously ascribe a lack of political will to reform, or a determination to silence all critics, to governments which, in fact, are less bent on crushing any manifestation of political pluralism than they are limited in their capacity to reform state institutions so as to make them more accountable and transparent. The Palestinian Authority (PA) is a good example. A recent study suggests that many of the abuses committed by the Palestinian security services since 1994, reflect less a desire by the PA to subordinate society than it does the deficiencies in the way these services are organized and staffed (Rubin 1999: 56).[3] Human rights abuses sometimes are due less to a regime's intentional repressive proclivities than to problems within its police and security forces, including lack of professionalism, adequate training, and monitoring mechanisms. In such environments, reform of institutions in question may be just as critical to the curbing of abuses as strengthening of human rights monitoring groups.

The 'Excesses of Demands Can Be Highly Destabilizing' Argument

Countries that are faced with an explosion of political demands, which cannot be satisfied because of the weaknesses of the existing political institutions, may find that frustration related to such a situation may lead not to democracy, but to growing unrest. This unrest may lead to potential violence, which is likely to make the regime even more reluctant to broaden political space. The case of Egypt, during the first half of the 1990s, illustrates, to some extent, such a scenario. In general, whenever the structures through which the processing of demands can take place lack effectiveness and influence, the call for greater freedoms is likely to be replaced by maximalist, non-negotiable claims, and moderate participation will easily be displaced by violent strategies. In societies characterized by widespread political alienation and fragile political orders, stimulating demands may even contribute to governmental collapse and chaos.

History also reminds us that excess of demands relative to the capacity of the political system to satisfy them can result in the breakdown of the existing democratic systems. Where governmental institutions and political parties display a weak capacity to respond to societal demands—and that is certainly the case in numerous Arab countries—a vigorous civil society may accelerate the erosion of an already fragile political order rather than spreading liberal values. Going back to Germany's experience, Sheri Berman shows that the collapse of the Weimar regime was largely a product of the weakness of its state institutions, and of their inability to respond to the demands placed on them by numerous and dynamic voluntary associations.

Throughout the 1920s, German governmental institutions showed themselves largely unresponsive to calls for economic and political change. Meanwhile, established political parties lacked any significant grass roots organization and support. Active only at election time, these parties were seen, by the middle classes, as dominated by unrepresentative elites, and as having been hijacked by particularistic, narrow-based interests. The perceived shortcomings of these parties prompted their natural constituencies to turn instead to voluntary associations as a way of articulating their demands and becoming involved in public affairs. Civil society thus became a sanctuary from, and the main alternative to traditional politics. However, as civil society flourished, it placed additional demands on already weak and overburdened political institutions. When these institutions proved incapable of satisfying these demands, their legitimacy was further undermined.

The result, Berman argues, was a highly organized and mobilized population increasingly dissatisfied and frustrated with traditional political structures. Consequently, the deadly combination of high levels of civic activism on the one hand, and ineffectual and unresponsive governmental institutions on the other, progressively corroded the foundations of the existing political order, and facilitated the rise to power of an anti-system party, the NSDAP, which made a deliberate and successful effort to harness civil society in order to subvert democracy.[4]

In short, many analysts' view of civil society remains shaped by the recent experiences of Eastern and Central Europe in the late 1990s, and Latin America during that same decade. In both regions, civil society often played a key role in mobilizing resistance to authoritarian regimes, forcing the leaders to engineer political openings, and, in most cases, helping bring these regimes down. Yet, it is important to keep in mind that a robust civil society pressing demands on a weak, democratizing government may also overwhelm it, and destabilize, if not destroy, the frail but promising democratic experiment.

The 'Civil Society Does Not Contribute to Pact-Making' Argument

Civil society's contribution to building democracy is usually limited by the fact that it is not typically a critical player in the signing of the 'pacts' or 'political settlements' which historically have established democracies. Before a society can be suddenly exposed to the risks, uncertainties, and rough-and-tumble of democratic politics, the main political actors must first reach among themselves certain basic compromises over the rules that will govern their competition for power. The main purpose of these rules is to determine how political disagreements will be settled, and how power will be shared among contending groups. Only after such understandings have been reached can greater competition and political participation be introduced into the system, without threatening to undermine the political order.

The political elites that attempt a democratic transition without previously engaging in any pact making will usually put themselves and their country under greater risks, as the example of Algeria between 1989 and 1992, demonstrates (Quandt 1998). Similarly, the experience of Yemen between 1990 and 1994 shows that pacts signed in haste and/or characterized by basic misunderstandings about power-sharing are likely to engender severe political crises rather than democracy.

What needs to be emphasized, here, is that these political settlements—especially the agreements reached over the constitution, the electoral law, and the laws regulating political parties, voluntary associations, and the press—provide the framework within which civil society operates. They, therefore, shape the opportunities offered to civil society to take action but also present the constraints under which it will have to operate. Yet, civil society itself does not usually play a direct role in the striking of these bargains. The latter are typically not reached by civil society activists, but by political leaders. This is a fact that seems to hold true both across history and cultures (Foley and Edwards 1996). Therefore, even a donor interested in fostering civil society needs to nurture the arenas within and through which these settlements can be reached. The prospects for a viable democratic system, in general, and a vibrant civil society in particular, depend largely on the extent to which these bargains are sound and how they leave no major issue unresolved. Furthermore, what analysts call 'civil society' is never a monolithic entity; more often than not, it consists of groups that have conflicting agendas and priorities. In this context, strengthening civil society may not lead to democracy, but to increased social fragmentation and dissension, unless the groups that make up civil society have already agreed on the rules of the political game. But such agreements, as has just been suggested, are usually not achieved by civil society, but by political leaders operating within arenas located on the 'supply side' of the political system.

It also should be noted that no matter how vigorous and dynamic civil society proves to be, it might find itself powerless to prevent the collapse of a promising democratic experiment, and prevent violence, if political bargains reached by elites break down. In Yemen, when the political crisis between the General People's Congress (GPC) and the Yemeni Socialist Party (YSP) intensified in the wake of the 1993 elections, civil society exerted tremendous energy to mobilize public opinion behind reconciliation attempts. It spared no effort trying to bring reluctant leaders on both sides to the negotiation table. Using all the mechanisms available to it—including mass conferences, public rallies, workshops, round-tables, publications, and petitions—it strove to foster a national dialogue, put forward concrete proposals to resolve contested issues, and sought to forestall the looming military confrontation (Carapico 1998). In the end, however, all of these endeavors were to no avail. They failed to prevent a violent resolution of the crisis, which was followed by new restrictions on civic activism.

If the securing of pacts among political elites is therefore critical to both democracy-building and the preservation of autonomous space for civil society, donors wishing to nurture the latter cannot afford to ignore the supply side of the political system. In countries where a dialogue between incumbent and opposition elites has not yet begun, donors must take steps to encourage it, with a view to reaching the pacts or bargains discussed in this section. When that dialogue is under way, donors must help move it forward. To do so, they have little choice but to strengthen those 'supply side' arenas, such as the legislature, in which that dialogue usually takes place.

The 'Political Sensitivity' Argument

Donors often feel that it is far more sensitive for them to support civil society's strengthening activities than to help reform state institutions so as to make them more transparent, accountable, and representative, thereby enhancing their capacity to contribute to good governance and democracy building. Assistance projects that directly aim to stimulate political demands can be threatening to host governments. They may be perceived as unacceptable interference in the affairs of a sovereign state, and/or risk engaging the donor too directly in sensitive political areas. They can even be counterproductive, causing host governments to retaliate against the associations that benefit from the assistance, making governments even more fearful of engaging in dialogues with opposition and civil society elites, and undermining the process of trust-building between state and civil society, without which democratization cannot succeed.[5]

It is easier for donors to claim that working with the supply side of political systems is politically neutral. For instance, strengthening a legislature, in which a variety of political forces compete, and helping it become more representative, capable, and central to the political system can be described as far more politically neutral than assisting NGOs (or, for that matter, political parties) that represent specific constituencies and promote certain policy agendas.

Demand-oriented strategies also tend to put donors in the awkward position of having to select certain groups and the constituencies they represent for support, while excluding others. This situation may naturally fuel resentment among those who see themselves and their agendas as being neglected by the providers of assistance. In general, civil society assistance programs often force donors to choose between the types of organizations they will support. Should they sponsor a wide, representative array of organizations in civil society, including those whose nature and objectives may not be consistent with those of the donors (Islamist groups, for example, in the case of donors from the United States) or should donors restrict that assistance to organizations whose goals meet with the approval of the donor? Either scenario contains serious potential risk for the donor: supporting groups that work against the preferences of the donor, or excluding them from assistance but then incurring their wrath.

Working with the supply side of the political system does not raise these problems. For instance, the legislature and the judiciary institutions are mere arenas within which policies are made (as in the case of a piece of legislature) or rules implemented (as for the judiciary). They do not take part in the democratic game. They do not represent particularistic interests—or, at least, they should not, and, if they do, the purpose of assistance might be specifically to remove that bias. However, they are institutions whose smooth functioning is absolutely essential to any democratic political system.

Because supply-side activities are less threatening to host governments, they are more likely to be accepted by them than attempts to stimulate demands. Supply-oriented assistance programs make it easier for donors to project an image of impartial facilitators, akin to the role of mediators in international conflicts. In fact, negotiated transitions to democracy are somewhat analogous to resolutions of inter-state conflicts. Incumbent and opposition elites are wary of one another. They have little experience with productive mutual interactions. Thus, they often welcome impartial, third-party efforts to promote resolution of problems that arise during their discussions.

Choosing Between Advocacy Groups and Service-Oriented Associations

When donors do seek to further promote democratization and good governance through civil society-strengthening projects, they are usually faced with having to choose between two different sorts of groups to support. The first consists of advocacy groups that press explicitly political demands such as transparency, accountability, respect for due process and human rights, and progress toward the rule of law. These groups typically recruit overwhelmingly among young, western-oriented and often western-educated urban professionals and intellectuals dissatisfied with the traditional political class. They tend to be most active in the capital and the largest cities, and direct most of their efforts at the national government.

The second main category of NGOs consists of service-oriented, grass roots associations. Less concerned with the national arena than with enhancing the well being of their respective communities, these self-help groups provide vital socioeconomic, relief, welfare, or humanitarian services, or seek to promote local development through the acquisition of basic skills and the organization of income-generating activities.

Although civil society assistance packages can involve support for both types of groups, over the last decade, aid professionals have been engaged in an ongoing debate regarding the contribution that each kind of association can make to democracy-building and good governance. This section will be sum up where the debate stands and especially show how it applies to the Arab world.

The Case for Advocacy NGOs

Aid practitioners who recommend focusing on advocacy NGOs point first and foremost to the unfortunate reality created by continuously diminishing funding for governance and democracy-strengthening activities overseas, especially in the Arab world. In the United States for instance, over the past few years, the field of democracy and governance has endured the most successive cuts in the foreign aid budget. Of all regions, this process has disproportionately affected the Arab world. Within the Arab world, only Egypt enjoyed a protected position throughout the 1990s, largely because of its role in the Arab-Israeli 'peace process.' More recently, the West Bank and Gaza also have received special attention. However, once Egypt and Palestine are taken out of the picture, very little U.S. funding remains to finance democracy- and governance-related projects in the Arab world.

This process has intensified pressures on USAID officials to become far more selective when deciding which democracy- and governance-related projects should be funded. Against this backdrop, those aid professionals who urge concentrating on advocacy NGOs, usually begin by asking the question: "How can a donor who can only draw on a very limited pool of funds best enhance prospects for democracy and good governance?" The answer, according to them, is: "by supporting the groups that address core democracy and governance issues and champion structural, systemic reforms"—that is, advocacy groups.

These 'advocates of advocacy' do not deny the merits of service-oriented and community-development NGOs: these groups tend to make a more immediate difference in people's everyday lives, especially the lives of marginalized, disadvantaged constituencies (poor populations, battered women, abandoned or abused children, mentally or physically disabled persons, etc.); they produce concrete improvements in vital areas such as health and education; and they help make up for the blatant deficits of state institutions in social areas. However, supporters of advocacy groups are quick to point out that service-oriented associations only make a marginal contribution to enhancing overall prospects for democracy and good governance. Their benefits in those areas lie, at best, on the margins. While they compensate for some of the deficiencies of the countries' political and governance systems, they do little, if anything, to draw attention to, and help eliminate, the structural shortcomings that produce these problems in the first place. In short, they only tackle the symptoms and not the root causes of the serious systemic flaws. No matter how praiseworthy and beneficial their grass roots charitable and relief efforts might be, and no matter how much dedication they reflect, they do not help reform the system. In the end, a multiplicity of more or less disconnected community-based initiatives is unlikely to ever evolve into a broad-based movement for change. In fact, they argue, community-development associations are sometimes riddled with parochial and primordial values that stand in the way of modern notions of citizenship.

Therefore, along the same line of reasoning, donors will, they emphasize, obtain far greater returns on their democracy and governance investments if they focus on advocacy groups whose activities usually encompass: agitating for fundamental, structural changes in the rules of the game; disciplining the state and holding government officials accountable by taking on the role of a watchdog; sustaining the public's appetite for reforms; explicitly engaging in the broadening of civic space and the protection of legal rights; articulating a compelling vision and agenda for reform; helping advance ideas of transparency, representative government, and rule of law; challenging intellectual, political, and cultural taboos and outdated ideas that thwart progress; exposing abuses of authority and seeking redress for them; publicizing the failings of the political class, thus pressuring parties and politicians to modernize their discourses and programs; acting as a source of new ideas and debates regarding key issues and choices facing the country; and forcing the government to pay greater attention to some pressing governance- and democracy-related issues, which otherwise might be left not addressed.

Finally, some analysts remind us that "working at the local level is difficult for USAID and other aid organizations, [in that] such work requires a more detailed, nuanced knowledge of the recipient society than aid projects directed only at the national level" (Carothers 1999a: 230). Consequently, it is easier and, in some ways, less risky for a donor to engage in civil society-strengthening projects that target advocacy NGOS, active on the national arena. When intervening at the grass roots level, a donor is more likely to misunderstand the realities on the ground, and open itself up to manipulation by actors, who may successfully misrepresent their goals and secure support for projects that may, in fact, be at odds with the donor's overall objectives.

The Case for Service-Oriented NGOs

Supporters of service-oriented NGOs tend to highlight the shortcomings that advocacy groups frequently display. Their misgivings toward advocacy groups stem, in part, from the latter's small membership and audience. In fact, according to some observers, advocacy groups are often effective at attracting donor funding not because they enjoy popular support or have a major impact on their respective societies, but, for the most part, because they are led by articulate, well-connected and westernized individuals, who know how to articulate their goals in a language that donors can understand and to which these donors are likely to be very receptive. Some analysts even argue that, more often than not, advocacy groups were created by donors; they would not exist in the absence of the external funding that made it possible for them to emerge, irrespective of whether or not they enjoy any indigenous support (Ottaway and Chung 1999: 107). In the past decade, according to these analysts, the emphasis that donors have placed on civil society projects, combined with the limited ability of civil societies to absorb external funding, has encouraged the proliferation of NGOs that do not contribute, in any meaningful way, to genuine political reform.

From this perspective, the most important shortcoming of many advocacy NGOs is their artificial nature, and, therefore, their lack of sustainability. Frequently, these fragile, elite-based entities—often entirely dependent on outside financing—will not be able to survive the shrinking of foreign aid budgets in the West. They are doomed to wither away as donor funding runs out. When they disappear, they will leave behind no significant record of achievement, having at best highlighted the insufficiencies of the state and political parties. However, they would have not been capable of generating a genuine dynamic for change.

Supporters of service-oriented NGOs do not only highlight the limitations of advocacy groups. They also emphasize the independent contributions that grass roots associations, engaged in charitable, humanitarian, or development activities can make to enhance prospects for democracy and good governance. First, they note, in countries characterized by a low governmental will to reform—that is, where the state feels, at best, ambivalent toward structural political reforms, and constricts the space within which advocacy groups can operate—there may not be any alternative for donors, who wish to support civil society, but to work with community-based groups. This is particularly true where the donor fears alienating the host government and is unwilling to exercise outright pressure on it to reform—whether because doing so would be contrary to the donor's perceived strategic interests, or because it might destabilize an ally and benefit hostile forces.

The United States' civil society assistance program in Egypt illustrates this kind of scenario (see Al-Sayyid 1999). In this particular case, the United States is unwilling to risk antagonizing a friendly regime that supports its overall policies in the region. U.S. assistance to advocacy groups is ruled out on several grounds: first, the Egyptian government would not look favorably on U.S. support to such groups; second, the freedom of maneuver that these groups enjoy is extremely limited and there is little that technical assistance could do to change that reality; and third, many of these groups oppose key U.S. policies in the region, particularly with respect to the Arab-Israeli conflict. The result is a civil society assistance program that focuses on strengthening the capacity of service-oriented NGOs.

In such controlled political environments, donors may, however, still be able to facilitate limited, incremental democratization by supporting development- and service-oriented NGOs. Advocates of civil society projects, built around community-based associations, acknowledge that the democracy and governance benefits of these activities might only be marginal, and that they will take some time to materialize. Nevertheless, they point out that such projects often constitute the only viable option for donors, who are concerned with minimizing the potentially disruptive impact of their civil society assistance. In addition, activities that center on local and development-oriented NGOs concerned with economic and social issues facilitate synergies with other components of the donor's overall assistance program to the targeted country. They may also act as a counterweight to radical and anti-democratic forces that seek to capitalize on poverty to expand their appeal. It is well known, for instance, that in the Arab world, Islamist forces often owe part of their success to their ability to meet basic needs in areas such as health, welfare, and education. A donor concerned with this phenomenon may find in it a justification for supporting alternative service-oriented NGOs. The donor may believe that strengthening these organizations is more consistent with enhancing prospects for democratic development.

Focusing on two USAID initiatives targeted at Tunisia and Egypt, the discussion will now focus on the potential democracy- and governance-building benefits of civil society projects that concentrate on community-development associations. These presumed benefits fall into two main areas: (a) the fostering of local level partnerships between the government and civil society actors—partnerships which, in turn, may generate a broader dynamic conducive to democratization; and (b) the capacity for activities that begin as grass roots development initiatives to develop into advocacy.

In 1993–94, USAID was in the midst of its first genuine, explicit attempt to encourage democratization and good governance in the Arab world. As part of this endeavor, the agency had launched in 1992 its Democratic Institutions Support (DIS) program. This critical mission of this project was to provide technical assistance in the design of democracy- and governance-related strategies and activities. Out of that project came a compelling conceptual framework that rendered support allocated to local service-oriented NGOs a critical component of a broader effort to foster democratization and good governance in selected Arab countries. Although Tunisia was a hostile environment for democratization building activities to take place in 1994, donors wanted to see the DIS project implemented there. However, before looking at how the project had been set up, it is first essential to describe the logic behind it.

The activities envisioned under that framework were essentially attempts to capitalize on the two critical ways with which several states in the region were responding to severe fiscal crises. First, they were explicitly encouraging service-oriented NGOs to take on some of the social and economic responsibilities that had previously been assumed by governments—in areas such as health, education, welfare, income-generation, urban rehabilitation, and infrastructure development. Second, they also were showing a greater propensity to decentralize responsibilities, while at the same time pressuring municipal authorities to become more responsive to community concerns, by, among other means, collaborating more closely with grass roots groups in identifying and resolving local problems.

In such contexts, the DIS project argued—and especially in those countries where limited will to reform on the part of the host government ruled out civil society programs emphasizing advocacy groups—assistance might instead focus on two new goals. The first would be the strengthening of the internal capacity of NGOs engaged in meeting community needs at the local level. The objective here would be to help these groups become more effective in representing grass roots interests, incorporating citizen input, and carrying out projects in ways that would not only benefit disadvantaged constituencies, but also involve these constituencies more closely in the design and the implementation of activities. Ultimately, with the same reasoning, such endeavors might create among the individuals and communities affected a sense of empowerment—that might generate a broader dynamic for change.

The second goal of assistance to service-oriented NGOs would be to facilitate partnerships between local government and community-based associations. It was envisioned that these partnerships would materialize in joint initiatives in order to identify and resolve specific, concrete problems at the local level. The hope was that these partnerships would foster an atmosphere of trust and a sustained dialogue between local government officials and elected representatives on the one hand, and community leaders on the other. Over time, as more fruitful interactions would take place between civil society and government officials, each would come to better appreciate the benefits of constructive cooperation. As the state would become more sensitive to the merits of involving civil society in meeting public needs at the local level, it might also become more willing to allow it to play a greater role in the discussion about national issues. In short, a multiplicity of local partnership initiatives might nurture a broader culture of dialogue, especially between reform-minded government officials and civil society leaders. This process might develop over time into a national movement for change, creating a friendlier environment for civil society, as a whole, to expand progressively its role in shaping public policy.

The logic that has just been described was reflected in a 1994 DIS project aimed at increasing NGOs' participation in municipal decision-making in Tunisia (USAID/Washington 1994). Tunisia's political and economic context at the time seemed particularly conducive to such activities. Since 1989, the Government of Tunisia (GOT) had significantly constricted the political space at the national level—a policy driven largely by a fear that the Islamist movement was best positioned to take advantage of a political opening. Neither parliament nor the legal opposition parties seemed to offer viable vehicles through which a pluralization of Tunisia's political system could take place.⁶ Meanwhile, the government had tightened its control over the country's once vibrant and autonomous trade union (the Union Générale des Travailleurs Tunisiens—UGTT) and the region's first human rights organization, the Tunisian League of Human Rights (LTDH). Such a situation significantly curtailed the freedom of maneuver available to donors interested in supporting political reform.

Simultaneously, however, financial and political constraints were pushing the GOT to decentralize certain governmental functions and encourage the private sector and NGOs to play a greater role in the delivery of municipal services. Decentralization and privatization were driven by both fiscal imperatives and political considerations. The former called for more cost-effective means of meeting the demand for social services at the local level. The latter required the state to become more responsive to local needs, and to provide more outlets for citizen involvement in public life at the grass roots level. Consequently, while political reform was stalled at the national level, NGOs—especially those engaged in micro-enterprise development, job training, and urban development—were given somewhat greater latitude to articulate demands at the local level. The GOT was now looking upon such NGOs as avenues, through which both community efforts and donor funding could be mobilized in order to meet community needs. For the first time since independence, the government was showing a readiness to break away from its centralized, elitist, top-down approach to policy-making and implementation, and was seeking to encourage NGO activity at the grass roots level—although only in non-politically sensitive areas.

The people in charge of project design within the DIS project encouraged USAID to seize this limited opportunity for promoting political reform in an environment that was otherwise hostile to democracy-building activities. Although acknowledging that Tunisian service-oriented NGOs remained weak and subject to varying degrees of state control, the project designers concluded that the most dynamic of these NGOs, especially in the fields of the environment and economic development, offered the only existing mechanisms through which local interests and concerns could be articulated and made to bear on public policy-making. The report that came out of this reflection thus recommended identifying pilot municipalities, in which USAID might initiate activities aimed at enhancing the technical capacity of grass roots NGOs and at creating development-oriented partnerships between them and municipal authorities. Faced with a state unwilling to open up the political system at the national level, with opposition parties devoid of genuine popular support, with a co-opted trade union, and with the absence of political space within which advocacy NGOs such as the LTDH might operate, the report argued that such a strategy—though likely to generate only limited and gradual progress toward democracy—was the only available option for donors to help expand popular participation in public policy-making.

USAID's civil society assistance program to Egypt also illustrates how, in a relatively closed political environment, a donor might seek to encourage incremental democratization by relying on service-oriented NGOs. Such an approach stems from the assumption that community-based and local development associations usually have an impact that goes well beyond service-delivery. They provide individuals with attitudes and skills, which, over time, may empower them to become more forceful in articulating certain political demands. Consequently, what begins as social work or poverty alleviation can evolve into advocacy.

Thus, the primary stated goal of USAID's civil society strategy in Egypt is not to contribute to democracy-building, but "to improve the quality of life for poor and disadvantaged groups" by strengthening the internal capacity of private and voluntary organizations (PVOs) and community development associations (CDAs) (USAID/Egypt 2000). However, this strategy also involves a more or less explicit attempt to enable these PVOs and CDAs to transcend the functions to which they have traditionally been confined—providing relief and social welfare—and to prompt them to take on advocacy roles. According to its proponents, there is some evidence that this approach is beginning to yield results. For instance, a report on activities carried out in the context of this strategy between October 1997 and September 1999 points out that, in several instances, projects that began by focusing on vocational training and community development led to important changes in attitudes and behavior, which in turn, led to advocacy-type efforts (USAID/Egypt 2000). For instance, some of the CDAs and PVOs which were receiving assistance, have begun to petition the government for changes in laws on issues ranging from child labor to divorce and alimony payments procedures. In Upper Egypt, women, participating in development-oriented NGOs, have been empowered to raise issues such as female circumcision, early age marriage, and the right of women to hold identification cards (which are required for voting and securing loans). According to the report, the capacity building and training activities carried out by USAID contributed to these transformations by strengthening the ability of PVOs and

CDAs to represent the interests of their constituents, while at the same time impressing on the associations' members the importance of engaging in public advocacy. The report concludes that, over time, "more and more PVOs and CDA . . . have themselves become advocates of advocacy" (USAID/Egypt 2000). In other words, they have come to realize that drawing the attention of the media and of public opinion to their needs, while lobbying government officials for changes in existing laws, are natural extensions of, and necessary complements to, their development activities. Furthermore, USAID's experience suggests that when this process takes place, donors can easily weave advocacy-support activities into their development-oriented ones, by providing targeted NGOs with some of the skills and know-how that may enable them to become more effective in articulating their concerns to both decision-makers and the public at large.

Finally, some will argue that the gradual integration of advocacy objectives into civil society projects, which began as development-oriented ones, provides several advantages. First, community-based associations are more likely to develop grass roots support than advocacy groups, which tend to be elite-driven. Second, these associations can gather credibility by accumulating a strong record of concrete achievements at the local level before they take on advocacy roles. And third, they are also likely to be seen as less threatening to governments than advocacy groups, especially when their activities have led to joint initiatives with local and regional officials; the trust built through such projects may greatly facilitate the task of service-oriented associations as they progressively engage in advocacy. In short, rooting advocacy activities in development projects may provide these activities with a stronger foundation, a broader base, greater legitimacy, and, through the positive relationships created with government officials, a greater likelihood of effecting changes in the policy arena.

Conclusion

For donors, the main implications of the arguments and the evidence that have been presented in this paper are twofold: one relates to the proper mix between 'supply-side' and 'demand-oriented' activities, and the other concerns the respective merits of advocacy NGOs and service-oriented ones.

With respect to the former point, the paper suggested that assistance strategies that emphasize civil society (i.e., the demand side of the political system) would usually be well advised to include supply-side activities aimed at strengthening the capacity of existing political institutions to process and respond to political demands. In fact, the more advanced the process of transition to democracy is, the more assistance packages ought to pay attention to the supply-side of the equation.

When the transition to democracy has not yet begun, when governmental will to reform may be lacking, when civil society is under siege and/or blatant human rights violations take place, making civil society a primary beneficiary of assistance may be particularly appropriate, if only to redress the imbalance of power between the state and society. Even at that early stage, though, some supply-side projects might be needed, since they may be essential to the launching and sustaining of a national dialogue between state and society, and between government and opposition elites. After all, these negotiations can be greatly facilitated by support for the institutional arenas within which they typically take place—from local councils and provincial assemblies to national legislatures.

Supply-side activities become even more vital once political space has been broadened, and the transition to democracy is already under way. At that point, and for the reasons that were examined in the second part of this chapter, it becomes critical to strengthen the effectiveness and representative nature of those institutions through which: political participation and contestation takes place, demands can be converted into public policy, and governance can be improved. In fact, donors should not wait until that stage before providing these institutions with the support they need to become more capable. Instead, 'pre-positioning' them may both avert subsequent breakdowns and reinforce the political commitment to move toward a more democratic government. Unless the political institutions, which are central to democracy and good governance, have been strengthened beforehand, they may prove unable to discharge effectively the enhanced responsibilities with which they are usually invested when the transition moves forward. At that stage, problems and popular disillusionment generated by poorly functioning political structures might bring a fatal blow to further democratic progress.

Just as demand-side assistance strategies usually call for supply-side activities, local development associations (as the last section of this chapter suggested) can take on advocacy roles as well. In Morocco, for instance, some of the most dynamic community-based associations, today, are neighborhood associations—associations de quartier. These associations initially emerged to deal with pressing, concrete concerns such as the preservation or rehabilitation of green spaces, the maintenance of public order, the cleanliness of streets, as well as employment-, health-, and development-related issues. However, they also have engaged in advocacy activities ranging from campaigns to lobbying municipal authorities and elected representatives and asking them to account for persistent problems and unmet public needs. Conversely, a prominent advocacy group, also located in Morocco, like Transparency Maroc (or "Moroccan Association for the Fight Against Corruption") has explicitly sought not to limit its action to advocacy, but to also formulate concrete proposals around curbing corruption in specific sectors or institutions. Indeed, Transparency Maroc has been solicited by certain corporations (such as the Office Chérifien des Phosphates) and government bureaucracies (the Ministry of Public Works and the Ministry of Education) to carry out activities designed to improve transparency within these institutions.

In short, a new generation of NGOs is increasingly blurring the line between advocacy and service-oriented organizations. Just as donors should be careful to design assistance strategies that pay due attention to the complementary relationships between supply and demand, they may find that this new generation offers the greatest returns on their democracy- and governance-promotion investments in the Arab world.

Notes

* Associate professor of government, Colby College. Some sections of this paper draw on the material contained in a monograph co-authored with Abdo Baaklini and Robert Springborg. See Abdo Baaklini, Guilain Denoeux, and Robert Springborg, *Democratization of Arab legislatures: A Developmental Agenda* (Albany, New York: Center for Legislative Development, 1999).

1. Adopted in 1957, this code gives drastically unequal rights to men and women, and legalizes discrimination against women in such areas as marriage, divorce, child custody, and inheritance.

2. According to Carapico, the first one was concentrated in the port city of Aden during the last two decades of British colonialism (i.e., from approximately the end of World War II until 1967), and was reflected in the multiplication of trade unions, syndicates, clubs, and political parties. The second occurred in North Yemen during the 1970s, and witnessed an explosion in the number and activities of local self-help groups, mutual aid networks, and community-improvement associations.

3. For instance, there are very few checks on the authority of local commanders, who tend to be very intolerant of criticisms of their actions and behavior, and do not hesitate to detain individuals or close down newspapers whenever they feel they have been slighted.

4. In the end, whether civil society dynamism fosters or threatens democracy depends largely on the broader political and institutional context within which that civil society operates. Berman's hypothesis in this regard is worth quoting at some length here, as it should be pondered by analysts of civil society in the Arab

world: "If a country's political institutions and structures are capable of channeling and redressing grievances and the existing political regime enjoys public support and legitimacy, then associationism will probably buttress political stability by placing its resources and beneficial effects in the service of the status quo. . . . If, on the contrary, political institutions and structures are weak and/or the existing political regime is perceived to be ineffectual and illegitimate, then civil society activity may become an alternative to politics, increasingly absorbing citizens' energies and satisfying their basic needs. In such situations, associationism will probably undermine political stability by deepening cleavages, furthering dissatisfaction, and providing rich soil for opposition movements. Flourishing civil society activity in these circumstances signals governmental and party failure and may bode ill for the regime's future" (Berman 1997: 427).

5. Faced with a donor determined to give priority to civil society organizations in the delivery of assistance, the host government may skillfully steer it—without the donor always realizing it—toward associations that are directly or indirectly controlled by the regime. If such entities then become the main recipients of foreign aid programs, the very purpose of external assistance—which is to redress the imbalance of power between State and society—will be defied.

6. In the parliamentary elections of March 1994, all the opposition parties combined had captured a mere 2.27 percent, of the vote, following a contest in which administrative interference had not impacted significantly on the results.

Part Two

NGOs of the Arab World: Between the Democracy Question and the Social Question

Chapter Five

From Inertia to Movement: A Study of the Conflict over the NGO Law in Egypt

Viviane Fouad, Nadia Ref'at, and Samir Murcos

This study examines the negotiating process, which took place between the Egyptian government, represented by the Ministry of Social Affairs on the one hand, and the Non-Governmental Organizations (NGOs)[1] on the other. These debates were about the law regulating NGOs' activities in Egypt. On May 1999, the promulgated Law 153/1999 is one of the latest initiative undertaken by the government of Egypt to further regulate the activities of associations and NGOs. Although this law did not change drastically the philosophy behind the NGO law, it generated some positive aspects for the civil society and its relationship with the state. This study traces the arguments and conflicts over the law back to the 1980s, with a particular focus on the period from May 1998 until the enactment of Law no. 153 in May 1999. It was during this period that direct negotiation between the two parties became possible. Moreover, this period witnessed the beginning of the forum for NGO activity, which was fostered and articulated by an alliance of both advocacy groups and civil organizations.

This negotiating process was a new experience, from a philosophical point of view in the history of the relationships between civil society and the state because of the new strategies and mechanisms it introduced, which reflected a new dynamism in civil society. This is important to the study in terms of deducing its results and assessing the ability of civil society to effect real transformations in social development, bring about social change, and firmly instill the values of participation and citizenship both at present and in the future.

We will first analyze the historical context of the relationship between the state and civil society by highlighting the circumstances which enabled the emergence of a civil society in Egypt. We will then try to focus on the new movement started by this civil society in order to stimulate political and civil participation and guarantee the freedom to associate without restrictions. The analysis will take into consideration the social, economic, and political changes, which occurred both at the local and the international levels. The content will also consider the repercussions of the changes on the relationship between the state and the civil society. The study is based on the dialectic of conflict and on the negotiations of both parties, in so far as it reflects, in reality, the essence of these changes.

State and Civil Society in Egypt: A Historical Overview

We cannot talk about civil society without mentioning the state in general and especially when discussing Egypt. Both the political experience and the literature related to the subject demonstrate that the coexistence between the state and civil society is, most of the time, dominated by the state. Despite this reality proved by facts and history, one must be conscious of a fundamental truth: the state and civil society are not two divided and different entities but are, in fact, closely related to each other. Each state, each regime has a civil society. Moreover, a deeper understanding of the word 'political' reveals that civil society is indeed a part of what is political. In other words, it is impossible to fully understand the fate of civil society and the impacts of the internal and external factors without grasping the evolution of the state (Ghalyun 1992).

What Nazih-al-Ayyubi refers to as "the functional centrality and the concentration of power" (al-Ayyubi 1989) constitutes one the fundamental aspects through which the administrative and political Egyptian patrimony has evolved over the centuries. One can trace this trend in Egypt right from the pharaohs, through the Greek, Coptic, and Islamic eras to the foundation of the modern state under Muhammad 'Ali's regency.

From Muhammad 'Ali's access to the throne in 1805, a new era started. The new state distinguished itself by the regime it founded. It was a centralizing and exclusive regime, which took over, very quickly, every aspect of the economy: agriculture, industry, and commerce (al-Ayyubi 1989). It also took charge of the organization of the state and created *divan* (ministries). While the state was being modernized, new social and economic forces, as well as major intellectual and cultural movements, emerged. As a consequence, a non-official press expressed itself, and associations and other entities like trade unions and political parties were created. The issue of foreign domination had been substantial for the emerging Egyptian civil society. One can even talk about a popular civil movement that faced its apex during the 1919 Revolution.

This movement later expressed itself on the political level through the Wafd Party, and through Bank Misr on the economic level (al-Ayyubi 1989). However, this movement of social forces could neither maintain the acquired assets of the liberal era, nor pursue the evolution of Egyptian political life. Thereafter, Egyptian society faced a crisis, which allowed the Free Officers to mobilize and take control in 1952. The role of the state became larger and the new regime followed the steps that Muhammad 'Ali had previously established.

Consequently, one assisted at the consolidation of the central government and at the concentration of power, which was to operate the economic and social development, but not the political field.

Indeed, political action was nationalized to the benefit of the leader (*al-hakim al-za'im*). The 1953 Law declared the dissolution of all political parties. In 1964, Law 32, known as the Law of Association was promulgated. Under this law, even the local institutions created by the government for youth, professionals, and workers simply became extensions of the state.

A New Mobilization of Civil Society: The Eighties and the Nineties

The period between the 1980s and the 1990s has witnessed many radical transformations both at the local and international levels. These transformations have an impact on the status of civil society in Egypt, on the nature of its functions, and its relations with the state.

National and International Transformations

At the international level, there has been an increased interest in civil society institutions, also called the 'third sector,' over the last twenty years. Moreover, the organizations faced a real development with regards to their size, influence, and power. This period saw the emergence of movements and organizations that supported and defended universal causes, such as human rights, the environment, women's rights, issues related to development, and international emergency relief. Finally, international funds increased their budget dedicated to the association sector from $1 billion in 1970 to $16 billion in 1997 (Abdallah 1999).

These transformations had a direct effect on Egyptian NGOs and associations. They gradually began to enjoy international moral recognition and material support. Moreover, these transformations generated a new field of actions, which were destined to produce political and social change. This is how the 'advocacy' and the 'protest' NGOs were created in Egypt. The creation of a network of both local and international organizations, offered these NGOs the possibility to exchange ideas and show solidarity with organizations across the country and around the world. It has also enabled them to access documents and international treaties, which can be used as references in order to exert pressure and defend certain rights. At the same time, the existence of this network raises many questions and debates about how foreign financial support to these NGOs makes their legitimacy and autonomy questionable. Moreover, their transparency, efficiency, and ability to be representative are also sometimes doubted.

At the local level, Egypt underwent many political, social, and economic transformations during the 1970s. The transformations had substantial repercussions on civil society in general, and especially on civil organizations. Although the autocratic and bureaucratic state apparatus remained, the growing influence of local and foreign interests started to manifest and organize itself in different groups. The interference of foreign interests and their alliance with both the elite and the state organs excluded large sectors of society—the middle class, workers, and peasants—who had previously benefited from 'Abd al-Nasser's policies (Thabit 1996). The new network of interactions and relations organized and defined, to a large degree, the political environment and its orientation. This is how, the policy for economic liberalization (infitah) was set up in the 1970s, and in the 1980s, political and economic reforms and Structural Adjustments Programs (SAPs) were implemented according to the International Monetary Fund. The programs entailed economic liberalization, privatization, encouragement of private capital, the weakening of the public sector, and the increasing integration of the Egyptian society and economy into the world market economy (Thabit 1996).

While all this was happening, the state withdrew from certain sectors; particularly the service sector, healthcare, housing, and education. State intervention in the economy was also reduced and all subsidies on products were removed. At the same time, the state's role in the legislative and security fields did not diminish; in fact, the developments in these fields were quite to the contrary. This is how legislature was created in order to attract both foreign and local private capital. At the security level, in order to maintain the political stability of the regime, a repressive policy toward popular protest was set up. The regime was threatened by the intensification of social imbalance, poverty, and marginalization of the lower classes, all of which came along with the economic reforms (Thabit 1996). Therefore, although the state since the 1970s has become weaker because of its dependence on foreign aid, it has not lost its security and legislative powers. Consequently, new legislation restricting liberties and limiting the actions of civil society were passed. These new laws were promulgated despite a greater margin of liberty in terms of freedom of speech and civil action, which had been forged over the last twenty-five years (Khalil 1993).

These evolutions reflect back on the relations between the state, NGOs, and civil society. The state has shown greater interest in civil organizations because of a combination of factors: the orientation of the state, its diminished role with respect to production and social sectors, and the changes within the international arena. The state now invites these organizations to participate in development. It releases more authorizations allowing the creation of these organizations, which then receive foreign subsidies. However, the public authorities are, in reality, only limiting their action to the fields of social services and policy enforcement, leaving the NGOs to fill the gaps created after the state stepped back from these social services. Moreover, the state is encouraging, on one hand, the involvement of these organizations in the traditional domains of production, which increases national revenues, but on the other hand, it imposes all sorts of restrictions to stop the development of civil society and its development into an autonomous actor, which would redefine its relationship with the state (Abd al-Fadil et al. 1996).

In other words, the role of these organizations cannot go beyond what we can call a 'complementary role' because they are still under the state's control. Law no. 32 of 1964, which enables the state to control the organizations and the activities of the organizations, is still valid. It also can be highlighted, that some members of different political movements left these movements and entered the NGOs and civil associations during the 1980s. This passage corresponds to the emergence of a new arena of civil action, which is represented by contesting organizations, such as the ones fighting for human rights, women's rights, and the environment. Most of these organizations are registered as 'civil societies'—regulated by the civil code—in order to escape falling under the legislation of the Ministry of Social Affairs. The relationships they maintain with the state are characterized by tension and conflicts because of the problems these organizations raise in terms of civil rights, politics, and social issues. Public authorities fear the negative image of the state that they create and pass on to international institutions, especially the U.S. and the European Community, which have repeatedly denounced the violations of rights by public authorities.

Civil Organizations and the Law on Associations

Human rights associations and new forms of civil societies took shape from the mid-1980s to May 1998. The beginning of the confrontation and conflict over the NGO law can be traced back to the mid-1980s when the Egyptian government refused to register two organizations: the Arab Human Rights Organization and the Egyptian Human Rights Organization. The Ministry of Social Affairs refused to register them on the grounds that the environment did not require such assemblies, in accordance with Law no. 32 of 1964. The two organizations then took several steps. They filed a suit in the administrative State Council court in 1987, protesting the refusal of the Ministry of Social Affairs to register the Egyptian Human Rights Organization. The director of the Center for Legal Studies and Information on Human rights was then assigned by the Egyptian Human Right Organization to file a suit in the State Council, declaring Law no. 32 of 1964 unconstitutional. In 1991, the two organizations, together with the branch of Amnesty International in Egypt, formed a committee to amend the NGO Law. This committee charged Amir Salim[2] to publish a critical study of this law and of a new bill, and it became one of the first documents published on the question.[3]

The turning point in the confrontation over the NGO Law between the states and the NGOs was during the International Conference on Development and Population (ICDP) that was held in Cairo in 1994. During the preparations for the conference, the private assemblies and NGOs, which had been founded as civil societies, had, for the first time, the opportunity to meet and get to know one another.

The state had objected to the participation of Egyptian civil organizations in the conference but changed its position after the insistence of the conference organizers. This international conference was an opportunity to present issues related to the Egyptian civil society and NGO activity in particular. It was also an opportunity to discuss Law no. 32 of 1964, at the local and international levels. Before the conference was held, the government had modified three articles of this law.[4] However, it is believed that these amendments were to appease the campaigns demanding the cancellation of this law, without making any real changes in the relations between the state and the NGOs.[5] The government was obliged to publicly announce at the international conference its intention to reconsider the law in order to broaden democratic activity and remove the restrictions that obstruct the independence of NGOs' activity.

This conference raised concerns for the state as it offered more freedom of movement and action for NGOs and raised the issues of Law no. 32 of 1964. After the conference and during the preparations for the Fourth World Conference on Woman that was due to be held in Peking in 1995, the state narrowed the scope of NGOs' activity and attacked the human rights organizations and civil societies. For instance, in January 1995, the Egyptian Foreign Ministry informed donor institutions that it was strictly forbidden to fund assemblies and NGOs, which were not registered in the Ministry of Social Affairs and were not regulated by the NGOs' Law no. 32 of 1964. The Legislation Department in the Ministry of Justice, during the same month, drafted a memorandum that declared illegal all institutions and centers that had been registered as civil societies for public utility, and stated that they should be subjected to Law no. 32 of 1964. This was followed by a fierce media campaign led by official organs from the Egyptian Ministries of Foreign Affairs and Interior against organizations and assemblies working on human rights issues. This followed the annual report of the U.S. State Department on Human Rights in 1994 that accused Egypt of many human rights violations. The media campaign accused those involved in human rights issues, of providing the international organizations with information that affected Egypt's reputation. They were accused of depending on foreign funding, of supporting predominantly political activities, and of seeking to please international funding institutions. The media campaign also said that the principles of human rights were not observed among the members of these organizations, as was evidenced in the violent internal differences and the mutual accusations traded by members of the Egyptian Human Rights Organization during its fifth general assembly in 1994. The authorities also restricted the activities of human rights and woman's NGOs.

In response to this campaign, the representatives of eight human rights organizations[6] denounced the measures of the government that were aimed at besieging civil rights institutions. They condemned the memorandum prepared by the Legislation Department in the Ministry of Justice and took several steps to counter this campaign. The legal experts succeeded in rebutting the decree of the Ministry of Justice and the state agreed not to enforce it. These organizations criticized the state, which forbade feminist associations working with civil societies from attending the Fourth World Conference on Women. This was reported in the foreign media, and the state withdrew from the fray when it realized the negative effects that such a position could have. It allowed them to take part in the preparatory meetings of the conference.[7]

In spite of these battles, between March and October of 1995, there was an initiative to create an environment for dialogue between the government and the assemblies and NGOs. United Nation's Children's Fund launched this initiative and its aim was to draw up a strategy to strengthen the role of Egyptian NGOs and to start a dialogue on Law no. 32 of 1964 through a series of meetings and symposia. While civil societies and NGOs took part in the meeting, no real progress was made.[8]

However, the state took no concrete steps to reconsider Law no. 32 of 1964 until 1997. Only at this point did the Egyptian government agreed to include this law among the laws that would be revised.[9] The Ministry of Social Affairs issued Decree no. 38 for 1997, to form a committee under the chairmanship of Counsellor Muhmamad Fathi Nagib composed of fifteen leading specialists. The committee was assigned the task of studying social legislation and preparing bills. It was to start its work with a bill to replace Law no. 32 of 1964. The formation of this committee created the impression that the new law was being democratically implemented in consultation between the state and representatives of civil society.

Law No 153 of 1999: Exerting Pressure in Negotiations

Several NGOs learned that the government secretly intended to enact a new law on NGO activity without consulting any of the concerned NGOs. The new bill contained new restrictions on the activities of NGOs, although there were a few articles that eased or alleviated some of those contained in Law no. 32 of 1964. The campaign that was launched against the new law marked a qualitative turning point in the activities of NGOs and human rights activities. A broad alliance was formed that brought together civil society organizations and centers active in the field of human rights, and NGOs that were involved in social development. They united in pursuit of one common goal, through an independent initiative separated from any foreign party, and with their own financial resources and effort. They relied on a democratic mechanism in planning and implementing a prolonged one-year campaign. This campaign and the negotiating process with the state can be divided into two distinct phases.

The First Phase

During this phase, human rights organizations and civil societies were, in particular, active. The government was supposed to present the bill to the People's Assembly before the parliamentary recess in June 1998. Thus, there was very little time for action. During this phase, several practical steps were taken. Statements were issued and studies were conducted to reject the new bill. These shed light on the problematic and negative impact of the new draft law on NGO activity. A statement defending the independence of NGO activities was signed by twenty NGOs, which were mostly civil societies.[10] This was followed by a Declaration of Principles to defend free and independent NGO activity. Sixty-seven NGOs and civil society organizations signed this declaration. It affirmed the right to freely form assemblies and NGOs and asserted that these NGOs were legal according to the constitution, and international agreements and conventions. It rejected any tutelage of governmental and administrative departments and affirmed that NGOs' activity should be independent. It further stated that public activities were political in nature and demanded a democratic environment that would allow free movement and innovation. A copy of the new declaration was sent to the minister of social affairs. Furthermore, the group of human rights organizations published legal and constitution-related studies about the new bill.

A media campaign was launched in the state-owned, party-owned daily press and weekly magazines. NGO activists, Egyptian intellectuals, and well-known writers took part in this campaign that criticised the new draft law on the grounds that it violated the right of free action for NGOs and democratic principles. Part of the media campaign also involved organizing a press conference to explain the shortcomings of the bill.

In addition, meetings of NGOs were arranged to discuss the bill and reach a common stand about the needs of NGOs and the dangers of this draft.[11] International NGOs were also contacted in an attempt to mobilize international pressure against the bill.

The first steps of the campaign were taken speedily and forcefully; different fronts were involved and various methods were used. There was an attempt to build local pressure that would prevent the bill from being submitted to the People's Assembly. These steps were successful; the government postponed the presentation of the bill to the People's Assembly. Broad-based discussions started and the issue of democratic NGO activity was brought to the public's attention. While some people believed that international pressure during this phase was the decisive factor in the state's retraction, others believed that the internal pressure was equally decisive and that the state was taken by surprise by the speed and forcefulness of the local campaign.

At any rate, the state opened the door to dialogue and negotiations with NGOs. Two encounters were arranged between the minister of social affairs, Dr. Mervat el Tellawi and the representatives of NGOs and of civil assemblies in June and July 1998, in Cairo and Alexandria. Representatives of eighty assemblies and centers were present. Most of them had signed the Declaration of Principles on NGOs' Activities. The aspects and results of these encounters can be evaluated as follows:

1) The government, as represented by the minister of social affairs, tried to dissipate the angry revolt that had broken out when the news of the bill had been leaked. The minister tried to give the impression that she was willing to hold a dialogue and negotiations and that the NGOs and assemblies could take part in drafting the NGO law. Four NGOs' representatives were included in the drafting committee of the new law.[12] The minister also announced her willingness to look into a number of demands and recommendations.[13]

2) Some of the documents on the new bill were not available to most NGOs and assemblies taking part in the meetings, and especially during the first one that was more like an interrogation session.[14] The second meeting, which was held in Alexandria, was marked by greater clarity of vision. The NGOs considered it to be the beginning of contact and they forcefully criticized the draft law.[15]

3) No clear measures were laid down to choose the negotiators representing the NGOs, but they were directly nominated. Nor was a clear and well-defined mechanism set up to follow the proceedings in the drafting committee or to make the negotiators accountable. However, the fact that these representatives of the NGOs were included in the committee was perceived as a contribution to "the creation of communication channels between the institutions of civil society and the concerned executive bodies."[16]

In July, a new blueprint for the NGOs' law appeared. It contained some amendments, but did not meet the most important demands of the NGOs.

The Second Phase

The NGOs taking part in the campaign believed that the first phase had succeeded in stopping the bill from becoming a law and had provided the necessary information about it to the associations and NGOs. A number of representatives of NGOs had been included in the drafting committee. The second phase started when these NGOs began to feel that their efforts had brought them some gains, and that they had to build on these gains and develop them positively and effectively. They also had to increase the number of participants in the campaign, and find an organizational framework for this campaign. Two different points of views were highlighted:

The first trend was supported by the human rights organizations, which believed that the campaign should be limited to the five big human rights organizations[17] and five other NGOs (later there was a slight increase in number), provided that these latter were big and influential. This strategy depended on unifying the efforts of this small number of institutions in a narrow organizational framework, as they were considered stronger, more effective, and more experienced. External pressure would be a helping factor in the negotiations to pressure the government.[18]

The second trend was supported by human rights organizations and the other civil societies, which believed that the campaign should not be confined to the human rights organizations, but that NGOs directly affected by the law should also be included. It was essential to strengthen the link between human rights activities and activities for social development. This trend was based on a strategy that sought to unify the efforts of these organizations in a democratically established broad organizational framework.[19]

The second trend succeeded in founding what was called the Forum for the Development of NGOs' Activity in August 1998, with sixty-seven NGOs and assemblies as members. Membership later increased to 104 institutions from twelve governorates. The forum was founded during the first constituent conference that was held in the headquarters of the Upper Egypt Society for Development and Education at the invitation of twenty centers and NGOs. The participants agreed on definite objectives and principles that were not only about the bill but also on the rights to form organizations and to foster NGOs' activities. In addition to monitoring the developments related to the new bill, the forum defined its mission as a "constant effort to activate NGOs' action in our society, protect our democracy, develop its mechanisms, and coordinate methods between organizations." An organizational structure was formed, a coordinating committee was established, and a plan of action was drawn up. However, the forum remained a flexible framework that allowed everyone to express their opinion, and to vote and settle differences by agreement. The most important measures, tools, and mechanisms of action that were agreed upon during this forum were as follows:

- Preparing files of documents related to the bill and the articles that should be amended, which were distributed to political parties, trade unions, professional syndicates, members of the People's Assembly, the media, and important personalities.
- Publication of a bulletin for the forum that reported all new developments, informed the societies involved of what had been achieved, and covered the news of NGOs in all governorates.
- Invitation of members of the People's Assembly, and especially those who were on the Committee for Religious Affairs, to attend the conference of the forum that was held in October 1998, and the conference that was held in Minya, at the invitation of the Coptic Evangelical Organization in November 1998. The members of the People's Assembly promised to invite representatives of the forum to an information session with the Committee of Social and Religious Affairs.

The new blueprints (from September 26, 1998) of the bill were discussed during the two conferences. Discussions were also held with NGO representatives in the consultative committee to draft the law. Dr. Fathi Naguib, the chairman of the Drafting Committee was invited to attend the Minya conference and discuss the articles of the bill as contained in the blueprint.

The final communiqué of the conference was sent to the national press, the opposition press, and a number of local and international news agencies. It was also sent to members of the People's Assembly, members of the Drafting Committee of this bill, a number of important public figures and the minister of social affairs.

Naturally, there were impediments to the action and performance because the participants were volunteers. This created difficulties at the administrative and executive levels in terms of increasing membership and increasing contacts with the mass media.

Lack of financial resources was another obstacle. The forum financed its own activities. Another difficulty was that many assemblies did not have modern means of communication. There were also the many forms of pressure that were exerted by the government on the assemblies and

NGOs. This created a state of anxiety and fear. A media campaign was launched in November and December 1998, which concentrated on the issue of foreign funding and linked it to 'dubious' activities, corruption, profiteering, and harming national security.

Civil society received a surprise on May 14, 1999 when the Council of Ministers approved the bill on associations, which did not correspond to what had been agreed upon by the Drafting Committee. Although some kind of negotiating process between the state and the organizations of civil society took place with respect to the bill, the Council of Ministers went ahead without considering the three published modified versions of the law, taking into consideration some of the civil society's demands. Instead, the bill was then being presented before the People's Assembly. This created a strong feeling of being deceived and a number of similar reactions from the forum, the human rights organizations and some other institutions and personalities. They can be summarized as follows:

A group of representatives of NGOs[20] and members of the forum to develop NGOs' activity declared a hunger strike in protest of the new law.

Four NGOs' representatives, who were members of the consultative committee to draft the law—Dr. Adel Abu Zahra, Dr. Tarek Ali Hassan, Counsellor Mohamed Abdul Aziz al-Gindi, and the lawyer Amir Salim—issued a statement, in which they affirmed that "the Drafting Committee had reached a text that met the minimal demands of all parties, but the bill that had been declared was different from the text agreed upon. We disclaim our responsibility for it."

Ten human rights NGOs and centers issued a statement that attacked the new bill and was titled: "In whose interests do we undermine NGOs' activities in Egypt?" committee coordinating the activities of parties and political forces issued a separate statement titled, "No to the Law on Societies." This statement demanded that the discussion of the new law be postponed and a dialogue started between the parties, the political forces, and the NGOs. It also called for a conference to be held promptly that would bring together NGOs, human rights centers, and parties.

The Forum to Develop NGOs' Activities held a conference in Cairo that was attended by human rights organizations, during which they rejected both the manner in which the new law was issued and its contents. They took a decision to send a delegation to the Peoples' Assembly to demand that the discussion of the new bill be postponed. Files were also sent to some members of the Peoples' Assembly that were used during the discussion of the law in the assembly. In spite of these efforts, Law no. 153 of 1999 was passed and the campaign came to an end. In order to analyze the negotiation process, three questions were raised.

Who Were the Negotiating Parties

Any negotiating process has principal and secondary parties, visible and unseen parties, who greatly influence the negotiating process. In this case, the visible parties were, on the one hand, the Ministry of Social Affairs, as represented by the former minister and its representatives in the joint committee to draft the law (the representatives of the government), and on the other, the representatives of NGOs, and members of the forum to develop NGOs' action. This study has dealt with the influence of the behind-the-scenes actors on the results of the negotiations. (Such parties are the security services in general, such as the police, for example.)

What Was the Subject of Negotiations

The answer to this question reveals the positions of the negotiating parties and the contesting interests. A reading of the successive blueprints of the law and the final law itself, as well as the comments, criticism, and proposals published by the NGOs will reveal three main aspects that were discussed.

1) The independence of NGOs' activity: the right to form and declare their association, freedom of activity, administrative and organizational independence, and the right to form local, regional, or international alliances and ties.
2) The economic aspects of NGOs' activities.
3) Organizations that are not subject to the old NGO law (no. 32 of 1964), and especially, civil societies engaged in human rights, women's affairs, etc.

There were two different concepts adopted by the parties. Articulating the governmental point of view, Burhan Ghalyun declared that the construction of the state and the nation has shortchanged the autonomy of civil society and threatened its right to exist. The elite classes believed it was the state's obligation to interfere in all societal matters, leading to a repression of civil society. Any collective cultural, social, and economic initiatives thus became a political activity (Ghalyun 1993). This framework is particularly close to that of the modern Egyptian state, which is the legitimate heir of the revolution of July 1952.

Such a vision considered civil society to be a natural extension, or an inseparable part, of the state, that was bound by the desire and will of the government. It is almost similar to the postion adopted by the governmental parties during negotiations with NGOs.

On the opposite side, in the NGOs' conceptualization, civil society is considered a major independent structure that has the right to participate, alongside the Egyptian state, in development issues. It even has the right to hold the state accountable and assess its performance on the basis of "The Declaration of Principles Governing NGOs' Activity."[21] This declaration states: "Non-Governmental Organizations are one of the main tools which individuals could use in public actions. By nature, public action is political action, whether it is related to human rights, working with special groups or taking part in development, in order to protect the rights of individuals or groups support certain policies, form pressure groups to protect the rights of individuals and groups, or form groups to pressure decision-making centers."

These two opposing visions of civil society can be clearly traced, as reflected in the three aforementioned aspects, in the different blueprints of the bill and Law no. 153 for 1999 as it had been adopted and enacted.

The Independence of NGO Activity

a) The right to form and declare an organization

The first question that emerged during the negotiation proceedings is: does any group with social interests and objectives have the right to officially form and declare itself to be an NGO by merely notifying the administrative authorities or should there be prior permission from these latter?

Although most blueprints of the law state that any group has the right to declare itself an association by merely notifying the administrative authorities, yet both the blueprint, presented by the Council of Ministers to the People's Assembly, and the law, which was enacted, supported the government point of view. The administrative authorities have the right to register or reject the association, while on the other hand the group of founders have the right to challenge this decision in the relevant court within sixty days.

b) Freedom of activity and the fields of action

The first blueprint of the law prohibited NGOs from practicing any political activities: "political activities were subject to the laws regulating political parties" (Article 11, May 1998, copy of the law).

The paragraph of this article had faced extensive criticism from the NGOs, who believed that some of their activities, by their very nature, were related to political activities. Such activities are, for instance, the organization of debates and symposia, to which political figures are invited, or some of the activities practiced by the human rights organizations to supervise elections or monitor the mechanisms of democratic development and the political impediments to this progress. This text also contradicts Article 55 of the constitution, which grants the right to form associations or societies without restricting activities of a political nature.[22]

Some blueprints of the law agreed with this view. The phrase, "activities that were political in nature" was omitted from the blueprint of September 26, 1998. Instead, it contained the following: "practicing political activity in infringement of the law regulating political parties." However, the blueprint presented by the Council of Ministers to the People's Assembly, and the law that was passed, restricted activities that were political or related to syndicates: "Any political or syndicate-related activities can only be exercised by the political parties and syndicates" (Article 11 of Law 153 for 1999).

c) Administrative independence

The blueprints of the law defined the regulations of the NGO, regarding the board of directors and its quorum, the duration of a session, regulations for renewal, the right to oppose candidates for membership of the board, etc., whereas the NGOs believed that it was the general assembly of the associations that should have the right to define the regulations of the NGO, according to its own nature and internal circumstances.[23]

d) The right to form sectorial and regional unions

The blueprints of the Law met the demand of NGOs and allowed the formation of several sectorial unions in the same region (blueprint of September 26, 1998), but it did not allow the formation of several regional unions. None of the blueprints of the law granted the freedom to form the general union of NGOs without a decree from the President of the Republic.

The law that was passed not only prevented the formation of regional unions and the formation of the general union without a decree from the President of the Republic, it also prevented the formation of several sectorial unions in the same governorate. The NGOs who were involved in the negotiations considered this to be a restriction of the freedom of civil society to form unions based on the NGOs' initiative, rather than forming them as an extension of the executive power of the state.

The Financial Aspects of NGOs' Activity

In practice, it is difficult to distinguish between two issues: the independence of NGOs' activities and the independence of its economic aspects. The funding of NGOs was a matter to which the negotiating parties attached great importance. The press and television also covered the discussion on this question. Already, before the start of the negotiations, two diverging points of view were reported in the press, in the official journals *(al-nasharat al-kawamiya)*, in the opposition bulletins, and NGOs' reports. The first point of view opposed foreign funding and cast aspersions on all activities that received foreign assistance (especially in the field of human rights). They were accused of profiteering, corruption, damaging the reputation of Egypt, carrying out foreign plots, and undermining national unity and cohesion.

The point of view that supported foreign funding refused to evaluate the activities of NGOs, based on its financial sources, whether the latter are local or international. The criteria used were related to the objectives and essence of the activities and the extent to which they fulfilled the priorities of the national agenda, the level of democratic management, and their impact on national development. At the same time, these advocates refused to describe everything from the West as colonialist. They also refuse to ignore the international democratic development movement that has evolved in the United Nations and is expressed in the international conferences on environment, health, woman's and children' rights, poverty, etc. Furthermore, they refuse to believe that the greater part of foreign funding that Egypt receives is obtained by the state. However, they do support the idea that democratic monitoring of NGO activities should be through internal NGO mechanisms. This could be achieved through openly declaring budgets and financial sources, and national monitoring mechanisms so that every citizen can monitor the NGOs' budgets.[24]

It was clear therefore, that the two points of view on foreign funding were prominent in all the blueprints of the law. None of the blueprints gave NGOs the right to receive foreign aid unless they had obtained the approval of the administrative body. The law also stipulated this. The NGOs considered this as a restriction of its financial independence and demanded that it should be enough to notify the administrative body of the funding, while keeping open budgets and accounts of expenditure. Furthermore, members and users of the NGOs, and the public prosecution would have the right to sue the NGO's person in charge for any financial corruption.

Regarding those civil organizations that were not subject to the old NGOs' law (Law no. 32 of 1964), that is civil societies, the bill was considered to be a move by the state to to tighten its control on these organizations. Thus, the state insisted on adding an article stipulating that every group whose objectives or activities were similar to those of NGOs, even if it assumed a legal form that was different from that of NGOs and institutions, should amend its regulations and apply for registration in accordance with the Law. Many of those working in human rights organizations considered this text to be harsher than that of Law no. 32, under which many non-profit civil societies had been formed.

What Was the Power of the Negotiating Parties

By negotiating power, we mean the ability to influence the other party in order to realize the immediate and strategic objectives of the negotiation process. These aims are the sum of material strength and real influence and the competence to pursue negotiations despite the historical, economic, social, and political context. In this case, we can be guided by the former equation as an analytical tool to understand the negotiating powers of the two parties involved and grasp the final result.

On one side of the negotiating process stands the Ministry of Social Affairs, representing the central government of Egypt, with all its bureaucratic organs, mass media, and its legislation arsenal related to political and civil participation. Its apparent structures are civil while its essence is governmental (such as the General Union of NGOs and the regional and sectorial unions that have been inherited from the 'Abd al-Nasser system). It has technical experience, technocrats to draft legislation, and a governmental legislative group in the People's Assembly.

The government strategy has approved what we can call a 'containment strategy' to quiet, appease, understand, and make good use of the contradictions of the NGOs. The legitimacy of the cause defended by the state is reflected in the concept of national sovereignty and social cohesion.

On the other side stand the private organizations—advocacy organizations, civil societies, and the NGOs, that is, the organizations most aware of the impact of the law on their activities and existence. They launched the first initiative to discuss the law and created the Forum for the Development of Civil Action. The NGOs also had good political and legal experience, which enabled them to provide an accurate analysis and detailed criticism of the various blueprints of the law. They also presented alternative drafts.

However, there were significant points of contention regarding the legitimacy of the NGOs in the forum. For instance, they tried to involve the civil associations in the process, but, in reality, the percentage of member associations of the forum remained meager compared to the total number of NGOs—14,000 associations, including non-active and inefficient organizations. This was used as a reason to attack and question the legitimate representation of the forum and the NGOs' position vis--vi s the l aw

The second difficulty was the issue of foreign funding. The international environment gave financial resources, technical skills, and practical experience to many NGOs, especially advocacy and mobilization organizations. However, the argument of foreign funding was used to undermine the legitimacy and credibility of the NGOs in the negotiations. To a great extent, it reflects the reality that the local material and moral support of civil society institutions is mostly associated with charity projects, services, current and urgent activities (especially those associated with religious institutions).

However, there is little awareness of the importance of human rights and development that have long-term cumulative and strategic returns, especially, in a political and legislative environment that restricts such an approach. Furthermore, the social groups that can give local funding (and especially the business associations) have different objectives and interests from the NGOs involved in human rights and development work.[25] This situation illustrates the inability or failure of these NGOs to interest local funders who have money and interests in human rights issues. On the other hand, we find that charitable and religious NGOs are able to obtain funds, not only from businessmen, but also from the middle and lower classes.

The NGOs' forum, therefore, decided to rely wholly on its own funds and members' subscriptions and rejected foreign funding, affirming instead the values of self-reliance and enhanced participation. In other words, while international institutions provided the NGOs with material and moral support in the first phases of the campaign against the bill, this support was not so strong in the last phases of the campaign. This strengthened the NGOs' negotiating position. However, the lack of financial resources hampered these organizations ability to perform administrative and executive missions and to communicate, coordinate, and follow-up on tasks and activities. With regards to the negotiation strategy adopted by the NGOs, we can say that it was one aimed toward mutual gains for both parties. After evaluating the real material strength and influence of each party,[26] they used negotiating mechanisms, tactics and pressure by forming alliances and networks of interested parties (such as the Forum for NGOs' Activity) drawing from the former political experience of activists in advocacy and mobilization organizations and the grass roots experience of the NGOs' members.

They contacted and informed members of the People's Assembly of their position in this negotation process and sought their support during the discussion of the law in the People's Assembly. In actuality, the session in which the law was discussed turned out to be dynamic and the viewpoint of the NGOs was presented through the documents they had sent to the members of the People's Assembly. Some women members of the NGOs also went on a hunger strike and there was a protest rally in front of the People's Assembly. Furthermore, they successfully used means of electronic communication to promote international coordination to serve their cause.

Conclusion

A final reading of the results of negotiations, which led to the enactment of Law no. 153 of 1999, should emphasize four main points:

- The Egyptian government maintained the essence of its philosophy vis- -vis NGOs' activity. There was some flexibility, reflected in withdrawing some of the powers of the administrative bodies and making the judiciary an arbitrator between the administrative bodies and the NGOs.
- The state in Egypt succeeded in bringing the human rights organizations under the umbrella of the new law.
- The NGOs gained some experience in organizing networks, and in pressuring and negotiating with the state.
- The margin of free movement, which was allowed by the law on 'civil and commercial societies,' was lost. Here we are referring to civil societies which registered as associations as opposed to NGOs in order to avoid falling under the regulations of Law no. 32/1964.

This analysis of conflict and negotiations between the state and NGOs reveals that several problematic issues on both the theoretical and the practical levels are yet to be solved. Some of these issues include: the role and independence of civil society, the role of the state, the democratic climate, and the interaction between local and international variables. All these subjects require further theoretical research as well as practical action. What is certain from this study is that the phenomena analyzed here represent a new experience in Egyptian political life: the relation between the state and civil society.

Notes

1. We shall use the term Non-Governmental Organizations (NGOs) to refer to the non-governmental organizations registered in the Ministry of Social Affairs and human rights assemblies registered as non-profit civil societies.
2. Lawyer Amir Salim is a lawyer and the director of the Center for Legal Studies and Information for Human Rights.
3. The study was titled, "Right for associations: Critical study on this association law, unconstitutional exception of this law, and projects related to a new law on associations."
4. These modifications were to prevent employees of the Ministry of Social Affairs who were working in the administration of these NGOs from being board members and to prevent members of the local councils also from being members of the NGOs' board of directors. Also, the minister of social affairs, who was president of the General Union of NGOs, was to be replaced by a president and a council to be appointed by the President of the Republic.
5. Shahida el-Baz, 1995.
6. The Arab Human Rights Organization, the Ibn Khaldoun Center, the Cairo Center for the Study of Human Rights, the Egyptian Society for Enlightenment, the Center of Legal Assistance for Human Rights, the Human Development Center, the Egyptian Human Rights Center, and the Egyptian Human Rights Organization.
7. Shahida el-Baz, 1995.
8. Interview with Dr. Hala Shukrallah, an NGO activist, 1999.
9. It seems that the main motive was not so much to respond to local demands to amend or revoke the law in order to encourage greater NGOs' activities. It was, rather, an attempt to contain the human rights organization and civil societies that had become active during the past few years, giving the state cause for concern. Egypt was also very sensitive about its image in world public opinion and was eager to appear to be a liberal state.
10. They were al Nadim Center for Psychological Treatment and Rehabilitation of Victims of Violence, the Center for Egyptian Woman's causes, the Center for Studies on the New Woman, the Center for the Egyptian Woman's Causes, the Center for Means of Communication Suited to Development. The forum of organizations for the Development of Woman, the Helwan Center for Social Studies, the Center for Legal Studies and Information on Human Rights, the Cairo Center for Human Rights Studies, the Center for Legal Assistance for Human Rights, the Human Rights Center to Assist Prisoners, the Land Center for Human Rights, the Egyptian Human Rights Organization, the Arab Programme for Human Rights Activists, the Development of Democracy Group, the Society for the Protection of the Alexandria Environment, Osiris for Rural Development and Protection of the Environment and Life, and the Center for Trade Union Services.
11. See Massirat tatwir al-amal al-ahli wa qanun al-jam'iyyat al-ahliya al-gadid. (Cairo: The Forum to Develop NGOs' Activity, March 1999).
12. They were Dr. Tarik Ali Hassan (Zeinab Kamel Hassan Institution, Cairo); Amir Salem (Center for Legal Studies and Information on Human Rights, Cairo); Counsellor Mohamed el Gindi (Society for Freedom to Develop the Community,

Alexandria); Dr. Adel Abu Zahra (Friends of the Environment Society, Alexandria.)

13. The minister of social affairs agreed to a recommendation presented by the NGOs' representative on the annulment of Article 36 bis, which enables the minister of social affairs to appoint any number of members to the NGOs' board of directors. She also said that she was prepared to reconsider a number of clauses prohibiting 'political activities' and revises the 'duration' and not the 'principle' of criminal penalties in the infringements of NGOs' actions. See Massirat tatwir al-amal al-ahli wa qanun al-jam'iyyat al-ahliya al-gadid.
14. Interview with Dr. Suzanne Fayyad, an NGO activist, 1999.
15. Interview with Dr. Adel Abu Zahra, the Friends of the Environment Society (Alexandria) and meeting with Dr. Hala Shukrallah.
16. See *Massirat tatwir al-amal al-ahli wa qanun al-jam'iyyat al-ahliya al-gadid.*
17. The Egyptian Human Rights Organization, the Cairo Center for Human Rights Studies, the Center for Legal Assistance for Human Rights, the Arab Center for the Independence of the Judiciary and Lawyers, and the Group for the Development of Democracy.
18. Meetings with Dr. Hala Shukrallah, Dr. Suzanne Fayyad, Professor Azza Suliman, Dr. Mohamed Hassan Khalil. Also see a document dated July 15, 1998 by Nagid al-Bor'i, a lawyer who was also the director of the Group for the Development of Democracy entitled al-Juz' al-thani min al-hamla, did qanun al-jami'yyat.
19, Meetings with Dr. Hala Shukrallah, Dr. Suzanne Fayyad, Professor Azza Suliman, Dr. Mohamed Hassan Khalil.
20. They were Dr. Suzanne Fayyad, Dr. Aida Seif al-Dawla, Ms. Rahma Rifaat and Ms. Leila Youssef.
21. *Massirat tatwir al-amal al-ahli wa qanun al-jam'iyyat al-ahliya al-gadid* 10, 11.
22. Ibid., 33.
23. Ibid. See the remarks on the blueprint of the NGOs' Law 16/3/1999, 49–51.
24. Ibid. See the introduction.
25. Amani Qandil, "al-Mujtama' al-madani fi Misr," in *al-Mujyama' al-madani -l-watan wa dawrihi tahqiq al-dimuqratiya*, ed. B. Ghalyun. (Cairo: Markaz Dirasat al-Wihda al-Arabiya, 1992), 22.
26. There are a number of strategies used in the negotiating process. See: *al-Tafawud wa-l-tafawud al-tanmawi*. Cairo: Fustat Center.

Chapter Six

Hegemony and Counter-hegemony in Egypt: Advocacy NGOs, Civil Society, and the State

Nicola Pratt

In the last decade, scholars, practitioners, and policymakers have given a lot of attention to the question of the contribution of non-governmental organizations (NGOs) to governance. The discussions over NGOs and governance have reflected growing concerns about how to cope with the rapid social, political, and economic changes entailed by globalization. Globalization challenges traditional forms of governance, based on a system of national, sovereign, territorial-bound states. NGOs play an important role within these political transformations because they represent a new form of political actor, whose sphere of action is both sub-national and supra-national. NGOs raise hopes of new forms of citizen participation and managing social and political change. Simultaneously, NGOs challenge the autonomy of nation-states and raise concerns about transparency and accountability.

Earlier approaches to this question were very optimistic and NGOs were heralded as the panacea for all ills—from underdevelopment to lack of democracy. NGOs were seen as possessing a multitude of positive attributes that the state did not possess, such as smallness of size, proximity to those who had been previously excluded from the development process, and an ability to create a public sphere in which individuals at the 'grass roots' can participate (for example, in English, Brown and Korten 1989, Korten 1990, Clark 1991, Edwards and Hulme 1992, Kandil 1995a, Fisher 1998; and in Arabic, the series of studies published by the Ibn Khaldoun Center for

Development as part of the "Civil Society in the Arab World Project" 1995, and Kandil 1995b). By the mid-1990s, the NGO backlash had begun. Many recent writings, both in the West and in the Arab world, have characterized NGOs as elitist and corrupt organizations with no accountability, dependent on western funding, and promoting western agendas. At best, they are seen as merely inefficient and unable to cope with the huge task that was originally set for them at the beginning of the 1990s (for example, in English, Stewart 1997: 11–34; and in Arabic, al-Masri 1998, 1999).

Two different concepts of the place of NGOs in civil society and the relation of the latter to the state underpin the above writings on NGOs. The 'optimistic' approach to NGOs and governance places NGOs within civil society, often conflating the two. Civil society is viewed as a level playing field, where individuals enjoy basic liberties of freedom of expression and assembly. Diametrically opposed to civil society is the authoritarian state. According to the 'NGO optimists,' any strategy for promoting good governance or democratization must be based on the expansion of civil society at the expense of the state. Since NGOs are more or less conflated with civil society, this strategy translates into the advocacy of strengthening and increasing the number of NGOs.

The 'skeptic' approach to NGOs and governance is based on a variety of theoretical positions ranging between a reconsideration of the above liberal notion of civil society on technical grounds (such as Stewart 1997) to a rejection of liberalism in favor of more communalistic notions of civil society and the state (al-Masri 1998, 1999). The 'technical' position agrees that NGOs have the potential to belong to civil society and strengthen civil society in order to contribute to good governance. Nevertheless, this does not mean that NGOs are contributing to good governance at this moment. Rather, NGOs are in need of various technical reforms in order to bring them to a position, in which they are capable of making an effective contribution to good governance. These reforms should be designed to increase transparency, accountability, organizational strength, and efficiency.

The 'communalistic' position is in fundamental conflict with the liberal position. It regards liberal notions of NGOs, civil society, the state, and good governance as the latest means by which the West undermines the strength of sovereign nation states in the 'Third World.' This position perceives civil society and the state in an organic relationship promoting the strength of the nation-state. NGOs are a threat to this organic relationship where their objectives are to promote individual citizen interests. NGOs are acceptable to the communalistic position where they carry out activities that are appropriate to the objectives determined by the nation-state.

A minority of more recent writings on NGOs attempt to overcome the disadvantages of the above positions by examining questions of power within civil society and between civil society and the state (for example, Whaites 2000: 124–41, White 2000: 142–55). In these writings, civil society is neither an entity apart from the state, as the liberal approach contends, nor is it subsumed within the state, as the communalistic approach insists. Civil society does not necessarily strengthen good governance; neither should it be regarded as promoting the non-differentiated interests of society within the nation state. Finally, NGOs are not the only elements of civil society. However, they should not be excluded from civil society when their objectives are considered to be in conflict with the 'interests' of the nation-state.

Here, I use the Gramscian concept of ideological struggle implied in the terms 'hegemony/counter hegemony' to understand the production and reproduction of power structures that link civil society and the state and determine the nature of governance. Civil society is characterized here, as the sphere in which discursive (or ideological) conflicts occur, contributing to the creation of power structures. NGOs and other elements of civil society produce power structures within society through their discursive practices—that is, their ideological beliefs and how these are acted upon. These discursive practices can be grouped according to their approach toward the hegemonic discourse used to reproduce the dominant power structures. The discursive practices of NGOs may contribute to the reproduction of power structures that enforce the hegemony of the state. Simultaneously, NGOs may act to counter state hegemony through their rejection of the dominant power structures.

This paper focuses on a group of Egyptian advocacy NGOs that are attempting to bring about change in the nature of governance. Despite the fact that advocacy NGOs represent a very limited number, being less than fifty organizations out of Egypt's approximately 15,000 registered NGOs, they are significant in that they have been at the center of a high-profile debate about the role of NGOs in Egypt. This paper attempts to evaluate the contribution of this group of NGOs to governance by examining their discursive practices in relation to the hegemonic discourse. This paper begins by defining the concepts of 'hegemony' and 'counter hegemony' and proposing how these may work in the Egyptian context. Then, the methodological implications of these concepts are briefly examined in relation to this study and there is a description of how fieldwork was conducted. The following four sections present the results of this fieldwork. Finally, there is a brief conclusion that evaluates the fieldwork results in relation to the objective of examining the contribution of advocacy NGOs to democratic governance in Egypt.

Do ning the Concepts: How Does Hegemony Work?

For the purpose of this paper, hegemony is taken to be the 'ensemble' of discursive, economic, and institutional structures through which rulers exercise their power. These structures are constructed through consensus backed by coercion (Gramsci, 1971: 161). They must appeal to the interests of society as a whole or a majority of society, and not only to the interests of the ruling elite. These mechanisms, according to Gramsci, are located within the institutions of civil society, for example, interest associations, the education system, the media, and NGOs. Mechanisms of coercion are located, according to Gramsci, within the state as political society (Gramsci 1971: 12).[2]

In postcolonial Egypt, the state has exercised hegemony through a combination of a nationalist-patriarchal discourse, the institutional framework of corporatism, and the economic structures of the public sector. The nationalist-patriarchal ideology is based on the idea that the regime is the sole legitimate representative of the nation's interests and that the nation's interests are politically supreme. The consequence of this ideology is that the rights of individuals or of particular groups, within the nation, such as women, workers, or Copts, have been suppressed on the grounds of national security, as defined by the regime.

This ideology supported the institutional framework of Egyptian corporatism. This is characterized by state-dominated, hierarchical, monopoly interest organizations, such as the General Federation of Egyptian Trade Unions (GFETU) and the National Federation of NGOs. The institutional framework of corporatism facilitated state penetration and control over the economy. The regime used state control of huge economic resources to distribute social and economic benefits, such as food subsidies and guaranteed employment. These benefits reinforced the idea that the regime was protecting the nation's interests.

These three elements are not completely autonomous, but mutually constitutive. Therefore, changes in one of the elements of the hegemonic discourse leads to changes in the other elements. Since the end of the

1980s, the pressure of economic liberalization has begun to dismantle the state-led, nationalized economy. However, rather than threatening regime hegemony, these developments in the economic sphere have led the regime to compensate by strengthening the ideological and institutional elements of the discourse.[3]

Hegemony is not only produced by the rulers. The ruled participate in the reproduction of the hegemonic discourse through their beliefs and actions. They perceive the hegemonic discourse as either in their interests or as the natural order of things. For example, public sector workers have suffered repression at the hands of the state security forces for their autonomous protests against the loss of benefits entailed by the dismantling of the public sector. However, workers continue to call for the restoration of the public sector even though the public sector is a part of the regime of hegemony that denies public sector workers their rights to freedom of association and expression in the defense of their interests (Pratt 2000). Similarly, working class women continue to promote a division of labor based on biological differences as a way of 'coping' with changing economic conditions that disempower them within the household. This is despite the fact that this division of labor is a fundamental part of the patriarchal discourse that maintains women's oppression within society (Hoodfar 1999).

However, hegemony can never be total; otherwise, the world would never change. Moreover, in today's world of global communications and international migrations, hegemonic discourses within one nation state cannot exist impervious to the discourses in other parts of the world. For example, Egyptian government officials must now include concepts of gender empowerment and women's rights in their discourses, because of the widespread use of these concepts at United Nations conferences (including the International Conference on Population and Development hosted by Egypt in 1994). Nevertheless, these concepts are not reproduced in the Egyptian governmental context in the same form that they are originally produced in other locations. The government inserts these concepts into the hegemonic discourse in such a way as not to challenge it.[4] However, by acknowledging the existence of these concepts, the regime opens the way for challenges to the hegemonic discourse by those from within civil society, such as advocacy NGOs, who define alternative meanings for these concepts and who perceive the dislocations within the hegemonic discourse brought about by these alternative meanings (Waltz 1995: 220–25).

In this way, civil society is not only the location of mechanisms of hegemony but also the site for the resistance against hegemony, or counter hegemony. Counter hegemonic projects aim to rearrange and recast the meanings of the hegemonic discourse. They emerge from the hegemonic discourse but may draw on ideas and resources from outside it in order to bring new interpretations to existing concepts. Counter hegemonic projects aim to provide blueprints for an alternative society. In other words, they strive toward hegemony.

Since the mandate of advocacy NGOs is to propose new policies and practices to improve the social and political conditions of citizens, I believe that the concept of counter hegemony is useful for positioning the discourses of advocacy NGOs in relation to the dominant power structures supported by the hegemonic discourse. A counter hegemonic project would seek to make absolute changes to the conditions that form the basis for exploitative and oppressive power structures. A project that is not counter hegemonic, in the sense that it accommodates or fails to challenge some aspect of the hegemonic discourse, would contribute to the reproduction of the hegemony of exploitative and oppressive power structures.

Methodology

The above theoretical and conceptual framework has methodological implications for how we study NGOs. Given the importance of discursive practices in the creation of power structures and the importance of power structures in determining the nature of governance, it is necessary to concentrate on how those discursive practices that may contribute to democratic governance are created. This involves examining the belief structures of individuals working within NGOs toward a change in the nature of governance.

NGOs consist of independent social actors who bring their own meanings to the work of their organizations. These meanings are produced within the context of the political and social conditions in which NGOs operate. They also influence NGO strategies in dealing with other actors, whether other NGOs, political parties, state institutions, or the international community. In other words, it is not possible to interpret the actions of NGOs without understanding the meanings that influence these actions. I argue that advocacy NGO activists bring shared meanings to their work concerning social and political change for the sake of democratic governance. These shared meanings constitute a discourse on democratic governance. This discourse interacts with the hegemonic discourse to either reproduce existing conditions or to create new conditions. This dialectical relationship is an important factor in shaping the future of governance in Egypt.

The fieldwork for this paper is based on literature produced by open-ended interviews with twenty advocacy NGO activists in eighteen Egyptian advocacy organizations working in various fields, such as: human rights monitoring, legal aid services, psychological rehabilitation of victims of violence, partial care for working children, rights education, human rights research, women's rights, child rights, rights of Copts, workers' rights, rights of peasants, rights of prisoners, and health and environmental rights.[5] The sample is numerically small but, I believe, qualitatively significant in that the persons interviewed represent some of the most active organizations in the Egyptian NGO community. Moreover, it is these NGOs that are often at the canter of heated debates in society over the role of NGOs.

In the process of sorting the data into some sort of order, I had to let some views slip between the cracks of my chosen categories. The choice for inclusion and exclusion of data is based on my conceptual framework of hegemony and counter hegemony. The hegemonic discourse represents the context in which the discourses of NGO activists have emerged and are developing. Therefore, I have used the three elements of the hegemonic discourse, which are nationalist, as a way of ordering my research data. In relation to each element, I have attempted to ascertain whether NGO discourses contribute to a counter hegemonic project or not.

From the interviews conducted and the readings of the literature produced by NGOs, I discovered four main themes within the discourses of NGO activists. These are:

- Autonomy from political society, that is, the state and political parties.
- Post-nationalism as a critique of nationalism.
- The deconstruction of the public versus private dichotomy as a critique of patriarchy and nationalism.

The deconstruction of the civil and political versus economic and social rights dichotomy as a basis for oppressive practices against workers and peasants.

In the following sections I will elaborate on the content of these discourses before drawing a tentative conclusion about the position of these discourses in relation to the hegemonic discourse and their potential for contributing to democratic governance.

In Search of Autonomy: Beyond Political Society

Almost all the NGO activists I spoke to were members of organizations that prior to May 1999 were not registered with the Ministry of Social Affairs as an association but were registered under the civil code as civil companies. A May 1999 law regulating the activities of civil associations made the pursuit of civil society activities through companies illegal (with a possible penalty of imprisonment) and almost all these advocacy organizations expressed their intention to register with the ministry as an association and one actually completed registration. Since the May 1999 law was struck down by the Supreme Constitutional Court in June 2000, all the advocacy organizations, except for the organization that had already successfully completed registration, maintained their civil company status.

All the activists I interviewed had chosen to register as civil companies in order to escape interference by the Ministry of Social Affairs. The original law regulating NGO activities, the infamous Law no. 32/1964, grants the ministry wide-ranging powers to intervene in the work of NGOs, to the point of even appointing ministry officials to the boards of NGOs. The law also contains articles restricting the plurality of associations (only one association carrying out a certain category of activity was allowed in each district) (see Salem 1991). The choice to register as a civil company was a clear demonstration by advocacy NGOs that they oppose government powers to control civil society.

Advocacy NGOs also feel that they have been driven by the government's declared hostility to their work to register outside the remit of the Ministry of Social Affairs. The government regularly issues statements, in which advocacy NGOs, particularly human rights groups, are accused of tarnishing Egypt's reputation abroad. Occasionally, the government goes further than statements in harassing advocacy NGOs. In 1991, the government used the powers of Law no. 32/1964 to dissolve the Arab Women's Solidarity Union after the latter had issued statements against the Egyptian government's involvement in the 1991 Gulf War. In February 2000, the secretary-general of the Egyptian Organization for Human Rights (EOHR) was referred to a state security court on charges of accepting foreign funds without the permission of the Ministry of Social Affairs. For many advocacy NGO activists, this signaled that the government would not tolerate any more internationally embarrassing criticisms of its human rights record by Egyptian NGOs (press release by eight human rights groups, February 19, 2000).[6]

The only advocacy organizations I spoke with that registered with the ministry under the old law (and were not dissolved) were those addressing child rights, health, and environmental questions. The fact that they were under the remit of the ministry did not seem to limit their activities in this sphere because the government did not see their work as a threat, although they were calling for policy changes. As one child rights activist expressed: "We use the space provided to us by the government to mobilize around the issue of child rights. The government, the president, and the president's wife have identified child welfare as a priority for the government and we can use this to our advantage."

The non-threatening appearance of an organization's work can mean that the ministry bureaucracy leaves you alone. However, once the government's suspicion is aroused, it can use its powers to limit an association's activity. A health and environmental association had been part of the NGO coalition opposing the May law and soon afterwards, the ministry, for the first time ever, refused permission for the association to receive the second installment of a grant from the Canadian International Development Agency (*Cairo Times,* March 2–8, 2000).

The attempts by many advocacy NGO activists to avoid interference by the state come from a belief in the illegitimacy of the regime and the regime's complete infiltration of state institutions (with the qualified exception of the judiciary). The NGO activists I spoke to, all regard the state as undemocratic, corrupt, or arbitrary. The regime passes anti-democratic laws and uses them in an arbitrary way to help its supporters and dissolve its opponents. Some of the activists interviewed had suffered arbitrary and anti-democratic laws as student activists in the 1970s and 1980s. Some had been detained or tortured on the basis of their political work. To work under the tutelage of the regime entails, to many NGO activists, opening oneself up to the corrupting and anti-democratic influences of the government. However, working within the framework of the civil code, subjects one to the rule of law as enforced by the judiciary.

NGO activists have also chosen to work outside of state tutelage because they do not believe it is possible to accomplish their goals within state institutions. For example, a group of psychiatrists working within state hospitals experienced, first hand, that it was impossible to get hospital authorities to write a report stating that a patient had suffered torture. This led them to set up an NGO that could provide this service. One of these groups told me that she thought that it would be impossible to reform the medical profession from within because it had been completely corrupted. An NGO activist working on workers' rights had chosen to work within an NGO framework because she saw the General Federation of Egyptian Trade Unions as totally controlled by the state and beyond reform. This same person had been fired from her job in a public sector factory for strike activity in 1989.

All the NGO activists I spoke to believed that the government had proposed the May 1999 law to take away the autonomy of NGOs working outside the framework of the ministry. Even those who intended to register their organization with the ministry (before the law was appealed) were afraid that they would no longer be able to carry out their activities as they had as civil companies.

It is not only hostility to the state that is demonstrated by NGO activists. There is also hostility to political parties. It has often been said that the rise of advocacy NGOs since the late 1980s is a result of the problems within political parties. The state's strict regulation of both the creation and activities of political parties have left them with almost no constituency. They also suffer from lack of internal democracy and an aging leadership. One activist told me that she and a small group of younger members of the Tagammu' Party had their membership frozen in the late 1980s because they tried to democratize the party.

When asked whether political parties should support the activities of advocacy NGOs, many activists replied that political parties are irrelevant and that they are only interested in issues of human rights, and other issues addressed by advocacy organizations, when it serves their political interests. For example, the Socialist Labor Party (an Islamist party) makes a big fuss about Islamists being tortured in prison but denies freedom of expression to those who dare to question any aspects of orthodox Islamic teachings.

Even where NGOs cooperate with political parties over certain issues, such as the Constitutional and Political Reform Committee, NGO activists constantly stress their independence from political parties and the danger of political bias to the credibility of the NGO. When pressed about the nature of cooperation, some NGO activists are skeptical about the commitment of political parties as institutions to certain human rights issues even though some individuals from those parties cooperate with NGOs on such issues. One NGO activist sums up the problems of cooperating with political parties within the Constitutional and Political Reform Committee:

There are agreements between the government and some political parties over the number of seats [allocated to them] in the People's Assembly. This means that political parties are not really working for long-term political reforms but rather they are more interested in gaining five or ten seats [in the next parliamentary elections].

Many NGO activists also stated that they had joined or formed NGOs in order to escape the political divisions that characterized student politics. In the words of one human rights activist who has since left the EOHR: "When I joined the EOHR, it was the first time for me to work alongside people of different political backgrounds. We were all united by the idea of human rights."

Several other NGO activists first experienced NGO involvement through the EOHR. This experience established many of their fears about open membership organizations and the risk of political infiltration. The EOHR became subject to much-publicized internal wranglings from 1993 to 1994 over the issue of the 'politicization' of the organization. One section of the membership accused some members of attempting to turn the EOHR into a political movement. The debate was not settled in a peaceable way and, consequently, many members left the organization. These events provide bitter memories for many NGO activists. One activist echoes the words of many ex-members:

> A political faction within the EOHR claimed that they were saving the EOHR from politicization, from being taken over by a certain underground grouping, while it was they who were politicizing the EOHR by rigging elections in favor of certain political factions. Since then, the work carried out by the EOHR has had nothing to do with human rights. It has been led by political interests [of the factions running the organization].

These bad memories have led NGO activists who were affiliated with the EOHR to purposefully build their organizations in a way that could avoid such partisan politicization.

The NGO activists I spoke to showed either hostility or suspicion to existing political parties and to state institutions. These NGO activists are attempting to create a civil society that is independent of interference from political society, whether from the state or from political parties.

Nevertheless, this does not mean that NGO activists are non-political or anti-political. The work of advocacy NGOs, as noted by some activists, can be considered political because it deals with crucial issues of power relations in society, such as between citizens and the state. Their rejection of political society may be considered a rejection of the state corporatist framework that currently characterizes political society and much of civil society.

Nevertheless, this does not mean that NGOs are substitutes for political parties. Advocacy NGOs are blurring the boundaries of civil and political society by addressing their work from the perspective of civic and political concerns. Many of the activists I spoke to believed that working within the framework of an NGO, rather than a state institution or a political party, was necessary in order to be able to address their work in a more holistic way. Many advocacy NGOs combine research/monitoring and advocacy with services that address the problem in question. For example, many organizations monitor and research rights violations, while offering legal aid, therapy, partial care, or even financial help to the victims of violations and to their families. They do not consider it possible to do such work within a state institution or political party.

However, the attempt to build organizations outside of the state corporatist framework and to protect their organizations from government and political infiltration has left advocacy NGOs open to criticisms of lack of transparency and accountability, not only from their opponents but also from NGO activists themselves. One of the activists I spoke to believed that registration with the ministry as an association would help to build stronger civil associations based on democracy, transparency, and accountability. However, another activist, when asked about the problems of closed organizations versus membership organizations, believed that membership organizations do not necessarily create a democratic organization, as demonstrated by the experience of the EOHR.

The Postcolonial Experience: Beyond Nationalism

Almost all of the NGO activists that I interviewed had been active in the student movement during the 1970s and 1980s, mainly as leftists or Nasserists, prior to becoming involved in NGO work in the late 1980s and throughout the 1990s. The experience of being part of the student movement during this period has had an important influence on shaping the ideas and actions of these activists. Within the discourses of NGO activists, it is possible to discern attempts to work through and overcome the problems experienced by the student movement and the major national leftist political currents of Nasserism and Marxism.

The postcolonial period began with hopes of social justice and freedom from colonialism. However, nationalist aspirations in this regard were frustrated by the 1967 military defeat at the hands of Israel and the loss of Sinai. The 1967 defeat led to student calls for democracy and greater participation in decision-making for society, and later (in 1971–73) to calls for transparency in the elite decision-making process concerning the confrontation with Israel. Following the 1973 victory, leftist and Nasserist student concerns continued to revolve around democracy, as well as opposition to Sadat's pro-American turn and the open door economic policy. Through this period, the national question continued to be raised and reshaped by the student movement, as a question of political democracy, of national sovereignty, and of social and economic justice (Abdallah 1985: 152, 189–91, 224–26).

However, in the context of a patriarchal nationalism, where the interests of the regime (as patriarch) are identified with the nation's interests, demands for national sovereignty are used to bolster regime power to the detriment of the freedoms of the rest of society. Denial of political freedoms was justified by the regime because of national security. Moreover, a tension existed between student activists and orthodox Nasserist and Marxist thought over the legitimacy of political democracy. One NGO activist tells me:

> Our, de facto, attitude as students was to defend patriotism and democracy. But we lived the contradictions of this because our leaders used patriotism against democracy. Because of Nasserism, we were led to believe that democracy was a 'bourgeois' idea. Marxist thought supported this.

'Bourgeois' not only referred to a class but also to the 'bourgeois countries,' that is western capitalist nations. Therefore, political democracy was not only discredited as being 'foreign' to the project of Nasserism, but also as belonging to the 'imperialist' enemy. The dichotomy was established: national/authentic/authoritarian versus imperialist/non-authentic/democratic. The political Islamist movement that grew in the 1970s also supported this dichotomy. The political Islamists also rejected ideas that were deemed to be western in origin, such as democracy. Within the parameters of nationalist political thought, there appeared to be no legitimate space for the student movement in search of democracy.

Moreover, from the mid-1970s, throughout the 1980s, leftist and Nasserist trends within the student movement were subject to repression that prevented them from forging strong links with other sections of society. Legal political parties (such as the Tagammu' and Nasserist parties) were limited in their outreach activities by restrictive legislation.7 Simultaneously, Marxist political parties were outlawed on the basis of an article in the constitution that did not permit the formation of parties based on a class ideology. Finally, the fall of the Soviet Union in 1989 did much to discredit the power of leftist thought in generating a democratic movement among wide sections of society.

Faced with a political impasse, one NGO activist says:

> In the late 1980s] thoughts [for forging links with the people] shifted to being where people were, that is, in the syndicates and in communities. However, the people who started to move into these new areas lost links with the left-wing organizations. Therefore, it was important to develop an organization that could do advocacy work.

The organizational framework for advocacy adopted by this and many other activists was that of an NGO. Moreover, in many cases, the content of advocacy became centered on a discourse of human rights, rather than that of leftist or Nasserist political thought. The beginnings of a human rights discourse in Egypt may be traced back to the establishment of the EOHR in 1985, some of whose early members were student activists from the 1970s. Many of the NGO activists I talked to, first came into contact with the concept of human rights through the EOHR, which defended them or their friends and colleagues. In particular, in 1989 the EOHR played a strong role in defending workers and political activists against state repression during the famous iron and steel strikes.

The adoption of a human rights discourse can be interpreted as an attempt by political activists to revisit the unanswered demands of the student movement. In other words, human rights represent a paradigm shift that enables former student activists and others concerned with the national question to overcome the contradictions inherent within it. The human rights framework solves the problem of reconciling national sovereignty with political democracy by recasting the national question. The first step of this recasting is the replacement of the notion of the supremacy of the nation with the supremacy of the national citizen as human being. The attainment of political democracy is no longer dependent on the regime safeguarding national sovereignty, but rather on the guarantee of the rights of all Egyptians as human beings.

The second step of this recasting is to deconstruct the West—that is, the traditional enemy of Egyptian national self-determination—in order to demonstrate that the West is not always a threat to Egyptian interests. This deconstruction allows the prioritization of democracy as an Egyptian concern over that of national sovereignty. The NGO activists I interviewed have embarked on a process of 'de-essentializing' the West. Whereas nationalist movements struggling against colonialism tend to reproduce the essentialized, 'racialized' discourse of the colonialists (Fanon 1990: 171), NGO activists may be seen as the creators of a post-nationalist discourse struggling against essentialized, 'racialized' nationalist discourses.[8] One NGO activist notes:

> People think that everyone in the West supports capitalism, but western society is pluralistic and not all the same thing. Many of the organizations in the West have ideas that are similar to ours regarding socialism and human rights. . . . People in the West are not a copy of their governments.

Moreover, NGO activists see links with organizations in western countries as a necessity in the current era of globalization. In this context, global links empower Egyptians in achieving their rights, rather than threaten their self-determination. As a workers' rights NGO activist asserts:

> The links with non-governmental organizations strengthens the [workers'] movement here, as well as the movement there. European workers' organizations need links with Southern organizations against transnational corporations, which impose bad working conditions on workers everywhere.

Attempts to go beyond nationalism do not mean that advocacy NGO activists ignore disparities of power and injustices within the world. They use the discourse of human rights to defend victims of oppression, whoever the perpetrators may be. Advocacy NGOs have been at the forefront of using a human rights discourse to condemn oppression, in particular Palestinians facing Israeli occupation and Iraqi people suffering the effects of western-imposed sanctions.

The Cairo Institute for Human Rights Studies (CIHRS) organized the first International Conference of the Arab Human Rights Movement, held in Casablanca, Morocco, in April 1999. A working paper presented at the conference, entitled, "Economic Sanctions and Human Rights," condemned sanctions, not on the basis of anti-imperialism or Arab nationalism, but as a violation of all international human rights covenants, including those addressing civil and political rights, social, economic, and cultural rights, child rights, and women's rights, in addition to the Geneva Convention (Sha'aban 1999: 9–10).

Under the title "Peace and the Rights of Peoples and Minorities in the Arab World," the final conference declaration states: "The rights of the Palestinian people are the proper standard to measure the consistency of international positions toward a just peace and human rights" (CIHRS: 8).

On this basis, some NGO activists condemn international human rights NGOs for failing to adopt clear human rights positions against the violation of Palestinian or Iraqi rights (Hassan 1999: 5). The suggestion by some Egyptian NGO activists to use networks between international and local human rights NGOs to encourage consultation and cooperation aims at overcoming the reproduction of the North/South dichotomy within the global human rights NGO community (Hassan 1999: 4–5).

Advocacy NGO activists use the idiom of human rights as a means of expressing new types of relations that they do not see as subscribing to essentializing nationalist discourses of the West versus the Arabs, or North versus South. NGO activists regard their advocacy of human rights as a new form of political discourse that goes beyond the limitations of previous discourses based on nationalism, whether Nasserist or Marxist. The supremacy of the Egyptian citizen as a human being clearly opposes notions of the nation, embodied by the regime, as supreme. The construction of such a discourse opens the way for a promotion of democratic political change in Egypt, as well as for calls for international justice and peace.

Challenging Patriarchy: Making the Private Public

Until now, we have looked at the ways in which Egyptian NGO activists seek to challenge the ideological and institutional supremacy of the regime through the advocacy of human rights within the framework of an NGO. This discourse, constructed around the themes of autonomy from political society and post-nationalism, seeks to reconcile the contradictions of historical demands for democracy and self-determination. It de-essentializes the West and questions the supremacy of the regime as the protector of the nation's interests.

Simultaneously, Egyptian NGO activists are attempting to 'de-essentialize' the Egyptian nation. They are seeking to demonstrate that Egypt is not one nation, in the sense of comprising a homogeneous group of individuals, but is made up of different groups and classes, such as women, workers, and Copts, each with different needs and particular rights. Moreover, democracy and self-determination are not only questions of public institutions and public policies, but also of personal relationships, particularly within the family.

The post-1967 student movement never raised the question of women's rights and equality in its demands to the regime. This was partly a result of the regime having co-opted women's demands from the pre-revolutionary women's movement. These demands included rights to political participation, rights to equal pay, and rights to child care services, which were all adopted by the post-1952 regime into legislation (New Woman Research Center 1996: 26). In other words, it appeared that women had been granted their demands and they were now free to participate alongside men in the student movement, calling for democracy and self-determination.

Moreover, the failure to raise demands specific to women's position in society was supported by the failure to raise the issue of gender within different ideological currents within the student movement. Both Marxist and Nasserist trends assumed that once women were granted equal rights in the public sphere, this would automatically grant them social equality. This position ignored the question of gender inequalities within the private sphere. In addition, both Marxism and Nasserism prioritized either the class struggle or the struggle for national self-determination over that of any other struggles, including that of the struggle for women's equality (El-Saadawi 1997: 235–41).

Nawal El-Saadawi, one of the founders of the Arab Women's Solidarity Association (AWSA) in 1982 (one of Egypt's first independent feminist organizations since 1952), challenged the exclusion of gender from Egyptian political trends by prioritizing the struggle against patriarchy within the struggles against capitalist exploitation and imperialism. In a 1981 paper that was adopted as AWSA philosophy, El-Saadawi argued:

> The progressive nature of the appeal for the creation of an Arab women's political movement and its revolutionary content are

embodied in the fact that the appeal is a response to genuine democratic principles, authentic Arab nationalism and true socialism. It is also a response to accepted human values. This is because it gives voice to the needs and rights of half the society, and is a response to the severest forms of open and hidden oppression exercised by half against the other half, that is, by men against women. Its progressive nature is also due to the fact that it is a response to class, group, and professional oppression—since the vast majority of Arab women are peasants, workers, or poor toilers—and it is also a response to national oppression—since Arab women are a part of the Arab nation, which is subjected to exploitation by international capitalism and Zionism (El-Saadawi 1997: 241–42).

Attempts to bring awareness of women's rights into political struggles, especially in the face of the growing Islamist movement, led former student activists to establish informal groups in the early 1980s, which later developed into NGOs devoted to promoting the rights of women. In the beginning, these groups were primarily concerned with promoting women's political and public roles in society. Their activities included studying the history of the Egyptian feminist movement, developing a feminist discourse for the Egyptian context, consciousness-raising to encourage women to enter public life, building a strong feminist movement, advocating legal reforms, and promoting women's writing (New Woman Research Center 1996: 36–41).

The establishment of women's rights advocacy NGOs represented a break from the de-politicization of women's issues that had occurred under the post-colonial regime. From 1952 onward, women's organizations became almost exclusively concerned with providing services and charity in the fields of mother and child welfare, community development, and religion and culture (New Woman Research Center 1996: 26). In contrast, women's rights advocacy NGOs established their interest in women's political and civil participation and the wider legal and political structures that inhibit such participation. This new form of women's activism challenged prevailing notions of women's interests as lying exclusively in the private domestic sphere. Similarly, child welfare has been traditionally addressed from the perspective of providing services and charity. NGO activists working within a framework of the international child rights covenant see their work as a break from the traditional model: "We see our role as empowering children and young people to make the changes in society that are necessary to guarantee their rights."

Advocacy NGOs are not only challenging patriarchal nationalism by promoting issues concerning women and children within the context of political and legal structures. By the mid-1980s, women's rights advocacy groups began attempts to break down the patriarchal division of public and private by bringing so-called private or family issues, into public debate as a political problem. In 1985, these groups joined with other women's rights activists to form the Committee for the Defense of Women and the Family, in response to imminent amendments to the law governing marriage and divorce—the personal status law (New Woman Research Center 1999: 349).[9] This was in contrast to the lack of activism during the passage of the 1979 amendments to the personal status law—Law no. 44/1979, often referred to 'Jihan's law' after the wife of President Sadat (Bibars 1987: 39). From 1993 onward, encouraged by a series of international UN conferences dealing with women's position in society, some women's rights NGOs began to become involved in working groups on other 'family' issues such as domestic violence and female genital mutilation (New Woman Research Center 1999: 359–60).

While efforts to promote the rights of women in relation to their political participation and legal equality has largely avoided controversy on the national level, the discussion of those issues regarded by patriarchal society as pertaining to the family has met with substantial opposition, and even attempts at suppression. For example, when some Egyptian women's rights NGOs submitted a report to the 1994 International Conference on Population and Development (ICPD) and then again at the Beijing UN Conference on Women in 1995 on the extent of domestic violence in Egypt, the official Egyptian delegation, headed by Mrs. Suzanne Mubarak, denied the existence of domestic violence. Egyptian NGO activists campaigning against female genital mutilation have faced widespread animosity from traditionalist, religious, and nationalist forces, to the concept of abolishing the practice. Similarly, attempts by women's rights NGOs and other women's rights activists to lobby the government to grant women more rights within the personal status law have been consistently met with fierce opposition from conservative sections of Egyptian society. The most recent demonstration of hostility to granting women more rights within the family, were the debates in January 2000 surrounding amendments to the personal status law procedures.[10]

The opposition toward bringing so-called 'private issues' into the public domain has often been accompanied with accusations that Egyptian women activists are implementing a western agenda.[11] These reactions are a consequence of the centrality of the public/private dichotomy within nationalism. In the struggle against colonialism and western threats, the private sphere became the repository of national culture, protected from the corrupting influences of the enemy, with woman as its guardian (Chatterjee 1993: 120). Nationalism characterizes marriage and divorce laws, female sexuality, and family relationships as issues to be kept away from politics and public discussion, especially in front of western representatives, even if Egyptians disagree with some of the practices that happen within the private sphere. These are perceived as necessary measures in order to protect Egyptian national culture—the foundation of the nation'—from western cultural invasion (Hetata 1997).

Attempts by women rights and child rights advocacy NGOs to make 'public' some private issues challenged nationalist—patriarchal discourse. However, their actions can also be read as challenging the discourse of 'post-nationalism.' Insofar as post-nationalism does not attempt to deconstruct patriarchal representations of the nation, it can be seen as being complicit with nationalism in the exclusion of the private sphere as an object of political struggle. Many of the women's rights and child rights NGO activists I spoke with joined or founded NGOs working on women's and child rights because they perceived these issues to be marginalized by existing advocacy NGOs. One women's rights activist told me:

> Some people do not understand the concept of particular rights for women. They think that all problems will be solved by civil and political rights, which is why a women's center is necessary. You can't solve the problems of society without solving the problems of women.

My own experience of attending seminars and conferences, organized by advocacy NGOs, supported this statement. During the annual 1999 Intellectual Forum of the EOHR, a member of a human rights organization stated that the role of human rights NGOs was to defend civil and political rights, not women's rights, or child rights, or social and economic rights. The existence of guarantees for political and civil rights would enable women's associations, trade unions, and other special interest groups to organize and defend their own rights. It was also notable that at this conference, only four women were invited to speak (out of a total of approximately 48 speakers) on a special session concerning women.

All NGO activists I spoke with, declared support for all international human rights covenants, including the Covenant on the Elimination of all Forms of Discrimination against Women and the Child Rights Covenant, without reservations. Some NGOs advocating human rights in general have programs related specifically to women rights or deal with women's and child rights in their press releases when specific issues are raised, such as amendments to the personal status laws or the promulgation of a new law on the child. However, women's and child rights within the context of NGOs working on civil and political rights or social and economic rights tended not to raise the issue of patriarchy within their work; their approach to advocacy work did not consider the particular problems faced by women and children because of patriarchy.

The discourse of advocacy NGOs working on women's and child rights does not only challenge patriarchal nationalism by redefining the boundaries of the political sphere that underpin the concept of the nation as supreme; in addition, it challenges the discourse of post-nationalism by deconstructing the nation. This new feminist discourse interrogates the discourse of post-nationalism by addressing the differences engendered within the national political terrain by patriarchy. However, patriarchy is not the only differentiating element within the political terrain.

From State to Market: The Challenge of Human Rights in the Era of Globalization

Unlike patriarchal nationalism and state corporatism, the state-dominated economy with its accompanying system of patronage, has been slowly dismantled over the past decade. Through this economic infrastructure, the government provided Egyptian citizens with guaranteed jobs, subsidized goods and services, and rent controls on agricultural land and housing leases. However, since 1991, when the Egyptian government agreed to an Economic Reform and Structural Adjustment Program (ERSAP), a number of measures have been implemented that remove these socioeconomic benefits. Those measures with the greatest political impact have been the privatization of public sector enterprises, leading to redundancies and removal of employment-related monetary and non-monetary benefits; the removal of administratively-decided rents for land tenants, allowing landowners to raise rents considerably and to evict peasants from their land; and the removal or reduction in subsidies of many goods and services.

These measures represent a huge reversal in the postcolonial political economy. The implementation of land reforms and legislation to protect the rights of workers from the early 1950s to the early 1960s were keystones in the postcolonial economic order and provided the regime with substantial moral authority to its claims of representing the nation's interests. So much so, that the national trade union became a vehicle for government control over workers, rather than a vehicle for representing workers' demands. Similarly, independent peasant organizations were not allowed to be formed.

There has been almost near consensus across the political spectrum that the economic and social rights of working people represent the essence of nation-building in postcolonial Egypt. Student demands following the 1973 war included calls to protect the social and economic gains of working people in the face of Sadat's open door economic policy (Abdallah 1985: 224–26). The Tagammu', Labor, and Nasserist parties contain various special committees or unions devoted to workers' and peasants' issues; all pledge commitment to legislation that protects the rights of workers and peasants, and all have opposed recent reforms that have undermined this protection—including the dismantling of the public sector.

Since the early 1990s, certain advocacy NGOs have been focusing their work on the violations of social and economic rights resulting from the ERSAP. These violations include: increasing levels of poverty as a consequence of reductions in subsidies, increases in rents, loss of land, and redundancy. Approaches to advocacy work against these violations have tended toward research and monitoring of the social consequences of ERSAP, particularly for marginalized sections of society, such as the urban and rural poor, women, and children. Another approach has been to provide legal assistance to victims of social and economic violations, particularly workers suffering from arbitrary dismissal, often related to the restructuring of the public sector in preparation for privatization.

Other advocacy NGOs have concentrated on defending the rights of workers, farmers, and their allies, to freedom of expression, freedom of association, and freedom of peaceful demonstration in the course of protecting their interests. For example, the EOHR was active in defending workers who were arrested, injured, or tortured by state security during the Helwan iron and steel strikes of 1989 and the Kafr al-Dawwar textile factory 'sit-in' of 1994. A number of human rights NGOs campaigned in defense of political activists and peasants arrested during 1997 for mobilizing against changes to the agricultural rents law.

The linking of violations of civil and political rights to violations of social and economic rights in the context of ERSAP constitutes a specific challenge to hegemonic discourse. Within patriarchal nationalism, workers and peasants only have legitimate claim to social and economic rights, and not political and civil rights. The reasons for this dichotomy can be attributed to the fact that, after 1952, the regime granted workers and peasants many rights. Therefore, the regime considered workers and peasants as having no need for autonomous political action because the regime was the guarantor of their interests. Second, the regime granted workers and peasants these rights in recognition of their important contribution to the economy, which was central to nation-building. Autonomous political action would threaten the continuity of the contribution of workers and peasants to the economy and therefore violated national interests. Even in the era of ERSAP, the Egyptian government continued to delegitimize autonomous political action of workers and peasants, by continuing to criminalize and suppress it using coercion, as well as claiming that the government will protect the interests of these people.

Opposition by advocacy NGOs to violations of the rights of workers, peasants, and marginalized social groups (both civil and political, as well as social and economic) not only challenges aspects of patriarchal nationalism that have existed since the beginning of the postcolonial era, but also interrogates the neo-liberal discourse of many international organizations and western governments, that claim that the transition to a market economy in Egypt (and other parts of the world) will guarantee human rights, democratization, and civil society.

Within neo-liberal discourse, ERSAP has a role to play in enabling countries to participate in the process of globalization, represented as a panacea for many ills. According to neo-liberals, globalization generates unprecedented levels of global wealth that provide a necessary foundation for the growth of democracy; unprecedented levels of global interactions through new media technologies, which publicize human rights violations internationally, making it difficult for governments 'to get away with it'; and, globalization undermines the power of the nation-state in general, setting free the forces of citizen groups within a global civil society. Contrary to this list of attributes of globalization, one NGO activist argues:

Globalization does not mean democracy but the control by transnational corporations of labor markets, of the movement of labor, and of the movement of goods. Globalization means more profits for transnational corporations and more poverty for the poorer nations. Now we live in an era that is against trade unions and social movements. Globalization is against democracy.

Implied in this analysis of the bases for democracy, is the need to eradicate social and economic injustices resulting from a class system that privileges one class (capital and landowners) over another (workers and peasants). NGO activists see ERSAP as encouraging class inequalities by promoting the interests of business and landowners over the interests of workers and peasants. As one NGO activist indicates: "The government gives business-people tax breaks, builds new cities for them [in the desert], and provides them with all the necessary infrastructure, such as electricity and pavements, and at the same time it stops workers from forming trade unions."

While rejecting the neo-liberal discourse on globalization, NGO activists advocate an alternative model of globalization, based on democracy and the power of civil society. This alternative consists of struggling against the policies of the World Trade Organization (WTO) and other international financial institutions that harm the interests of working people, of forging links with trade unions and NGOs in other countries, who are struggling toward the same goal, and of ordinary people having greater access to information to use in their struggles against oppression and injustice. For many NGO activists, the Seattle anti-WTO demonstrations in November 1999 provide the model for this alternative model of 'globalization-from-below.'

Nevertheless, while democracy and an empowered civil society provide an alternative model of globalization, Egyptian NGO activists I spoke with, do not clearly advocate an alternative economic model to the neo-liberal market, nor the patriarchal nationalist state-led economy it seeks to replace. Having rejected existing political ideologies based on experience of their negative effects on human rights, advocacy NGO activists find themselves in a post-modern/post-Soviet ideological void. Not even the 'grand narrative' of universal human rights can provide them with an alternative economic model. This tension within the discourse of alternative globalization makes it easier for advocacy NGOs to concentrate on the citizenship aspects of the model, rather than its economic power relations. This gives the impression that advocacy NGOs are not really that concerned with the rights of working people. In the words of one activist:

> The problem with human rights and women's rights organizations is that they are too interested in political and civil freedoms, but the topic of workers' rights is a very thorny issue for them because it makes problems for them.

However, some NGO activists recognize this tension and its sources, but are unable to put forward an alternative model for their work. One activist confessed to me:

> There's no doubt that there are problems [with the intellectual reference of our work], whether with the [international human rights] covenants, the constitution, or Egyptian legislation. However, we have to have some intellectual reference for our work.

Despite the limitations in the discourse of NGO activists regarding an alternative model of globalization, the construction of a discourse that links violations of the rights of workers, peasants, and marginalized social groups to particular economic models challenges both nationalist assumptions that the regime is protector of the interests of all members of the nation and neo-liberal assumptions that the free market is the protector of the interests of all citizens. Like women's rights activists, those that advocate the rights of working people also interrogate post-nationalist assumptions that democracy exists external to relations of power within the national terrain. Access to democratic rights for working people depends upon their position within relations of economic power, as structured by the economic system.

Conclusion

This paper sets out to ascertain whether Egyptian advocacy NGOs are counter-hegemonic organizations or whether they propagate existing hegemonic relations through their discourses. The basis for current regime hegemony in Egypt was broken down into mutually constituting elements of a national—patriarchal discourse, state corporatist institutions, and a state-led economy, which is now being replaced by a neo-liberal market economy. Various advocacy NGO activists challenge regime hegemony through their discourses on post-nationalism, autonomy from political society, patriarchy, the dichotomization of rights, and alternative globalization. Taken as a sum total, these various discourses can be sewn together to create the beginnings of a counter-hegemonic project challenging the notion of the supremacy of the interests of the nation that justifies undemocratic practices against all citizens and political exclusion of women and working people.

This nascent counter-hegemonic project is based on the deconstruction of several dichotomies that underpin the hegemonic discourse: the Arab world/the West; political society/civil society, private sphere/public sphere, and civil and political rights/social and economic rights. Many of these dichotomies were constructed in the context of colonialism and the anti-colonialist struggle. Anti-colonial nationalist discourse sought to challenge racist stereotypes by inverting dichotomies produced within colonial discourse. While this was a useful tool in the struggle against colonialism, it quickly turned into a tool for oppression in the postcolonial context. The discourses of NGO activists represent attempts to move beyond these dichotomies by deconstructing them.

Nevertheless, these efforts at constructing a counter-hegemonic project are limited by the lack of an alternative economic model that would remove the material bases for unequal power relations within society. Unlike Antonio Gramsci in the 1920s, NGO activists working in a post-Soviet/post-modern era are not willing to advocate emancipation from capitalism based on Marx's philosophy or any other grand narrative.

Notes

1. This paper is part of my ongoing research for my Ph.D. dissertation, "NGOs, Civil Society, and the State in Egypt in an Era of Globalization," funded by the Economic and Social Research Council, U.K., in the Department of Politics, University of Exeter, U.K.. I would like to thank my supervisor, Dr. Salwa Ismail, Mr. Didier Monciaud, and Dr. Nadje Al-Ali for their comments on earlier versions of this paper.
2. It is also possible to identify coercive mechanisms located within institutions of civil society, for example, 'honor killing' by male family members. Similarly, mechanisms of consensus can be located within political society, for example, the parliamentary system.
3. For example, over the last ten years, the regime has strengthened corporatism by increasing its control over corporatist institutions. This is demonstrated by a 1993 law reducing the autonomy of professional syndicates and a 1995 law increasing government control over the labor unions. Similarly, this and other legislation strengthen the patriarchal-nationalist ideology by criminalizing independent political activity and freedom of expression. The regime's increased control over

the ideological and institutional elements of its hegemony compensates for its decreasing control over the distribution of economic and social benefits because of the introduction of neoliberal economic reforms.
4. This process is similar to that termed 'relocalization' by Dina El-Khawaga. The term refers to the process of incorporating a 'foreign' concept into a local environment. According to El-Khawaga, this process consists of a reframing of the concept according to the value systems of the society. See El-Khawaga, 1997: 233–34.
5. The fieldwork for this paper was conducted over the period from December 1999 to March 2000. The interview respondents remain anonymous and they are all referred to by the female gender, although some of their organizations are mentioned by name where the issue discussed has been published. I am deeply indebted to them all for having given up their time to speak to me and I apologize now that this research may not fully represent the diversity of views within the advocacy NGO community.
6. Among the human rights community, it is widely believed that the charges were meant to punish the EOHR for attempting to publish a report on 'sectarian strife' in an Upper Egyptian village in January 2000. Following the charges against the EOHR secretary-general, the EOHR president changed 'sectarian strife' to 'civil strife' at a February 15 press conference, aware of the controversial nature of implying that Egypt has a problem between its Muslim majority and Christian minority (for more details, see Cairo Times, February 24–March 1, 2000). The EOHR had already refused in December 1999 an award from the U.S.-based Freedom House for its previous report on allegations of torture in the same Upper Egyptian village in 1998, rejecting Freedom House's notion that Copts constitute a persecuted minority in Egypt. In 1994, the Ibn Khaldoun Center was forced to change the venue of its international conference on minorities from Cairo to Cyprus because of a huge backlash in the Egyptian press against the idea of categorizing Egyptian Copts as 'minorities.' Coincidentally, the newsletter of the Ibn Khaldoun Center for Development Studies (an NGO that has actively promoted the rights of religious minorities) and the newsletter of the EOHR were both issued with confiscation decrees in January 2000, shortly after the tragic events in the Upper Egyptian village (see EOHR press release, January 19, 2000).
7. Law no. 40/1977 on political parties.
8. For further discussion of the 'post nationalism' discourse, see Ghandi, 1998: 122–40.
9. For a detailed account of the committee's activities and demands, and the passage into law of the personal status amendments of 1985, see Bibars 1987: 138–150.
10. The amendments were passed (in a modified form from the government's proposed bill) by parliament on January 26, 2000 and ratified by the president on January 30, 2000. The proposed bill would have allowed women to travel abroad without their husband's permission. Among the most important of the accepted amendments is that which allows women to seek a divorce without cause if they renounce their financial rights. See the debates in the Egyptian press over the amendments during this period.
11. Many international women's conferences have witnessed sharp divisions between 'western' and 'Third World' women over priorities within feminism. Some have characterized this debate as consisting of two positions: that western feminism is

more concerned with women's sexuality and that Third World feminism is more concerned with 'bread and butter issues' about women's material existence. For example, see, Gilliam 1991: 216–20. However, the writings of Egyptian women's activists do not present these issues as diametrically opposed, but as connected and mutually reinforcing. For example, see El-Saadawi 1980: 1–2; New Woman Research Center 1998: 170. Egyptian women activists talk about the problem of being labeled 'western' and attempts to be 'authentic' in Al-Ali 2000, 47–50, 189, 208–15.

Chapter Seven

Islamic NGOs and the Development of Democracy in Egypt

Abd al-Ghaffar Shukr

Democracy is the key to economic or social development, to a real modernization of society, to social justice and to people's participation. The Arab people have been fighting, for over two centuries, to break the vicious circles of backwardness, foreign domination, social inequity, exploitation, and division. But every time, their hopes are dashed against the wall of personal despotism, military or tribal. Some people imagined that democracy could prevail in the Arab world if only political parties could exist, newspapers could be published, and parliamentary elections could be held. They thought that democracy could be proclaimed by political power and that it would be established quickly. However, democracy is a way of life, a way of working society, which cannot be reached without the implication of society as a whole and without all the democratic principles being part of citizens' and social institutions' behaviors. Consequently, democracy is a historical process, which is spread over a relatively long period of time, and can, in certain phases, face a regression due to the obstinacy of certain forces trying to stop it.

It is within such context that the importance of civil society becomes obvious. Civil society reinforces the democratization process in the Arab world in general and in particular in Egypt. There are numerous studies on this topic, however none of them analyze one of the most important aspects of this issue, which is the Islamic NGOs and their relationship to democracy. Their services attract thousands of citizens. Moreover, their importance within civil society is constantly increasing, which is calling on them to play a much more substantial role in reinforcing democratic values among their members—people who deal with them or benefit from them. This paper focuses on the relationship of Islamic NGOs to democracy in order to respond to the following questions:

- What are the essential conditions for democracy to be established in the Arab world? What part does civil society assume in this domain?
- What is the position of the Islamic NGOs with regards to this process? Why did they acquire a certain interest in democratization process of Egypt and the Arab countries?
- Are there any precise indicators, which highlight the type of relationship existing between the Islamic NGOs and democracy? If so, what are these indicators?
- How do these Islamic NGOs create fora to reinforce democratization?

These conditions can be determined once the concept of democracy has been defined. Very broadly, democracy can be defined as being essentially a framework that peacefully manages the nascent conflicts and competition within society. This is not just an addition of individuals; it is composed of social classes, which are united by certain relationships and converging or diverging interests, which generate fights and conflicts. If society cannot solve its conflicts peacefully, especially those linked to accessing power, they risk violence, and ultimately civil war, endangering society and its citizens.

Society is democratic when it has a good network of economic, social, political, and cultural relations; when it is capable of managing the interactions between individuals and social classes, between society and the state and finally between the different types of power—executive, legislative, and judiciary. As a result, the question of democracy is relative. It is, therefore, a historical progressive process, which starts when a society guarantees a minimal and efficient political participation to all citizens without exceptions and which develops and matures when the democratic principles stabilize. Democracy is not confined only to politics. It entails certain values for the citizens to follow such as respect of differences, recognition of others, equality, tolerance, dialogue, and compromise. Moreover, we could not talk about democratization without the creation of institutions promoting such lifestyle, without the declaration of democratic values and without the establishment of mechanisms enabling their enactment.

Society can only learn and embrace democratic values if citizens are educated on what democracy entails via practical activities; if people acquire the experience which teaches them the values of a system based on dialogue, collective action, acceptance and critique, team work, and respect toward majority opinion. Within this context, civil society and NGOs in particular have a huge responsibility. They represent an ideal framework to disseminate and experiment with democracy in a way that includes women as a fundamental component of society. The nature of civil society endows it with a very importance role in the democratization process. Civil society can be defined as a gathering of free organizations, founded on volunteerism, which both occupies pubic space between family and the state and obliges the values and the norms of respect, compromise, tolerance, and good management of diversity and difference. In this sense, the organizations of civil society, which bring people to participate in public actions, are qualified as being, in a way, the infrastructure for democracy as a way of life and as society's way of working. The internal life of these organizations, including NGOs, offers the opportunity to educate people on democracy. This training is done in different ways: volunteering to take public action, practicing a collective activity; expressing one's opinion; listening to what others have to say; participation in the decision-making process; voting at elections to chose the leaders of the institutions or associations; accepting the results of the elections, whether they correspond to one's opinion or not; participating in the definition of the aims of the organizations, of their priorities, area of control, and the evaluation of their results.

Thus, democracy can be built from the bottom, in a manner that progressively includes the whole population. So, what is the position of the Islamic NGOs on this process? Why have they gained a special position within the democratization process in Egypt and in the entire Arab world?

The Role of Islamic NGOs in the Transition to Democracy

These NGOs are important in the area of non-governmental activity for the various services they provide: education, health, and social services for millions of citizens. They also provide financial assistance and aid in kind—such as the *zakat* and *sadaqa* banks—and contributions to many marginalized social groups, especially widows, orphans, the elderly, and the disabled. Furthermore, they organize *hajj* and *'umra* (pilgrimage) trips and provide religious classes, cultural lectures, and opportunities to participate in sports. These NGOs have distinguished themselves due to their capacity to constantly increase the financing of their activities and to compensate large numbers of citizens for the withdrawal of the state from what used to be free public services, such as education and health care. This has led the NGOs to expand their activities in the rural and urban areas of many governorates. Their number and proportion, compared to the amount of NGOs in Egypt, are steadily increasing. In the 1960s, Islamic NGOs accounted for 17.3 percent of the total number of NGOs. In the 1970s, they represented 31.2 percent and, by the end of the 1980s, they accounted for 34 percent. Today, 67.3 percent of all these Islamic NGOs are based in eight governorates: Cairo, Giza, Alexandria, Qalyubiya, Minufiya, Sharkiya, Asyut, and Minya. Eight-two percent of the Islamic NGOs in these governorates were founded during the 1970s and 1980s. Therefore, any study of civil society in Egypt should pay special attention to Islamic NGOs—particularly if the study is on the relationship between social institutions and the development of democracy.

This paper will discuss Islamic NGOs based on two main criteria: the name of the organization and the classification of its activity. Thus, by Islamic Non-Governmental Organizations, we mean:

- NGOs with a name that contains the word Islam or any or its derivatives such as Muslim (Islamic).
- NGOs with a name that contains one or more names that are generally associated with Islamic heritage, culture, thought, or history (Heritage-related).
- NGOs that were formed as part of the activities of a mosque, and were named according to the mosque's name (Mosque-related).
- NGOs, whose main—but not singular—purpose is to facilitate the *hajj* and the *'umra* (Pilgrimage-related).
- NGOs that teach the holy Qur'an even though they may carry out other activities (Qur'an teaching).

Central NGOs that have many activities (Sunna-related). Examples of these include: the Legitimate Society to Assist Those Working in the Fields of the Holy Qur'an and the *Sunna* of the Prophet (al-Jam'iya al-Shar'iya li-Ta'awun al-Amilin bi-l-Qur'an al-Karim wa-l-Sunna al Muhamadiya), the Young Men's Muslim Associations (Jam'iyat al-Shuban al-Muslimin), the Young Women's Muslim Associations (Jam'iyat al-Shaabat al-Muslimat), the Society to Preserve the Holy Quran (Jam'iyat al-Muhafaza 'ala al-Qur'an al-Karim), the Society of the Muhammadi Clan

(Jami'yat al-'Ashira al-Muhammadiya), and the Society of the Supporters of the *Sunna* of Muhammad (Jama'at Ansar al-Sunna al-Muhammadiya).

As we have said, a study of the Islamic NGOs' relationship with democracy acquires special importance in view of the increasing non-governmental activities they carry out and also because of their increasing number. They attract millions of Egyptians and they are associated with different social groups, creating a sense of belonging and loyalty between the members and the leaders of these societies.

Islamic NGOs' Role in Democracy

This paper focuses on the role of these NGOs in teaching their members democratic values and will analyze whether their internal functioning can be understood as contributing toward instilling democratic behaviors that can then be transmitted to society in general. This paper seeks to analyze the influence that these NGOs have on the democratization process and on the people who deal with them and on those who use the services they provide. The question is whether they invite these people to take part in evaluating its activities, defining priorities, and monitoring performance. In other words, does the internal structure of the NGO function according to the principles of democracy? The aspects of this role can be gauged by the following criteria:

1. The extent of real growth in active and effective membership of the society.
2. The attendance rate for the annual general assembly, the highest authority in the NGO.
3. Rates of new membership to the board of directors.
4. The level and scope of voluntary work in running the activities of the NGO.
5. The decision-making mechanisms and the daily running of the NGO.
6. The extent of women's participation in the activities and management of the NGO.

In defining general indicators related to these aspects of the activities and management of Islamic NGOs, we shall rely on the results of a field study[2] for a sample of Islamic NGOs. The sample consisted of 27 NGOs in Cairo and Dumyat. Although we cannot generalize these indicators because their scale is too small, yet, we can use them to trace general aspects of this phenomenon, especially as they are similar to results reached by previous studies on NGOs in Egypt and the Arab world.

The research made a critical study of the following aspects: the reasons for the establishment and success of the Islamic political movement, its effects on the activities of Islamic NGOs, the relationship of this movement with Islamic NGOs, and finally, women's position in Islamic non-governmental activities.

The Field Study Sample

In view of the objective difficulties encountered when conducting field research in Egypt and the difficulty of basing the research on a large representative group, the research group decided to investigate those Islamic NGOs research group members had personal relationships with, in order to reach a more accurate estimation. The sample contained ten NGOs from Cairo, nine from Minya and eight from Dumyat. There are very many NGOs in these governorates, and all these NGOs fit the classifications that we used to define an Islamic NGO (Islamic, Heritage-related, Mosque-related, Pilgrimage-related, Sunna-related, and Quran teaching).

Here is a list of these NGOs:

Cairo Governorate:
Al-Jam'iya al-Shar'iya bi-l-Matariya / Jam'iyat Sherif al-Islamiya bi-l-Sahil / Jami'yat al-Wa'yy al-Islami bi-l-Sahil / Jam'iyat 'Ibad al-Rahman bi Madinat Nasr / Jam'iyat al-Ikhlas al-Islamiya bi-l-Sharabiya / Jam'iyat al-Nasr al-Islamiya bi-l-Khalafawi / Jam'iyat Dar al-Arqum bi-Madinat Nasr / Jam'iyat Dhat al-Nitaqain bi Madinat Nasr / Jam'iyat al-Shubban al-Muslimin bi Ramsis / Jam'iyat 'Umar ibn 'Abdul 'Aziz bi Madinat Nasr.

Minya Governorate:
Jam'iyat 'Ali ibn Abi Talib—Bani Mazar / al-Jam'iya al-Khayriya al-Islamiya—Deir Mawas / Jam'iyat al-Shuban al-Muslimin—Minya City / Jam'iyat al-Iyman wa-l-'Ilm al-Islamiya—Samalout / Jam'iyat al-Huda al-Islamiya—Minya City / al-Jam'iya al-Khayriya al-Islamiya Bani Mahdi / Jam'iyat al-Birr wa-l-Taqwiya al-Islamiya—al Birgaya / al-Jam'iya al-Islamiya li-l-Islah wa-l-Tawhid—Minya City / Jam'iyat al-Salam al-Islamiya—Malawi.

Dumyat Governorate:
Jam'iyat al-Shaykh 'Amr li-l-Khadamat al-Diniya wa-l-'Igtima'iya /

Islamic NGOs and Democracy in Egypt

Jam'iyat Da'wat al-Haq al-Islamiya / Jam'iyat Ansar al-Sunna al-Muhamadiya / Jam'iyat Kafalat al-Yatim wa-l-Tanmiya / Jam'iyat al-Ri'aya al-'Igtima'iya wa Taysir Shu'un al-Hag wa-l-'Umra bi Hayy al-Nasiriya / Jam'iyat Tahfiz al-Qur'an al-Karim wa Taysir Shu'un al-Hag wa-l-'Umra bi Qism Rabi' / Jam'iyat al-Shubban al-Muslimin / al-Jam'iya al-Shari'iya li-Ta'awun al-'Amilin bi-l-Kitab wa-l-Sunna bi Kafr al-Ghab.

Research Tools

The team used two different research methods:

1. Index for observation and in-depth study of Islamic NGOs.

    First, the team concentrated on the official documents of each association (including forms for facts related to the month, data about the board of directors, the activities officially registered in the records of the NGOs, data on the last general assembly, budgets, and membership) in order to know the objectives and official activities of the NGO and obtain information on the members of the administration board.

    In addition to these direct questions, the researcher made field observations on issues such as: the relation of the mosque to the NGO; slogans and newspapers on the bulletin board; the appearance of members and activists in the society; the relationship between men and women in the society, whether they mingled freely or were separated; and the extent of women's participation in the activities of the society.

2. Index on interviews with members and activists in the NGO.

    This index attempted to find out the opinion of active members in these societies through direct dialogue, the main points of which were recorded. The questions of this index focused on a number of main issues: the motives for membership or taking part in the activities of the NGO; the relationship with other institutions and organizations in society; the attitude to women's participation in NGOs action; and the role of NGOs in society.

General Indicators on the Relation between the Islamic NGO and Democracy

The field study revealed a number of indicators on Islamic NGOs and their relation to democracy through the six main areas that we have referred to before and which are:

The Extent of Growth in Active and Effective Membership of the NGO

A number of factors and, chiefly, the extent to which members participate in its activities, starting from planning and ending with the implementation and monitoring of performance and election of leaders can gauge the democracy of any social institution. It can also be gauged by the increase of the number of active and effective members from on period to another.

According to the results, 21.4 percent of all NGOs have seen their memberships decrease from year to another. Thus, 78.6 percent of the NGOs in the sample had registered a very meager increase in the number of members. This could not be attributed to a real growth of the association, as much as it could be attributed to the fact that the membership of the NGO was a condition to benefit from its activities: such as sports in Gam'iyyat al-Shubban al-Muslimin (Young Men's Muslim Association) or going to the 'umra and *hajj*, or subscribing to projects to build mosques or care for orphans. Thus, the increase in membership in these societies does not reflect an active and effective membership. The growth in membership is sometimes due to an increase in the branches of the NGO such as al-Jam'iya al-Shar'iya. This increase can be explained by the fact that these branches built new mosques. Proof that this growth in effective membership is not real can be seen from the fact that, with the exception of some NGOs that make provision of their services conditional upon membership, the members of the other societies are no more than a few tens (from twenty-seven to 215). This is a clear indicator that the NGOs do not appeal to the masses. It also indicates that their leaders have a limited ability and lack interest in attracting new members.

The Attendance Rate for the Annual General Assemblies

Growth in membership is an indicator of the ability of the NGO to attract new activists. Participation and attendance at the annual general assembly (the highest authority in the NGO, according to the law) indicates the degree of effective participation by NGO members in shaping its orientation, defining the priorities of its activities, monitoring performance, and electing leaders. The results of the field study in this connection revealed the following: in 17.9 percent of the NGOs in the sample, (about a fifth of the sample) the attendance rate at the last general assembly in 1998 was 50 percent. In 82.1 percent of the sample, the attendance and participation rate varied between 3.8 percent and 41.8 percent, that is, less than half of its members. However, the real attendance rate was much lower than this, as a result of granting power of attorney for attendance at the general assembly to complete the quorum. Most of these powers of attorney were formal. It should also be noted that the high attendance rates at the general assembly were usually associated with a very limited number of members, no more than forty in most cases. In these cases, therefore, attendance of 20 members would achieve the quorum for the general assembly. At times only ten members attended and achieved a 50 percent attendance rate using powers of attorney. In other words, those who attended the general assembly were, in many cases, no more than the board of directors.

These figures indicate that the meetings of the general assembly, the most important organ for participation in the NGO, are merely formal and reflect no real or effective participation of members. As a result, the management and policies of these NGOs are in the hands of a selected few, who have been on the board of directors for many years.

Rates of New Membership to the NGOs' Board of Directors

In any institution, democracy is also reflected in the rate of change among its leaders, to bring about the rotation of leadership among the largest number possible of members, to train them in leadership skills and experience. Hence, these members would be qualified and experienced enough to play a leading role in activities outside the NGOs. This would create new leaders for all sectors of society and enhance the development of democracy in general. The development of democracy would be even more enhanced if NGOs send an increasing number of their members to take part in the Local People's Councils or the People's Assembly. Field results indicate that, in this area, the Islamic NGOs play a very small part. This is clear when we follow the duration of the term of office of some board members, during which they control the decision-making process, for example, posts like board chairman, deputy board chairman, secretary, and treasurer. The results show that:

Over 47 percent of all leading board members have been in office for more than ten years. The percentage of those who have been in office for more than five years is 80.8 percent. A large percentage of those board members have been in office since the NGO was founded. This explains why very few people dominate these NGOs, why the leaders remain unchanged, and why, therefore, the NGO fails to supply society with new leaders.

The age of these members ranges from thirty-five years, as a minimum, to seventy-eight. Young people are thus absent from decision-making institutions and from the daily management of Islamic NGOs, while the future of society relies, to a large extent, on training young leaders to take effective decision and action. If the NGOs do not offer young people the opportunity to acquire leadership skills and do not introduce them to democratic practices, they have failed to fulfill one of their main roles in society and do not contribute to the development of democracy.

The Level and Scope of Voluntary Work in Running NGO Activities

Voluntary work in an NGO provides the basis of active membership as does the level of member participation in its activities, monitoring its performance, defining its objectives and priorities, and taking part in the management. If there are more personnel with salaries than volunteers, this reflects a major deviation from the principles along which NGOs were formed. This transforms the NGOs into institutions that provide services in return for remuneration, which is very different from their real mission in society. For instance, their mission could be to provide the citizens with an opportunity to voluntarily take part in a collective action and thereby discover means to solve their problems, satisfy their basic needs and complete a necessary activity.

However, the results of the field study revealed the following: 33 percent of the NGOs included in the sample only rely on volunteers. This is a very low percentage considering the fact that the essence of Islamic NGOs is considered to be voluntary work, which is seen as the base for their activities. It is to be noted that two-thirds of these volunteer-run NGOs are in the governorate of Minya, where severe security restrictions on Islamic NGOs are imposed, as a result of the violence and armed attacks perpetrated by some extremist Islamic political groups. This has caused the financial resources of these NGOs to shrink, preventing them from employing personnel. Also, there were fewer people who wanted to work there because of the fear of the security forces. The following statistics are important: 51.9 percent of all the NGOs in the sample rely on civil servants who were detached from and paid by the Ministry of Social Affairs; 66.7 percent of the associations in the sample rely on salaried workers.

The NGOs that rely entirely on voluntary work—including the level of the board members—only constituted 14.8 percent of the total sample. This is the real percentage reflecting relatively better participation in the NGOs. It was seen that the voluntary participation of members in running these NGOs and carrying out their activities certainly gave them more opportunity to take part in shaping the orientations, defining the priorities, and monitoring the performance of the NGOs.

Thus, it can be said that most of the NGOs covered by the sample had, in fact, become employment institutions and did not take part in training people to participate in public work—which is their expected role so as to promote the development of democracy for all.

Decision-making Mechanisms and the Daily Running of the NGO

With regards to this criterion, the sample reveals the domination of a small elite. It was found that this small group also made decisions on policy matters and the priorities of the NGO. Therefore, there were no broad opportunities for others to take part in the decisions and in the definition of the orientations. This can be seen in the following facts:

a) The board of directors alone has real authority and makes all decisions in 63 percent of the NGOs in the sample.

b) The chairman of the board supervises the day-to-day management and takes decisions to run the NGO in 85.2 percent of the cases in the sample.

c) In 26 percent of the NGOs in the sample, the board chairman alone assumes this responsibility.

d) This percentage becomes 37 percent, if we add the NGOs, whose day-to day activities are supervised by the board chairman and assisted by the director. The latter's role does not go beyond the duties of a civil servant and he never takes part in decision-making.

Women's Participation in NGO Activities and Management

The position embraced by the association with regards to women has an impact on the democratization process and on the efficiency of their efforts for development. It is therefore necessary to offer women opportunities so they can participate in the different fields of national activities, especially those tackled by civil society institutions. These latter mobilize the efforts of the local population to foster efficient participation with respect to social and economic problems, and also help people solve their difficulties on their own. However, women's participation is restrained by the dominance of a traditional conservatism based on gender discrimination, which forbids women to take part in public life to the same degree that men do. This is what was observed in the Islamist NGOs, which were dominated by a certain conservatism—in reality, a deep expression of social discrimination.

According to them, women's original duties are in the household: to build the Muslim family and bring up new generations in the spirit of Islam. Within this framework, women can assume other roles provided that they do so while observing Islamic restrictions, such as modesty and decorum, not mingling with men, and ensuring that there is nothing in these other roles that conflicts with their original role.

That the Islamic NGOs view women's participation in this way was clearly revealed by the results of the field study. A poll was conducted among a number of NGO activists such as the board chairman, the secretary, the treasurer, board members, founding members, and the administrative director. They were asked about women's participation in NGO activities and the results were as follows: 7.7 percent said that women should take part with no restrictions; another 7.7 percent of them said that women should not take part in NGO activity as their role is at home; and 69.3 percent said that priority should be given to the home and if women had enough time and effort, they could take part under certain conditions. Some of these conditions included:

- Their activities should only be restricted to working with women and children.
- Women need to respect the laws of the shari'a and respect Islamic customs.
- Their participation should be essential to support the family.

A deeper analysis of these views revealed that among the leaders who had said that women could take part without restrictions were heads of NGOs that did not allow women to become members.

Another poll was taken with this same sample about the participation of women in the board of directors and the results showed that while 15.8 percent approved the participation of women without restrictions, 10.5 percent believed that only men should serve on the board of directors, and 73.7 percent approved of women's participation on the board under certain conditions, such as:

- Women could take part in women's societies that were geared to serving women and children.
- They could take part in women's societies provided that they observed Islamic restrictions.
- They could take part provided that their primary and original role at home was not affected.

We can see therefore that the great majority of Islamic NGO leaders placed restrictions on women's participation and leadership. In studying the situation as a whole, we saw that women's participation in the NGOs or on their board of directors, or even their attendance to the general assemblies was very low.

In the NGOs covered by the poll, the membership of women ranged from 2.3 percent to 7 percent. Women's attendance at the last general assembly in 1999, ranged from 3.4 percent to 9.9 percent. It should be noted that a large percentage of women who attended consisted of paid employees and, for the most part, they attended in order to reach the required quorum, or when a larger number of votes were needed. In terms of the representation of women on the board of directors, 92.6 percent of the boards had no women members. With respect to women's participation in voluntary activities, it ranged from 5.3 percent to 12.9 percent. The percentage of women working as paid employees, however, was much higher. It ranged from 16.2 percent to 52.2 percent. Most women who worked as paid employees were involved in activities related to women and children; as such they worked as supervisors in nurseries, instructors in ateliers, and as cleaning women, nurses, or doctors.

It is clear from the above figures that, in general, there is no real role for women in the NGOs—beyond their performance of certain limited duties in return for a salary and under the supervision of the male elite that controls the NGOs. Islamic NGOs are like other NGOs with respect to the low participation of women. However, women's participation in Islamic NGOs is less than in other NGOs with regard to membership on the board of directors, attendance at the general assembly, or even general membership. In a field that covered 1,084 general NGOs, women formed 22.4 percent of the membership in the general assemblies, and 18.8 percent of these NGOs had women members on their board of directors. These rates are less in NGOs devoted to social assistance and are much less in cultural, scientific, and religious (including Islamic) NGOs, where only 7 percent of the them had women serving on their board of directors (Quandie and Ben Néfissa 1994)(Shahida el-Baz et al., text presented before the NGO Committee to prepare for the Fourth World Conference on Women, 1995, oral presentation).

From the July 1993 report published by the Central Agency for Public Mobilization and Statistics (CAPMAS) and 1989 statistics on NGOs that received government aid, it was clear that the highest percentage of women's participation was in NGOs geared to care for the family or work on issues around birth control (43.6 percent participation in the general assembly and 41.8 percent participation in the board of directors). These were followed by NGOs devoted to child and maternal care, traditional charities, and social aid societies. The lowest percentage of women's participation was in cultural, scientific and religious (including Islamic) NGOs: with only 14.4 percent participation in the general assembly and 7.98 percent participation in the board of directors (Ben Néfissa and Qandil 1995).

The results from this study on Islamic NGOs correspond, despite the small size of the sample, to the general indicators mentioned above, and are the expression of the insignificant feminine presence in the general assemblies and their almost non-existent participation at the level of the board of directors. Based on all of the findings outlined above, it is possible to conclude that:

> Most of the Islamist NGOs of the sample count on individual membership, which is for most of the time inefficient and low. They count on paid work for their activities, within which dominates a civil servant mentality and not a participatory attitude, especially when it comes to making a decision. The real power is maintained by a small circle of people, whose positions are likely to be open to new members only in cases of emergency, such as death or an extended stay abroad. Within these small circles, the main protagonist is the director of the administration board, who monopolizes the role for many terms. Consequently, they are elitist NGOs despite the vast amount of services and activities they offer.[3]

How Do Islamic NGOs Become a Field for Democratization?

In terms of their relationship with democracy, these NGOs are not different from many other civil society institutions, which are also elitist organizations controlled by a small circle of leaders. The latter do not allow members to participate in the definition of the objectives and the priorities of the organization, nor to control and evaluate their efficiency. Consequently, most NGOs, Islamic or not, do not play a significant role in the democratization process of society. All efforts to reform, which would enable these associations to effectively participate in the democratization process, should not only be confined to associations but should be extended to all of society in general. Such reform is composed of different steps: recognition of the supremacy of the law and the right of the law; respect for pluralism in both the political as well as in the cultural spheres and trade unions; respect for the independence of popular initiatives and the alleviation of all restrictions stopping a powerful and independent civil society from existing; respect for all civil, political, economic, and social liberties and rights; the diffusion of democratic culture and the existence of free democratic media.

Despite this vast program for the democratization of all of society, it is possible to prescribe a formula for a common action strategy for all civil society institutions. It, seems essential not to let civil society become a mere substitute for the state, when it is a question of supporting the poor and minimizing the problems linked to structural adjustment programs. It is important to amend the existing laws on associations and civil society in order to give them genuine autonomy; create a regional level of common technical organs structures in charge of scientific research and information producing; train new executives and improve the current leaders; coordinate the common campaigns dedicated to promote civil society and let the people know the problems faced in this matter; facilitate a regular communication between civil society and the decision-making nucleus; organize frequent conferences on the main problems faced by civil society; guarantee the coordination between the different civil societies in the other Arab countries to forge one civil society, which would officially be present in the institutions of the Arab League, and which would have a role to play in the strengthening of the relationships between the Arab states on democratic bases.

Notes

1. Vice president of the Arab Research Center.
2. This field study was part of a research on Islamic NGOs in five Arab and African countries: Egypt, Sudan, Tunisia, Algeria, and Morocco. The filed study was conducted by the Arab Research Center in 1999. The research team which carried out the research on Egypt consisted of Abd al-Ghaffar Shukr, coordinator; Dr, Amin Abdul Khalik, former director general of societies in the Ministry of Social Affairs; Anis al-Bayya', deputy director of social affairs in the governorate of Dumyat; Hassanein Kishk, researcher in the National Center of Social and Criminal Research; Azza Khalil, researcher at the Arab Research Center; Dr. Emad Siyam, expert in Jam'iyyat Nahdat Ta'lim (Education Revival Society); and Dr. Huweida Adli, expert at the National Center for Social and Criminal Research.
3. From Imad Siyam, who helped Shukr with his research.

Chapter Eight

NGOs and the Reform of the Egyptian Health System: Realistic Prospects for Governance or a Pipe-dream?

Sylvia Chiffoleau

The Egyptian health system—one of the lynchpins of the social role of the national state—has recently had its principles and efficiency severely questioned. Its services were supposed to benefit the very poor, to guarantee an equitable and just provision of health care, but it has failed to deliver on both counts. As for the development of the private health sector that has been accelerating for the past two decades, it cannot be relied upon to cater to disadvantaged groups because the costs are too high. Yet, the problem of the Egyptian health service's limitations grows more critical as each day passes because of the ongoing epidemiological transition,[1] which could unleash a flood of increasingly diverse and sophisticated demands on a system that cannot even meet basic needs. Faced with this dilemma, the Egyptian government appealed to the international authorities. The latter, headed by the World Bank, proposed a comprehensive reform of the health system, based on the principles of governance, with room for the views and actions of NGOs. This paper seeks to explore the realities of NGO participation in the new health system being set in place.

Reforming the Egyptian Health System: An International Partnership

Health issues used to be mainly a domestic question, but it has never been completely absent from the international agenda. The states, for security interests, have pre-emptively equipped themselves with information and monitoring systems in an effort to contain the spread of infectious diseases and epidemics. That concern, along with the institutions and legal conventions emerging to address it, led to the creation, after the Second World War, of the World Health Organization (WHO): the UN specialized agency whose mission is "the attainment by all people of the highest possible level of health." While the ideal may sound utopian, concrete programs have nonetheless come into being and been taken into account in the implementation of health policies, especially in developing countries. For example, the Expanded Program on Immunization (EPI)—carried out in cooperation with UNICEF since the mid-1980s—became a central plank of public health policy in Egypt and managed to substantially reduce the country's infant mortality rate. These aforementioned agencies which drains considerable amounts of funds (from international donors and private investors) have a significant influence on the definition of health policy.

Bilateral cooperation, in addition to the role of international health agencies, is another way in which western models influence domestic health policies. The agency whose involvement in the field of health in Egypt has been far greater than any other is the United States Agency for International Development (USAID). In the late 1970s and early 1980s, USAID assistance concentrated on extending access to health care services for underprivileged rural and urban populations. In 1983, the focus of its priorities shifted to reducing infant mortality. Meanwhile, it has supplied some $208 million in support of family planning programs—a permanent feature of American aid policy since 1975—making USAID Egypt's biggest donor in this area (USAID 1994).

The World Bank, after having long remained minimally involved in the health sector—where, in theory, it lacks a mandate for intervention—launched a clear offensive in the late 1980s and, above all, the early 1990s. The starting point came in 1987 with a report titled, "Financing Health Services in Developing Countries—An Agenda for Reform" (World Bank 1987). While reasserting the need to pursue structural adjustment policies, it marked a shift toward a broader interest in the social and human aspects. Work then began to establish a financing, co-ordination, and research mechanism, culminating in the "World Development Report: Investing in Health" (World Bank 1993), which took stock of world health and health care systems, noted the negative effects of structural adjustment programs on social—especially health—policies and, hence, signaled the World Bank's effective entry into this field of action. The Bank's health system reform projects, once lambasted for failing to reach disadvantaged groups, had now become a policy priority. It advocated a range of measures based on its underlying neo-liberal principles: that state intervention in the health sector should be minimized, private-sector development should be encouraged, costs should be controlled, and so on (Koivusalo and Ollila 1997).

In 1993, the planning department at the Egyptian Ministry of Health and Population (MOHP) began working within the framework of a USAID-funded project with Data for Decision Making (DDM)—a unit attached to Harvard University's School of Public Health—to carry out an evaluation that would lead to improvements in public-policy planning and development. One of the six stated goals was to analyze problems encountered in the health sector and finalize a strategy for reforming Egypt's health system.

Two years later, in 1995, USAID's central authorities selected a consortium of consulting firms—including DDM—to conduct the surveys needed to launch its own health system reform strategy, a project prioritized in its five-year plan (1995–2000). The Partnerships for Health Reform (PHR) project set out to enhance knowledge on health problems and propose solutions for Africa, Asia, Latin America and the Caribbean, the Middle East and Eastern Europe. Emphasis was placed on reforms that complied with USAID strategic objectives for family planning, maternal and child health policy, and AIDS-related activities. In 1997, DDM activities in Egypt came within the framework of the PHR project (with which the MOHP had joined forces).

Meanwhile, in 1996, the Egyptian government was wary to multiply evaluations of the health system, which was deemed deficient because this weakness could affect the state's legitimacy relying on its social role. Consequently the Egyptian government asked the World Bank—which, by that time, was involved in health-related activities—to explore the possibilities of a loan to finance the surveys needed to evaluate the flaws of the health system. In June 1996, the Bank delivered a report stating that such a loan would indeed be granted so long as the Egyptian government consented to a comprehensive reform of the national health system, which, in the Bank's view, was structurally too fragile to just apply limited and spontaneous actions. Given the scale of the project, the World Bank called for the involvement of other donors. USAID, already engaged in a similar project in Egypt, joined the partnership; so did the European Union, which was in the process of establishing its post-Barcelona[2] cooperation policy. All evaluation work, carried out prior to this partnership, especially by DDM, was used for a wide-ranging survey of the health sector. The conclusions served as a basis upon which a project for reforming the entire Egyptian health system was drafted. The project details, along with financing agreements between the three main donors, were finalized in June 1998, and a pilot application phase was launched for field-testing in three governorates.

This experience represents both a breakthrough in terms of partnership between aid donors and also a test of what is conventionally referred to as 'governance.' The ideological ties between USAID and the World Bank produced a framework for this reform that became instrumental in bolstering the ongoing economic liberalization process. It called, inter alia, for a shifting of responsibility between the state, civil society, and market forces within a system where new actors would join in the decision-making process and help to enact public policies. One of the ground rules in this scenario was that NGOs actively involved in the field of health should be invited to take part in the debate and should implement the modalities of health system reform. Having already been tempted to encourage closer NGO participation in development programs for some years, and given the importance of the non-governmental sector in the social arena, the international organizations working in Egypt were quick to give it a try. Their pilot projects, however, produced mixed results with respect to the NGOs' ability—in the short to medium term—to interconnect with relatively large-scale and efficient development programs.

Limited Mobilization of Egyptian NGOs by International Organizations

International organizations have grown increasingly more porous to the influence of multiple actors, which emerge beyond their institutional borders, and among which the NGOs play an important role. The newly acquired strength of international NGOs (INGOs) has been officially acknowledged through the granting of consultative status to intergovernmental organizations competent in their area of interest: the Economic and Social Council of the UN (ECOSOC), European Commission, World Health Organization, etc.). Meanwhile, during the major conferences of recent years (Rio de Janeiro, Cairo, Copenhagen[3]), local—often referred to as "Southern"— NGOs have demonstrated their energy and desire to take part in the political interplay at both national and international level. Their increasing visibility and the liberal precepts guiding the international organizations have prompted the latter to seek direct contact with NGOs on the ground in developing countries. Not only are they deemed more capable of having an effective impact on grass roots communities often excluded from public social services, but they also make it possible to introduce international funding without having to pass via the states, thus avoiding the cumbersome red tape involved in working with states (Smouts 1995). With that in mind, the international organizations and bilateral cooperation agencies in Egypt have, over the past few years, been carrying out a series of evaluations aimed at gaining greater insight into the local NGO milieu, and gauging the extent to which that milieu can be mobilized for the sake of social development. Notwithstanding the history and scale of Egyptian associations, a genuine, effective, and wide-ranging partnership has been slow to establish.

Once again, it was USAID—with its longstanding, deep-rooted involvement in Egypt—that launched the quest for more extensive contact with NGOs. True, USAID already happened to be working with a number of large Egyptian NGOs, but now it was a matter of carrying the logic of collaboration to hitherto unprecedented lengths. In May 1991, the governments of Egypt and the U.S. reached an agreement whereby some $20 million of direct funding would be earmarked for Egyptian associations—on top of the traditional sums made available to the Ministry of Social Services for redistribution to local NGOs. Notwithstanding the agreement, however, the Egyptian state was reluctant to relinquish its role of intermediary between the international organizations and local NGOs, and USAID found it hard to break out of its close circle of favored NGOs, due to an inability to register new beneficiaries for its aid (Sullivan 1993).

At the 1995 Copenhagen Conference, U.S. Vice President Al Gore launched the New Partnerships Initiative (NPI), a project designed to boost the capacity of NGOs, small businesses, and local authorities in the South with logistical and financial support from American NGOs and, in doing so, create a vast environment that could play an effective role in development projects, especially those geared to helping disadvantaged groups. Within this context, USAID launched an evaluation of the Egyptian NGO sector with a view to establishing a partnership between American-Egyptian NGOs, as recommended by NPI guidelines.

Via the intermediary of an American NGO, the National Council of Negro Women (NCNW), an aid and grant scheme was made available to a number of carefully selected4 Egyptian NGOs, who also received technical assistance and training within the framework of this partnership. According to its report, this pioneering experience can pride itself on having achieved, and even exceeded, its original objectives: thirteen Egyptian NGOs selected (against a target of at least ten) and twenty-eight grants provided (originally to have been at least twenty). The selected NGOs, however, had quite a specific profile; they represented a small minority of NGOs. They tended to be large, mainly Cairo-based and already professionalized, associations with a relatively long history of working with international organizations or bilateral aid donors: the Coptic Evangelical Organization for Social Services (CEOSS)[5] Association for the Protection of the Environment, Muslim Young Women's Association, etc.). As for the grants distributed in the health sector, these mainly went to Muslim associations involved in curative action (expansion of a private general hospital in al-Arish; a health center for Zabalin neighborhood families and adolescents) as opposed to the specific focus of USAID's own priorities: primary health care and prevention (USAID 1995).

Other international organizations have confirmed how few NGOs appear eligible for recruitment to carry out large-scale development programs and make rational use of financial aid in keeping with the donors' criteria. A UNICEF survey of the Egyptian NGO sector, for instance, underscored the enormous potential of Egyptian NGOs, pointing out that they were already playing a considerable role in development (UNICEF 1994). However, it found out that very few of them are genuinely active, enterprising, or innovative; these were the ones that happened to be connected to international donors or INGOs, or else emerging through the initiative of modern professionals experienced in management and administration. The majority—a *fortiori* the closest to grass roots level and hence geographically most remote from the decision-making centers—knew nothing of the procedures to follow in order to obtain funding from donors (UNICEF 1994). Hence, UNICEF and USAID both emphasized the need to provide (especially managerial) training prior to distributing financial aid. Most international organizations have, as it happens, been publishing training manuals for NGOs in the South for a number of years with a view to striking a balance between the objectives and modus operandi of both parties.

It was only a matter of time before the World Bank began showing interest in the Egyptian NGO sector. In order to support the Social Investment Fund initiatives prioritizing NGOs' participation—and with the consent of the Ministry of Social Services—it commissioned a consulting firm to evaluate their capacity to take part in development activities, foster popular participation, and protect vulnerable social groups from the negative effects of structural adjustment policies. The first part of this project, called "Egypt PVO Sector Study" (World Bank 1994), concentrated on drawing up a financial profile of Egyptian associations operating in three of the country's governorates (Sohag, Sharqiya, and Giza). This report highlighted the fact that NGOs, contrary to a widespread belief, were generating large revenues. This cast the role of state aid in the PVO sector and, hence, the latter's dependence on the former, in a quite different light. The total NGO revenues for the year 1992 were estimated at $85–110 million, that is, an average annual income at least eighteen times greater than Ministry of Social Services subsidies. The total state aid to the NGOs in the three governorates studied accounted for less than 10 percent of the sector's overall revenues, with foreign aid amounting to just 5 percent. Two-thirds came from the NGOs' activity revenues and private donations. So, the NGOs' greatest asset and most tangible contribution to national development appeared to be their capacity to mobilize local resources for investment in local actions. But the report also drew attention to the fact that of the plethora of NGOs registered in Egypt, no more than a fraction had such strong fund-raising abilities.

In its theoretical expositions on the role of NGOs, the World Bank has identified their main strengths as lying in their ability to reach the most disadvantaged and geographically remote communities; to innovate and adapt standard program models to local needs; to act as mediators in the transfer of technologies developed elsewhere; and to foster local participation in the elaboration and implementation of public programs. However, the study's diagnosis with respect to the case of Egypt showed that local NGOs fell far short of that ideal. Indeed, it considered that they were not ready yet to fulfill such functions. As a result, rather than dwelling on the financial aspects—ultimately less crucial than they might appear—the report recommended that particular attention be paid to training professional managers, enhancing managerial and organizational capacities, fostering leadership within communities, and decentralizing the main agencies out of Cairo: a key requirement for developing local, grass roots associations.

Indeed, it is at the base, in rural areas especially—the weakest and poorest level of society which need social services—that associations (especially efficient ones) are most scarce. The second part of the study, commissioned by the World Bank, "Egypt PVO Social Assistance: Direct Aid to the Poor" (World Bank 1995), recognized that NGOs had—albeit recently—begun playing a significant role as social service providers, but that this role was somewhat unevenly distributed. In the three governorates studied, for instance, only 41 percent of the sampled NGOs were found to be devoting a share of their funds to social aid; most of them were Islamic associations. With regards community development associations, they are the least spenders in the social arena. Moreover, a mere fraction of NGO-generated social aid was reaching the rural poor, the bulk of it being concentrated in the cities where the Islamic associations are predominant. In 1992, no more than 10 to 15 percent of total NGO revenues was going toward social security; meaning that the government remained the chief contributor to the Egyptian welfare system.

Despite unanimous agreement that the Egyptian NGOs' really do have the potential to participate in the country's development, there is still a long way to go before that potential can be effectively and, above all, swiftly mobilized. A huge gap exists between the prevailing views on attaching greater value to the active involvement of NGOs—their participation in the decision-making processes and carrying out social action—and the realities of the situation with respect to Egyptian NGOs, very few of which are fit to play such a role. The partnership between the state, international organizations, and NGOs, though much vaunted as a key principle of governance, is in fact showing little sign of life. A similar gap (between declared principles and the bona fide participation of NGOs in the processes co-established by the Egyptian government and the donors) has been revealed through the reform of the health system.

Health System Reform: NGOs Left Out of the Picture

Broadly speaking, the strategy for reform aims to tackle four main areas: social security cover and financing, provision of health care services, rationalizing the system's organization and administration, and the pharmaceutical sector. Financing and health care services hinge on a proposal to offer universal cover regulated by a national health insurance fund. The latter, however, would be limited to a 'package' of basic preventive and curative services, theoretically tailored to the specific needs in Egypt. Any services not included in the 'package' would have to be covered by other means, for example, personal financing, private insurance, or intervention on the part of employers. Any affair should no longer be strictly dependent on the Ministry of Health, as access to this basic health care should also be available from a whole range of sources such as private-sector doctors and clinics, NGOs, and so on, within a competitive environment overseen by the health insurance fund.

The reform program, discussed by the Egyptian state and the donors hardly makes any direct reference to NGOs themselves. Regarded as a branch of the private sector, they are framed in terms of the "patient-as-client" medical model, and very little is said about any specific action undertaken by the NGOs. This silence is partly due to the fact that the reform program's initiators lacked a clear idea about the profile of the NGOs working in the field of health in Egypt. The numerous studies, conducted by both the world of academic research and international organizations, have served to broadly outline their strengths and weaknesses, geographical locations, or even financing methods. They have shown what a highly heterogeneous milieu this is, with its few efficient NGOs and plethora of modest, more or less active, ones whose daily practices are extremely hard to grasp, not least in the field of health. But in the typologies used to classify NGOs by activity (Ben Néfissa and Qandil 1995), while health activities—for example, mother and child care, care for the disabled, family planning—may well have figured among the most recurrent headings, no light is shed on the work actually being done.

In reality, the extent of NGO involvement in health sector activities appears to have been exaggerated by the prominence of clinics run by the religious—mainly Islamic—organizations. Those institutions apart, only a handful of big development-oriented NGOs have the resources to set up and staff health-care facilities. The rest—the overwhelming majority of NGOs registered as being in any way attached to the health sector—lack the means to own such facilities. At best, this restricts them to running education and training programs, a role that most are unwilling to play, if only because of their lack of competence to run such activities.

The profile of the NGOs genuinely active in the field of health, however, does not suit the health system reform program's priorities. On top of the reform program's agenda, is guaranteeing people's access to decent health services, particularly to those who were previously excluded from the system. Essentially, this means ensuring access to health services for the underprivileged rural populations. Yet the most efficient health-sector NGOs, headed by the Islamic association clinics, are very similar to private doctors. They are all based almost exclusively in urban areas, where almost all private doctors are located. Besides, they are strongly interlinked, with the same practitioners often found moving from one type of institution to another within the framework of a dual practice. Since the public health service tends to favor urban areas, most NGOs find themselves based in places where public amenities are in more plentiful supply, while both NGOs and private-sector practitioners are rarely found in rural areas where such amenities are highly needed.

Health-oriented NGOs reflect another characteristic feature of the Egyptian medical profession as a whole, in that their demographic balance is tipped in favor of specialists to the detriment of general practitioners. Fewer than 20,000, or 15 percent of, Egyptian doctors are estimated to be delivering primary and preventive health care on a more or less full-time basis. Moreover, they are employed almost exclusively by the public sector. As a general rule, the predominance of specialists poses a problem with respect to Egypt's pathological profile, which still requires a great deal more primary health care, and is seriously obstructing efforts to implement reform aimed at curbing deficiencies at grass roots level. The reform program is accompanied by a training scheme specifically for 'family doctors,' a term chosen in an effort to boost the image of a practice that has become relatively uninspiring as a vocation. Without the emergence of this new class of practitioner, little real progress can be made toward the participation of NGOs (and the private sector in general) in strengthening the primary health care system.

A final characteristic feature that health sector-oriented NGOs have in common with the health system as a whole is their general tendency to prioritize curative over primary and preventive health care. This is hugely typical not just of the private sector—whose general scheme the NGOs have largely reproduced—but in the public sector too. The Ministry of Health and Population pours some 50 percent of its resources into hospitals and curative services as opposed to just 20 percent into preventive medicine and mother and child care—a field in which the NGO and private sectors scarcely figure at all (for example, the former devotes no more than 4 percent of its activities to immunization). Added to the inordinate amount of attention paid to curative services, is the bias toward urban areas referred to earlier in this chapter. Not only are the private and NGO sectors lumped together in cities, but the public sector largely tends to prioritize them too. The government spends twice as much per capita in urban areas than in rural areas, despite the latter being far less well equipped than the former in terms of health care facilities. Moreover, public money is going to the governorates and regions with the lowest infant mortality rates. The system, as it stands, grants the smallest amounts to the regions that are poorest in terms of health indicators and facilities alike; the few NGOs present on the ground are powerless to fill the breach.

In this context and according to the above characteristics, the NGOs working in the health sector are nowhere near ready for the role ideally mapped out for them by governance-related guidelines. Rationalizing health systems theoretically calls for the mobilization of the private and association sectors to offset the shortcomings of the state, and—on the pretext that they are best placed to grasp the needs of, and have a more positive impact on grass roots communities—to reach excluded groups. However, in Egypt's case, NGOs hardly feature in the field of primary and preventive health care, especially in rural areas, that is, among the most disadvantaged groups. The reform program, when dealing with the redevelopment of health care services, is also less than forthcoming on the role of NGOs, preferring to concentrate instead on shifting the focus of the state and the public sector to the task of strengthening weak links within the health system. The reform program is therefore contradicting a number of its original defining guidelines.

Interest may be converging on the potential of NGOs to participate in development, and surveys may be proliferating with a view to understanding them better and bringing them into partnership with international organizations. Nonetheless, at the current time, NGOs remain afflicted by serious structural problems that prevent their effective mobilization and ability to play a significant role in the field of health. This brief overview has shown them to be primarily urban-based and curative-oriented, with religious (mainly Islamic) clinics as the norm. Their services and facilities (not to mention salaried employment structures) are cast in the traditional mold, and geographically fail to make up for the deficiencies of the health system. They can of course be incorporated into the new system (managed by the national health insurance fund), but will not help redress the most blatant failings in the current distribution of health care services. As for the smaller NGOs occasionally found working on the ground (especially in rural areas), neither the experts responsible for the preliminary evaluation of the health system nor the authors of the program for its reform, have regarded them as being reliable at all.

Before any NGOs working in the field of health can really be improved and mobilized, the medical profession must first make a genuine commitment to voluntary work, which seems a highly unlikely prospect. There has, in effect, been little development on that front to date: the 'best working' health facilities being the clinics run by religious organizations that pay their practitioners—often more (sometimes much more) than they stand to earn in the public sector. Doctors choosing to work with associations tend to go for the large, professionalized NGOs and are more willing to act as program managers than devote themselves to practice in the field. Smaller NGOs, on the other hand, can rarely afford to pay a practitioner.

It seems hard to imagine any large-scale mobilization of doctors to work on a voluntary basis for small NGOs, even by multiplying the types of paid practice. Indeed these NGOS are established in disadvantaged neighborhoods or rural areas where doctors already have enough trouble surviving. A more realistic option for those NGOs would be to mobilize non-medical voluntary staff, particularly if they are seeking to develop a vocation in preventive services. But these too demand skills and abilities that even the rare paramedics emerging from the official training system have great difficulty mastering. An agreement therefore needs to be reached to launch a major voluntary worker-training program that could pave the way to effectively improving NGOs' intervention capacities in the field of health. International organizations are very well aware of this; practically all of them prioritize actions geared to training the members of NGOs.

NGOs appear to have been cast aside by the health system reform program. Actually, at its present stage of implementation, NGOs' participation is, above all, seen as being instrumental: a means to support the governance approach advocated by donors. The truth is that health-related NGOs are not being widely mobilized, and no more than a few have proved capable of filling the breach left by the public health service's shortcomings. Although not often directly referred to in the texts, NGOs are in fact involved in the ongoing thinking, and even some of the action. Some of the larger NGOs are participating in the follow-up committee set up by the Ministry of Health and Population. Moreover, once they have been properly identified, the masses of smaller NGOs can embark upon a process of improvement and change geared to resolving their weaknesses and ultimately becoming fit for a part in the new health system, not least in the field of training. An evaluation of the second (pilot application) phase of the reform should help to establish whether such a process is under way, and to gauge the extent to which Egyptian NGOs, as a whole, are any nearer to being eligible for a hands-on role in the governance of that system.

Notes

1. The epidemiological transition is characterized by the decrease of the mortality rate which is caused by infectious and parasitologic diseases (e.g., diarrhea, measles, respiratory infections) and by the increase of pathologies which are linked to the

risk factors (e.g., obesity, smoking, hypertension). Developing societies accumulate their own pathologies with the ones prevailing in developed countries.

2. The post-Barcelona period is the time that followed the first Euro-Mediterranean Conference which took place in Barcelona in November 1995, during which the Barcelona Declaration was adopted settling the bases for the Euro-Mediterranean partnership.

3. The United Nations Conference on the Environment and Development (UNCED), Rio de Janeiro, 1992; the United Nations Conference on Population and Development (ICPD), Cairo, 1994; the United Nations Conference on Social Development (UNCSD), Copenhagen, 1995.

4. The NGOs that could register for the competition should be dedicated to development, registered with the Ministry of Social Affairs, have an influence on the targeted groups, and have a decent level of administration and management skills.

5. The CEOSS began as a literacy project in 1950. It is one of Egypt's largest development organizations, providing integrated approaches to poor communities in areas of economic, agricultural and environmental development, health care, and education.

Chapter Nine

New NGOs and Democratic Governance in Palestine: A Pioneering Model for the Arab World?

Dina Craissati

The contemporary expansion of NGOs in the Arab world is spectacular: it is estimated that they have grown from less than twenty thousand in the mid-1960s to around seventy thousand by the early 1990s. Several factors have contributed to this dramatic growth: the weariness of crisis-overwhelmed Arab states in meeting the socioeconomic and political needs of their populations; the expansion of an educated Arab middle class with the qualities and impetus needed to build NGOs stepping into the realms neglected by the state; external western political and financial support of privatization (and of NGOs as a form of private enterprise); and liberalization policies and growing margins of organizational freedoms (S. Ibrahim 1995). It is now conventional wisdom in academic circles and among activists alike that such growth is a determining contributor to democracy and an essential factor for the needed socioeconomic changes in the region. For the so-called donor community, and especially the World Bank, Arab NGOs are becoming a vital component of processes of "good governance."[1]

The Objective

The aim of the present article is to provide a framework for a more differentiated understanding of the relationship between democracy and civil society[2] (and particularly NGOs as one of its components) in the Arab region. It will feature a new kind of actor or NGO (close to what one may call a new social movement—NSM—here, specifically engaged in radical politics) and show how it potentially contributes to a new democratic culture, to policy change and to genuine sociopolitical and economic transformation.[3]

Focusing on the Palestinian case, and more specifically on the field of health, the present article highlights how the three models of democracy (liberal, socialist, and radical politics) are reflected in different forms of collective action. In this sense, the Palestinian setting provides a relevant heuristic case study, since from the 1970s onward grass roots organizations in the West Bank and the Gaza Strip have been engaged in building social— and possibly autonomous—infrastructures and patterns of organization in various sectors. These organizations gradually raised the banner of social issues within the Palestinian national movement, prompting fundamental changes within Palestinian society and opening up channels of confrontation and negotiation between themselves, other actors in society, as well as formal Palestinian Liberation Organization (PLO) bodies—and now the Palestinian National Authority (PNA). The significance of the Palestinian case lies, furthermore, in the unique context of Palestinian contemporary history. It offers a possibility to analyze the relationship between civil society and formal politics because the Palestinian state is still 'in the making.'

Through such analysis, the hope, on the one hand, is to contribute to the advancement of knowledge concerning the potentiality of NSM-type NGOs (and hence of a new democracy) in the Arab region. On the other hand, it is to extricate analysis of democracy in the Arab world from the particularism and parochialism to which these NGOs are often constrained, and to link the region and its particularities to wider international discussions on new social movements and democracy. Thereby, the aim is also to bridge the gap between what is considered 'Northern-centric globalization' of democratic values and Southern attempts at forging democratic realms amidst cultural and fundamentalist hegemonies.

The following account is structured into four parts. Part one introduces the three models of collective action in Palestine. Part two presents the specific context of social movements in Palestine and the structural conditions for their development, situating the empirical account provided in part three on Palestinian collective action in the field of health. Part four concludes this chapter drawing on the findings of the research.

Three Models of Collective Action in Palestine

This chapter explores three models of collective action in the field of health in Palestine. They relate to the three models of democracy—liberal, socialist, and radical politics—and, here, are labeled as integration, rejection, and challenge.

The integration model relates to liberal representative democracy. It is founded on a formal legal framework for the protection of liberties, accompanied by a conservative approach to social duties and an abstract and neutral conception of egalitarianism and tolerance. Political participation mainly centers on the formal political processes, which protect constitutional rights. Economic liberalization and rational technocratic outlooks to development guide and support the functioning of such a paradigm. The type of collective action associated with this model is either based on voluntary charitable societies enhancing traditional norms and consolidating conventional forms of organization, or on pressure groups competing for their particular interests to be included in and allowed access to politics. The model is one of integration because it does not endanger the prevailing economic, social, and political system. On the contrary, it seeks to further people's adaptation to sociopolitical opportunities and constraints, as well as their compliance with the standards of formal democracy.

The rejection model refers to socialist neo-Marxist democracy. It is based on the principle that civil and political rights can only flourish if balanced by socioeconomic rights. Hence, democratic processes are steered toward the necessity of achieving economic egalitarianism and social justice, possibly at the expense of individual liberties. Political participation is geared toward the building of social power through political mobilization. Market-oriented capitalism is rejected in favor of a strong interventionist welfare and/or nationalist state as the vehicle for directing a planned economy and achieving national independence. According to Dina Craissati, the type of collective action highlighted in such a model is that of idealized grass roots organizations acting within an over-politicized society, united by the project of mobilizing large sections of society and conquering social power to change the economic and political order. Collective action is only evoked in reference to its relationship with political action, either in terms of withdrawal from politics into civil society (an anti-institutional fundamentalism) or in terms of seizing political power. The model is one of rejection because it implies the creation of societal breaks through revolutionary mobilization and a large scale totalizing confrontation to either reject or capture state power.

Finally, the challenge model is linked to radical politics or on the politics of self-limiting radicalism. It is a challenging model because it puts forward a new legitimacy that defies old conceptions of democracy as well as conventional and institutionalized forms of enacting politics. This model also poses a challenge because societal stakes are defined around the combination of conflicting dimensions of democracy. Societal claims include the reconciliation of positive and negative rights, the renewal of social solidarities, the building of active trust, and the embedding of egalitarian and access politics in meanings, values, and identities. The model entails an ongoing rethinking of the welfare state around generative politics.[4] It provides a framework for active social commitment, autonomy and innovation, investment of economic resources in societal sectors and social initiatives, and decentralization of political power. Finally, the model constitutes a challenge.

With regard to the Palestinian case, these three models can be revealing at different levels. First, they can enrich the understanding of what is controversially called, in the literature and in Palestinian society, 'mass' or 'popular' voluntary organizations, and now, NGOs. This analysis places all these organizations of civil society in relation to each other and assesses the quality of their action. Some organizations in Palestine do not necessarily represent a democratic challenge despite their wide social constituency and membership, provision of social services, or organizational capacity and active NGO network.

Second, the delineation of social movement characteristics out of mass organizations and NGOs in Palestine solves the dispute around their 'politicization,' that is their use to further national and political aims. In a context of national liberation, the whole of society becomes tainted by the national struggle, and any social actor can hardly bypass this. Furthermore, the still weak institutionalization of state structures and political parties in Palestine creates a 'political market' in which all forms of organization become a potential constituency. However, the difference between one 'politicized' mass organization (or NGO) and another, becomes the quality of their collective action; their capacity to prevent politicization and to create social democracy—which remains constrained by the national movement and its political offshoots; and their ability to articulate a national societal struggle in order to build a political society (the state infrastructures working for politics) out of the politicized community (the people themselves).

Third, and in view of the actual phase of state building, the radical politics approach raises different questions concerning prospects of democracy in Palestine that go beyond normative liberal concepts. Hence, it will not be enough to ask the preliminary question as to whether or not state formation in Palestine will be accompanied by representative democracy and respect for human rights. The examination of democratic prospects should go a step further by addressing the quality of a liberal democratic constitutional state. In other words, are there new social movements in Palestine capable of breaking away from conventional models of the welfare state, which have been historically carried by national liberation movements, and are they capable of proposing alternative forms of societal and state organization? Are there new social movements in Palestine capable of enriching the actual democratic debate, which is centered on demands for human rights and formal democracy? Can they address the political and economic essential questions while simultaneously taking necessary measures to adequately and responsibly manage the state?

New Social Movements and the Political Landscape in Palestine5

NSM-type NGOs, as a type of agent involved in collective action in Palestine, should be examined within the development, since the late 1970s, of three intertwined frameworks of national, political, and economic liberalization. First, there is the evolution of new forms of social organization to resist military occupation and to prepare for the future Palestinian state. Second, the more 'political' strategies and struggles of the PLO, and later the PNA, influenced the path of social movements. Third, the emergence of an NGO movement within the present context of state-building, peace-making, and international aid is now marking democratic politics in Palestine. It is argued in this section that these frameworks have, to different degrees, overshadowed and at times diverted the stakes pursued by NSM-type NGOs, and that a more refined analysis is needed to unearth the radical politics in which they are engaged.

The Politics of Resistance and Liberation

By the mid-1970s, gradual awareness of the destructive socioeconomic effects of the Israeli occupation led to the adoption by the Palestinian national movement of a *sumud* (or steadfastness) program. It aimed at mobilizing the population in the Occupied Territories to build an infrastructure of national institutions in order to sustain a process of self-reliance and of disengagement from the occupation. However, the way this strategy was promoted by the PLO leadership from 'outside' the Occupied Territories brought forth criticism and resistance from progressive forces on the 'inside.' Although the *sumud*, through the external fund allocations of the

Jordanian-Palestinian Joint Committee created in 1978, bolstered agricultural, educational, medical, cultural, and other social institutions, it nevertheless led to uneven development and social differentiation. Moreover, it also supported traditional institutions and charitable societies that failed to address the needs of the most deprived sectors of the population.

Sumud muqawim (or resistance sumud) thus appeared as an internal reaction to what has been called the static sumud of the outside. It was to be based on the local needs and priorities articulated and defined by those facing occupation on a daily basis. Young university-educated professionals, who came from refugee camps, villages and small towns, led mass organizations, which had become the expression of *sumud muqawim* by the late 1970s, and had proliferated across several socioeconomic sectors. On the one hand, these organizations challenged traditional, nationalistic and elitist patterns of development through the mobilization of the poor, especially in the villages. On the other hand, these NGOs mobilized attention through alternative, decentralized, more open and democratic structures, through grass roots voluntary work, and within a spirit of egalitarian social transformation. When the Intifada began in 1987, they could provide the organizational basis and the agenda to sustain the movement. The challenge of static *sumud* by *sumud muqawim* could thus be considered the first kind of societal rupture created from within the national movement by mass organizations.

In turn, the Intifada (together with the Declaration of Independence of 1988) bolstered the creation of a multitude of centers and projects geared toward community, human resources, and institutional development, research, and advocacy—complementing the strategy of *sumud muqawim* with the notion of 'development for liberation and building the future Palestinian state.' Such institutions differed from charity-oriented societies in their developmental approach, but also from mass organizations, as they did not have a broad-based membership. Their aim was to provide specialized support and technical assistance and training to other organizations, to charitable societies, to grass roots committees and to various unions and cooperatives. Often called 'professional' centers, they were, for the most part, composed of a network of dedicated intellectuals, academics, and professionals committed to challenge the established order, but also dedicated to foster genuine and sustainable development in Palestine. Furthermore, most centers had paid staff and funding primarily came from international aid.

The politics of *sumud muqawim* and of liberation as reflected in mass organizations and professional centers should be viewed with more scrutiny in light of the 'politics of meaning' adopted by NSM-type NGOs. Indeed, as will be demonstrated, the radical politics approach as used in health-related organizations in Palestine can deepen our understanding and assessment of the actions of these organizations and centers. This approach can help to identify the alternative forms of democratic practices that have existed in Palestine since the 1980s and that are likely to make genuine, contributions to a democratic Palestinian future.

The Encroachments of Political Action

The second setting in which mass and other organizations emerged and evolved is more 'political' and linked to two major developments since the mid-1970s. First, the progression of political strategies and the intensification of political struggles within the PLO have played an important role in furthering mass organizations, while on the other hand restraining their social action. Second, the creation of embryonic state structures, since the Madrid peace process in 1991 and after the first Oslo agreement in 1993, has marked the beginning of what one may call interactions and confrontations between state and civil society.

In 1993, mass mobilization became part of the PLO's political strategies when at the eleventh session of the Palestine National Council, the national movement included political struggle next to armed struggle in its program of national liberation. Furthermore, the mounting Israeli repression against members of political organizations in the Occupied Territories led to the recognition by the national movement, that clandestine and strictly political action would be limited, unless supported by open structures of mass organizations addressing the needs of the people. The Palestinian Communist Party (the Palestinian People's Party—PPP—since 1991) was the only political force with its leadership and its main base 'inside,' in the Occupied Territories. It took a pioneering role among the forces on the left to develop such strategy and build alternative mass organizations. When the success of such mobilization became obvious, it was followed, albeit at differing levels, by all political forces of the national movement.

However, the political and factional divisions afflicting the national movement since the 1980s, and especially after the Lebanon war in 1982, intensified the politicization of the popular movement, which came to reflect its deep divisions. Mass organizations proliferated, became divided into four (and later five and six) contending and parallel fronts (according to the main political trends within the PLO) and duplicated their efforts in each of the sectors of society in which they were active.[6] Even the professional centers, which stemmed, for the most part, from the initiative of independent groups, frequently did not escape identification by Palestinian society with political fronts. Although the Intifada created an environment to overcome rival parallel work, 'factionalism' escalated again following the Madrid negotiations in 1991 and the Oslo agreements in 1993. The Intifada continued to influence what became the NGO movement, albeit in a different way. NGOs came to be seen and criticized as bases for the interests of weakened factions and political parties unable to address the challenges brought by the PNA's authoritarian intrusions and the continuous breaches in the peace process.

Such politicization has often furthered the political mobilization of constituencies at the expense of developing and sustaining societal meanings, and, as a result, has blurred different dimensions of the struggle. Before state structures came into place, following the Madrid negotiations, the PLO represented and integrated the various Palestinian political, military, and social movements into a unified national struggle. Now the separation between the state and civil society has become a complex process because the national liberation struggle is still pervasive and the distinction between the PLO and PNA remains undefined. This phenomenon most often dilutes the distinctions (especially at the analytical level) between national struggles, politicized/ 'factional' struggles, and those located at social/societal levels.

The politicization of mass organizations was further complicated by the ascendancy of Fatah within the national movement since the mid-1970s and its efforts to increase its leading influence in the institutional make-up of the Occupied Territories. This phenomenon was especially active in the mid-1980s through the creation—or reactivation—of PLO-linked para-state structures. These latter took the form of higher councils, general unions, and later, after Madrid, they became the technical committees, which were to prepare for self-rule and acted as governmental bodies. This domination continued through the formalization of the state-building process with the creation of the PNA in 1994, and the formation of the Palestinian Legislative Council (PLC) as well as the appointment of the new cabinet in 1996. Because Fatah also had 'its' mass organizations (and now, during the second uprising, it is the major force in mobilizing people at the popular level), it symbolizes, in a way, the tensions inherent to the evolution of a national movement into governmental and state structures. It has also represented the rising trend, since the establishment of the PNA, of cooptation and control of what came to be a dynamic 'non-governmental' sector.

However, the degree of politicization has varied from one sector to another (labor, students, youth and voluntary work, women, health, agriculture, and education) and from one political front to another (Fatah, PFLP, DFLP, and PPP). It has varied according to the structural configuration of each sector, the conception of political and social-developmental work of each political front or party and, but no less important, the capacity of each organization to dissociate its actions from partisan politics, to create autonomous social realms and to uphold the societal stakes it articulated. Indeed, as will be demonstrated in the case of the health sector, this was essential for the survival and vitality of these organizations. This is where the first seeds of friction between the 'social' and the 'formal political,' or between a still-to-be-articulated civil society and the state, can be traced back to.

Several additional constraints emerged for the democratic politics of NSM-type NGOs within such a tense context. Since Oslo, there have been mounting assertions by the PNA that 'non-governmental' institutions were unnecessary now that a government was assuming its role. The PNA initiated efforts to extend what it considered its legitimate authority over various socioeconomic sectors and to control NGOs and their relations with donors. The move was also part of a strategy to restrain NGOs as potential fronts for political opposition, especially from those factions that rejected the peace agreements. They also occurred within the semi-anarchic and arbitrary space within which the PNA operates, and which is also characterized by human and political rights violations as well as bureaucratic corruption and mismanagement. And last but not least, the prospects of cooperation and alliances between the PNA and Hamas. (The PNA buys political approval in return for illicit control over social sectors, such as education, family, and personal status issues) represent major battlegrounds for endeavors to shape the democratic citizenship of the future Palestinian state. This is especially so today, with the current environment of the second uprising, which has been heavily marked by confessional and religious dimensions.

The NGO Movement and the Present Context of State Building in Palestine

This leads to the third context in which radical politics in Palestine should be located: the emergence of an NGO movement after Oslo and the articulation of what has now come to be called Palestinian civil society. Within the course of 1994, a variety of more than seventy organizations in Palestine, from charitable societies to mass organizations, unions and professional syndicates, and development, research, and advocacy institutions organized into an NGO coalition, the Palestinian Non-Governmental Organizations (PNGO) Network. The PNGO Network is now an officially organized framework with around 120 member organizations, with a mission statement and objectives, approved by-laws, a general assembly, a steering committee, a financed structure and a coordinator, and various public activities. The concept of NGO as used by the network is defined in a very loose way so as to include numerous and different groups and institutions working outside the formal governmental sphere and outside the 'profit-making' sector.

Since its creation, the NGO movement has been engaged at various levels of shaping democratic processes in Palestine: addressing general issues of political democratization, especially through securing a law that protects its room for action; working on issues of NGO accountability and professionalism; defining relations with international donors; and all this amidst endeavors for a just peace. However, despite their laudable achievements, NGOs have been criticized, often superficially and in a wholesale manner, as jumping on the bandwagon of foreign agendas at the expense of the national struggle and genuine socioeconomic development.

In 1995, the Ministry of Social Welfare emerged as the regulating ministry in charge of NGOs. It issued (in collaboration with the Ministry of Justice) a Draft Law Concerning Charitable Societies, Social Bodies, and Private Institutions, which brought a high degree of state control on NGO activities and on foreign assistance to them. In addition, the PNA created its own controlled NGO network (comprised mainly of Fatah-linked organizations) in 1996 and initiated press campaigns against PNGO, accusing its members of being factional, lacking transparency, and corrupted by international aid into lucrative and prestigious work places.

Since then, the PNGO Network has been fighting for a legal system that guarantees the right of NGOs to exist, to operate autonomously, and that secures their independent sources of funding. It has also been challenging the PNA to adopt a constructive role by recognizing the complementary role of NGOs next to the PNA in state building and development work. It held several events on the question of NGO regulation and legislation related to that sector, elaborating on the accomplishments of NGOs and their role in resistance under occupation, as well as in building the future Palestinian state. It produced discussion papers, newspaper articles, and press releases, as well as an alternative NGO draft law; it organized conferences and forums; it lobbied within the international community, the PLC, and among the political factions; and it built a coalition with the conservative Union of Charitable Associations. The result was that the PLC ratified a more liberal NGO law in 1998, and then signed it in January 2000. Although the PNA created a Ministry of NGOs composed of members loyal to the regime—after it signed this law, the present Palestinian NGO law can be considered one of, if not the most liberal, in the Arab world.

This success could also be a consequence of the NGOs' ability to effectively deal with two sets of contradictions. First, while fighting at the national level for the creation of a Palestinian state (and hence state institutions), Palestinian NGOs have been simultaneously engaged in struggles with that state at the level of political democratization. Second, while mobilizing against PNA charges of corruption, the PNGO Network has opened up a public space to debate the democratic functioning of NGOs. The issue of 'factionalization' and its negative effects are now openly addressed, as this phenomenon was perceived as providing NGOs with a cover for non-transparent (and hence undemocratic) operations. Related to this is the issue of professionalism, which was seen to be negatively affected by appointments based on political affiliation instead of professional merit. The suggested cure for these ills is now propagated in terms of healthy internal electoral processes, administrative public accountability and transparency, meritocracy, professionalism, efficiency, healthy planning, and economic viability.

However, Palestinian NGO endeavors, especially the moves toward institutionalization (through the creation of permanent centers, as against the previous informal decentralized structures; the increase in salaried personnel; and the emphasis on training, capacity-building, and governance issues), are now criticized as 'narrow' development work. They are perceived as a retreat from the popular grass roots and voluntary nature that used to characterize mass organizations. Moreover, they are seen as being satellites of political parties, recruiting only the privileged. Finally, they have the image of a 'donor-imposed political conditionality' centered on skills and efficiency. What has come to be called the "professionalization" of NGOs is unraveled as rooted in their integration into a global "NGO culture" promoted by international aid and foreign agendas in support of a "depoliticized" peace process (Hammami 1995, 2000).[7] It also explains the relative "absence of civil society" and the incapacity of Palestinian

NGOs to mobilize the masses and provide leadership in the present second uprising (Hammami and Tamari 2000).

However, a more thorough analysis is needed to assess the performance of Palestinian NGOs if one is to differentiate between them and appreciate some of their accomplishments. The above criticisms scratch the surface by taking institutionalization and mass mobilization as the criteria for success or failure. The institutionalization processes do not represent a negative sign; for some NGOs, this transformation could be part of what Offe calls the "organizational maturity" phase of a group or movement (1990). Such a phase is an extension of the spontaneous, informal, and decentralized organizing of the 1980s and results from the expansion of the activities of Palestinian NGOs. The 'professionalization' of action could be central for the functioning of NGOs, which now need to question achievements and to seek ways of consolidating them. But they do not say much about the quality of social action nor do they address the deeper meanings and visions underlying the actions developed by some of these NGOs. Similarly, mass mobilization is not a criterion for appraising the effectiveness of struggles. It can be argued that it is not the role of NGOs to mobilize masses, especially now that the lines between state structures, political parties, and civil society institutions are being drawn. It can also be argued that NGOs that focused on mobilizing political constituencies rather than on the articulation of societal stakes depended on the fortunes of political parties and factions and on the legitimacy of political opposition.

Following the Oslo agreements, PNA institutions have been understandably attracting most of the external funding in order to develop into governmental structures in various areas of civil administration with a capacity to formulate and implement socioeconomic policies.[8] NGOs, as the main recipients of international aid programs before Oslo, were penalized because it was (rightfully) considered that they could not easily shoulder projects that needed to be intensified. However, the PNA leadership has been facing huge problems of institutionalization and has been unable to create clear, efficient, and accountable administrative procedures and decision-making channels to manage international aid. In such an environment, funds were not only slow in their release, but donors are now turning to NGOs as efficient and flexible low-cost technical managers of foreign aid. Concurrently, the neo-liberal international development trend of furthering 'good governance' and civil society is also at play in Palestine. In February 1997 for example, the World Bank established a $15 million NGO

Trust Fund. Moreover, owing to pressure from international aid agencies, the PNA is now moving to use international monies within structures of joint funding, that is, through grants to NGOs.

The implications are poignant and double-edged. While international aid is an important material resource and furthers the autonomy of NGOs, it also undermines the sovereignty and authority of Palestinian statehood. In addition, such aid represents a discretionary mechanism to influence the course of the peace treaty (Abu Sido and Ghali 1995), or in other words, to use economic agreements as a bait or substitute for the achievement of political rights.[9] Palestinian NGOs here face challenges on contradictory fronts. First, there is the need for efficient coordination of national budgets and funds while fighting against their centralization and misuse. In their struggle against the inefficient PNA bureaucracy, in their criticism of its control and of corporatist tendencies, and in their fight for access to resources, NGOs face the need to create a constructive relationship with the PNA in order to secure the necessary state intervention in socioeconomic development and state-building and to define a complementary role for NGOs in public welfare.

The second challenge is the urgency of addressing the quality and content of international aid agendas, of PNA welfare politics, and of NGO intervention in the development field. This is an issue where it will not be enough to ask whether state formation in Palestine will be accompanied by welfare policies, since, at this juncture in Palestinian socioeconomic development, the risk of giving economic and technocratic indicators priority over social ones is very tangible. The neo-liberal, market-oriented strategy of donors is aimed at NGOs as a means of privatization and of rolling back the state in terms of welfare provision, as cheap, competent, and efficient sub-contracting agents of development services, and also as buffers in the face of the explosive situation in the region (Hawkins 1997). The controversial issue here is how to cooperate with the World Bank, while preserving the state—against privatization policies—and suggesting alternative forms of state and societal organization. The PNA policy orientation in this regard is also an obstacle, as it represents a conservative welfare approach with its insistence on non-state providers of welfare, family responsibilities, and social networks for material support. Women are valued within the frame work of their family responsibilities and mothering tasks, and NGOs are regarded as charitable societies assigned top-down duties in the provision of services. Furthermore, the welfare outlook of the PNA is based on mechanical planning and neglects the constant reproduction of asymmetrical resource distribution.[10]

This is an area where Palestinian NGOs are still weak and have yet to articulate their struggles, but where the spaces available to them should not be underestimated. This is all the more pressing in view of the dramatic socioeconomic losses incurred through the second uprising and the present crisis in Palestinian history. The sustaining of resistance will greatly depend on the capacity of Palestinians to reshape socioeconomic policies and interventions.[11]

Community-based Health and Health Politics in Palestine[12]

The health sector in Palestine reveals much about the possible scope of NGO activities in terms of sustaining resistance and redefining policies. This sector saw the emergence, in the 1980s, of what one may call the 'committees' movement that challenged the biomedical and engineering approach to health care that was offered by Palestinian hospitals and charitable societies, and which was supported by *sumud* funds. Such a biomedical approach was doctor-heavy, urban, hospital-based, purely cure-oriented, and technical, neglected primary health care work and the most deprived sectors of the population, worked within the limited boundaries of military laws, and understood the occupation to be the major cause of the deteriorating health care system.

While the medical committees did not deny the importance of curative medical establishments, they stood for redressing the balance toward preventive medicine and health education, based on the needs and participation of the population in the countryside. Such a task had to also include the active involvement of women, and bypass the boundaries imposed by military laws through mobile and small unregistered permanent clinics and a network of decentralized democratic grass roots committees made up of voluntary health professionals and other activists. By renewing the concept of health, they insisted on linking it to socioeconomic conditions, thus exposing the inequalities within Palestinian society, which have been hidden by the external and unifying threat of occupation. Although primary health care was, at a later stage, adopted by the medical establishment—partly due to its success and partly due to its promotion by international aid agencies—this change did not come with the new societal vision and the creative mobilization of the medical committees. These committees were, as a result, the best equipped to successfully respond to the emergency situation of the first Intifada in the late 1980s.

The Union of Palestinian Medical Relief Committees (UPMRC) was at the vanguard of the movement promoting the new health vision, setting an example in 1979 for the other committees that followed in 1985, the Union of Health Work Committees (UHWC) and the Union of Health Care Committees (UHCC). This, in turn, set the stage for the politicization of the primary health care sector, as each of the three unions were identified in the Palestinian community as affiliated to one of the three PLO left fronts, the UPMRC to the People's Party, the UHWC to the PFLP, and the UHCC to the DFLP. Moreover, the establishment in 1989 of the Health Services Council (HSC) was regarded as an initiative by Fatah to create its own competitive primary health care body.

Since then, it has been common talk in the Occupied Territories that primary health care activities were based more on political mobilization and ideological considerations than on health needs and professional work. This has led to inefficient duplication and unequal distribution of services and resources. However, such allegations, while they do carry several elements of truth, have overshadowed the differences between the four primary health care organizations, and the contributions of some of them to the development of the new vision of health and the struggle against factional politics.

The Politics of Meaning [13]

The work of the UPMRC includes various traits of NSMs and represents a model of challenge to the Palestinian medical establishment and to mainstream health thinking. Through stages of experience and through creative responses to changing needs and realities, it developed a more sophisticated version of primary health care, going beyond the 'egalitarian and access' politics of *sumud muqawim*. Moreover, the UPMRC represents a break, on a second level, from the traditional hierarchical and centralized approach to health. These changes took place as a result of active and continuous work on changing attitudes toward health and health professionals and after bringing and articulating new values around the relationships between doctor, nurse, health worker, patient, and community. Projects included the training of midwives and the setting up, in villages, of training centers for health workers, women's health, community-based rehabilitation, and school-level health programs. These programs are all geared toward empowering the patient and the community regarding health problems, while acknowledging and respecting the creative capacities of health workers. This project is also a conscious departure from dependent and hierarchical ways of perceiving doctors, health professionals, and technological equipment. One of the most visible achievements within such a trend is the emergence of women leaders at all levels of activities.[14]

Furthermore, despite recent institutionalization processes (for example, the hiring of salaried personnel)—an unavoidable development in the expansion of health centers and programs—UPMRC staff insist that this does not displace voluntary work and that the organization is always revitalized by democratization efforts. What is also interesting is that the UPMRC is very active in promoting and sustaining its vision of health with facts, training, skills, sound research methods, and professional attitudes toward community work. It entails, in other words, the embedding of instrumental rationality in community-based health. The 1990s have been considered by the UPMRC as a developmental phase, in which the expansion of projects has required planning and specialization. While concentrating on developing models and visions of intervention for the Palestinian health sector, it also created an NGO offshoot, the Health Development Information and Policy Institute (HDIP), to carry out the tasks of information sharing and information gathering, supervision, research, and shaping public policy. During the second uprising, the UPMRC could take the lead in addressing the health crisis through first-aid campaigns and other interventions.

Finally, the motto of health 'free of any factions' has remained at the heart of the UPMRC's projects, and it has refused to join several health coalitions on the basis of political representation. It works, cooperates, and coordinates its activities with numerous health institutions—from hospitals, university centers, charitable societies, women's organizations, counseling centers, and other health NGOs. It is also one of the founders of the PNGO Network and is very active in its steering committee. Through its collective action, it has been able to construct new identities and alternative social practices in health, and create democratic social spaces and health committees around health centers in villages—made up of organizers, health professionals, and health workers. While all these individuals might not be members of or directly linked to UPMRC, according to one of the UPMRC doctors, they carry its 'heart.' Perhaps the pinnacle of such work was the celebration of the twentieth anniversary of UPMRC in November 1999, which was attended by twelve thousand people, including youth groups, trainees, health workers, community leaders, ministers, and members of the PLC and local municipalities. The celebration did not only acclaim good health, but also social organization, self-reliance, and democracy.

On the other hand, the UHWC and the UHCC remained at the first level of *sumud muqawim* or of 'access' politics to health. They provide primary health care services while not actively and consciously working at changing attitudes or promoting a new vision toward health and health professionals. They represent a model of intervention, which can be depicted as one that rejects, but does not challenge the mainstream 'bourgeois' health set-up. The concept of primary health care remains self-evident and has not developed as a result of a rich and long experience with the communities, nor is it complemented with an articulated health-related concept of community empowerment. Community involvement and women's participation have certainly been part of the discourse, but only for mobilization purposes. They have not been linked to societal change and to projects of autonomous self-help. Primary health care, in the case of the UHWC and the UHCC, has remained at the level of servicing the people.

This primary health care approach can be characterized as an undefined mixture of revolutionary leftist and nationalist political culture, what Salim Tamari (1992) would call "radical populism." On the one hand, this approach contests the Palestinian traditional and elitist establishment that works within the confines of Israeli regulations and, in the case of private clinics, does not address the socioeconomic needs of the deprived. On the other hand, the mobilization of the largest number possible of health professionals, workers, and activists in the face of the coercive Israeli occupation remains the main challenge for the members of the UHWC and the UHCC.

Despite the trend since 1991 toward more professionalism in health work, activists of both organizations continued to see features of radical populism as their main trait and continued to underscore political mobilization. Thus, the social spaces they created through the different health clinics and projects could not offer much resistance in the face of politicization. This in turn crystallized their weaknesses when, after the Gulf war and the Madrid peace process, political strife within the PLO intensified and several institutions in the Occupied Territories had to face budget cuts. The painful necessity to close clinics, the drive to orient the work toward more professionalism (rather than toward mobilization), and the urge toward being 'represented' in health coalitions all seem to have diluted the struggle for the survival of their health vision in the name of a struggle for physical (and political) survival.

The Health Services Council, the fourth primary health care organization identified with Fatah, embodies the integration model of primary health care in the sense that it provides primary health care services in rural areas, but by integrating such services to the elitist view on health. According to the president of its board of directors, "medicine is medicine" and there are no differing approaches to primary health care. The approach of the HSC is clearly in line with the biomedical approach: developing specialized clinics with sophisticated equipment. Its work is based neither on voluntary grass roots work nor on participation of the village community. It is constituted only of clinics with paid staff, which are, in effect, a reorganization and convergence of old traditional clinics previously supported by the *sumud* funds into more geographically centralized ones. There is therefore hardly any difference between the work of the HSC and the one of charitable societies. There is even some overlap in their membership and part of their structures.

The Politics of Influence

The primary health care models of the four different organizations also reflects on their relations with the Palestinian health authorities and the Palestinian Ministry of Health. The impact of Palestinian state-building process, prompted by the 1991 Madrid negotiations on the health sector is best exemplified by the 'intrusion' by the Fatah-controlled 'official' bodies of the 'outside' into the social spaces created in the Occupied Territories. In 1992, the health sector witnessed the development of a National Health Plan and the creation of a Higher Health Council (equivalent to a health ministry), both under the auspices of the Palestinian Red Crescent Society in Cairo and its offshoots in the Occupied Territories. The official explanation for such state projects was the need for an 'alternative' to the low-standard, politicized, and inefficient health services under the occupation; the necessity to plan, monitor, coordinate and implement health services in the absence of accountability and effectiveness; the importance of regulating health funding; and preparing to take over the health sector from the Israelis.

A critical appraisal of the National Health Plan and of the Higher Health Council's structures and functions in fact reveals major trends toward a nationalist, strongly interventionist, and centralizing welfare state. Additional distinctive features are an engineering, biomedical, and bureaucratic approach to health, with traditional paternalistic views on leadership. This vision overlooks notions of community involvement and empowerment, marginalizing the achievements and innovative contributions of the committees' movement in primary health care, and most importantly, it did not see a need for such a movement to exist after the establishment of a Palestinian Ministry of Health (created in 1994).

At first, such state endeavors were met with strong reactions by all four primary health care organizations on the basis that they were not undertaken in consultation with the wide array of bodies working in the health sector in the Occupied Territories. However, beyond this level of opposition, the three models discussed above came distinctly into play when the organizations were given a formal role in the development of the National Health Plan and a seat in the Higher Health Council.

The integration model of the HSC was reflected in its total rallying behind the authorities (there was also some overlap between its members and the founders of the Higher Health Council), and the opposition has been dependent on the formal role its members obtained in the development of the National Health Plan and on their representation in the Higher Health Council. According to the president of the HSC, "primary health care, as in all Arab states, is for the state, for the Ministry of Health." As for the director of the HSC, he stated: "Palestinian NGOs will have no reason to exist after the establishment of a Palestinian government; some NGOs will develop into a government, some will cease to exist." In 1994, the HSC and its clinics merged their resources into the PNA Ministry of Health.

As for the rejection model of the UHWC and the UHCC, it can be seen in their ambiguous blend of a nationalist unifying view and a strong opposition to unilateral moves by the health authorities from the outside. On the one hand, both organizations have participated in the National Health Plan Commission. On the other hand, they have refused to join the Higher Health Council because of its undemocratic and partisan constitution. However, the stakes of their struggle have remained at the formal level of democratic participation (and thus of political recognition). They have not gone much further to criticize the content of the National Health Plan or to articulate a clear vision of their function in the future Palestinian state. They are against the government unless it is democratic (in the liberal sense of the word). They envision their role in the future Palestinian state depending on the quality of such a future government, and on the way the national question is going to be solved. If there is to be a Palestinian state, they would see no contradiction in joining the Ministry of Health.

The UPMRC went beyond the level of criticism of the undemocratic and politicized character of the National Health Plan and the Higher

Health Council. It questioned the substance of the National Health Plan and challenged the health authorities with its alternative community-based health project, which calls for the existence of autonomous health groups next to state health structures. Through several confrontations with the health authorities, confrontations which, unlike the case of the UHWC and the UHCC, are accompanied by the struggle for the maintenance and development of autonomous action; the UPMRC has been pushing and lobbying for a new vision of democracy in the health sector. Such a vision does not only require the election of a minister of health, but also the negotiation and consultation between social forces and governmental structures. These national decisions concerning health are influenced by the models created by such social forces and should take into consideration the demands of the grass roots for more and other health services.

For the UPMRC, the issue of centralized health structures is of prime concern. On the one hand, they agree that the Ministry of Health should run a number of centralized structures, such as infectious disease and vaccination programs, standardization of services and quality control (always with the aim of achieving social equity and putting an end to uneven development). On the other hand, for the UPMRC, decentralization does not mean breaking down the health system into districts; rather it implies the allocation of resources to health NGOs and empowering the people to make decisions concerning their health. There should be space left for NGOs to function in order to maintain creativity and prevent bureaucratization. The relations between centralized and decentralized health structures should be based on complementarity, cooperation, and democratic coordination. Professionalism, cost-effectiveness, and sound distribution of resources are stressed in planning and coordination. In addition, the government can and should rely on the expertise of NGOs and learn from the models they create, and there should be a contractual relation between the two that would allow NGOs to share their experience.

The UPMRC is now successfully engaged in diverse collaborative projects with the Ministry of Health. It has managed to make the health sector in Palestine one of the few, in which there is mainstream coordination between its diverse actors, especially between the Ministry of Health and NGOs.[15] The HDIP is currently acting as a center for information and surveillance of the health care system and is involved in concrete relations with the Palestinian health authorities to influence health policies through policy-oriented research. For example, the Policy Dialogue Project initiated in

1996 makes cooperation and coordination easier between the Ministry of Health, NGOs, local community organizations, private hospitals and the United Nations Relief and Works Agency (UNRWA), and orients them toward the development of national health policies.[16] In this way, the UPMRC goes beyond the formal model of decision-making by creating an informal space where the needs of the underprivileged are continuously articulated and pushed, and by eventually producing a prototype for alternative forms of democracy in Palestine.

Health and Radical Politics in Palestine

Like in the West, the countries of the South have to face the need for rationing resources and controlling expenses in the field of health. Within this context, the two dominant models of democracy are actively competing and commanding the need for an alternative. The liberal health model favors individual initiative, competition, and efficiency in a system that provides a lot of stimulation but that is highly dependent on privatization and does not offer collective perspectives nor generalized and equitable coverage. In the Third World, such a system, encouraged by international aid, is leading to a rise in expenses, thereby restricting popular access to health services. The welfare state model is a system where the state controls regulates and finances health services and where access to health care is secured for all. Its disadvantages are the known plethora of specialized personnel, hierarchical structures, disincentives to health professionals, deteriorating health equipment, bad administration, and mediocre health services (Danzon and Poitrinal 1996).

The alternative health model goes beyond the economistic solutions to health and addresses questions of environment, life styles, mentalities, education, and knowledge in order to ensure both creativity and public access. In addition to the principle of treating illnesses, it supports the acting on environment and behaviors through legislation, education, information, and by developing coherent programs of illness prevention and health promotion. The model advocates the active participation and responsibility of the people in the improvement of their health, as well as the extension of the mission of health professionals beyond merely providing services to include their involvement with the individual and the community (Danzon and Poitrinal 1996). In other words, alternative health is closely connected to the notion of generative politics put forward by Giddens (1994).[17]

In turn, the aforementioned paradigms of integration, rejection and challenge in the field of health in Palestine may be linked to these three democratic health models.The liberal model (integration model), as carried by the HSC or by the elitist, technocratic, and biomedical establishment advocates a competitive private health care system based on individualized atomistic health services, top-down hierarchical relations between patients and doctors, and economic and technological solutions to health problems. It eventually retreated from basic socioeconomic support to the poor.The welfare state model (rejection model), represented by the UHWC and the UHCC, presses for a public health care system based on the egalitarian provision of health services and on egalitarian principles of health care, but within a nationalist populist conception of community mobilization which resembles the paternalist outlooks of the welfare state. Both models compete for influence within the Ministry of Health. Both carry the belief in access to health services, one through free market competition and the other through the public system of the welfare state. Both hold a narrow view of political action in the health care sector, which takes the form of either pressure groups that do not question the system or that of a single organizational principle for society that aims at the control of the state.

In Palestine, one can also observe emerging alternative democratic practices of health beyond the liberal and welfare state paradigms—as represented by the challenge model of the UPMRC. Such practices take the shape of informed self-care, autonomous and responsible health provision, and the creation of new solidarities through the active participation of the communities in the organization of health (in contrast to the individualistic approach of the hospitals, and also to the patronizing dependency-fostering solidarities of traditional welfare). The model casts health development within its political, economic, and social environment, considering health care within a holistic approach. It requires coordination with basic economic and educational infrastructures, stressing qualitative development over quantitative expansion of services, bridging preventive and curative health, and viewing basic primary health care and simple intervention techniques as more effective and cost-efficient than expensive and sophisticated equipment and structures. Not only is equal access of the poor and underprivileged to health a leading goal, but, the democratization of relations between health providers and health beneficiaries is also vital.The recognition of the capacity of ordinary people to treat common health problems and the appreciation of health workers trained outside formal health institutions is also essential.The UPMRC provides a vivid example of generative politics by insisting on complementary roles between the state and

NGOs, and between autonomous and public services, and by forwarding new ideas on decentralization of health resources.[18]

Through its community-based health model, the UPMRC has built enough independent strength to face the political establishment, not only on a professional non-partisan basis, but also based on new meanings in the field of health. In this sense, the movement goes beyond formal models of political decision-making processes, first by creating autonomous social spaces where the needs of the underprivileged are continuously prioritized, and more importantly, where renewed health relations and values are introduced. Second, the UPMRC enlists in 'self-limited' and radical health politics by engaging in conflicting relations and negotiations with the health authorities, and by establishing a framework for cooperation, dialogue, and sharing experiences and visions. Indeed, the emergence of such a type of NGO in the field of health has an impact beyond health, by advancing alternative forms of democratic and political action through concrete autonomous spaces of collective action between the citizen and the state.

Conclusion

This paper has examined a distinctive type of collective action in Palestine, which carries characteristics of NSMs and advances new forms of democracy beyond the integrationist model of liberal democracy and the rejectionist model of socialist democracy. In addition, it has demonstrated how the new democracy represents a contending model for the two others and touches on the politics of self-limiting radicalism. Four general findings emerge from this study.

First, Palestinian NGOs should be viewed within a different focus than that pervasive in the literature. They are not significant merely due to their increasing number and their presence on the ground, and they are not artificial phenomena of a "weak" civil society.[19] It is also not enough to assess them according to their mobilization capacity or their tactical (or opportunistic) response to political and economic opportunity structures. Palestinian NGOs carry the potential for forwarding alternative patterns of state and societal organization because they include elements that are struggling for alternative democratic models. The radical politics approach and the three models of integration, rejection, and challenge can help differentiate among the various types of NGOs and identify those that are potential leaders in societal change.

Second, radical politics in Palestine is not directly visible. This is particularly so, since the politics of influence is less obvious than the politics of meaning. There are two reasons for this. On the one hand, lobbies, interest groups, access politics, and national struggles are now dominating the public political scene in Palestine because of the urgency of defending the physical spaces created by NGOs. Moreover, the national question has not been resolved yet. This overshadows the politics of meaning and it blurs the distinction between the politics of influence, which is centered on societal stakes, and the politics of access, which is centered on particular (and national) interests. It creates ambivalence and tension between the orientations of NSM-type NGOs and the protest mechanisms of other NGOs. On the other hand, the process of state building is at a very embryonic and exploratory stage and additional experience has yet to be gained regarding the relationship between state and civil society.

Third, the research has indicated that the UPMRC, the organization said to be affiliated to the Palestinian People's Party, has developed interesting characteristics of NSMs. However, this does not mean that the relationship between the party and the movement is linear. It is interesting to note that, within the realm of the political left, the frailty of organizations related to the DFLP and PFLP has been matched by the weakening of these political fronts, while the strength of UPMRC was not matched by a corresponding upturn in fortunes of the Palestinian People's Party. Although the present research has not investigated the relationship between the party and the movement, it could at least note that the leaders of the UPMRC, perhaps because of their political background, were forcefully protecting their autonomy from the party and disapproved of the political exploitation of the organization. With respect to Fatah, the distinction between the political/national and the social movement is blurred.

Fourth, although contextual circumstances do play a role in the emergence of NSM-type NGOs, these latter also have a dynamic of their own beyond the preconditions of their birth. It is important to further the analysis around the hypothesis that civil society flourishes more in contexts where the state is absent or weak than in those where the state has a long tradition of regulation and centralization. The absence of a state in Palestine has indeed facilitated the development of such NGOs. However, state building gives them an opportunity to participate in the definition of citizenship. The fact that the PNA and international donors are paying attention to NGOs is not only due to political and economic considerations; it could also be a sign that some NGOs are proliferating as NSMs and as actors and makers of generative politics.

Tamari (1995) looks at Palestinian NGOs as part of a trend within a major rift stemming from the political disarray that prevailed during the first Intifada and the post-Intifada period. He indicates that the role of Palestinian NGOs is critical, both in sustaining grass roots development work and in putting brakes on the hegemonic tendencies and poor performance of the PNA. It has also been argued in the present article that the test for democracy in Palestine is closely linked to values of a new citizenship and the capacity of Palestinian NGOs to play a role in checking the powers of the PNA and building this democracy beyond grass roots development. If the outcome of this second uprising lies in the ability of political forces to shape its direction, then genuine national liberation will depend on the capacity of NSM-type NGOs to rise and reshape socioeconomic struggles.

In this sense, Bishara (1994) rightly warns against the 'fetishism' of Palestinian statehood and insists that the construction of the Palestinian state will not come through the peace agreement, but through the struggle for values of equality, freedom, the right to food, and women's right to control their bodies. Such a goal not only goes beyond the issue of statehood but also of nationalism altogether. This in turn prompts ideas to rethink nationalism and citizenship in the Arab world, which are in a state of deep crisis. Al-Khafaji notes that the problem of leftists and liberal intellectuals in the Arab region is that they have to identify ways to achieve the two largely dissociated objectives of radical social change on the one hand and democracy and the rule of law on the other hand. The Arab world has been plagued by either an "ultra-nationalism," which has viewed citizenship through the mystifying lens of state power and has hailed poor economic results at the cost of democracy, or an ultra-liberalization that is marginalizing more and more of the population, leading to wider identifications with parochial loyalties and radical Islamist movements (Al-Khafaji 1993). Consequently, citizenship has to be rethought beyond the classic notion of a nation's ability to integrate its population within national territorial boundaries and to ensure commitment to the nation (Deegan 1993).

Despite the undisputed right of the Palestinian people to fight for their national sovereignty and for a just peace, the democratic alternative in Palestine lies within a renewed national, economic, and sociopolitical struggle. Haidar 'Abd al-Shafi, the former prominent head of the pre-Oslo negotiating team and one of the most daring leaders of the democratic opposition, insists:

The critical issue is transforming our society. All else is inconsequential. [. . .] We must decide amongst ourselves to use our strength and resources to develop our collective leadership and the democratic institutions, which will achieve our goals and guide us in the future. [. . .] The important thing is for us to take care of our internal situation and correct those negative aspects from which it has been suffering for generations and which is the main reason for our losses against our foes (in Usher 1995: 82).

Not everything has already been said about social actors in Palestine, especially in the case of the health sector. Although NSM-type NGOs use channels of action ignored by proponents of liberal concepts of democracy, they are bound to be more successful than the lethargic political parties, the self-oriented interest groups or the radical fundamentalist movements. It is true that such Palestinian NGOs continue to face the challenge of protecting their gains. On the other hand, they have given an impetus to a new kind of democratic thinking within Palestinian civil society and between the state and civil society that will be difficult to contain. And this should not remain without consequence for a new democratic future in the Arab world. If, as Isam al-Khafaji (1993) mentions, effective radical change in the Arab world needs a rethinking of national sovereignty, maybe an eye should be turned to those who, through social action, are already rethinking it and struggling to achieve it in Palestine.

Notes

1. The World Bank introduced the term "bad governance" in 1989 to explain why structural adjustment programs largely failed in the Third World. Too much bureaucracy, corruption, and lack of accountability on the part of governments are accounted as the sources of economic inefficiency. Hence, "good governance" is seen as a remedy to this problem by emphasizing pluralism and the rule of law, and specifically the role of non-governmental actors in the promotion of an efficient capitalism (Kiely 1995).
2. For critical discussions on democracy and civil society in general, and in the Arab world in particular, see Cohen and Arato (1992), Giacaman (1993), Held (1987), F. Ibrahim (1995), Markaz al-Buhuth al-'Arabiya (1992), Markaz Dirasat al-Wihda al-'Arabiya (1992), Norton (1995–96), Sadowski (1993), Salamé (1991), and Wood (1990).
3. See Craissati (1998) for a detailed presentation of new social movements involved in radical politics. For additional theoretical sources on these issues, see Calhoun (1994), Cohen (1985), Cohen and Arato (1992), Eyerman and Jamison (1991), Giddens (1994), Held (1987), Kiely (1995), Kuechler and Dalton (1990), Lustiger-

Thaler (1989), Lustiger-Thaler and Maheu (1995), Maheu (1991, 1992, 1995), Melucci (1988), Roche (1995), Scott (1990), and Touraine (1984, 1995).

4. Anthony Giddeus. 1994. Beyond Left and Right: The Future of Radical Politics. Cambridge: Polity.

5. The following account on the political opportunity structures in Palestine is mainly based on intensive field research undertaken in the Occupied Territories between 1992 and 1994 and inquiries during several visits in the West Bank and Gaza Strip between 1995 and 2000. It is also based on the works of 'Abd al-Hadi (1992, 1994), Abu Sido and Ghali (1995), Baumgarten (1991), Bishara (1996), Brynen (1996), Byrne (1996), Dakkak (1983, 1988, 1992), Gresh (1988), Hammami (1995, 2000), Hammami and Tamari (2000), Hilal (1995), Hiltermann (1991), Hulilat (1991), Richards (1995), M. Robinson (1993, 1997), Tamari (1991, 1992, 1995), L. Taraki (1989, 1990), Usher (1995, 1997), as well as on diverse issues of Middle East International (London), Palestine Report (published by the Jerusalem Media and Communication Center), and Perspectives on the Palestinian NGO (PNGO) Network (newsletter published by the PNGO Network).

6. The main political trends within the PLO are the mainstream Fatah and the three fronts on the left: the Popular Front for the Liberation of Palestine (PFLP), the Democratic Front for the Liberation of Palestine (DFLP), and the Palestinian People's Party (PPP). The DFLP split in 1990 into two factions, one now called Fida (around Yasir 'Abd Rabbuh and very close to Fatah and Arafat), and the other around Nayif Hawatmeh.

7. For example, this has been particularly obvious in the "democracy projects" sponsored by international "democracy institutes or organizations." The democracy projects in Palestine consist mostly of workshops and training sessions for designing, promoting, and implementing democratic ideals, increasing voter awareness, encouraging free and fair elections and promoting constitutional and legal reform, centering on the aspects of "good governance" in terms of accountability, administrative efficiency, and economic credibility. They have led to the burgeoning of democracy institutes in Palestine, for which such programs were a means to attract funds. The trend is now regarded within some circles in Palestine as the "politics or discourse of defeat," that is, as a way to neutralize and depoliticize the national struggle by diverting it from political parties and issues of national liberation to "civic institutions" and issues of management (Byrne, 1996, Hammami, 1995).

8. For a detailed analysis of international aid to Palestine, see Brynen (1996).

9. Stork and Doumani (1994) account for this dilemma where Palestinians have been criticizing World Bank policies for years and are now turning to international donors as tactical allies to force Arafat to adopt a more rational approach in appointments and decisions instead of the nepotism that characterizes his functioning. Shammas, founding member of the Center for International Human Rights Enforcement, indicates how at this stage the World Bank represents an ally for Palestinians because "it can help hold the line against a non-accountable and non-professional Palestinian economic authority" (1994: 15).

10. See Giacaman, Jad, and Johnson (1995), who analyze the "Social Welfare and Recreation" chapter of the PLO's General Program for National Economic Development, 1994–2000.

11. The NGO movement has been active in the area of socioeconomic development through diverse activities. It has, for example, managed to insure that the NGO Trust Fund includes Palestinian NGOs in East Jerusalem, hence protecting Palestinian national interests against Israeli hegemony over the peace process. It has also managed to preserve some independence from the PNA in that it succeeded to have the "governance committee" of the NGO Trust Fund include a multilateral representation with heavy PNGO Network representation and to ensure that the chosen project manager remains independent of the PNA. The PNGO Network is also active in the World Bank NGO Working Group, the mission of which is to lobby the World Bank on development policies, to engage in dialogue with the World Bank on issues of poverty reduction and social development, and to define World Bank/civil society relations. Lately, the PNGO Network has created task forces to review NGO activities and develop strategies to address the socioeconomic crisis that accompanied the second Intifada.
12. The following account on the Palestinian health sector is based on in-depth interviews with health activists, officials, and administrators, as well as general observations made during field research. It is also based on the works of Barghouthi and Giacaman (1990), Giacaman (1989), and Robinson (1993, 1997). For a more detailed account, see Craissati (1998).
13. Terms according to Dina Gaissati.
14. The fact that these women are questioning relations of authority in their homes (and this has occurred at several instances) represents an important dimension of self-actualization and individual subjectivity, and as such is an invaluable rupture with dominant societal orientations.
15. For example, it is worth noting that the qualified workers employed by the UPMRC in the villages are now recognized by the Ministry of Health.
16. The UPMRC is also leading the Middle East and North Africa World Bank NGO Working Group.
17. This model is not new and has been promoted by the World Health Organization (WHO) and the UNICEF Alma-Ata Declaration of 1978.
18. This model is outlined, albeit not in the same phrasing, by Mustafa Barghouthi, Chairman of the UPMRC, in a document on the development strategy needed in the Palestinian territories (Barghouthi, 1993).
19. See Tamari (1995) on these two positions.

Chapter Ten

NGOs and 'Civil Society' in Palestine: A Comparative Analysis of Four Organizations[1]

Salma Aown Shawa

This chapter examines the changing roles of Palestinian Non-Governmental Organizations (NGOs)[2] in the context of increasing debates about the growth of 'civil society' at both the local and international levels. Drawing on an analysis of four recently collected organizational case studies of Palestinian NGOs, the paper argues that the rhetoric—used by donors and some activists, inside and outside NGOs—claiming that NGOs are the ones 'building civil society,' has been somewhat overstated. The reality is that Palestinian NGOs have gradually shifted from being organizations which served the community in multiple ways (including service provision, organizing, and campaigning) under Israeli occupation to currently shifting toward a narrower NGO focus on service provision as a result of institutional and environmental pressures, which have grown under the Palestinian National Authority (PNA) and the 'peace process.' Palestinian NGOs historically drew strength and legitimacy from the lack of a national government by providing services and acting as local leaders. Thus, they provided essential services as well as political and moral support to local communities. Following the establishment of the PNA, these organizations were thrown into confusion and have faced external pressures from the PNA, from donors, and from forces inside these organizations to 'let go' of their previous multiple functions, particularly their political roles.

The concept of 'civil society' is problematic in the context of Palestine. On the one hand, there are similarities with western discourses of 'civil society.'

NGOs are seen, within that context, as having the potential to spread civic and democratic values and challenge government policies. NGOS are also perceived as being able to help create a civil society. However, the internal structure of local NGOs are mostly based on vertical and hierarchical ties.

This chapter argues that despite these criticisms, some Palestinian NGOs are nevertheless attempting to hold on to or build some sense of a 'civil society role.' In addition to providing services (which is of course itself a useful function) some NGOs are also advancing agendas for social change (such as gender issues and a concern about poverty reduction). NGOs are also seeking to build links with local communities and to represent communities' interests before government and donors. Despite these partial attempts, the NGOs' capacity to build civil society has been overstated. There exist real problems in fulfilling the expectations found in the rhetoric of building civil society. These problems are centered on: (1) the narrowness of the prescribed role of NGOs in donors' and government discourses; (2) restrictions on NGOs due to the continuation of the Israeli occupation and the inefficiency of the PNA; and (3) structural problems within NGOs, such as the lack of democratic practices.

Context of NGO Development in Palestine

Historically, Palestinian NGOs (PNGOs) had a large share of service provision responsibilities to Palestinian communities. The absence of a national government led NGOs to respond to the political needs of the community as well. The Intifada (1987–1993) consolidated these roles as there were larger gaps in service provision and there was a dire need for local leadership. As a result of their contributions to service delivery, PNGOs received international recognition, in addition to the traditional subsidies they received from Palestinians and Arabs. This recognition was accompanied by financial support, which helped to sustain and develop them. The Gulf War (1990–91) followed by the Madrid peace process (1991–92) encouraged the PNGOs to give more attention to social and economic development and to start preparations for the nation-building stage. The transformation of NGOs started during this period and it was intensified after signing of the Declaration of Principles (DoP) in 1993.

Before the establishment of the PNA in 1994, PNGOs had a political role, owned economic resources, acted as development agents, and were involved in preparations for nation building. The establishment of the PNA was bound to change some of the NGOs' contributions—with some roles diminishing while others emerged. Among the roles that were compelled to change was their involvement in politics since the PNA wanted to ensure its legitimacy and control over this field. Among the new roles that local intellectuals and activists expected PNGOs to assume because of the changing political and social circumstances was the role of building 'civil society.' This expectation was based on the notion that the presence of a national authority was conducive to the emergence of a civil society and NGOs were the appropriate agents for carrying out this role. This expectation also stemmed from an international emphasis on the role of NGOs, or generally the 'third sector,' in building civil society, especially in transitions to democratic systems. Researchers, practitioners, and policy makers asserted that NGOs contributed to the process of 'building civil society' either by strengthening the rule of law or spreading the spirit of association and democratization. International donor support to PNGOs reflected also this new interest by dedicating funds toward 'building civil society'.

Thus, the transfer of power (despite its limitations) was expected to change the roles of NGOs and to encourage the emergence of a role in 'building civil society.' Given these expectations, this article investigates how the discourse on NGOs and civil society reflects on the contributions of NGOs to the community in the autonomous areas of the West Bank and Gaza between 1993-98. The article also tries to examine how actors, such as the Palestinian authorities, funding agencies, or PNGOs interpreted the role of NGOs in civil society and how these interpretations reflected on the practices of NGOs. The article argues that despite the vital services that PNGOs provided to Palestinian society, and despite having a potential in consolidating a 'civil society' in these areas, their contributions were limited. There were both external and internal limitations as will be discussed in this article.

Conceptual Framework

To analyze how the discourse on NGOs and civil society reflected on the contributions of PNGOs, this chapter examines three main questions. First, how donors' discourses on civil society could influence the roles of NGOs— and this involves a literature review on the global phenomenon of NGOs, specifically with respect to donor policies and their influence on NGOs and civil society. Second, how NGOs could contribute to building civil society on a practical level, which calls for an examination of the relationship between NGOs and civil society and a review of civil society theories. Finally, how NGOs as 'organizations' could contribute to this process.

NGOs and International Funding Agencies

The first part of the review is based on the increase in numbers of NGOs since the 1970s. These organizations tried to respond to contemporary challenges in their societies such as the inability of governments to satisfy needs, the dominance of market economies, the failure of structural adjustment programs, or the contraction of the welfare state. The rise of these organizations started to become more apparent since the World Food Conference in Rome in 1974, the UN Environment Summit in Rio de Janeiro in 1992 , followed by the Cairo and Beijing conferences (1994 and 1995) on population and women. According to the Johns Hopkins Comparative Non-profit Sector Project, in 1995, the non-profit sector in the twenty-two countries examined was a $1.1 trillion industry with 19 million full-time paid workers . The share of this sector in employment accounts for 7 percent of the non-agricultural labor force in Western European countries such as the Netherlands, Ireland, and Belgium. According to the United Nations Human Development Report, the revenues of NGOs in the U.S. were estimated at $566 billion, in Japan, $264 billion, and in the U.K., $78 billion . According to the same report, the total budgets of NGOs in developing countries were around $1.2 billion. In the Arab world, the number of NGOs in countries such as Jordan and Tunisia has more than doubled between the 1980s and the 1990s.

The rise of NGOs was accompanied by an increase in international aid from multilateral and bilateral agencies. For instance, NGOs' dependence on international donors reached 30 percent of their income in the mid-1990s . This dependence led to the emergence of international policy trends that prescribed expectations of NGOs. The priorities of donors shifted from relief to 'development' in the 1980s , while the 'new policy agenda' with its emphasis on the role of private institutions dominated the international aid arena in the beginning of the 1990s . These private institutions, whether being profit oriented or not, were seen as the appropriate mechanism for development. The most current development paradigm used by international aid organizations stresses both governments as well as 'civil society' in achieving development (World Bank 1998). The World Bank emphasized co-operation between the government, civil society, and the private sector in order to speed up the development process. Donors' emphasis on 'building civil society' raises questions on how their interpretations of NGOs' roles influence the latter's contributions through the allocation of resources and priorities. Thus, donor discourses constitute the first component of the conceptual framework, which affects the role of NGOs in civil society and eventually their contributions.

NGOs and Civil Society

The second component concerns the debates among practitioners, experts, and academics on the relationship between NGOs and civil society. Three stances on this relationship could be identified in these writings. The first group is composed of authors who advocate the liberal approach and consider the model of Toqueville as the appropriate model for analyzing the role of NGOs. The model of Tocqueville posits NGOs as trying to preserve the rights of people as against the inherent authoritarianism of the modern state. The model suggested that NGOs could ease the tension within civil society by grouping people according to their interests rather than their primordial ties . The second group argues that the neo-Marxist approach, based on critical theory and Gramsci's concept of civil society, were more appropriate. This group focused on the eminence of the struggle between NGOs and other actors and, consequently, saw a political role for NGOs . The third group is represented by authors who were skeptical of linking NGOs with civil society . This group criticized donor attempts to emphasize the role of civil society, and argued that donors aim to serve their interests through this discourse.

These debates go back to discussions on the role of civil societies in contemporary societies and their relationship with the state and the economy. Authors used different approaches to analyze contemporary civil society. For instance, Arato uses the post-Marxist approach; Keane combines Liberal and Marxist approaches, and Putnam builds on the Liberal tradition . The universality of civil society is questioned by several authors (Hann 1996), who try to localize forms of distribution of power deviating from the western concept of civil society. Other authors even questioned the presence of civil society and 'good governance' within western societies themselves and questioned whether they were not mere 'myths' (Wood 1997).

Since the most prominent rhetoric currently used to characterize the contribution of NGOs to civil society is the liberal approach, the analysis of NGOs' contribution to building civil society are: (1) spreading the association spirit; (2) spreading democracy; and (3) acting as a buffer between society and state. These functions will be used to measure the extent to which NGOs can practically contribute to the process of building civil society, which constitutes the second component of the conceptual framework.

Role of NGOs as Organizations

The third part of the conceptual framework involves how NGOs as 'organizations' can reflect the new role of building civil society. Thus, the review of the writings on organizations revealed that NGOs were restricted in fulfilling expectations of their roles because they are governed by their history and resources, their environments, and competing interests within the same field (Bourdieu 1977, Powell and DiMaggio 1991, Meyer and Scott 1992).

The discourse on civil society can help to transform these organizations, if, in parallel to their efforts to build a civil society, they adopt democratic principles within their own structures.

It can be deduced from the literature review that the contributions of NGOs can be affected by the discourse on NGOs and civil society in three ways. First, this discourse can change the roles of NGOs by new ways of distributing resources and new priorities established by funding agencies. Second, the discourse influences the relationship between NGOs and their governments and communities by prescribing certain interpretations of this relationship. Third, the discourse can affect relations within organizations. My hypothesis is that the discourse on NGOs and civil society can bring new strengths to NGOs if it expands these roles and if NGOs can practically play a vital role in spreading the association spirit and democratization, acting as buffer between society and state, and by internally transforming their organizations.

The Arab Context

Debates on civil society with regard to its interest and usefulness in the Arab world emerged in the 1980s among Arab intellectuals (Ibrahim 1993, 1995; Ghalyun 1993; al-Sayyed 1995). Most of these intellectuals were mainly interested in civil society as a tool for understanding the political impediments to democracy in Arab societies (Brynen 1995; Norton 1996). There were numerous debates among these scholars revolving around the definition of civil society. Generally, these definitions entailed a study of the organizational aspect of civil society, meaning non-governmental organizations. Authors perceived NGOs as a 'buffer' between the state and its citizens (Brynen 1995; Norton 1996).

Moreover, as the research on NGOs in the Middle East increased, questions of whether civil society had become more vibrant or not began to be raised. Researchers attempted to assess the impact of NGOs on social and political life and to historically examine the roles of NGOs (Kandil 1994).

Some authors discussed the organizational issues and the regional concerns of NGOs (al-Jabiri 1997, Madani 1997). Some others (Marzouk 1997) have looked more critically at the role of NGOs and concluded that "excessive politicization" of Arab NGOs forced them to reproduce the same authoritarian structures found in the Arab political life (Marzouk 1997).

Since the signing of the peace accord in 1993, there were discussions in the Palestinian areas on the changing roles of Palestinian NGOs, which focused on their role in civil society, development, and on their relations with the Palestinian National Authority (PNA). Advocates of the 'civil society' role of NGOs saw them as an embodiment of democracy. Some authors assumed that civil society existed by the mere fact of the presence of NGOs and political parties. Others thought that Palestinian 'third sector' organizations provided a strong base for building civil society because their interests were not limited to serving their narrow political interests but rather the interests of the whole society. Others negated the fact that there was a civil society in the Occupied Territories because of the historic absence of a state and considered these discussions mere 'simulation'. Some authors objected to applying a 'western' concept to a different environment without a thorough analysis of the compatibility of the subject matter and the method.

Some authors observed that the overlapping in the functions of NGOs as 'development agents' and 'civil society' organizations was an attempt to prevent authoritarianism of the incoming authorities due to the weaknesses of political factions. With the advent of the PNA, the "political field" had witnessed new "images," among which was "the romantic image of the institutions of civil society that act as a guarantor for democracy against authoritarianism" (Hilal 1998: 254). The author observed that NGOs along with international donors were developing a new 'ideology' that was based on development language and was intensified by the increase in poverty and inequality in the Palestinian society (Hilal 1998: 260). Other authors observed that the adoption of this 'ideology' of civil society was a result of the weaknesses and eventual defeat of leftist factions (Hammami 1995).

For other authors, the PNA could benefit from the experience of NGOs and use their services since its resources were limited and it could not fulfill all needs of society (Barghouthi 1994). Meanwhile, the latter author listed the threats that NGOs could face in the future. These threats included co-optation, centralization of authority, marginalization of NGOs, distortion of objectives for securing funding, and indifference to the Israeli occupation. On the emerging relationship between the PNA and NGOs, another author noted that the PNA displayed the tendency of 'controlling' NGOs, despite animosity among the ministries (Sullivan 1995). He observed that although Palestinian NGOs succeeded in temporarily withdrawing the draft law on associations in 1995 (also thanks to other factors such as the international pressure), it does not mean they succeeded. The author described the differences among NGOs and the PNA as 'cultural' since they resulted from differences in generations and in socialization (Sullivan 1995: 49). With regards to differences among social actors and their negative impact on building civil society, another author (Roy 1996: 255) described the struggle among social groups in the Palestinian society as one major obstacle to "building civil society" in the Gaza Strip.

NGOs formed coalitions such as the Palestinian NGO Network (PNGO). PNGO stressed the need to work in an environment were freedom of association was guaranteed and the independence of NGOs was ensured within a legal framework (PNGO 1995: 2–3). PNGO has issued several papers on how its members stipulated their relationship with the PNA through the legislature on charitable societies and NGOs (PNGO 1997: 13). One of the main criticisms of PNGO to the initial draft law was that it did not take into consideration the uniqueness of the Palestinian NGO sector as well as its diversity and multiple specialization and development approaches (PNGO 1997: 13). The case studies described below examine the narrow connection between the role of these organizations and the discourse on civil society.

The Case Studies

The research is focused on Palestinian NGOs during the period between 1993–1998 following the transfer of authority from the Israeli occupation to the PNA. The fieldwork was carried out between summer 1997 and summer 1998. The focus was on four NGOs working in the West Bank and Gaza: Agri Friends, Health Friends, Mother and Child Friends, and Rehab Friends. Agri Friends (AF) was established in 1983 in the West Bank and in 1987 in Gaza: Health Friends (HF) was established in 1985 in both areas, Mother and Child Friends (MCF) was established in 1991/92 in the Gaza Strip, and Rehab friends (RF) was established in 1980 in Gaza. Most attention was given to the Gaza Strip branches during this study.

RF was established as a charitable society, which was the most common form of Palestinian third sector organizations until the end of the seventies (according to 'Abd al-Hadi 1996). AF and HF were established as voluntary committees, which represented the second type of NGOs which emerged in the mid-seventies and beginning of the eighties ('Abd al-Hadi 1996). These committees were affiliated with political factions but supported the community as a whole. During the Intifada, the number of these committees multiplied and they attempted to fill the gap in governmental services supported by Palestinian, Arab, and international aid.

The Gulf crisis, which started in 1990, negatively impacted Palestinians and it led to the depletion of funds from most of the Gulf States. The Madrid peace conference convened in 1991 symbolized a shift in the political environment. According to some authors, the peace process led to the emergence of two distinct types of NGOs (Nakhleh 1994: 13). One type of NGO was prepared to take over official or semi-official functions—such as the high councils, research centers, and unions (Nakhleh 1994: 13). The second type continued to include personnel who were dedicated to voluntary work and committed to the importance of building civil society organizations (Nakhleh 1994: 13). MCF represented the second type of organization as well as the third type of PNGOs, which, according to Abdul Hadi, aimed to professionalize the work of NGOs (1996). The objective of the founders was to create an organization, which was unaffiliated with any particular political faction and was specialized in children's and women's issues. The interviews with these organizations focused on their directors, executives, some board members, and fieldworkers. Moreover, this study is also based on interviews with PNA officials, donors, and some beneficiaries.

Discussion of Key Findings

The findings of the research on Palestinian NGOs showed tendencies that resembled the main themes in the international discourse on civil society and NGOs. There were also differences stemming from the specificity of the Palestinian experience.

NGOs: Key Elements of Civil Society?

Most Palestinian NGOs under study stressed their role as key components of civil society. This emphasis represented a new tendency among Palestinian NGOs following the arrival of the PNA. It also represented the global phenomenon, among intellectuals, international NGOs, and funding agencies of highlighting civil society.

The first three NGOs (AF, HF, and MCF) emphasized the term 'civil society.' For HF, the importance of NGOs arose out of their role as key elements in 'civil society.' However, for AF, not all NGOs qualified to be part of civil society. NGOs had to prove their transparency, professionalism, and democracy to be constitutive of civil society. They had to, according the director of AF, "believe in the principles that they worked on [transparency]." Moreover, "Before we ask society for democracy or professionalism, we have to apply it ourselves.... Laws and systems, we have to apply them to ourselves" (from interview on June 8, 1998).

HF highlighted democracy, accountability and transparency as well. The director of MCF also stressed transparency and the possibility of the PNA to check on NGOs, on the condition that it did not interfere with the autonomy of these organizations. The director of HF explained that the organization was able to acquire credibility in the community through its high-level services and care of the poor and marginalized.

The concepts of 'democracy' and 'community participation' were linked to civil society. For HF, community participation was achieved by taking into consideration the needs of the community. The director of MCF stressed the importance of community participation for the role of NGOs in civil society:

> There is no need for any organization unless it has a strong relation with the local community. The survival of an organization is associated with the extent to which it participates with the local society in making and implementing its plans. We cannot make plans without involving the proposed beneficiaries of the project (from interview on May 19, 1998).

AF went a step further and showed that it organized 'workshops' in order to involve the community. AF interviewees also considered publishing organization reports and budgets in the newspapers, as a way to further involve the public. A person associated with AF showed how financial contributions from the public could be seen as methods of community participation. Community participation was also a method to raise funds from beneficiaries in order to help the organization to be less dependent on donors.

NGOs as Lobbying Groups?

Some NGOs advocated 'lobbying' for certain policies as a way of influencing politics. The strongest NGOs—the better-established ones—tended to focus on this function despite their acknowledgement that at some points the PNA lacked clear policies. The emphasis on lobbying was highlighted by the work of the PNGO Network—which AF, HF, and MCF were all members of. PNGO Network articulated its position on the role of Palestinian NGOs after the arrival of the PNA thus:

> NGOs are presumed to play an important role during the coming period as 'lobbying groups' continuously watching the activities of *al-sulta* (PNA) and following up on its adherence to democratic values and human rights. NGOs also have to strengthen societal sectors and increase their participation in the direction of more democracy in general national and private developmental decision-making (PNGO 1994: 3).

A second area for lobbying was in terms of influencing council members to change the draft law in accordance with the version put forth by the PNGO Network. The administrative director of AF explained:

> One level is to be able to do lobbying with the law. For example, instead of waiting until a law is enacted, we made a legal study comparing the work systems and laws that governed the work of *al-mu'assasat al-ahliya* (community organizations) in other parts of the world. Accordingly, we suggested the proposed bill for the relationship [between NGOs and the state] (interview with the administrative director, March 5, 1998).

A third area for 'lobbying' was in relation to the function of institution building. The director of AF stressed the role of the organization in 'training' the target group on lobbying. Lobbying was seen as a means to change policies and therefore, to build 'civil society.' Looking at lobbying broadly, MCF could be seen to be implementing this by convening public meetings with PNA officials, and where, mainly by women and children attended. During these meetings, issues of concern to the local residents were raised. However, these meetings were less effective because they solved individual cases rather than finding systematic approaches to problems within the PNA. An MCF board member explained, "problems were raised and some of them were solved on an individual basis . . . [but what persists is] the problem of *al-wasta* (informal connections)" (interview with staff-member, May 13, 1998).

The goal of influencing 'governmental policies' has been emphasized by international donors. These donors, especially USAID, considered influencing policies to be one of the main functions of NGOs in order to be considered a part of 'civil society.' One of the programs of USAID offered support to NGOs or non-profit organizations that were "interested in or are working on development and strengthening of the Palestinian civil society for the realization of a just, transparent and responsible governance system" (*al-Ayyam*, 7/21/1998).

Depoliticizing NGOs

Most NGOs interviewed tried to show their detachment from politics. For instance, the AF public relations officer explained how the decision to get away from politics was taken by the majority of the staff, who felt the negative implications of factional politics on the organization's work. He also related getting away from political factions with a move toward democracy and building civil society. Here, there was a juxtaposition of working in politics and building civil society. However, the issue of democracy was intertwined with civil society. Civil society was perceived as a step toward democracy:

> Seven years ago, we started to endure the political character that was ascribed to AF because of our relationship with political factions. This was one of the impediments to the development of the organization in a natural way. We, as staff and as administration at AF, started to think about how to address this point. There was a strong move by the staff toward thinking that the political dimension, or the political relationship between AF and any political faction, has to have its limits in a way or another. We also wanted to give attention to the social and development dimensions, to build a democratic society and to help in laying down the first blocks of a civil society (interview of the head of public-relations at AF, February 25, 1998).

The attempt to de-politicize NGOs was also apparent in the World Bank's approach. A World Bank official that oversaw the World Bank Trust Fund in the West Bank and Gaza said: "NGOs had played a strong role with respect to opposing the occupation [however, now they have to act as] as public service providers" (interview with the coordinator, May 7, 1998).

Both HF and MCF reiterated the negative implications of politics, and they contrasted 'politics' with development. RF showed its detachment to political affiliations and insisted on its role as a service provider. According to these organizations, de-politicization was needed in order to succeed in building civil society, or in the case of RF, to provide services. For the first three organizations, previous involvement in politics meant that the organizations were not capable of building a democratic society—'the first blocks of a civil society.' As shown, accountability and transparency had a better chance of taking place when politics was put aside. Therefore, these organizations were clearly saying to the PNA and donors that they had historical shortcomings–which they were willing to correct for the sake of gaining a better position in the new environment.

Reactions From the PNA

Despite acknowledging the role of NGOs in civil society, officials at the Ministry of Interior place pre-conditions on the involvement of NGOs in this role. At this point, differences started to emerge between the NGOs' conception of civil society and the PNA's views. One pre-condition that NGOs needed, according to the official, was to work in accordance to a national plan, while minimizing the number of NGOs operating. To be more efficient, NGOs had to work according to a national plan and there was no need for several NGOs:

> Because we have come out of occupation and we are in the phase of national liberation, the number of associations has to be proportional to our needs. For example, all associations for disabled people have to make a qualitative union. There has to be a general union in co-ordination with the World Bank and donor countries. For example, Egypt has only 70 associations. The multiplicity of associations is a theft (interview with the head of the NGO-unit, May 21, 1998).

The official believed that NGOs ought to co-ordinate with each other and form unions that helped them to comprehensively plan their activities because it was a 'national liberation' phase. The decreasing number of NGOs would provoke a reduction in trivial expenses. Moreover, NGOs had to be transparent and had to inform the PNA of their income and connections with external actors:

> We ask two things from the associations. We have to know the origins of both visible and invisible funding sources and they should

not have any relations with parties that may harm the sovereignty of the state or affect the transparency of *al-sulta* [the PNA] (interview with the head of the NGO unit, May 21, 1998).

Organizations had to inform the authority of their visible and invisible income. They also had to cut their relations with political factions, especially opposition factions. According to these officials, NGOs could play a significant role in civil society if they revealed their funding sources and if they were not affiliated with parties opposing the peace process.

Donor Expectations of NGOs in Palestine

Donors, for their part, also used the discourse on civil society and NGOs to express their expectations of NGOs and to implicitly influence their priorities. Definitions of civil society restrict the participation of NGOs in civil society to specific types of NGOs. These restrictions exclude a vast majority of NGOs from partaking in civil society. Thus, USAID introduced into its work the concept of civil society and put aside some funds for strengthening civil society in the mid 1990s. The agency, in 1996, developed, within its civil society unit, its definition of the concept to include a critical focus on advocacy . It has focused on projects associated with legislatures, elections, and influencing policies. This definition excluded most PNGOs since they were mostly service providers, with very few organizations having advocacy functions. USAID's four goals with regards to governance were:

> Increasing the participation of civil society organizations in public-decision making and government oversight; enhancing the capability of the Palestinian Legislative Council to perform functions of a legislative body; supporting more effective executive authority in legislation and public policy-making; and putting in place the foundation for decentralized local government.

USAID allocated most of the funds that aimed to strengthen governance to the PNA rather than to NGOs. Moreover, not all NGOs were civil society organizations according to USAID. The agency used Blair's criteria for differentiating between NGOs that were service providers and advocacy organizations . According to these criteria, most Palestinian NGOs were considered 'service providers' by USAID. Only a number of professional and research institutes could be considered 'civic organizations' that had a public interest. According to USAID, PNGOs needed to be trained in civil society before they could satisfy a public interest or civil society role.

However, the latest shift within USAID policy, is toward PNGOs, with an emphasis on co-ordination between NGOs and the authorities. It emphasizes co-ordination between NGOs and the PNA as the appropriate means for NGOs to be included as civil society organizations. PNGOs in this case had to show willingness to work with the PNA to be acknowledged as builders of civil society. NGOs had a crucial role, especially after the establishment of the PNA because of the deterioration in service provision and economic conditions. The deteriorating economic conditions after signing the DoP in 1993 put a burden on the PNA and NGOs. NGOs had to try to provide services and support the disadvantaged in society. As with the other programs of USAID, the target organizations for its aid were again mainly PVOs (Private Voluntary Organizations) working along with some Palestinian NGOs, which were eligible for receiving USAID funds.

Despite the USAID discourse on NGOs and civil society, PNGOs had a small chance of being accepted as part of civil society. First, very few PNGOs could play a role in civil society because most of them were service providers. Second, most USAID funding to the NGO sector was channeled through PVOs, which did not strengthen local NGOs and made them dependent on these PVOs. Third, USAID's support to the Palestinian areas was mainly directed toward the PNA with some opportunities for NGOs, if they coordinated with the PNA.

As can be seen, NGOs, PNA officials, and some funding agencies related the role of NGOs to building civil society. However, PNA officials and donors prescribed a set of conditions in order for NGOs to fulfill this role. These conditions centered on transparency, service provision, and detachment from politics. As will be discussed below, these interpretations of NGOs roles' in addition to objective conditions stood in the way of NGOs being able to carry out their potential in 'building civil society.'

Emerging Issues

The key findings revolve around two main themes in relation to the role of NGOs in civil society. The first theme revolves around the interpretations of NGOs' roles in building civil society and how these interpretations reflect on the actual contributions of NGOs. The second theme concerns the actual ability of NGOs to build civil society.

Local Interpretations of Civil Society

Regarding the views of interviewees on civil society and how they interpreted them, there were four main responses. First, there was a group of interviewees, who thought that there was a need to *adapt the concept to the local culture*. These interviewees stressed the importance of localizing concepts related to civil society. They justified transferring western concepts only if these concepts were transformed into forms adaptable to the local culture. The interviewees mentioned venues where people could be exposed to western culture through training, education, and reading books and journals. Training and education and insight were means through which this process took place. One example of transferring the concept to the local culture was to establish a new unit called the 'institutional development' unit at one organization. The aim of the unit was to transform the concept of civil society from a high level of abstraction to a practical level. The objective of the unit was to adapt the concept according to the needs of the targeted communities. However, the same interviewees cautioned against transferring western concepts without paying careful attention to how the transformation took place. The agent who made the transformation had to reach a certain level of maturity to be able to handle 'foreign' concepts without losing understanding of the local culture.

A second interpretation of the concept of civil society was that it was *absent in the local context and that there was a need to import it*. This group of interviewees believed that there was no Palestinian civil society and therefore, it needed to be imported from the West. For instance, NGO personnel declared that the community lacked some basic understanding of civil society concepts such as the understanding of a rule of law. Other NGO personnel noted that following the arrival of the PNA, they had shifted their attention toward teaching the targeted groups how to 'lobby' and not only how to 'produce.' This shift resulted from the need to influence the state and not to wait for the state to carry out its priorities. There were some donors who stressed the need to transfer the concept and create it in the Palestinian context. Donors declared that they were giving Palestinians 'aid' because they wanted to help them build a 'vibrant' civil society. These donors emphasized governance, legislature, and civil society as pre-requisites for being included in the international system.

The third interpretation of the concept was its *irrelevance* to the Palestinian areas. Some organizations did not use the term 'civil society'— or similar terms such as 'democracy' or 'accountability.' One organization highlighted the humanitarian nature of its work rather than its attempt to influence society. The reason for this was that its culture was closer to charitable organizations, which stressed welfare approaches. A number of PNA officials discarded the whole discourse on civil society because it did not add to the contributions of NGOs. The real significance of the concept, according to these officials, was the volunteerism that resulted from it. There were also some international NGOs that did not highlight the concept and considered their work to mean the same thing as 'civil society' without necessarily using the term.

The fourth interpretation of the concept of civil society in the Palestinian context was that *occupation was an obstacle* to the development of a civil society—unlike other colonial experiences, where civil society was inherited from colonialism. Most Palestinian interviewees stressed the impact of the occupation on impeding their attempts to build NGOs and eventually a civil society, even after the handover of power to the PNA. There was no mention of the Israeli occupation's attempt to build parallel civic institutions to attack organizations supported by the PLO, which, in the past had been operating from outside the West Bank and Gaza. Interviewees mentioned that the Israeli army stood in their way of carrying out their work because of the fear that they were political organizations. Because of the occupation, NGOs had to change their priorities to respond to the needs of their communities. They were forced to work in areas that were neglected rather than making their decisions according to their own priorities.

Can NGOs Build a Palestinian Civil Society?

Regarding the second theme, which revolved around the practices of NGOs in building civil society, most interviewees clarified that NGOs faced impediments during this process. These impediments prohibited them from fulfilling expectations and carrying out the functions of building a civil society, which were: spreading the association spirit, democratization, and acting as a buffer between the state and society. These impediments ranged from restrictions in the general environment, which surrounded NGOs, to restrictions within NGOs themselves. These impediments included Israeli restrictions on movement as well as daily interventions from PNA security forces. The obstacle in the policy environment included a lack of coordination among NGOs of different political beliefs and a lack of interest from the community.

The problems that prevented NGOs from carrying out their visions of building civil society also resulted from the conflicting expectations of the role of NGOs. For example, PNA officials, despite their rhetoric on encouraging NGOs, allowed security forces to continuously interfere in NGOs affairs. International donor viewpoints on civil society limited the possibilities for most NGOs to be considered key components of civil society. This advantage was only given to a handful of NGOs—those working in the field of advocacy. These differences in support for NGOs created a hierarchy and a sense of 'class divisions' among NGOs, which negatively affected the practical consequences of building civil society.

Impediments to building civil society also included internal problems within NGOs. Although some NGOs linked their attempts to build civil society by showing transparency and accountability in their internal structures, they were not entirely satisfied with their attempts. Only one organization tried to open up the decision-making process within the organization to include different stakeholders. One organization did not show any attempts to diversify its governing board or to change its members. All of them emphasized their attempts to detach themselves from their previous political affiliations as a sign of transparency and accountability—even though they did not carry out structural changes in their governance or reduce their centralized structure.

Conclusion

Palestinian NGOs were active before the arrival of the Palestinian National Authority. Their previous discourse focused on their roles as part of the resistance movement to the Israeli occupation. With the fading away of the first Intifada, and the beginning of the peace process, they shifted their attention toward 'development' issues, which included the promotion of social change. With the establishment of the PNA, these NGOs were thrown into confusion. Some of them started the process of self-limitation by detaching themselves from political factions, by founding income-generating projects or by confining their efforts to 'development' or 'civil society.'

Alongside these changes among NGOs and within their surrounding environment, there was a growing global discourse on the role of 'third sector' organizations in civil society. Some of the Palestinian NGOs took on this discourse because of their formerly politicized nature and their interest in social change; others felt that the discourse could help them to legitimize themselves in the new environment. Despite the prevalence of this discourse in some policy circles, on the practical level, PNGO efforts were limited. Actors such as the authorities and donors tried to confine the roles of these organizations to service delivery by limiting the available space for NGOs or by controlling their economic resources. The response of some NGOs was to highlight their withdrawal from politics as the pre-requisite for building civil society.

Finally, the findings show that the outcome of the emphasis on the role of NGOs in civil society was overstated. These organizations could not fulfill expectations of building civil society because of the impediments in their environment—and because of their own shortcomings. However, these findings should not minimize the contributions of NGOs to social change, changing regressive values, and attempts to draw links with their communities—all of which can have a long-term impact on the process of building civil society.

Notes

1. I would like to thank the Middle East Awards in Cairo (MEAwards) for supporting my research in Palestine in 1997–98 and the Aspen Institute, Nonprofit Sector Research Fund, Washington for supporting the writing up of this research in 1998–2000. Thanks are also due to Dr. David Lewis, Center for Civil Society, Social Policy Department, London School of Economics. I would also like to thank the Forum of Social and Economic Policy Research in Palestine (PRIP) and their reviewers; Dr. Ibrahim Abu Lughod; and the steering committee of the Conference on NGOs and Governance for their feedback on earlier versions of this article.
2. The term 'NGOs' will be used throughout this article to refer to organizations that are nonprofit and work in social welfare. NGOs form a subset of third sector organizations, which range from community based organizations to professional unions. NGOs in this article primarily work in social welfare and development and are indigenous organizations.

Chapter Eleven

Agency and Ideology in Community Services: Islamic NGOs in a Southern Suburb of Beirut[1]

Mona Fawaz

For almost twenty years now, Islamic organizations have made the front pages in the world's media, particularly in mainstream western news agencies. Deploying words like "terrorism" and "extremism," these media often portray the activities of Islamic organizations such as Hizballah and Hamas as singularly extremist and violent acts executed by brainwashed members.[2] This negative assessment has not only been diffused into popular culture but has also colored academic works, including 'development' literature, which has in general neglected to document any of the projects, working mechanisms, or approaches to poverty alleviation pursued by Islamic NGOs. It has instead focused on whether they fit within definitions of 'civil society' or not, and have commonly blamed them for the destruction of this 'civil society" in the countries where they have operated.[3] In these works, if Islamic NGOs are mentioned, whether in Lebanon, Egypt, Sudan, or Palestine, their projects and services are often described as "political co-optation." Ironically, the following definition taken from the mainstream U.S. news agency, CNN, is a good description of what Islamic NGOs do: "Hezbollah[4] (Party of God)—an Iranian-sponsored Shiite Muslim faction based in Lebanon [...] has sowed support in Beirut's Shiite Muslim, southern suburb by *creating a social welfare system*."[5]

Throughout the countries where they have worked, and as their growing popular support indicates, arrays of Islamic NGOs have spread in large numbers and developed often intricate and complex networks of service provision. In Lebanon, where Islamic movements have been significantly present since 1982, Islamic NGOs have provided a range of services that encompassed health care, education, drinking water provision, garbage collection, income generation initiatives, and many others. They have also placed local resident members, often formerly demobilized, into positions where they can actually act on their poor living conditions—by shaping their own process of service provision and organizing for their rights. Despite their record in Lebanon, these NGOs have received the same dismissive treatment mentioned above. For example, the 1997 United Nations Development Programme (UNDP) Lebanon report does not carry a single mention of these NGOs in its list of Lebanese service providing NGOs.[6] In the literature on Arab NGOs, these organizations are also often deliberately dismissed as political work or reactions to poverty, and are never examined as service providers.

This study attempts to provide a correction to this strong bias by building an understanding of the process of community development initiated by Islamic NGOs in Lebanon—specifically in a southern suburb of Beirut—in terms of community mobilizing and service provision. It also seeks to challenge the perception that politics cannot or should not mingle with service provision. While this argument has been made for international humanitarian (relief) organizations (Weiner 1998), it still lags behind in the examination of service providers, especially with small-scale local NGOs (Edwards and Hulme 1994).

In the choice of Islamic NGOs for my case study, I also aim to point out and challenge another bias in the literature on development. Indeed, in its choice of case study and the description of NGOs, literature on development has often emphasized a particular class of NGOs that are not, or which claim not to be, politicized or religious. It has therefore traditionally excluded a large class of service providers such as, besides Islamic NGOs, the Liberation Theology groups in Latin America, a number of African-American churches in the U.S., and probably many other similar cases. However, all these groups have at times been efficient service providers and community organizers all around the world. Thus, in defining the organizations I am studying as NGOs, I make a conscious choice to challenge the existing definitions. I hence apply in my case study some of the analytical lenses usually applied to NGOs—such as the analysis of the mechanisms of service delivery (agency), while I also introduce other frameworks (such as ideology) that, in my opinion, would often be useful in even less visibly politicized groups. Tying these concepts together, the paper argues that Islamic NGOs have used a combination of ideology and concrete mechanisms to further a responsive and flexible performance.

The chapter is organized as follows. It begins with a brief introduction of the NGOs, where I also introduce their geographic and political backgrounds and the projects they have tackled. It then moves to examine one type of project, self-sufficiency projects, and one organizational structure, "volunteer sisters" *(al-akhawat al-mutatawi'at)*. Projects and structures are examined by way of showing how both agency and ideology are used by these organizations and how they influence their performance. In both sections, I highlight some of the advantages and problems emanating from the strong political identity of these organizations. Finally, I conclude by summarizing my main points and suggesting directions for further research.

Background Context of the Study: Lebanon and the Southern Suburb of Beirut

Two main events mark Lebanon's recent history, its civil war (1975–91), and the struggle with Israel (including the declaration of the Zionist state in 1948, the influx of Palestinian refugees, the bombing since 1948, and the occupation of South Lebanon in 1978). While my aim is far from elaborating on this tumultuous history, it is important here to connect these events to the emergence of Hizballah in 1982, and its evolution from a marginalized military group into one of the leading political parties in the country—the leader of the military resistance against Israel, with twelve representatives in the Lebanese parliament and several officially affiliated mayors. Indeed, Hizballah's history is strongly connected to local and regional struggles.[7]

It is clear today that unequal regional development (development focused solely on Beirut) correlated with the systematic neglect of a number of religious communities, who were predominantly rural, was one of the main factors that precipitated the country toward the military strife. The Shiites, 80 percent of whom were rural at that time, constituted a large section of these neglected communities (Nasr 1985). As of the mid-1960s, a growing number among them rallied behind Imam Musa al-Sadr's movement for social justice and resistance to Israel (Norton 1987; Nasr 1985). This early local mobilization movement later constituted one of the largest pools of organization that Hizballah could build on (Norton 1987).

Hizballah emerged in 1982, as an offshoot, or reaction, to the Israeli occupation of the country and declared its military resistance to Israel (Fadl

Allah 1994). With this call, it immediately revived earlier mobilization groups and rallied along their lines. Hizballah's role, however, transcends the local boundaries. Unlike Imam Musa al-Sadr's movement, which called for changes in the Lebanese governance structures, Hizballah had wider regional affiliations that made it an integral part of the Islamic (Iranian) revolution.[8] It adopted in its ideological and philosophical orientations (Shiite) Islam as a mode of life and declared that it is engaged in a struggle to apply Islamic precepts within the general current (al-hala al-Islamiya) that seeks to build an Islamic society (Fadl Allah 1994: 36).

The organizations this paper addresses grew within this same political and religious (Muslim Shiite) environment and historical path. They were also affected in their creation and their operations by the same historical and political events. Before we look at them in more detail, I will introduce the geographic context of their activities.

Southern Suburb of Beirut

The southern suburb of Beirut is a zone of sixteen square kilometers, extending on the outskirts of Municipal Beirut, between the International Airport, the Mediterranean Sea, and the large industrial zone of Choueifat.[9] This area houses a very high concentration of residents, which reaches over 1,000 person/ hectares in Palestinian camps and in a number of informal settlements at the fringes such as Hay al-Sellom or Laylaki.

This high density of residents and the poverty of the area are relatively new features of the southern suburb of Beirut. Indeed, less than fifty years ago, the area was still predominantly agricultural land that gradually moved to house (until the early 1970s) a middle class, religiously mixed population (Yahya 1994). However, the area's relatively cheaper land prices and unregulated access made it the logical destination of many rural migrants. The civil conflict (1975) and the Israeli invasion of parts of South Lebanon (1978) precipitated migration to this area (Bourgey 1985).[10] The civil war also led to the subdivision of Lebanon, especially the metropolitan area of its capital city, into homogeneous sectarian religious enclaves controlled by militias of the same sects. The southern suburb of Beirut eventually became the logical destination for the displaced Shiites. During the years of civil war, most of Beirut city's growth was contained in this enclave (BTUTP 1993; Bourgey 1985).

By 1985, ten years after the beginning of the civil war, the population of the southern suburb of Beirut had more than doubled and became almost exclusively Shiite. It went from 140,000 inhabitants in 1969 to around 526,000 in 1993, accounting for at least one-sixth of the Lebanese population[11] (excluding the Palestinian camps).[12] It also became almost exclusively Shiite, thus moving from 32.8 percent in 1973, to above 90 percent in 1998 (BTUTP 1993). Simultaneously, during these years of war, the per-capita income of Lebanese citizens dropped by two-thirds, especially after the 1982 Israeli invasion of Beirut that heavily damaged the economic infrastructure of the country (World Bank 1997).

The unequal regional development was also manifested in the neglect of the suburb of the capital city that were transformed into strongholds of rural migrants. Long before and during the years of civil war, and in compliance with its policy of neglect, the Lebanese government was minimally involved in service provision in some of the poorest rural areas of the country. Between 1965 and 1982, Public agencies did not initiate any major public project in the southern suburb of Beirut. In fact, with the exception of a few decrees related to enlarging streets, not a single public intervention was even planned in the area. Furthermore, during the years of the civil war, especially in the 1980s, this policy was further accentuated with a series of attempts initiated at the central state level to evict informal residents from the area (estimated to be 40 percent of the population of that area)[13] and reduce its density (El Kak Harb 1996, Sharafeddine 1985, Yahya 1994).

The failure of the Lebanese state in providing services and the poverty of the residents opened spaces in the suburb for various political parties to win the residents' support by providing these missing services. Between 1975 and 1991, a large number of political groups entered the lives of the residents of the southern suburb of Beirut city (the political movement called Amal and the Progressive Socialist Party). Most of them provided, at some point or another, services to the community. Similarly, international, national, secular, and religious NGOs attempted at various phases to fill this need. The Islamic NGOs I am describing were part of these service providers. This research attests to how, over the past years, they have materialized their interventions with actual community mobilization and civic involvement.[14]

Methodology

I conducted the fieldwork necessary for this research during the summer of 1997 and December 1997–January 1998. Almost all the fieldwork was conducted in the southern suburb of Beirut where the headquarters of the Islamic NGOs were located.

I adopted open-ended qualitative questions as a format for the interviews conducted with residents, NGO members, political party members, government officials, and employees and planners who have worked on the southern suburb of Beirut. My analysis is also based on documents and evaluations conducted primarily by the Research and Documentation Center (CCSD)—a research center located in the southern suburb of Beirut, which is informally affiliated to Islamic NGOs and Hizballah. The center carries surveys of Lebanese areas populated with Lebanese Shiite communities and maintains a library and archives compiling data primarily related to the same areas. I also use the evaluation reports and pamphlets of these NGOs in order to draw figures and details of their work. Finally, I use the figures and stories compiled by a private planning office, the Bureau Technique d'Urbanisme et des Travaux Publics (BTUTP), located in the vicinity of the city and its southern suburb. This bureau has undertaken a number of projects in my study area, especially a large-scale study to improve the infrastructure system at the end of the civil war, between 1991 and 1993. This paper's conclusions are mainly tested through my personal observations of the area over the past years as a resident of Beirut.

Islamic NGOs of Resistance: A General Description

A cluster of over fifteen Islamic NGOs, all based in the southern suburb of Beirut, have coordinated, cooperated, and complemented their activities in order to develop and operate an active and complex network of service provision. As there is more than one breed of Islamic NGOs in Lebanon, and since this study is limited to the Islamic NGOs that explicitly support Hizballah's resistance in South Lebanon, I will refer to these NGOs as 'Islamic NGOs of resistance' in the rest of the paper. All of these Islamic NGOs of resistance are officially registered as non-governmental organizations or 'charities.' They are all registered with the Lebanese Ministry of Interior and abide by Lebanese laws that regulate non-profit organizations.[15]

These NGOs differ from most others in two key aspects. First, they all flaunt an openly political and religious identity. This openly politicized identity differs from the more common description of NGOs in development literature as 'non-politicized autonomous service providers,' who do not get involved in (corrupting) political activities. In fact, this politicization goes against some of the basic perceived relative advantages of NGOs, over the state: NGOs are independent from voting processes and are therefore able to provide "non-clientelistic" and more "dedicated" services (Berg 1987). Instead, Islamic NGOs, in the southern suburb of Beirut have exploited their religious political affiliations to further their activities.

Politicization appears also in the NGOs' identity as 'Islamic,' that is, they are part of the 'Islamic dynamic' *(al-hala al-Islamiya)*, the current trend of Islamic awakening that has been spreading in southwest Asia for almost half a century. This movement urges for the revival of Islamic values and rule in most aspects of daily life, especially in governance. It transcends the boundaries of particular countries to build a pan-Islamic movement in the entire region (southwest Asia). Hence, all Islamic NGOs of resistance have a strong affinity to the Islamic values promoted by the Iranian revolution and locally by Hizballah. Since they have developed as offshoots of the 'Islamic dynamic,' all these NGOs are strongly imbued in the values and precepts of the Islamic revolution. This is obvious, for example, in the advertisement pamphlets of these organizations that invariably include a picture of Ayatollah Khomeini (the late leader of the Islamic revolution) and an acknowledgment of his central role in their inception.

Islamic NGOs of resistance also portray themselves as 'resistance organizations.' They openly support the military resistance to Israeli occupation led by Hizballah in South Lebanon. NGO offices are plastered with pictures of martyrs—resistance fighters killed in the line of duty. In fact, these organizations perceive their tasks as complementary and intrinsic to the resistance movement led by Hizballah in sustaining and strengthening civilians in times of war. They claim to be building a "resistance society." Hajj Kassem Aleik, the head of one of these NGOs, explained:

> The resistance society is our vision. It is the task to build a society that will refuse oppression and fight for its rights. All the rest—water provision, garbage collection, and agricultural training—is only a working strategy.[16]

Second, these NGOs also differ from other Lebanese NGOs in the literature, because most of them were created as a subsidiary of a foreign—here, Iranian—NGO. In fact, their organizations were almost all created either by the 'mother' organization—an NGO based in Iran. A cluster of organizations that had developed earlier in Iran were all reproduced inside the southern suburb of Beirut in the years following the Islamic revolution of 1979. The NGOs in Lebanon reproduce the division of tasks, the classification of beneficiaries, and even carry the same names as those of the Iranian NGOs. They are thus duplicates of an existing elaborate model of service provision that has been gradually re-adapted to fit local circumstances.

Over the past twelve years, Islamic NGOs of resistance have closely cooperated and complemented each other's tasks to tangibly improve services (health, educational, urban) and living conditions. In the following paragraphs, the NGOs are classified in two categories. The first one gathers NGOs that offer multiple services to the population as a whole and the second unites others that only target specific people.

The Large Service Providers

This class of NGOs is designed to respond to particular "types of needs" such as health care, education, or urban services for entire neighborhoods. Among these organizations, Jihad al-Bina' (literary translated into jihad or battle for construction) is a 'development and construction NGO' that has undertaken, among other tasks, garbage collection, drinking water provision, and other large-scale functions. All of these services were provided in response to urgent needs of the residents. For example, this NGO undertook garbage collection during the last years of civil war (1988–91) in a number of districts in the southern suburb where municipal services were halted. The NGO also provided water at a time when a severe water shortage crisis had left the entire area without drinking water. The organization has since then provided free drinking water to a portion of the southern suburb's residents through ninety-six water tanks, each with a capacity of around two square meters, refilled daily once or twice by six water cisterns.[17] More recently, Jihad al Bina' has initiated an "environmental branch" that seeks the "embellishment" of the area by designing public squares and other common open spaces in the suburb.

There are many other NGOs, in this category. For example, al Haya'a al-Sahhiya (the Health Committee) provides health care services through a hospital that runs in the southern suburb and through various dental clinics (since 1987) and health care centers (the first was inaugurated in 1985), which are spread around the southern suburb of Beirut. Another example is Jam'yat Ta'lim al-Dini al-Islami (Islamic Educational Organization), which runs a number of schools, as well as educational and training programs (al-Mustafa high schools are among the largest and most efficient schools today).

NGOs Targeting Specific Beneficiary Groups

These NGOs are designed to cater to the multiple needs of specific target groups, rather than the entire community. Specifically, the three NGOs in this category have a large outreach among the poorest sectors of the community, who have been most severely affected by the sixteen-year civil war (1975–91), and the continuing Israeli occupation of Lebanon, which began in 1978. The specific target groups include the war martyrs and their families, who are served by al-Shahid (the Martyr), the war wounded and their families, served by al-Jarih (the Wounded), and the resource-less community members are served by al-Imdad (the Resource).

The oldest among these NGOs, is al-Shahid. It was founded in 1982, almost simultaneously with Hizballah and was soon followed by the other two organizations. All three NGOs provide the same types of services, namely health care, food subsidies, education, training, and micro-credit. The latter two services are part of an overarching 'self-sufficiency' program that al-Imdad has been promoting in the area.

Funding

In their funding, all the service-providing NGOs have relied on the same sources. In their initial phase, they all depended largely on Iranian funding to operate, either directly from their mother organization or indirectly through Hizballah. Today, they have moved to rely mostly on a number of local sources. Hence, these NGOs are mostly funded by the *khums*, the *zakat* and the *sadaka*, all forms of (obligatory) religious contributions paid by Shiite Muslims to the poor.[18] Through these religious channels, Islamic NGOs receive funds from within the local community but also from rich Lebanese expatriates and other Arab donors. The money is either directly collected by NGOs, or collected in the central office (the office of "Sayyed Hassan Nasrallah, the official representative of the Wali al-Faqi Sayyed 'Ali Khamenee"), from which it is redistributed to NGOs. In addition, these NGOs appeal directly to occasional donors through boxes distributed around the country. Finally, most of these organizations have income-generation projects, such as resorts or contracting companies that operate anonymously within the private sector and generate profit that is channeled into their services.

These characteristics of funding have an influence on the relationship between the local NGOs and the mother ones. Some of these NGOs, such as al-Shaheed or al-Imdad are secondary branches of mother NGOs in Iran.

They report to their respective bases in Iran and adopt policies from their own Iranian-based mother NGO. The Lebanese branches of this group of NGOs are also partially funded by the Iranian mother organization. At the same time, another group of NGOs have no administrative attachments to or financial dependence on their respective 'model' organizations in Iran. At the time of their creation, they adopted the name and experience of the Iranian organization but, in their tasks and policies, they do not follow the same projects or the same structure as the Iranian institution they were modeled after. These are for example, Jihad al Bina' and al-Hay'a al-Sahhiya. Jihad al-Bina' was first created by and affiliated to the Iranian organization of the same name, while al-Hay'a al-Sahhiya stemmed out of the local first-aid volunteer groups, who later adopted the foreign organizations' umbrella and name. Today, both of these organizations share the same relationship with their Iranian counterpart, which amounts mostly to sharing experiences and development lessons. These NGOs are in fact directly affiliated to Hizballah and abide by its decision-making. While Hizballah does not intervene directly in their tasks, it still looks at the general NGO's strategy, such as its choice of undertaking or dropping large-scale projects.

The Islamic NGOs and the State

The relation of Islamic NGOs of resistance to the state is complex and ambiguous, and warrants several research projects. Indeed, listening to the language of NGO workers, it seems that their relation to the state is characterized by a large dose of antagonism. It is not rare to hear NGO workers blaming the state's discriminatory development policies, corruption, and incapacity. A director of one of the Islamic NGOs told me:

> The government is acting like a private company. Civil servants contract their own companies to develop the projects that could generate profit for them and not for the citizens.

Throughout the interviews I carried out, these comments were very common. NGO workers often blamed the state for its lack of presence, for neglecting the poor Lebanese residents, and for excluding them from the Lebanese post-civil war reconstruction process. On the other hand, state agents also severely criticize the organizations and dismiss their services as entirely 'political.'

The antagonistic language however does not exclude cooperation in several spheres, such as in water distribution, where the Islamic NGOs buy water from the Public Water Agency at a subsidized price. In addition, since 1998, a number of the former NGO workers have run municipal elections and occupy positions in municipal councils or are mayors themselves. Many of the activities the mayors undertake are the continuations of their earlier activities founded in the NGOs.[19]

Self-sufficiency Projects

Given the scale and number of these organizations, it would be impossible to introduce and analyze their activities in one short chapter. I have hence chosen to analyze their performance through one of their most remarkable projects: the [financial] self-sufficiency projects. These are targeted income-generating projects carried out by organizations such as al-Imdad and al-Shahid. They include tasks like bread-making, cooking, sewing, carpet making, hairdressing, mini-stores, and many more. In the following paragraphs, I describe some of these projects in order to illustrate the ways 'agency' and 'ideology' interact in their design.

The Bread-making Initiative

A good illustration of the self-sufficiency projects is the 'bread-making initiative.' The bread initiative was started by al-Imdad, which sought to provide the means of livelihood for Umm Hassan, a woman abandoned by her husband. She was identified by the organization through a report from her neighbors. Umm Hassan wanted to work while staying at home with her newborn. When Abu Fadi, the self-sufficiency representative from Al Imdad asked Umm Hassan what she could do, she said she could bake bread. She was referring here to the rural Arab bread, which is baked using traditional methods and which does not need a large investment. The NGO gave her the oven for free and provided her with the necessary loan to purchase gas and raw materials. There is no interest on this loan because the Islamic law, the shari'a, forbids charging interests. The woman had to repay her loan over a period of ten months. The NGO did not require collateral since NGO workers consider the social informal ties they have with members of the community as a sufficient guarantee. Over the past two years, Umm Hassan has been baking bread daily. In the beginning, a social worker from the organization helped her distribute it in local restaurants. Since then, she has arranged for a neighbor to distribute the bread for her. At the time of our visit, a social worker from the organization was training her eldest son to do the distribution himself. The bread gave Umm Hassan the money to sustain her family and to repay her loan on time, which she did. Abu Fadi, the self-sufficiency representative, explained to us that the organization had allocated part of its yearly budget to do local small-scale projects. After seeing Umm Hassan's success, the organization had been able to replicate it in a number of other cases where women with similar skills were also able to earn a living.

Sewing Projects

Another example of income-generating initiatives is the 'sewing projects.' In these projects, the organizations gave families sewing machines for free. A large body of literature argues for the distribution of non-perishable assets and durable goods such as land or equipment as a longer term and more sustainable solution to poverty alleviation. Unlike food distribution and income transfer programs, which are generally seen as emergency relief solutions, non-perishable goods, such as a sewing machine, provide a useful income-generating asset that help poor people develop their own sources of livelihood (Sen 1987, 1996). Within this context, the organizations seek to distribute sewing machines to residents as a way to support the families' efforts to attain financial self-sufficiency. As in the bread-making initiative, the organization grants the family the necessary loan to buy the first round of materials necessary to start up. Here too, loans are interest-free and the payback period is generally around ten months. Sometimes, this grant is combined with training for one or more family members to develop their sewing skills.[20] Sewing projects are particularly interesting because the organizations have managed to create a market for the families' products within the Islamic schools in the country. For example, the schools and the summer training center run by al-Imdad use children's school uniforms sewn by the beneficiary families of the organization. Through this process, the organization has indirectly included the beneficiary families in the web of its own activities without having them directly affiliated to the organization. It has provided them with a real niche inside the NGO itself and allowed them to become suppliers of the organization, and therefore an integral part of its structure. The NGO was hence able to considerably enlarge its outreach and support base.

Grocery Stores

Over the past ten years, the NGOs have funded a number of mini-markets and local grocery stores spread out around the area. I visited four of these stores initiated by al-Imdad. Three of them began as small cigarette stands and grew into stores either located in an old shipping container inside an informal settlement or in the front room of a family's house. The conditions to grant credit and the loans were similar to the other cases. However, in these projects, the families often needed more substantial loans to open the store. In order to receive these loans, both of these organizations placed some conditions on their beneficiaries; they had to start up with a regular small loan, with which they would put up a cigarette stand. Only after they had proved their credentials and repaid this first loan would the NGO grant them the second and larger ones. Through this process, al-Imdad gave the families an incentive for repayment. Behind each of these cases was a story. The self-sufficiency representative of al-Imdad, who accompanied us during the visits to these stores knew them all. While he worked with the family to overcome its difficulties, the representative sought personal relationships to better understand their conditions and needs.

Hairdressing

The hairdressing initiative is a good example of demand-driven training programs. A number of young women, tired from inactivity and seeking a way to improve their incomes, were interested in this new skill and reported their interest to the organization. Al-Imdad funded and organized a local small-scale temporary training center in the house of one of the beneficiary families and provided the program for free. A volunteer worker in the organization, a hairdresser, took it upon herself to train the seventeen young women who enrolled in the program. She and other volunteers had generated the idea in the community and thus developed and supported it inside the NGO. For eight weeks, the volunteers in the NGO ran the training program for six hours a day. When this training was through, only six of the enrolled trainees were still interested in hairdressing as a business. Two of them applied for loans at al-Imdad and received them to start up their businesses. Now they are both running successful businesses and one of them owns her hairdressing salon.

Assessing Income-Generating Initiatives

The above descriptions of self-sufficiency illustrate some of the strategies, adopted by Islamic NGOs of resistance in their income-generating projects and more broadly, their approach to service provision. First, these NGOs are responsive to local needs and capacities. They seek to build on existing skills within the community in order to initiate income-generating projects and help families attain financial self-sufficiency. Unlike many employment-generating projects, where families are dragged into long training programs, which are pre-requisites for them to attain jobs in formal organizations such as factories, al-Imdad's income-generating projects build on the indigenous capacities of the families they support. "It is very important for us not to impose on a family any type of work," explained Abu Fadi, the head of the Beirut self-sufficiency unit of al-Imdad. "Instead, we encourage the families to choose something themselves. We would rather build on their own skills whenever we can, rather than compel them to learn additional things."

Besides respecting residents' decisions, the development literature has pointed to other positive aspects of these types of projects. For one, the practice generates faster results in income generation since families do not have to undergo a phase of training in a fresh skill at a time when they are struggling for survival. In this context, training only makes sense if it has an immediate application and could open up new channels of income generation. Therefore, the organization only resorts to training when residents request it themselves and if this new skill has proved to be needed in the market.

Another important aspect of self-sufficiency projects is that they are always undertaken with the solid backing of the structures of support provided by some of the Islamic NGOs of resistance, notably al-Imdad, al-Shaheed, and al-Jarih. These organizations provide beneficiary families with a safety net that consists of technical, emotional, and financial support, and help the family achieve its goals. First, NGOs do not separate between their respective self-sufficiency and social help wings. The majority of poor families often has health problems along with their financial problems and would hardly survive if they had to bear all the costs of both medication and daily needs. Therefore, as a first step, the NGOs provide them with health care while they ensure their own daily subsistence. Second, the NGOs provide vocational training to their beneficiaries when needed. Training could be directly supplied by one of the organizations, like the hairdressing program lead by al-Imdad, or through covering tuition fees in local institutes. Most of these training programs teach simple trades and skills such as sewing, cooking, rug making, embroidery, and others. Building skills also includes guiding the first steps of the family in running a business. Therefore, when al-Imdad provides a family with credit, the self-sufficiency representative, who approves the credit, also monitors the progress. While they undeniably build more dependence on the organizations, these interventions, nonetheless, also indicate an acute understanding of the living conditions of the residents and hence allow a wider support in the transition phase toward self-sufficiency. Third, the way in which these organizations provide markets through their own institutions to families seeking self-sufficiency (clothes for students in their schools, for example) blurs the boundaries between NGOs and their beneficiaries and hence makes them more approachable and available at the local level. Finally, the ability of these NGOs, to cater to diverse needs and services attests to a unique flexibility rarely encountered in such organizations.

Yet, the projects are far from attaining their goals of economic success, and income-generating projects show ambivalent financial results. When describing the success rate of these initiatives, the director of al-Imdad explained that only 25 percent of the projects "made it." By success, the director meant that the family had achieved financial self-sufficiency irrespective of whether it had managed to repay its loan or not. The director's calculations did not include the cost of labor and the many grants the local NGO had granted to the projects. Neither did they include the costs of medical services that the NGO also covered. Taking the bread-making initiative as an example, al-Imdad's calculations excluded the price of the oven and the costs of distribution and monitoring that were all incurred by the NGO. Yet, this project is considered among the NGO's most successful initiatives. Al-Imdad self-sufficiency projects' loan default rate was not more successful since it is as high as 80 percent. Many of the local grocery stores for example, continued to expand until they reached the point when they could not return their loans anymore. Only at that point did they stop, and settle on stable revenues that could cover their living costs without ever returning the loan. In all these cases, the NGOs did not include the costs of following-up, training, conducting the initial feasibility studies it had led, or even the loan deficit the family accumulated in assessing its success. Those accustomed to working in or reading about income-generating projects will not be surprised by the results that these NGOs have achieved. Indeed, it is generally agreed that it is unusual that such projects yield a significant income increase to the participants. It is even more rare that real economic benefits cover the costs of these projects, especially when they target the poorest residents (Tendler 1982, Vivian and Maseko 1994, Adams and Pischke 1992).

Yet, for the residents, many of the projects offer invaluable assets that the economic success or the efficiency of the projects does not reflect. This is especially due to the political framework in which these projects are inscribed. This framework mainly works toward challenging the level of dependency that residents had been confined to since moving in to the city from their rural areas. Indeed, Islamic resistance NGO workers not only physically support residents, as described in the previous section, but also seek to build ties with them and challenge their hopelessness. This is reflected in the language they use and the approach to poverty alleviation that complements the supportive structures with an appealing conceptual framework. NGO workers therefore speak of social justice, dispossession, and displacement. They have placed financial self-reliance in the context of challenging existing power relationships in the city and redefining the control of resources among residents. This definition of financial self-sufficiency as a means and not an end, and the position of such projects in the context of strengthening the communities' capacities to stand up for their rights are at the heart of the NGOs' success. This places them at odds with most other NGOs that equate "empowerment" with "financial self-reliance."[21] Instead, Islamic NGOs have managed, in this context, to develop a more elaborate vision of self-sufficiency that goes beyond an increase in financial means and places empowerment back in its original political context. Al-Imdad has viewed the self-sufficiency projects as a way to increase the community's control over its own means of survival. The effect is to reduce the family's dependence on anyone, whether the state or NGOs. "It is because we refuse to be insulted and oppressed anymore that we pursue these [self-sufficiency] projects," a social worker explained. "We are looking for our communities' self-sufficiency so we can build a real alternative, where we are recognized as equals and truly respected." Indeed, as long as it relies on external charity to survive, a community is unable to reclaim and enforce its own rights. On the one hand, people preoccupied with basic survival are often unable to think beyond their daily food. On the other hand, there is little chance that they can actually revolt against their scarce sources of survival (Salmon 1987; Abers 1996). In that sense, and again in those workers' understanding, self-sufficiency projects are an essential part of the process of building a resistance society, as they build into them the need for such a society to reclaim its own means of subsistence.

This switch in the understanding of service recipients has been extremely important in the tasks carried out by NGOs. For instance, the empowerment language has allowed organizations to target specific groups inside the community and maximize its projects' efficiency without the usual pitfalls of such initiatives. Indeed, whereas accurate targeting is often a potential way of tackling a problem directly and thus catering to the best form of support, many scholars examining strategies of poverty alleviation have denounced the psychic costs of social stigma and marginalization that are linked to participating in projects specifically targeting the poor. Indeed, these authors argue, singling out a community is very likely to generate resentment within the stigmatized community and political rejection from other groups, whose money is invested in programs that don't benefit them (Sen 1995, Skocpol 1991, Besley and Kanbur 1988, Wilson 1989). By tying self-sufficiency projects to the notion of resistance and hence directly linking the beneficiaries of these NGOs to this resistance, the organizations have transformed the task of service provision from charity into an absolute necessity. The organizations were therefore able to legitimize and gather support for the targeting process.

Yet, the adoption of politics as an implicit tool in projects doesn't come without a price. The main shortfall is the exclusion of those alienated by this ideological appeal either because they do not abide by the "Islamist" message of these organizations or because they do not constitute a potential political client (that is, they are non-Shiites) and are therefore not explicitly targeted. Hence, all the supported families of al-Shaheed are necessarily already supporters of Hizballah, since they come from families who have lost members to the struggle against Israel. In addition, most 'clients' of these organizations live in the southern suburb of Beirut, an area almost exclusively inhabited by Shiite residents, all of them potential voters for Hizballah. While the organizations claim inclusiveness and enumerate non-Shiite beneficiaries, it is unlikely that the latter constitute any significant number. To be sure, the organizations acknowledge this bias and blame it on the segregated and atomized nature of the city after the civil war; yet, nothing in their own policies seems to transcend the divisions of the city. To the contrary, some of their practices clearly go in the opposite direction. For instance, credit applications inquire about beneficiaries' religious beliefs and even question their religious practices (observance of dress codes, for example). In addition, the organizations' own explicit political identity, apparent for instance in the workers' dress codes or their level of discourse, repels many residents who do not want to commit to such a religious-political orientation. These political signals are also likely to influence residents in the long run, who even if they are not asked directly, still perceive the need to 'return favors' by voting for the political candidates of these groups. Hence, several residents indicated that they preferred to visit the local offices of the ministry of social services and other institutions, even if the latter are unable to provide them with the same level of support.

In short, the above description of self-sufficiency projects reveals, at the micro-scale, a model of services, in which ideology is used to facilitate targeting without stigma and to encourage residents to achieve project goals. In addition, the design of self-sufficiency projects highlights the capacity of NGOs to develop flexible, easily adaptable, and responsive projects that start from local skills and capacities and build from them successful projects. The capacity of NGOs to develop such projects is closely connected to their management model. Perhaps no single structure reveals the intricacy of the NGOs' design in its degree of decentralization, accessibility, flexibility, and capacity to build a safety net that supports self-sufficiency and reduces barriers between residents, beneficiaries, and NGO workers as much as the 'volunteer sisters.' The following section examines in detail the structure of the 'volunteer sisters.' It is presented here as an illustration of the ideological and structural (agency) tools that explain, to a large extent, the operational success of these organizations in service provision.

Volunteer Sisters

The 'volunteer sisters,' or *al-akhawat al-mutatawi'at*, form the outreach structure of the group of NGOs, which target specific types of beneficiaries: al-Imdad, al-Shaheed, and al-Jarih. Within each NGO, 'volunteer sisters' are part of the network of social workers, whose primary task lies in monitoring the NGO-beneficiary relations. The following section describes and analyzes the details of this structure.

Social Workers

The network of social workers in each of the three NGOs that target services is composed of five or six full-time (male) social workers in addition to over a hundred volunteer women. Men have a well-defined role: they keep regular office hours inside the NGOs, during which they mostly fill up beneficiary applications for loans or grants and approve/reject requests. The 'volunteer sisters' have flexible, open-ended tasks that require neither their presence in the offices nor specific working hours. Instead, they act as the informal liaison between social workers inside the organizations and beneficiary families. They are subdivided, within each organization, into 'geographic sub-units' that correspond to the neighborhoods where each 'sister' lives. Each of the sub-areas has a 'head-sister,' who coordinates the work of her fellow workers and reports back regularly to the male social workers inside the organization.

Two declared criteria are used to recruit 'volunteer sisters.' First, they need to be residents of the areas where they work. Second, they have to believe in the Hizballah ideology prior to working in the organization, which entails being screened by the political party as acceptable members of its social wing. (The latter condition entails a first screening: women have to accept Islamic values as understood by the political party, encourage the resistance of Hizballah in the South, etc.).[22]

Task Description

'Volunteer sisters' have two tasks that are both extremely flexible and were designed to accommodate the schedules of housewives and their volunteering activities. The 'volunteer sisters' visit the NGOs' beneficiary families in each of the geographic sub-units of the southern suburb of Beirut on a weekly basis. These visits are designed to ensure the family's proper reception of allocations and to learn about additional needs the organizations should provide for. The 'sisters' then relate rapidly to the NGOs any problems the family encountered, which allows for a quick response from the NGO.

However, the role of the 'sisters' extends beyond the services of the organization, to include any issue related to the family's well-being. Hence, during these weekly visits, the 'sisters' often develop personal relationships with the families and learn about problems and struggles that transcend the NGOs' services. Often, they get involved with children's schoolwork, and romantic or professional family dilemmas. They have thus somewhat customized the relationship between the NGOs and the families as they have adapted and catered it to the specific needs of beneficiaries. This role is particularly crucial when a family takes a loan for the execution of a self-sufficiency project. Under these circumstances, the role of a 'sister' becomes even more important since she is to ensure the family's well being and help overcome any impediments to the success of their income-generating initiative.

Through these visits and the close relations they develop with families, the 'sisters' also collected project suggestions and eventually initiated programs with community members. One such example is al-Imdad's hairdressing training program, described earlier. It was the 'sisters' who proposed this project to al-Imdad. Second, the volunteers create as an outreach structure in the wider communities of the southern suburb of Beirut. Since the 'sisters' are necessarily local residents of the sub-neighborhood where they work, they are immersed in the local networks of social relations—on which they can rely, in order to identify families in need or gather information about subsidies or grant applicants. In that sense, the role of their network is crucial in facilitating the difficult task of targeting beneficiaries. It represents a cheap and easy way to identify and assess real needs for potential beneficiaries, a problem most targeted programs struggle with. In fact, one of the most commonly reported shortfalls of targeted initiatives is precisely the prohibitive cost and complex task of determining accurately residents' incomes and checking real needs (Besley and Kanbur 1988). The 'volunteer sisters' allow the Islamic NGOs to easily overcome this difficulty.

Origins of the 'Volunteer Sisters'

Although the NGOs to which the 'volunteer sisters' are affiliated are modeled after and still affiliated to Iranian mother institutions, the structure of the 'volunteer sisters' itself does not exist in the original Iranian model. Moreover, the network of women working in the field of social services, these former are not affiliated to any of the Iranian mother institutions of al-Imdad, al-Shahid, or al-Jarih. In fact, this structure presents an example of a clear departure from the original mother institutions to adapt to the local Lebanese context.

When al-Imdad launched its operations in 1987, all social workers, including volunteers, were men and no woman was allowed to join the NGO's social workers section. During my interviews with social workers in the organization, I learned that the establishment of this structure among Lebanese NGOs was a subject of contention between the Iranian al-Imdad mother institution and its Lebanese offshoot. Indeed, when they started visiting houses beginning in 1989, the male workers felt they needed women who, according to one of them, "could relate more readily to fellow mothers, sisters, and friends." However, he added:

> The Iranian mother institution did not immediately accept enrolling women as part of the organization, as this structure was not part of the mother institution. It took us a year to convince them that it was entirely appropriate to include 'volunteer sisters.'[23]

In short, the Iranian mother institutions had to reevaluate their model and reshape their structures according to local Lebanese needs. While information about the negotiation process was not readily available, the existence of this dialogue by itself and the development of the 'volunteer sisters' as a central structure of the NGOs, clearly indicate that interaction and feedback from the local level is an essential element of how the organizations developed. It is even clearer today as the need for more members and increasing challenges, coming particularly from community members who want to participate in the NGO's activities without abiding by the political ideology—because they want to support resistance activities or help community members force on these organizations more inclusive standards. It is even clearer today as more people want to participate in the NGO's activities without abiding necessarily by their political ideology. These people want to help their community and support the activities of the resistance.

In addition to the two organizational tasks, the 'sisters,' by virtue of their affiliation to Hizballah, also relay information about the political party's events, such as political rallies or dinner banquets. "We act as a two-way information channel," a 'volunteer sister' explained. "We inform the NGO of the beneficiaries' needs and we inform the families we visit of Hizballah's activities." This task, while often unmentioned in NGOs, attests to the open political activities that NGOs help channel, and highlight, once again, the blurred division between politics and service provision. However, this political messenger task is more elaborate and subtle than it may appear at first. The next section details the role of politics and how it influences the performance of the 'volunteer sisters.'

Ideology in the Work of Volunteer Sisters

The relationship of Islamic NGOs of resistance to Hizballah acts as a major asset for organizational performance and influences their operations in several ways, as detailed below. While these observations cannot be generalized to include all volunteers, they appear to be applicable to many.

First, the political ideology is used by NGOs to develop a prestigious image of their work and hence act as a major incentive for many NGO members to volunteer time and effort. Participation in the work of Islamic NGOs is an indirect contribution to the Hizballah struggle for justice. While the political party mostly conducts armed resistance, the organizations support its activities by 'building a resistance society,' which would be committed to resisting all forms of oppression. Therefore, volunteering for any of these NGOs becomes a prestigious activity that bestows part of this prestige on the 'volunteer sisters' and encourages them to participate in the

NGOs' tasks. True, all 'sisters' would rather ascribe humanitarian motivations to their enrollment, but most also resolutely state political ones. This is not surprising since, as mentioned above, all sisters have been recruited directly from "Hizballah women, and have already had affiliations to a political mission prior to their involvement with the NGOs.

Second, the political ideology also generates among sisters a 'sense of mission' that encourages them to participate actively within the NGO's structures. Many of the interviewed sisters talked of "duty," "obligation," "responsibility," or a sense of "urge" when participating in the NGO's activities. The following quotes present an idea of one of the sisters' motivations:

> I love the idea of giving and sharing and I feel the urge to do it. This is why I enrolled. I will never leave the organization unless I feel I am personally unable to fulfill my tasks dutifully.[24]

Another 'sister' added: "It is our duty to participate in the resistance society."

The rhetoric of a 'sense of mission' is common in the development literature. Central figures in organizational analysis, such as Wilson, have argued that a "sense of mission" provides an organization with the basis for recruiting and socializing new members and relieves administrators from the burden of creating incentives. In short, the sense of mission generates commitment and enthusiasm for the employees and a strong incentive for good performance (Wilson 1989). The 'sisters' often said that the NGOs provided them with an effective space to channel their sense of mission: the duty to support the military activities against Israel, fight oppression, or, more simply, be religiously committed to helping others.

It is important to note that the sense of mission is not particular to 'volunteer sisters.' Indeed, many other Islamic NGO workers confirmed this idea. One of them, Hajj 'Ali Zein, working for Jihad al-Bina', told us that "the highest form of commitment is military resistance. It then trickles down to us in all these organizations. We all try to help as much as we can." Another worker in the same organization told us that "the presence of resistance is psychologically important to us employees in Jihad Al Bina'. It definitely energizes us." In short, the notion of resistance has helped these NGOs to switch from their image as one among many other charities to being a part of an organized structure of resistance that appeals to members of the local community precisely because it fights the same perceived oppressors.

Third, the political ideology, including dress codes, behavioral attitudes, and language serves as a major asset toward building an organizational culture strongly tied to the mission and goals of the political party. For instance, since 'volunteer sisters' are members of Hizballah, they have all adopted the dress code that was ruled by a jurisdiction *(fatwa)* of the late Imam Khomeini, which, in addition to the traditional veil, requires women to cover their chins and foreheads. Women have also adopted the traditional Islamic clothing: they wear long, formless, dark-colored dresses and entirely cover their arms and legs. The 'sisters' have also all adopted the behavioral attitudes ascribed to Islam: they don't shake hands with men and observe strict segregation with members of the opposite sex.

This dress code is particularly important for the 'volunteer sisters,' who are highly visible in the society. Indeed, through their dress code, they already embody a visual symbolic representation of the political ideology they promote. The 'volunteer sisters' are particularly aware of this aspect of their task and proudly endorse it.

> We constitute a main branch within the large [Islamic resistance] movement. The way we are dressed, the way we look, the way we talk are all indicators of our political commitment. When people see us, they often ask about Hizballah's resistance operations, for example.

Finally, the sisters have adopted the language perpetuated by the political party, and inspired again by the Islamic dynamic and the culture of resistance. It starts with the formulaic greeting, *"al-salam alaykum"* (peace be upon you), systematically used even in response to the other more casual greetings used elsewhere in the city. However, it builds into a much broader language adopted from the political ideology of the Islamic dynamic. They, for example, have relabeled poverty as the outcome of discriminatory state policies rather than poor people's lack of skills. Thus, the victims of oppressive structures are not hopeless, desperate individuals but rather active subjects who are resisting oppression—they are only perceived as "weak" *(mustad'afin)*. They therefore can enroll in organizations, and in doing so join a "resistance society," which "fights" the "oppression" and misery heaped upon them by biased social structures. Above all, this new language consciously challenges people's perceptions and hopelessness through rewording and redefining their position and role in the society.

On a more critical note, however, it is important to highlight that the way these organizations have used ideology, while extremely successful in promoting their work, can also be seen as somewhat exclusive and problematic. Indeed, the same literature that praises the 'sense of mission' and the organizational culture often elaborates on the difficulties of instilling them among the staff of the NGOs. Wilson, for one, describes particular examples of organizations, such as the FBI and the trouble they went through to instill this 'sense of mission' (Wilson 1985: 91–110). Islamic NGOs did not have to go through the same process. They have received this culture and mission from an existing political ideology and from the experience of resistance in the south of the country. If this political ideology eased the process of culture building, it however also had major drawbacks. Indeed, many residents refuse to receive the NGOs' services, precisely because they brandish such obvious political symbols. This is especially the case with the targeted initiatives that entail a strong personalized relation with the organization. Even more pronounced than this voluntary self-exclusion is the explicit process that excludes from the web of NGO workers all community members who are not willing to abide by the religious commitments of the NGOs, which include clothing, language, and other restrictions. In fact, the homogenization of the city during the civil war has allowed suspending this issue—since almost exclusively Shiite residents live in the areas where these NGOs provide services. There is therefore no real pressure from local residents who might be explicitly excluded. However, if the situation was to change, the strong and exclusive ideology of these NGOs could become a serious impediment to their relations with the community. In addition, the mission and the ideology are vulnerable to change since they are tied to particular historical conditions (resistance to the Israeli occupation of Lebanon). Hence, the eventual pullout of Israel from Lebanon could also create another challenging momentum and lead to the need to recreate new missions—which could mean possibly losing affiliates along the way.

Conclusion

I have argued that both political ideology and the organizational agency play central roles in the way these NGOs undertake their service provision. In terms of agency, the highly decentralized, flexible, and easily accessible structures are a main factor in the NGOs' success. First, the NGOs' highly decentralized structures allow for 'volunteer sisters' and self-sufficiency workers, themselves residents of the area, to choose and implement projects, and this explains the unusual responsiveness of these NGOs and their capacity to build on residents' local skills when they design interventions. In addition, the 'volunteer sisters' show the flexibility of the organizations both internally, in allowing for a flexible schedule that even busy women can abide by, to a flexible NGO-resident relation that caters to every family's crisis at its own pace. Finally, the recurrent presence of NGO members in the beneficiary's home and their presence as residents of the local neighborhoods facilitate access to NGOs and blur the boundaries between organizations and residents. As for ideology, it has been able to create the necessary mission, culture, and aura necessary to encourage community members to volunteer and workers to perform well. It has also facilitated some of the NGOs' tasks, such as targeting beneficiaries without explicit stigmatizing. These two processes were carried out simultaneously and together allowed the organizations to build the relationship of trust and cooperation they were able to achieve with the community.

To conclude, this research was based on a pioneering investigation of Islamic NGOs, in a context that perceives them negatively. It has sought to highlight some of their successful initiatives and working mechanisms. Particularly, it has challenged the grounds on which they are often dismissed (ideology) to show that ideology can actually aid more efficient service provision. Nonetheless, since the time this research was conducted, many elements have changed with respect to NGOs' performance. First, the penetration of the NGO workers, through Hizballah, into public structures of governance (especially municipalities) has introduced new dynamics in their operations that are worth exploring. How are boundaries drawn? Are there new channels of cooperation between public and (private) non-profit sectors? In addition, the recent events in South Lebanon (the massive Israeli pull-out), which had not yet unfolded when this paper was written, have raised questions relating to some of the main mobilization mechanisms of Hizballah as a political party and its affiliated NGOs. With the expected complete liberation of the South, how do mission, aura, and sense of commitment change? These are all issues that require further substantial research.

Notes

1. Besides all NGO workers and community members, who took the time to listen to my questions and explain their work, my special thanks go to Alan Shihadeh, Meenu Tewari, and Karim Kobeissi for comments on earlier drafts of this paper. All mistakes and omissions remain, of course, entirely mine.

2. This literature is extremely abundant in American mainstream media, for example The New York Times, The Boston Globe, and many others. For other sources, check Barsky 1995, Lamchichi 1995, or Miller 1997.
3. For example, see Lesch 1996.
4. There is no one way of writing Hizballah's name in English. I adopted this orthography (Hizballah) because the two parts that suggest clearly the word Allah ('God' in Arabic) as separate from Hizb ('party' in Arabic).
5. CNN: "Struggle for Peace" Homepage (emphasis added). (http://www.cnn.com/WORLD/struggle_for_peace/key_players.html No.palestinians)
6. UNDP report on Lebanon, August 1997.
7. These figures refer to the situation at the time the paper was presented at the conference in March 2000.
8. Although the Islamic revolution occurred in Iran, hence has a geographic specificity, it carries within its ideology and philosophy a strong expansionist push that transcends the local country-boundaries. For a detailed description of this movement, see Fadl Allah, 1990.
9. Beirut Municipal area is 17.2 square km (for the same population).
10. People fled other suburb that were then controlled by Christian militias or they fled rural areas, mostly from the South and the Beka'a, where Israeli warplanes and aggressions were the most active.
11. This figure represents roughly one-quarter of the Beirut metropolitan area residents. Some statistics affirm that the southern suburb contain 700,000 people but since there has been no official census in Lebanon since 1932, there is really no definite figure.
12. I have excluded the Palestinian camps from this study because they have, until lately, related to the jurisdiction of United Nations Relief and Works Agency (UNRWA) the and do not closely relate to services provided by these NGOs in the southern suburb of Beirut.
13. This is a controversial figure presented by Sharafeddine. This percentage in fact depends on the definitions and types of informal processes in place.
14. I reconstructed most of this history through interviews with residents and planners who have worked in the area.
15. The NGOs are all registered however under different, generic names. It is important to note here that under Lebanese law registration of non-governmental organizations is restricted to a declaration of foundation and does not require the sanctioning of the state.
16. Personal interview conducted in July 1997.
17. The NGO purchases the water from the Beirut Public Water Agency (a state agency) for a nominal "symbolic" fee and redistributes it on those tanks.
18. The khumus and the zakat are religiously mandated percentages on the income that all Muslim Shiites are mandated to pay for poor members of their communities. They are generally channeled through religious institutions. The sadaka is a benevolent and unspecified amount of money, similar to a donation.
19. In the presentation he gave at the Center d'Etude et de Recherche du Moyen-Orient Contemporain (CERMOC) in April 1999, Hajj Abu Said Khansa, the Ghobeiri Mayor and a former Islamic NGO worker, described the activities of his municipality. They were strikingly similar to those of the NGOs.

20. Al-Shahin runs a training center in the southern suburb of Beirut. The center provides particularly young women the proper training for sewing.
21. Vivian and Maseko perhaps best document this idea in their assessment of rural NGOs in Zimbabwe. The authors argued that many NGOs have uncritically adopted this definition of "empowerment" from the political right wing, and have consequently reduced "empowerment" to "enrichment of individuals." These NGOs have therefore missed the more fundamental definition of "empowerment" as a change in power and an increased control over one's own resources (Vivian and Maseko 1994: 14–15).
22. Over the past two years, the structure of the women volunteers in these organizations has been revised due to challenges in the local community that have led to more inclusive involvement. Non-Hizballah women were hence allowed in the organizations, training programs, and teaching positions. While they do not retain, to my knowledge, the same capacities that these sisters have, this development nevertheless indicates a change in the tight control over who works within these organizations.
23. Interview in 1997.
24. Interview in 1997.

Chapter Twelve

The poverty Alleviation System and the Role of Associations in Yemen

Blandine Destremeau

In recent years, tackling poverty has become a priority in Yemen. This orientation is justified by the dramatic evolution of the economic and social situation of the country since the Gulf War, which has generated a sharp increase in financial poverty. It has also drawn attention to the alarming state of social indicators, be it health, education, or access to social services (Table 1). Owing to its status of least advanced country, of being the poorest country in the Middle East, and to its demographic and strategic weight in the Arabic peninsula, Yemen is receiving growing financial support from international donors.

Nevertheless, the emergence of poverty as a leading concern in policy discourses cannot be dissociated from the fact that since 1995,[1] the country has submitted to a swiftly implemented Structural Adjustment Program (SAP), as these programs are launched by the International Monetary Fund. The state of 'economic restructuring' goes hand in hand with a marked intervention from international organizations, and with the adoption of the concepts and packages that they continuously produce. According to the prevailing new vision, poverty alleviation is tightly fit into international schemes and the main goal is the restructuring of what recently came to be called the old 'social safety nets.'

One of the main components of this vision is the idea of diversifying the actors involved in the safety nets, in order to challenge the functions of the central state, reduce public spending, increase efficiency and flexibility, and foster popular resources and creativity. As in most countries facing a similar situation, in Yemen too, associations[2] have been encouraged to multiply, along with various institutions articulating their activities and roles within a global framework of poverty alleviation.

This chapter seeks to contribute to the analysis of the 'poverty alleviation system' in Yemen, particularly the relationships between the main actors involved and the role assigned to associations and NGOs within this system. The research is based on documents, discourses, and information gathered through interviews, participation in various seminars and meetings, and field observation.

The first part of this study will present the 'poverty alleviation system' from an institutional point of view. While this 'system' is very close to that in other countries that have been involved in similar situations for years, the specificity of the Yemeni case resides, I believe, in the fact that it has only been a decade since these global schemes have been imported ready-made, and that they are being grafted onto social and political structures with little experience of foreign interference. The second part will focus on Yemeni associations, their types, and the setting of their existence and operation to try to grasp what their position and role are within the 'poverty alleviation system.'

The Context of Structural Adjustment

Yemen has been following a stabilization and structural adjustment reform program to which, the government, according to the World Bank, has shown "laudable commitment" (World Bank 1999).

A comprehensive economic, financial, and administrative reform program was set up in 1994 between the government of Yemen, the IMF, the World Bank and other donors as a response to Yemen's declining economic performance. Besides the effects of the Gulf War, the economy had suffered from the civil war, which drained resources away from development and damaged social and economic infrastructures. As a result, the balance of payment deficit increased, as well as inflation and unemployment, while foreign debt arrears reached alarming levels.

A stand-by arrangement was signed between the IMF and the government of Yemen for fifteen months over 1996 and 1997. After the government raised diesel prices and electricity tariffs, thereby prompting social protests and unrest, the IMF board approved an Enhanced Structural Adjustment Facility and an Extended Fund Facility covering the 1997–2000 period, with a view to expanding the role of the private sector by reducing the crowding-out effect of a large and inefficient government bureaucracy (UNDP 1998). The structural adjustment package consists of a classic combination of reforms of the tax and expenditure structures (including the removal of subsidies on basic consumption items), civil service, trade and tariff policies and administration, budget management, monetary policies and the banking system, as well as of the public enterprise sector through privatization.

The results of structural adjustment reforms in Yemen are considered satisfactory on the macroeconomic level. The GDP growth rate increased, while inflation and the budget deficit were brought down to very reasonable levels. The exchange rate was stabilized and the balance of payments improved. In 1996, the Paris Club granted Yemen debt relief for three years—starting from October 1997—with the notable effect of lowering the rate of debt service to its current account receipt (UNDP 1998; European Commission 1999).

However, the structural adjustment program has had a very negative effect on the population's well being, notably as a result of the important price rises, which drastically reduced the purchasing power of consumers. Additionally, unemployment is soaring, due in part to the slowdown in government hiring, but also to shrinking job opportunities abroad (Al-Maytami 1999). In addition to the economic, administrative, and financial reform program, some social measures were also planned in order to overcome the immediate negative effects of these reforms—so as to limit the social opposition that they would give rise to and, thereby, increase the government's leeway in implementing them. Human resources and social development were considered a priority, as a support to growth and employment generation, in a context of general backwardness,[3] very low human development, and alarming social indicators (see Table 1). This policy orientation was reflected by a significant rise in budget allocations to these sectors in 1997 compared to 1996. The momentum was unfortunately not maintained: the rise the following year was much lower, social spending was then drastically reduced in 1999 compared to 1998, and only marginally benefited from the windfall revenue increase due to oil price rise in 2000.[4]

The first Consultative Group on Yemen, gathering twenty-five international donors, met in Brussels in June 1997. Chaired by the World Bank in cooperation with the European Commission, it brought together representatives from many countries as well as various funds and UN agencies. The satisfactory economic performance of Yemen, its progress toward solving the debt issue and its consolidation of democratic political progress in particular were taken into account, in addition to the natural disasters Yemen had been exposed to in 1996 (UNDP 1998; European Commission 1999). During this meeting, the first formal one of its kind, assistance was pledged to Yemen for a three-year period. An Arab Monetary Fund facility was approved in 1997 for a period of two years. The World Bank increased its involvement in Yemen after its office was established in Sana'a in 1995 (European Commission 1999).

The Poverty Alleviation System in Yemen

The poverty alleviation system in Yemen presents itself as a set of interacting programs carried out or initiated by institutions of various statuses, not only in terms of their affiliation to the government—governmental, para-governmental, non-governmental, centralized, decentralized, etc.—but also of their relative position within this system: some give, some receive, some control, some are controlled.

As already mentioned, the poverty alleviation system is a process in Yemen. This does not mean that all its components are new but that those that were already in place are now expected to be linked with new institutions and fit within a global framework. As it will be shown later on, some programs or overarching structures are newly established, covering new specialized poverty-alleviating institutions and previously launched governmental programs. Their role is mainly to coordinate between various initiatives and to target the activities implemented toward their own formulation of what should be done against poverty.

The World Bank's Commitment to Poverty Alleviation in Yemen

The aim of the World Bank's commitment toward poverty alleviation in Yemen is mainly to get around the negative effects of structural adjustment on social welfare. This is to facilitate implementation of reforms and to ensure their success regarding social and political acceptability, the contribution of human resource development to economic growth and the distribution of growth benefits to the population through employment generation. It therefore consists of both structural reform measures and programs.

The core of the World Bank Group intervention in Yemen is economic, with administrative reform and support to the growth of the private sector.

Other aspects are addressed as well: gender- and poverty-focused projects in health and education, especially for girls and women; access to rural regions; and urban water management. The World Bank strategy in Yemen is considered to entail important risks in terms of political support, inadequate institutional capacity, domestic strife, and slow progress regarding governance. The first concern, in particular, has to do with the impact of structural adjustment on the impoverishment of the most vulnerable groups. The Bank's policy response to this risk is to create visible improvements that are meaningful in the daily life of Yemenis, such as providing funds for schools and health clinics and expanding support for public works, basic education, health, and water supply. These sectors are no longer in the context of productive value-enhancement of individuals, but rather in the context of the political pressure that impoverishment can exert on the structural adjustment process—if not checked by countermeasures. Another item that responds to the risks involved, and is also linked to poverty, is the fight against corruption, which diverts resources from investment, tends to foster social conflict, and reduces the efficiency of civil service.

In its first Country Assistance Strategy document of 1996, the World Bank expressed concern for poverty alleviation along two perspectives: firstly, under the label of "social protection," which covered civil works and a social fund project, and secondly, under the heading "sustainable human and natural resource development," which included investment projects in education, vocational training, agriculture, water supply, transportation, and flood rehabilitation. In 1998, following an evaluation of the first phase's results and a drop in oil prices, the government and the Bank began to work on a new 'country assistance strategy.' The four principles stressed in this plan are: selectivity, sustainability, partnership, and impact on poverty. The last point states:

> The strategy should bring early benefits to large parts of the society, particularly the poor. These benefits should be visibly associated with longer-gestation interventions, especially economic and administrative reforms.

These social benefits, the strategy notes, should concern education, health, and "other services most valued by Yemenis," with a view to strengthen the benefits of other objectives. According to the World Bank, in the framework of structural adjustment and as far as poverty alleviation is concerned, the Yemeni government has improved targeting of subsidies, greatly increased expenditures on basic education and health (up from 4.6 percent of GDP in 1996 to 9.7 percent in 1998), expanded public works, and established substantial cash transfer, community[5] development, and micro-enterprise programs for the poor (World Bank 1999).

A renewed commitment is made to improve girls' education and health, the latter consisting of spreading the use of contraceptives, improving safety of motherhood, child nutrition and immunization, community water and sanitation, and clinical care facilities. The Bank also supports the strategy of the Ministry of Health, with regard, in particular, to the decentralization of management of service provision, and to the setting-up of cost-recovery and cost-sharing schemes. Furthermore, the Bank is committed to upgrading poor areas by strengthening the communities' capacity to support themselves. Its main components consist of a public works project, irrigation improvements, an agricultural technology project, support to the Social Fund for Development, as well as contributing to the betterment of rural access and cooperatives. Additionally, the Bank involves itself in job creation, relying mainly on broad-based, diversified, and sustainable economic growth, with targeted interventions to promote productive private investment and employment.

The National Poverty Alleviation and Employment Generation Program

The National Poverty Alleviation and Employment Generation Program (NPAEGP) of the UNDP and the government of Yemen lies at the core of the poverty alleviation system, in the sense that from it stem, or within it, are incorporated most of the poverty alleviation institutions and programs. Its status is mainly that of a temporary program to set up the government or government-linked structures and institutions, which should tackle poverty alleviation on a rather permanent basis.

The NPAEGP was launched by the United Nations Development Programme (UNDP) and the document was signed with the government of Yemen in 1997. While the UNDP is by far its major sponsor, several other agencies also contribute to this project, including United Nations Capital Development Fund (UNCDF), World Food Programme (WFP), World Health Organization (WHO), United Nations Children's Fund (UNICEF), Food and Agricultural Organization (FAO), International

Labour Organization (ILO). It is particular as it is a joint UNDP-Yemeni government program[6] seeking to integrate all its elements within Yemeni governmental or non-governmental structures—the UNDP merely playing a supportive role in the country's effort to deal with poverty. This scope is shown by the fact that the poverty alleviation and employment generation program is housed in a building apart from UNDP premises, staffed with UNDP personnel, international experts hired for the purpose, as well as government employees sent by their administration. The National Program objectives themselves are embodied in four sectoral development programs: Social Development, Agricultural Development, Social Infrastructure Development, and Industrial Development. The UNDP-led program includes two types of intervention: building a national consensus and developing programs. As is generally the case, its format is rather complex. It has four components:[7]

- A national policy framework, including the establishment of a National Committee for Social Safety Nets (NCSSN), coming under the supervision of the Ministry of Insurance and Social Affairs; a Poverty Information Monitoring System (PIMS) to be implemented by the Central Statistical Office of the Ministry of Planning and Development; a National Action Plan for Poverty Eradication (NAPPE); and the Yemen Human Development Report, published in 1998, under the responsibility of the Ministry of Planning and Development.

- Labor policies and systems, which cover the establishment of a Labor Market Information System hosted by the Ministry of Insurance and Social Affairs and serving to establish a task network and support the restructuring and reinforcement of Regional Employment Offices; the strengthening of the Human Resources Development Unit of the Ministry of Planning and Development, and the enhancement of the National Program for Productive Families managed by the Ministry of Insurance and Social Affairs.

- The development of small enterprises and micro-finance, covering two dimensions: on the one hand, productive employment through the delivery of micro-finance and small enterprise support services, as a complement to the existing Small Enterprise Development Unit pertaining to the Industrial Bank of Yemen, and to the Social Fund set up by the World Bank. This program should constitute the main access line to credit by the poor. On the other hand, the creation of an enabling environment for small enterprises and geared to their 'institutional normalization.' This component primarily serves the 'informal sector,' where one-third of non-agricultural workers living in rural areas find their livelihood. A similar analysis can be applied to two-thirds of non-agricultural workers living in urban areas.

- Finally, the Regional Development component, covering the establishment of an institutional framework for participatory development, the reinforcement of regional institutions' capacity in planning and implementing development projects; the drawing-up and implementation of regional development plans; the setting-up of a Regional Development Fund, and support to Aden's low-cost housing project (in cooperation with United Nations Human Settlements Programme (UNCHS/HABITAT). The Regional Development program is run in coordination with a wide range of partners from within the government and among international organization agencies (including the FAO). However, although this component is rather autonomous from the ministry structure, it ought be integrated within the new structures and processes created through the implementation of the Local Authority Law (law of decentralization) approved by parliament.

The National Action Plan (UNDP and Government of Yemen)

The global policy framework of the poverty alleviation system, as far as the track followed by the UNDP is concerned, rests on the National Action Plan for Poverty Eradication, one of the elements of the UNDP-led five-year National Poverty Alleviation and Employment Generation Program. Its status is that of a guideline for government institutional reform, organization and functioning, so as to set up a 'poor-focused' type of governmental institution.

The NAPPE is still at an early stage: it exists on paper, drawn up by a team of international experts, and is presently being discussed by a technical committee made up of members of ministries, representatives of associations, and international consultants. Its goals are to provide general and specific orientations for concrete anti-poverty actions and intervention measures; to raise public awareness and political commitment regarding the poverty challenges Yemen is facing; and to facilitate identification of resources to fund the most urgent projects according to priorities. Some of its policies and components should be included in the second five-year plan (2001–2005) (Al-Saqour 1999b). In its final draft, the NAPPE presents itself as an operational plan articulating strategies, priorities, issues, determining factors, goals, beneficiary groups, and policy components into a complex matrix guiding action plans.

The NAPPE constitutes the operational arm of the Poverty Policy Framework outlined in a strategic paper prepared by the chief technical advisor of the program (Al-Saqour 1999a). This document analyzes the problem of poverty in Yemen and its causes; it provides statistics and lists the most affected groups along with the type of poverty they are facing and its determining factors. It also delineates poverty reduction policies according to three tracks. The first is the social welfare sphere—involving social safety nets, community-based development policies, subsidy and credit, upgrading, micro-enterprise business policy, and social information and social survey. The second track is focused on human capital—including social policies, education, training, population policies, as well as the 'culture of poverty' and empowerment policies. The third track is the economic approach—consisting of macroeconomic and microeconomic policies, taxation, investment, expenditures, wages and employment, informal sector and regional development. Clearly, all three of these tracks are intertwined and complementary.

The Social Safety Nets (Government of Yemen and Various Donors)

Social Safety Nets refer to a variety of measures, programs, and institutions that contribute in different ways to alleviate the various forms of poverty in the short-, medium-, and/or long-term. All of them are supposed to be fitted into Yemeni government policies, budgets, and routines, although they are, perhaps in an increasing way, dependent upon external formulation and funding.

'Social safety net' is a phrase stemming from poverty analysis and alleviation terminology drawn up since the beginning of the 1990s, and more specifically from the realization of the negative impact of structural reforms on poverty. Their existence is contingent upon the designation of poverty as a phenomenon within the specific context of globalization in the last decade. In fact, when poverty alleviation was still not a goal in itself in Yemen (as in many other countries) but was implicitly incorporated into a wider framework for development, social progress, and fight against 'backwardness,' there was no such term as social safety net. The former policy led by the government, although neither explicitly formulated as a poverty-alleviating one, nor formally called 'safety net,' typically consisted of subsidies on staple foods and basic social services,[8] cash transfers, which could be received directly or through charitable associations, or as *zakat* redistribution during the month of Ramadan, and expenditures on social sectors and government employment. Today all of these are considered as inadequate, either in their conception or in their implementation, since the government cannot—or is perceived as no longer being able to—sustain them. Moreover, structural adjustment requires a reduction of public expenses, and the ideological climate has changed from a state-led developmental approach to a more privatized and pluralistic set-up. Former 'social safety nets' are being drastically restructured, not to say dismantled, to be replaced by a set of seven programs,[9] some new, some already in place but being fit into the overall framework and covering most of the aspects listed in the first track above.

The first program is the Social Welfare Fund established in 1996 and managed by the Ministry of Insurance and Social Affairs. This fund distributes financial support and cost-exemption cards to legally defined categories of individuals, mainly women without male support or families, whose main expected breadwinner is disabled, and unable to earn an income. Entitlement to these minimal funds is supposed to be determined after a social inquiry has been made. The main funding sources for this program are the government, zakat, private donations, as well as external grants.

The second program is the Social Fund for Development created in 1997 at the initiative of the World Bank, with the aim of supporting employment generation, small-scale income-generating projects, community and social development, and associational activities. Its main backers are the International Documentary Associations (IDA) and the Arab Fund for Social and Economic Development, the Dutch government, the Organization of Petroleum Exporting Countries (OPEC), the United States Agency for International Development (USAID), the European Commission (EC), and the Yemeni government. The Social Fund has mainly financed micro-enterprise development, equipment for community schools and clinics, and women's literacy training.

The third social safety net is the Public Works Program established in 1996 for a period of four years with the support of the World Bank. Its main purpose is to create employment and income opportunities for low-skilled workers.

The fourth program, already mentioned, is the National Poverty Alleviation and Employment Generation Program supported by the UNDP.

The fifth program is part of the Ministry of Insurance and Social Affairs, called the National Program for Productive Families. Funded by public monies (and in 1999–2000 with a UNDP contribution), it focuses on training beneficiaries (in this case, mostly women) chosen from among the welfare recipients most liable to benefit from such training and able to provide for their own needs through work.

The sixth component, which is not really a program as such, consists of NGO activities. This issue is covered in the second part of this paper.

Finally, the seventh safety net is the Small-Scale Credit Units launched through local associations.

A centralized body has been planned[10] by the poverty alleviation and employment generating program in order to coordinate specific poverty alleviation structures and programs: the National Committee for Social Safety Nets (NCSSN). It should allow for the improvement of current policies and projects, eliminate redundant work, increase local participation, gather and circulate information, and also undertake planning and evaluation (Al-Saqour 1999c). The NCSSN is made up of two groups: the first brings together dignitaries and prominent leaders who stand for moral and political commitment, whereas the second is entrusted with administration, follow-up, technical decisions and daily tasks. The whole structure comes under the supervision of the Ministry of Insurance and Social Affairs, but the president of the NCSSN is the prime minister. At the governorate level, the NCSSN is represented by steering committees headed by governors and gathering representatives from the Ministry of Insurance and Social Affairs, the Social Fund for Development, the Labor Union, and civil society. International experts are to be involved for a one-year period in building up its structure. In the document prepared in order to set up this institution (Al-Saqour 1999c), it appears that the understanding of social safety nets is wider than the field defined more narrowly in the policy framework outline.

A comment may be made concerning beneficiaries and coverage of social safety nets: the most dynamic schemes, that of the Social Fund for Development in its micro-enterprise development component, and that of micro-credit and small enterprise development address population groups enjoying entrepreneurial assets, that is resources to invest, skills, but also sufficient self-esteem and positive representations of themselves and the environment. This is to say that these programs do not target or prioritize the poorest of the poor. The latter are assumed to be taken care of by the welfare fund, that is by cash transfers amounting at the end of 1999 to one sack of flour a month per family. These transfers are formally restricted to families, most often to women-headed households earning no other revenue (including from begging), a condition that is deeply flawed considering the dismal level of the amount handed out. Any additional revenue leads to the cancellation of the right to welfare. Thus, the most wretched of society are caught in a poverty trap. Starting in 1998–99, the Ministry of Insurance and Social Affairs launched extensive social surveys to establish a revised (and extended) list of beneficiaries, and to follow up on their socioeconomic condition so as to avoid undue transfers.

Social assistance schemes addressing so-called 'structural poverty' prove themselves unable to pull the poorest, most deprived, and helpless categories out of poverty. Individuals considered able to work, especially women, are supposed to be led to find employment or, under certain conditions, to follow training programs such as those conducted by the Productive Family Program. The latter has been running for quite a number of years (since 1988 in North Yemen), and now covers both the urban-based North and the rural-based South, with up to eighteen different branches to train women in skills other than the traditional sewing and knitting. This scheme is particularly interesting as it attempts to draw assisted families out of severe deprivation into productive activities and is unique in bridging the institutional gap between, on the one hand, the 'recoverable poor'—through employment, credit, and small enterprise development schemes, and, on the other hand, the 'irrecoverable poor' kept within charitable set-ups that have little chance to transform their material and social conditions. Standing somewhere between welfare and incitement to productive activity, it is starting to coordinate its actions with the Social Fund for Development in order to enhance the integration level of its beneficiaries into the labor market and find outlets for the products of its training workshops. But it was plagued with a lack of funds due to a dramatic rise in the poverty rate that was left unmatched by a similar increase in resources. In 1999–2000, it benefited from a UNDP grant for the first time.

However, social safety nets suffer from their budget and social limitations, including their dependency upon conditional foreign funding in the face of the major phenomenon that poverty represents in Yemen. The anti-begging campaign launched in Sana'a a few years back is a good example of these constraints: the beggars, taken off the streets, have been housed separately in two government-rented houses for men and women; whereas the children have been sent to a home used as an alternative for youth serving a prison term and where they can benefit from a basic education and some professional training. Thus, beggars depend upon low social support from the government since nothing is really being done in terms of their reintegration into social and economic life or for their health care. Their only way out for now is if a relative guarantees—by offering to support them—that they will not resort to begging again.

Limits to the efficiency of social safety nets in tackling poverty should not be considered only from a quantitative point of view. Rather, one should wonder whether palliative measures can ever replace structural redistributive reforms in altering the mechanisms creating and perpetuating poverty. Furthermore, the poverty alleviation system itself generates biases that reduce its capacity to fulfil its publicly claimed goals.

Information and Competition

An overview of the poverty alleviation system reveals some of its main weaknesses. Primary among them is the fragmentation of this systerm. The system aims at reaching the local level, more precisely the target groups identified through various surveys and studies conducted by either international organizations (such as the Poverty Information and Monitoring System), research centers (often depending either on the same organization, or on government institutions), or ministries. In recent years, the Ministry of Insurance and Social Affairs has conducted extensive social surveys to identify the rightful beneficiaries of its welfare system. The Ministry of Planning and Development, and particularly the Central Statistical Organization, has conducted comprehensive surveys aimed at measuring poverty either directly or indirectly. Two large-scale household budget surveys were conducted in 1992 and 1998, which are supposed to serve as a main basis for interventions and follow-up of poverty and poverty alleviation measures.

However, among different institutions, data is seldom collected on comparable premises or following similar methodologies, and consequently, the findings show many discrepancies. Various criteria are used by government services, donors, and organizations to select their target groups and the local bodies they wish to support. The 'poor' counted by the World Bank to provide statistics on poverty in Yemen (head-count index and related indicators) are not the same as those considered as such by

Economic and Social Commission for West Asia (ESCWA) or the UNDP, for example, that both use a different method to define and measure poverty and thus come up with different results (Table 1). The basis used by the social services of the Ministry of Insurance and Social Affairs is more social than statistical, since it takes into consideration both family income and whether or not the household includes potential male breadwinners: as in other Arab countries, the beneficiaries are first and foremost widows or divorced women.

Groups or individuals eager to make funding requests find it difficult to get proper information and a clear knowledge of what is required from them, or even to understand what is the rationale of donors or government offices, why several schemes may cover a limited area, while other areas in the country are totally neglected. Similar to a market in its functioning, this rather opaque situation feeds a competition where the social capital of needy groups (including sometimes their capacity to pay for intermediaries) and their access to information (often kept secret), play a more crucial role than the real needs or 'capacities' repeatedly advocated. Running from office to office, maintaining the necessary social ties, and attempting to seize all opportunities are very time-consuming tasks. And small organizations, especially the newly established ones, tend to spend more time trying to access support funds than building their project on the ground. In other cases, the capacity of local notables to forward their demands does result in a project being implemented. But since the running of projects or the provision of personnel for a school or a health center depend on yet another administration, the infrastructures may remain unused until they become dilapidated or obsolete.[11] Fragmentation of information, schemes, and institutions further tend to discriminate between organizations established in main cities, or between people who have access to the power circles (through tribal ties or relatives in high administrative offices) and those who do not. Local associations may afford a unique location close to their constituencies, but NGOs, as organizations linked to the international scene need to have their main office close to international organizations and ministries. And such a requirement takes away a significant portion of their budget (cost of an office and a guest house for personnel, trips to and from the field, etc.) and draws them far away from their operational field.

The other logical weakness is that of coordination and consistency. The local offices of ministries and government schemes are supposed to cooperate in a given place and to coordinate with local non-governmental organizations (branches of international NGOs or Yemeni associations) and community representatives on common areas of interest and intervention. However, their different logics sometimes prevent smooth cooperation, and there have been many cases of tensions and even entrenched warfare. For example, in one location, registration of associations at the local office of the Ministry of Insurance and Social Affairs is outright blocked if the board does not accept representatives of the ruling political party among its members. And this is despite the fact that the Social Fund for Development demands formal registration in order to back a funding request. Or, in another case, authorization from the local representative of the Ministry of Health has proved very difficult to obtain, although an international NGO project implemented by Yemeni NGOs had been previously approved by the Ministry of Planning and Development. In rural areas, training programs for social workers of various types sometimes result in producing skilled but unemployed individuals, as, in times of budget cuts, the Ministry of Civil Service tends to become a besieged fortress, granting positions to well-connected applicants only.[12]

The issue of coordination leads to the question of the prospects for networking Yemeni associations into a coherent social and civil fabric, with a stronger potential for action than single unaffiliated associations. However, the context and the overall scheme favor competition and fragmentation over cooperation, thereby weakening this potential.

The Role of Yemeni Associations in Poverty Alleviation

Associations, and more generally civil society organizations are not new phenomena in Yemen. Popular charitable associations distributing alms to the poor, literary circles, professional syndicates, women's organizations, migrant groups based on common origin, and local development associations or cooperatives are found across the country, and have existed since the early decades of the twentieth century (see, among others, Beatty, Al-Madhaji, and Detalle 1996). The 1990s represent a turning point in their number, role and diversity for mainly three types of reasons. First, the context of unification deepened the contact between various legacies and experiences. Second, the formal institutional founding of liberalism and pluralism created a constitutional—and somewhat legal—framework for associations of all kinds. Third, the set-up of structural adjustment and, with it, poverty alleviation constituted a powerful lever for the blossoming of bodies of various types entrusted with implementation, organization, local relations, etc.

Associations in Yemen: A Mixed Category

The number of associations has dramatically grown in Yemen in recent years. No official statistics are available yet on their current number. But a major survey sponsored by the Social Fund for Development is being conducted by the Ministry of Insurance and Social Affairs and should lead to the creation of a detailed database. Some researchers and organizations have also attempted to create databases of narrower scope: thematically or geographically. Sources, including the administration most involved, agree on a total of around 2,500 non-governmental bodies registered by the Ministry of Insurance and Social Affairs, as compared to a few hundred some years ago, and only a handful three decades ago. This increase can be linked to several factors. The major one is undoubtedly the fact that the 1991 constitution of the unified republic allows pluralism and free association within democratic structures. There is also the fact that the structural adjustment program created a demand for Yemeni NGOs serving as 'grass roots' and 'civil society' partners for international organizations that provide them with financing schemes.

However, this official statement and the objective facts the latter covers should be examined more closely. The first issue concerns the types of organizations that are registered as associations. According to Al-Harazi (1998), whose typology we will use—without totally adhering to it—Yemeni associations can be classified into four kinds:

- Social associations: they are involved in issues that can be considered both social and political in nature, such as social affairs, family, and human rights.
- Professional syndicates and unions, most powerful among which are the teachers' unions. The latter's role in poverty alleviation is undoubted, since one of their major struggles has centered on the level of wages, which, in most cases, does not allow teachers to live above the poverty line. Also included in this category are student unions and that of journalists, medical doctors, pharmacists, and lawyers. Al Harazi places the Women's Union in this type, although they seem better placed among social associations.
- Trade unions and syndicates, which are very numerous when the professional, local, and establishment branches are all taken into consideration.

Their total number approximates two thousand. Interference by central authorities appears to have prevented the General Union of Workers' Syndicates of the Republic from playing a significant role regarding workers' demands and slows the process of issuing a law for these bodies or holding elections in the union. The local sections, on the other hand, continue to show commitment and resistance on the part of the workers.

- Welfare and cooperative associations, which include three sub-types: the generalist welfare associations, the local associations, based in a governorate or a district; and the very small ones, based in an urban neighborhood or a commune. According to Al Harazi, they cover various types of activities, such as purely charitable work, more specialized ones such as for the disabled, hearing- or speech-impaired, the Red Crescent, and finally a "miscellaneous" category, including handicrafts, housing, consumption, agricultural, medical, and fishermen's associations.

In Al Harazi's classification, what would be called 'NGOs' in the definition we put forth in note one, seems to be missing or ill-suited to the categories of "cooperative and charitable associations" and "social associations." This problem reflects the novelty of the phenomenon coupled with their international funding; neither allows an accurate definition of their outline and place within the overall set-up in Yemen. Types of associations that appeared after the unification of Yemen are also missing in Al Harazi's classification. These were strengthened during the political crisis of 1992–94, and probably make up the most politicized associations defending the foundation of civil society, democratization, and defence of human rights. According to Thaira Shalan (1999), these are, more than other types, subject to pressure, if not downright harassment from central authorities. Consequently, after the 1994 civil war, some centers and institutes advocating human rights and democratization did not register with the Ministry of Insurance and Social Affairs. Wishing to escape its control and the lack of autonomy it entails, they preferred to register instead with the Ministry of Culture or unions. Usually, such institutes and centers do not take the status of associations but consider themselves as consultancy, expert, information, or training structures.

Some associations (and probably even the majority according to main sources) are offshoots of government or political parties and linked to some components of the state apparatus through clientelistic ties, which jeopardize their autonomy and tend to determine their positions, actions, and relationships with other associations. The government actually created some associations so as to undermine the activities and credibility of pre-existing ones and to put forth a discourse different from that of potentially more 'subversive' organizations. In other cases, there is evidence that members of official parties or security forces have joined associations in large numbers in order to alter the ballots, influence the votes, and/or to know what is being said. This seems to play a role in the associations' weak democratic character.

Local associations that are formally registered are often limited in scope—to the implementation of one micro-project in a village for instance. They are also likely to be closer to the local population and to the expression of their needs and are therefore more participatory than others engaged in a wider range of activities. Some of these associations, however, do cover a wide gamut of activities and stand for real social stakes, such as the association for the defense of old Sana'a. Yet, others are local branches of associations found nationwide, such as the *islah* (the major opposition party, with an 'Islamist' agenda) Charitable Association, or the Hail Said (Yemen's major industrialist) Productive Families Charitable Association. Local associations include local professional defense groups, defending citizen's interests (for fishermen and farmers, for example) but also types of cooperative groupings seeking access to government support or group-purchasing of tools or supplies. They also cover 'investment' associations, whose activity is to gather under the patronage of one or several individuals the savings and gold of families in order to invest them and distribute the benefits to stakeholders. Considering the risks involved, their low rate of profitability, and the rumours of embezzlement or outright robbery that circulate about these projects, it would seem that the reputation of 'investment associations' is somewhat tarnished. 'Community committees' make up a special kind of local association in the sense that they may be formed for a limited purpose and time period and are closer to a tailor-made local mobilizing movement than an association per se.

The case of charitable associations is interesting as it is probably the one that developed the most in recent times. Interviews show that the legal possibility of registering and the chance to get support from the Ministry of Insurance and Social Affairs have prompted many individuals to set up *jama'yat* in order to grant a formal framework to their charitable activities or social objectives. Local notables are setting up associations that distribute grants collected from merchants to the poor of their area. Middle- or upper-class women organize training or hobby activities for poor women in city quarters, or decide to set up services among population groups suffering from injustice and marginalization. Some of them are effectively 'Ramadan associations'—as they are sometimes contemptuously called—since they distribute food and cash to the poor only during the holy fasting month. Yet, others do play an active role in implementing development and poverty alleviation projects at the national level and have the required connections to donors to obtain financial support and escape a purely charitable agenda. It is typically the case of the already mentioned *islah* or the Hail Said associations.

Many Yemeni associations stem from local notability or interest groups not always reflecting the real demands of the population, while they may actually be serving their needs. Some, however, can be considered as community-based or grass roots, even though participatory processes are often limited in their midst. The first task of many associations wishing to foster a participatory process, as a means of empowerment and reinforced legitimacy, is to reach out to villages, raise awareness about needs and means to improve a situation, then try to convince the locals to use their services, and also to participate in their activities. As far as I know, the most active in this regard are women's associations and those established for marginalized groups, perhaps because they formulate their needs also in terms of social integration and access to rights. Overall, the associational form still seems too young in Yemen for participatory and grass roots movements to emerge spontaneously in this shape. Social demands are still mainly conveyed through more clientelistic/paternalistic channels: people would turn to the local *shaykh* or a charitable association instead of organizing themselves to further their demands.

The Legal and Political Framework

It is often argued that the confusion felt among the different categories of associations would be solved if a law would clarify the matter. The present law, ruling the status of associations, dates back to 1963 (in North Yemen), which has allegedly become inadequate since unification in 1990 and since the new phase of democracy and pluralism (Shalan 1999).[13] It is apparently not compatible with the unified constitution of 1991, revised in 1994, that grants freedom of expression, political pluralism, and freedom of the press and association. This legal vacuum points to the huge legislative work required in the changing environment of the nineties, not only in relation to the overall national setting (unification, pluralism, civil war of 1994, etc.) but also regarding the many political interests at stake and the specific structural adjustment toll. Decree 18 of 1994 covers the professional syndicates, but neither the unions nor the associations. In 1998, a bill on charitable associations and foundations was proposed by the Ministry of Insurance and Social Affairs, which forwarded another version of it to the World Bank. The draft has been met with criticism and has raised many debates, mainly since the associations felt that a lot of its articles gave the government the right to interfere in their activities and jeopardized their freedom. In 1998, a consultation round was set up between the three parties involved—the government, the associations, and the World Bank—but no agreement could be reached until the end of 2000.

In 1995, a law on cooperative (agricultural, housing, and handicrafts) associations and unions was passed after much discussion but less turmoil, and this is probably due to the fact that the case of cooperatives is much more straightforward and involves less political stakes. It should be added that a local authority law concerning associations, often called 'governance law' was approved at the beginning of 2000. It provides a framework for development management at the local level (governorate and districts) and seeks to increase the transparency, efficiency, and coordination of, among other things, poverty alleviation schemes, mainly through increased local participation. It is not yet clear how this new 'governance' framework will be incorporated with local safety net committees, local administration, central government, and finally associations. Moreover, the question on how long this formal setting will take to be implemented and alter procedures and functionings remains.

Whatever the shortcomings of the legal framework are, some of the main problems and limitations of associations may come from enforcing the constitution and the practical relevance of the laws. One problem concerns registration, which has been decentralized and controlled by governorate branches since 1992. The criteria used for registration and the fate of each applications differs widely from one place to another—not to mention the long delays until registrations are entered in the central file and made effective. In fact, some associations have been operating for years without a license and some are not required to abide by the provisions of the law, which is considered arbitrary and generates lack of trust from associations (Beatty, Al-Madhaji and Detalle 1996).

Furthermore, and as Thaira Shalan (1999) mentions, since the state constantly attempts to control NGOs to take away their independence and seeks to create divisions within organizations it does not approve of, including political parties, simply a new law seems insufficient to grant associations freedom of existence and activity. According to the same author, groups affiliated to a political party allied with the central authorities obtain the right to register, whereas those wishing to establish an independent organization, association, or league do not. Requests are also refused when certain personalities on the board or among the founders are not agreeable to the Ministry of Insurance and Social Affairs, and when applicants refuse to remove them from their list of members. Shalan notes the fact that some association members consider that the Ministry of Insurance and Social Affairs acts essentially as an intelligence agency, aiming to infiltrate their work and favoring the establishment of other organizations to undermine real NGO and voluntary activities. She also asserts that when the government manages to benefit from international subsidies, it distributes these funds to certain organizations at the expense of others and keeps the major part to finance its own activities or for personal use.

On another level, the law seems unable to bring transparency within associations. In many of these, heads are not elected but appointed, or elections have not taken place for a long time. Shalan states that association presidents generally control the resources available to the associations. The amounts are unknown to the members and no reports are published and delivered to the constituencies; only donors enjoy this privilege. The absence of internal democratic procedures seems to plague a vast majority of Yemeni associations, and far from being related only to a matter of 'capacity,' this appears to be intrinsically linked to the very nature and *raison d'être* of many of them. As already mentioned, for some of these associations, this attitude has defensive purposes, as they feel threatened by being taken over by 'official members' from central administration.

Without questioning Thaira Shalan's assertions, which are in fact validated by other sources as well as by some of the cases I came across and by some information I received during interviews, I do not have the means to verify cases of outright pressure, manipulation, or fund embezzlement. However, it seems important to suggest some background elements and analysis.

The fact that the state, as it fights against the centrifugal potential of associations, tries to harness them to its ends and to enhance its capacity through civil society institutions, forms part of the history of North Yemen (Chaudhry 1997). Attempts by the state to control nascent or established civil society organizations is in fact, a rather expectable phenomenon in countries enjoying only limited democracy and submitted to internal and external pressure for political liberalization. In present-day Yemen, it also has to be related to the turning point of the 1994 civil war, which generated a heavy strengthening of state domination and a consolidation of its control over potentially dissident political forces. The first few years following unification have been characterized by a pluralist balance, which has allowed the development of independent civil and political forces. This situation also made it possible to make demands for greater political participation, a fairer allocation of resources, and a constituency for social welfare, women's rights, unionism, secularism, and a new social contract; in other words, the re-emergence of civil society after many years of authoritarian rule, as shown by the fact that numerous regional conferences and meetings were held at the height of the crisis (Rougier 1999, Carapico 1998). According to Rougier, the political pluralism Yemen got after unity may be, firstly, the consequence of a social pluralism seeking official recognition; this social movement could exploit the potentialities offered by the birth of a unified territory previously impossible to imagine (109). The need to strengthen the institutions of civil society was mainly emphasized by smaller parties with little or no role in formal ruling institutions (Carapico 1998).

This fine balance was totally destabilized by the social and economic crisis of 1992–93, and then destroyed by the 1993–94 political crises, and the strong momentum in favor of the respect for the rule of law was muffled. The drift away from empowerment of civil society, as planned in the constitution and claimed throughout the popular mobilizations of 1993–94, is linked to the campaign of retaliation and the offensive led by the northern forces against the southern-based Socialist Party. As a result, a special regime void of any legal reference was set up. Such veering away also has to do with the fact that the defeated South, more than victorious North Yemen, carries a legacy of institutions, civic commitment, peaceful civil movements, and organizations partly crushed in the process. It is difficult to contend that, compared to the 1990–93 period, democracy has been losing ground since the 1994 events, and that the regime has evolved toward more authoritarianism.[14] For Carapico, "civic potential lies in the very breadth and diversity of models and ideologies alive in body politics" (1998: 243). Thus, she continues, "in Yemen's contemporary political society, a wide array of historically rooted political tendencies vie for seats in parliament and for influence in the courts, the schools, the intellectual imagination, and public opinion."

In other respects, and whatever the evidence of actually unlawful or abusive practices toward associations may be, discourse on them is significant as well. The whole backgrounds depict the fact that the law is clearly not the major implementing power superseding other interests, but is nevertheless becoming a moral reference for action. Certainly, as in many countries in the Arab world, pluralism has become a reality in Yemen, while effective participation and "real" democracy are still wanted (Korany and Noble 1998). Therefore, pluralism tends to offer an ideal ground for factional strife. But the new "political correctness" requires an unavoidable legal—and legitimizing—cover, just as reference to democracy has acquired a very highly symbolic value in Yemen as in the rest of the region (Brynen, Korany, and Noble 1998). It remains that in a period of liberalization and weak political accountability the availability of financial support only increases competition between the various government and non-government parties involved. It thus comes as no surprise that the law may be used for the defense of private and/or political rather than 'neutral' collective interests.

NGOs' Role According to External Assistance Program Documents

The description of the poverty alleviation system gives the impression of a complex combination of many elements. One of the questions raised is the effective functioning of the articulation between these components, knowing that their interests are not necessarily the same. However, looking more closely, it also appears that it is highly concentrated around two poles: the government and international organizations. Certainly, with regards to national policies (subsidies, employment, and social spending), most of the government's old ways of tackling poverty have been weakened. The ministries and department in charge of poverty alleviation have, on the contrary, received a boost. Moreover, newly created bodies tend to strengthen the Ministry of Planning and Development in particular, and to a lesser extent the Ministry of Insurance and Social Affairs. Ironically, when one hears of decentralization and state withdrawal from the social realm, the main poverty alleviation programs tend to increase the governmental institutions' capacity to intervene.

This impression is supported by the fact that, although the World Bank states that "collaboration with development partners is essential" and that "the strategy should maximize the potential synergies of joint or coordinated efforts with other development agents, including private enterprise, NGOs, and official development assistance" (World Bank 1999), the Bank only mentions two types of partnership: first and foremost, the one with the government, including building the capacity of public administration, a task, which fits with the Bank's mission; and, secondly, that with substantial donors. As far as the Bank's participatory approach goes, NGOs are also mentioned within the Country Strategy paper in terms of an "inclusion of those affected by a proposed project or policy in the design phase at the community or stakeholder level," and also with respect to the "delegation of an appropriate level of responsibility to local stakeholders in implementation."[15]

Turning to UNDP cooperation with the Yemeni government for poverty alleviation, several statements have been made concerning the role of NGOs (Al-Saqour 1999a). The first one asserts:

> NGOs and other society institutions, at this period, are not fully established and incapable of supporting and administering any sort of target in their localities. They need assistance to expand the provision of welfare service delivery, and to build their capacity before handing over any kind of anti-poverty activities to them (17).

Further on, the same paper notes that, although NGOs are "quite active in the area of in kind-type social assistance programs," the lack of coordination and complementarity between NGO programs, individual initiatives, and government welfare programs, as well as their lack of cooperation and resources, hinders NGOs' participation in social safety nets.

In the section "Development Cooperation" of its Country Strategy Paper for Yemen, the European Commission states its intention to focus on "implementation of sectoral reform programs in human resources-related fields, such as vocational training and health, contribute to poverty alleviation and stimulate economic activity in Yemen, especially at the small and medium enterprise (SME) level, through helping set up a Social Fund and a Social Safety Net together with other donors and concentrate more aid on gender- and women-specific issues" (EC 1999). Looking at the chart titled "Community Contribution toward schemes carried out by NGOs," one notices that the EC has steadily supported NGO projects in Yemen, although irregularly in terms of number of projects (one in 1990 and seven in 1993) and total funds granted (with a marked increase in 1998). The EC is the largest multilateral sponsor of

NGO activity in Yemen. Since the beginning of cooperation with the country, 4 percent of funds allocated have gone to NGOs. The associations receiving this aid and in charge of the projects, however, are all international NGOs from Europe.

On the other hand, the main bilateral donors (the Netherlands, Japan, Germany, and Great Britain) all show a strong commitment to support grass roots projects, either through funds specifically earmarked for them, or on sectoral budget lines.

External Assistance and the Role of NGOs: A Case Study of the Year 1997

In a document mentioning the level and destinations of external assistance from all sources to Yemen for 1997 (UNDP 1998), it can be seen that the level of aid allocated to Yemeni NGOs amounted to 0.29 percent of the total for 1997. It cannot be known whether this aid was received directly, indirectly (that is, through another NGO, for example), or whether some further distribution took place downstream. But the rest of the assistance went either to the implementation departments of the ministries involved, or directly to authorities, organizations, institutes, and companies, depending on the donor government.

The same document provides interesting details about the situation of NGOs regarding external assistance for the same year, which can be considered as a relevant case study since it witnesses to the setting-up of the basic institutional tools for structural adjustment. One can notice (see Table 2) that the areas in which Yemeni associations have been funded are typically linked to women (education, training, awareness programs), children (education, training, prison, disability), and refugees. Although supported NGOs' projects do not directly pertain to the health sector, some of the activities do. However, one important remark should be made concerning poverty alleviation: clearly, associations are supported only in activities related to human poverty—which used to be called 'basic needs'—along with some involvement in vocational training in the prospect of improving living standards and incomes. But they are not funded by external assistance to operate in productive sectors, such as industry and agriculture, or in trade and transportation. This can be understood as reflecting either the fact that these sectors are mainly the domain of cooperatives, or the lack of popular initiative in these sectors—but it can also be seen as some kind of exclusion of NGOs from these areas mandated by donors.

A rather clear division of labor thus appears between, on the one hand, the main economic actors including government and the private sector and, on the other hand, the social realm of associations, circumscribed in its scope and means. Even in the social sectors, NGOs remain a marked minority in terms of funds and number of projects. From the data available in the UNDP document for 1997, which can be considered as rather comprehensive, it can be concluded that the role of local NGOs in poverty alleviation remains rather small in Yemen.

The Mediation of International NGOs

What actually comes out of interviews, is that the relationships between donors and local NGOs, are to a large extent, supposed to be established through intermediary bodies, be it the Social Fund for Development, other micro-finance schemes, or more specifically, international NGOs. The latter, whose number, now reaching around twenty-five in Yemen, has witnessed rapid growth in recent years, are among the main agents implementing poverty alleviation programs and projects. They are also entrusted with enhancing community organizations, reinforcing representation in these local structures, teaching their staff the procedures for setting up a project and accounting books, etc. Some capacity-building seminars have been organized directly by donors, and funds have been distributed either directly or, more importantly, through international NGOs. In the context of structural weakness of local associations, international NGOs come as the main link and route to access these funds, sometimes in a patronizing fashion, and in other cases, in subcontractual relationships, where international NGOs are also expected to monitor the use of funds when the local counterpart, as is often the case, has little experience in this matter. Differences can be observed between the policies and practices of international NGOs in their dealings with local associations, according to their level of financial dependency or autonomy,[16] which, to a large extent, determines their ability to apply their own programs and methods or that of their donors. No more than five or six international NGOs presently operating in Yemen finance their activities and overhead expenses from their own resources, and can therefore afford to follow a rather independent agenda. The others are heavily dependent upon donors' funds, and can be considered as implementing agencies rather than 'real' NGOs. The financial autonomy versus dependency of international NGOs affects the sustainability of the local activities they support. Whenever the latter depends on short-term funding (as it is the case for European

NGOs financed through the European Commission for Humanitarian Operations (ECHO), the emergency fund of the EC), programs involving local partner associations run for a number of months and —have no choice but to manage the financial ups and downs to which they are submitted.

One of the main biases of this set-up is that it prompts competition at several levels: between international NGOs competing for funds; between local NGOs also competing for funds as well as access to information about international NGOs, intermediary bodies, and donors; and finally competition between local and international NGOs, the former often feeling discriminated against and suffering from a lack of trust and credibility. A few Yemeni associations have succeeded in building rewarding relationships with international organizations and NGOs. They are those whose names are well known and are regularly invited to international events and seminars. They enjoy a good reputation built not only on their actual capacity as associations, but also on the social capital prominent members have managed to acquire because of their own social and family connections. Concerned with their own survival, international NGOs turn out to be more or less committed to actually building the capacity of local associations or organizations at the grass roots level so that the latter are able to carry on their activities after the former have left. The interviews I conducted with Yemeni associations often convey the feeling that they are constrained in a relationship of dependency owing to their alleged lack of experience. Furthermore, they claim being indiscriminately suspected of lacking transparency and accountability, while other poverty alleviation agents seem to fare little better.[17] They mention being kept away from decision-making circles and fund allocation, a process that apparently takes place between international 'partners' and government institutions, with little possibility of interference, agency, let alone control or participation, from local associations. In some cases, international organizations have interfered in their local partner's activities and in the choice of their main executives (Shalan 1999). Often, they have the capacity to push NGO activity in one specific sector or another through their funding agenda. In addition, it would seem that the distance often kept between international NGOs and their 'local partners' would prevent the latter from benefiting from the former's experience and from learning from the various stages of project conception, implementation, and evaluation. These feelings were even more clearly observable in the study carried out some years ago by Oxfam on how local NGOs felt about donor support (Beatty, Al-Madhaji, and Detalle 1996).

Conclusion

Understanding the role of associations in poverty alleviation in Yemen requires taking into account, not only their technical role in implementing projects and programs, but also in a wider perspective, the room that is left for them to fight for political, civic, economic, and social rights. This is why I felt that the analyses and hypotheses presented in this paper had to include questions about politics and the overall set-up of poverty alleviation. Two main factors weigh on the capacity of Yemeni associations to significantly alter the creation and perpetuation of poverty in the country, and to fulfil the role of building a civil society: the political control they are submitted to and the position they are assigned in the 'poverty alleviation system.' Both tend to merge to offer a technical and moral vision of poverty, thereby squeezing out political analysis and solutions and curtailing in-depth changes in the economic, social, and political order.[18]

Development, within the framework of the poverty alleviation system, holds an inherent paradox. Certainly, this system provides avenues of participation, legal protection of associations' existence, and an active role for NGOs, in addition to being their main prospect for financial support. However, this set-up also imposes a conventional and restrictive framework, which has, to some extent, confiscated from alternative voices the capacity to articulate the issue of poverty and the possible solutions to it, and turned it instead into a single version that is valued as if it were a universally valid doctrine. In the midst of fierce competition for funds, tending to divert their main focus from genuine development and social change to concern about their own survival and submission to their backers' implicit and explicit views and ways, Yemeni associations are left with a mere 'subcontracting' role. They are thus encouraged to look up to donors, competing with each other, often in a rent-seeking attitude, instead of investing their energy primarily in advocating their values and catering for their constituencies' needs and demands. Hierarchical organization, fragmentation, and competition hinder rather than boost Yemeni associations' role and capacity to transform the mechanisms of creation and perpetuation of inequalities, marginalization, and poverty.

On the other hand, fighting the political control of the state appears as a necessary step in the historical construction of civil society through social movements, and Yemeni society already has quite a bit of experience in this matter. "The State does not provide a legal-institutional framework for civil society; to the contrary, civil society counteracts the military

Table 1: Basic social indicators and poverty estimates in Yemen

	Year	Unit	Value	Source
Total population living below poverty line	1998		19.1%	World Bank, World Development Report
			36.4%	1999/2000, UNDP 2000, Basic data on
	1999		37.7%	Yemen is based on national statistics.
Urban population living below poverty line	1998		36%	World Bank*, UNDP 2000,
			31.8%	Basic data on Yemen is
	1999		34%	based of national statistics.
Rural population living in poverty	1994		30%	UNDP Human Development Report
	1998		37.7%	1995, UNDP 2000, Basic data on
	1999		38.9%	Yemen is based on national statistics.
HDI Ranking	1997		148	UNDP 1999
HPI –1 Ranking	1997		78	UNDP 1999
Real GDP per capita	1997	PPP^{19} US$	810	UNDP 1999
Female real GDP per capita	1997	PPP US$	579	UNDP 1999
Male real GDP per capita	1997	PPP US$	1038	UNDP 1999
GNP per capita	1997	US$	270	World Bank 1999
Distribution of income: share of lowest 20%; share of highest 20%	1998		6%	World Bank, World Development
			49%	Report 1999/2000
Adult literacy rate (over 15 years)	1997		42.5%	UNDP 1999
Female literacy rate	1997		21%	UNDP 1999, UNDP 2000. Basic data
	1998		33.85%	on Yemen is based of national statistics.
Male literacy rate	1997		64.2%	UNDP 1999, UNDP 2000. Basic data
	1998		68.75%	on Yemen is based of national statistics.
Gross schooling rate (all levels)	1994	% of	52%	UNDP 1999, UNDP 2000. Basic data
	1998	population	59.2%	on Yemen is based on national statistics.
Access to safe water	1990–97		61%	UNDP 1999
Access to health services	1990–95	% of population	38%	UNDP 1999
Access to sanitation	1990–97		24%	UNDP 1999
Life expectancy at birth	1960	Years for 1,000	35.8	UNDP 1999, UNDP 2000.
	1997	live births	58	Basic data on Yemen is based
	1999		60.1	of national statistics.
Infant mortality	1960	per 1,000	175	UNDP Human Development
	1997	live births	75.3	report 1997, UNDP 2000.
	1998		72.7	Basic data on Yemen is based
	1999		70	of national statistics.
Rural areas	1999		73.9	
Urban areas	1999		54.4	
(Middle East)	1998		49	World Bank*
Annual population growth rate	1998		2.9%	World Bank*
Annual growth rate of labor force	1998		3.4%	World Bank*
Unemployment	1998		27–30%	Middle East Economic Survey 19/04/99

* unknown source, quoted by Volpi and Detalle 1999.
Note on the table: these are selected indicators, but other estimates exist, often conflicting with those presented above.

State," writes Sheila Carapico (1998: 252). The prospects for this social and political process to take place and for the potential of associations to develop are hopeful. This is largely because one of the major demands of the Yemeni population focuses on services, and the tradition of self-help and local mobilization are still deeply embedded in society, whatever the degree of expectation toward the state. Furthermore, extra-governmental realms, including tribes, are still alive in Yemen as an alternative to failing state institutions. Beyond the provision of technical services, a political focus and the politicization of social resistance are probably the best means for Yemeni associations to play a greater role in poverty alleviation.

Duration	Objectives of the Project
1993–97	Training women in literacy and small enterprise management skills
1993–97	Education of women in health literacy and economics to prepare them for small enterprise loans
1993–97	Protection of the cultural heritage of Yemen
1993–97	Basic education and home/community-based income opportunities for returnee girls with alternative education and vocational training
1993–97	Provide working/begging children with alternative education and vocational training
1993–97	Vocational training and educational services for women and children

Sector of Assistance	Number of Projects	
Agriculture, forestry, and fisheries	Total	NGO
	39	0

Sector of Assistance	Number of Projects	
Area Development	Total	NGO
	9	1

NGO Projects

Duration	Objectives of the Project
1993–97	Empowerment of women's groups, supporting their participation in various workshops and conferences, skill training to enable them to make decisions and income generating activities.

Sector of Assistance	Number of Projects	
Industry	Total	NGO
	8	0

Sector of Assistance	Number of Projects	
Energy	Total	NGO
	9	0

Sector of Assistance	Number of Projects	
International Trade in Goods and Services	Total	NGO
	1	0

Sector of Assistance	Number of Projects	
Domestic Trade in Goods and Services	Total	NGO
	1	0

The Poverty Alleviation System in Yemen

Sector of Assistance	Number of Projects	
Transportation	Total	NGO
	10	0
Sector of Assistance	**Number of projects**	
Communications	Total	NGO
	11	0
Sector of Assistance	**Number of Projects**	
Social Development	Total	NGO
	34	8

NGO Projects

Duration	Objectives of the Project
1993–97	Strengthening and extension of services of the Yemen Family Care Association (improve family planning)
1993–97	Institutional development and capacity building of local NGOs working with disability, especially in advocacy and networking
1993–97	Improve knowledge of children's rights, and monitoring of convention implementation
1993–97	Aid to children in prison/custody, reduce or abolish prison sentences for children, improve legal protection, support rehabilitation
1993–97	Support to the Society for the Physically Disabled, provide opportunities for integration, education, playing and social activities for disabled children
1993–97	Conference for women who played a role in the 1997 elections to draw lessons and draft a plan of action for the improvement of women's political participation
1993–97	Strengthen the capacity of Hodeidah Women's Union to offer effective services
1993–97	Improve opportunities for social and economic development of women in Aden governorate

Sector of Assistance	Number of Projects	
Health	Total	NGO
	65	1

NGO Projects

Duration	Objectives of the project
1993–97	Improve the standards of mother and child care services in one Aden clinic

Sector of Assistance	Number of Projects		
	Total		**NGO**
Disaster Preparedness	5		0

Sector of Assistance	Number of Projects		
	Total		**NGO**
Humanitarian aid and relief	26		5

NGO Projects

Duration	Objectives of the Project
1993–97	Assist refugees Living in Yemen, camp construction, health and educational services, food and nutrition, social counseling
1993–97	Basic facilities and humanitarian needs to Somali refugees, self-reliance and empowerment of women
1993–97	Rehabilitation of Shabwa drinking water sources after severe floods (2 projects)
1993–97	Oxfam activities in rural women's development, marginalized groups and readiness for emergency

(Source: UNDP 1998)

Notes

1. In 1995, Yemen was just coming out of five years of major turmoil. In May 1990, the previous two parts of the country were unified. However, the historical project stumbled on the Gulf War and its dramatic consequences for the country: a deep economic crisis. The political crisis only became worse and culminated in a civil war in May 1994. It is only after the reaffirmation of the political authority in Sana'a, then able to muffle opposition, that the social adjustment program became feasible.
2. For the purpose of this chapter, associations—formally constituted and registered as non-profit, non-governmental groupings of citizens with various types of goals or aspirations—will be distinguished from NGOs—tentatively restricted to associations engaged in development, poverty alleviation, or advocacy activities, and in contact with the 'international scene,' that is, international donors, discourses, NGOs, seminars, etc. However, the distinction is not always easy to make, as will be explained in this chapter.
3. 'Backwardness' is a term that was frequently used in the studies concerning the years before the revolution and is still very widespread among the various experts and researchers when they describe the situation of Yemen's countryside. In spite

The Poverty Alleviation System in Yemen

of its normative and value-laden character, it will occasionally be used in this chapter.

4. Significantly, the 32 percent rise in public revenue expected for 2000 as a consequence of the oil price rise was mainly allocated to raising defense spending by 101 percent. The defense budget for year 2000 shows a threefold increase over 1996, while civil service benefits from a 31 percent rise and health, education, and social services by only 14, 15, and 23 percent respectively, in marked decline over 1997 and 1998 (Middle East Economic Survey, January 31, 2000).
5. The meaning and scope of the term " community " will not be discussed extensively in this paper. However, as will be made clear, it will be used in its now conventional but largely implicit meaning of 'people living together in a given location,' regardless of whether or not they actually have common or competing interests, or feel and act as a community.
6. Support to the National Program to Alleviate Poverty was formally expressed in Ministerial Cabinet Resolution 168 of 1998. Its executive agent is the Ministry of Planning and Development, and the implementing agents are the ILO, FAO, UNIDO, and United Nations Office for Project Services (UNOPS) (Al-Saqour 1999c).
7. Most of the following elements will be mentioned again further on in the paper, as fitting within the global system.
8. Subsidized items consisted of one-third of households' average expenses on basic food commodities, which themselves absorbed an average of two-thirds of households' budgets. The reduction of subsidies on rice and sugar, which took place in 1994, and that on wheat, flour, petroleum products, electricity, and water that took place in 1995, greatly affected the purchasing power of households (Ministry of Planning and Development and UNDP 1998). Measures taken in following years had a similar impact, only increasing consumption and human poverty.
9. Some components of the more traditional health and education services organized by the government can be considered as indirect safety nets, with regard to human capital upgrading, in addition to literacy and training programs, water provision, and feeding schemes.
10. It was formally created and its tasks outlined by Ministerial Cabinet Resolution 15 of 1998.
11. In a case I came across, a rather influential mountain village succeeded in obtaining three different water distribution systems. However, none of them were working.
12. Several stories collected show the skewing of civil service recruitment toward individuals who could mobilize and pay intermediaries.
13. For more details on the association law, see Beatty, Al-Madhaji, and Detalle 1996.
14. The defense budget was to be increased by over 100 percent in 2000 compared to 1999, a threefold rise over 1996. See note 2.
15. World Bank, 1999, Country Assistance Strategy of the World Bank Group for the Republic of Yemen. Report 19073-YEM, Middle East Department, MENA.
16. According to the UNDP report quoted above (UNDP 1998), in 1997, eight international NGOs actually contributed funds for development in Yemen, mainly in the fields of health, social and human resource development, and humanitarian aid and relief. Their total contribution represented 0.32 percent of total external assistance (multilateral UN system: 76.5 percent; multilateral non-UN: 5 percent;

bilateral assistance: 18.2 percent). Multilateral UN system assistance had significantly increased over 1996, while multilateral non-UN and bilateral assistance had relatively decreased.

17. International NGOs, perhaps more than donors, prompt this bitterness, and this is for several reasons: they distribute less funds than donors and are in a position similar to that of local associations; they carry out activities that local NGOs often feel they could do just as well—or better—themselves; they are in an ambiguous position regarding the discourse they hold and the social distance/proximity they keep with local populations. Whether their personnel is made up of volunteers with low pay who remain ill-understood by the rural or marginalized groups in which they are settled, or on the contrary, display fancy life styles (cars, drivers, guards, etc.), the integration of international NGO project settings into 'local communities' is often problematic. Furthermore, international NGO project settings 'in the field' become a de facto part of local politics, all the more so when they represent stakes revolving around power and money. However, their capacity to understand their own role and to construct a vision of these stakes tends to be blurred by a number of factors, among them: their belief in 'doing good'; the cultural distance between them and remote population groups; the common assumption that local populations can actually be considered as 'communities' despite the power relationships within each 'community.'

18. According to Sheila Carapico (1998), external pressures from international partners and sponsors of Yemen, particularly the U.S., in favor of democratization and political pluralism have at best been quite minimal; their concern for stability in the peninsula and their relations with Saudi Arabia weighing more than their commitment to democratization and human rights.

19. Purchasing Power Parity: PPP dollars are an artificial monetary unit, which allows international comparisons by equalizing the purchasing power of any currency according to the level of prices in any given country.

Chapter Thirteen

NGOs in a Country Without a Government: Islamic Movements and Aspirations to Replace the State in War-torn Somalia*

Marc-Antoine Pérouse de Montclos

It is always difficult to talk about NGOs in a war-torn country, especially one in which the machinery of state has ceased to exist. Somalia provides some interesting perspectives on this situation. It has been without a government since the collapse of the Siyad Barre dictatorship in 1991. In the north of the country institutions have been set up that might pave the way for reconstruction, but the south is still mired in chaos and is regarded as an empty shell by the international community, which has recognized none of the structures that presently exist in Somalia.

In such a context, what kind of collective actor can serve the interests of civil society? Where no government exists it makes little sense to talk of NGOs, since any organization is automatically non-governmental. This is not because an NGO is defined solely in relation to the state, but because power vacuums create a basic situation in which voluntary associations are more active in performing their mission of filling gaps in the state, and in which political movements have more opportunities to consolidate their footing in society by providing public services.

From the list of existing associations and movements, we shall, at the outset, exclude the western organizations working in Somalia, and also the armed factions and warlords, whose dynamic of competition, looting, and violence, is contrary to goals of reconciliation and reconstruction. Having done this, we can distinguish two categories of voluntary associations. The first one, often financed by the Somali diaspora, has philanthropic intentions and supplements inadequate public services such as health care, food supply, education, and agricultural support. Some associations of this type emerged when humanitarian agencies arrived 'en masse,' at the time of the 1977 Ogaden War against Ethiopia. Officially, there were eighteen NGOs in Somalia in 1988. Later, many wanted a share in the largesse being dispensed in the south of the country by the United Nations operation being set up between 1992 and 1995. During that time, almost 940 local NGOs were recorded.[1] Meanwhile, in Somaliland, which was busy rebuilding an independent state in the north without the approval of the international community, a similar development occurred: Somaliland counted 493 social, non-profit-making agencies in 1998, compared to four in 1992.

In this chapter, however, we shall focus our attention on the second category of associations, which is more difficult to define. It comprises organizations that have worked out a comprehensive blueprint for society and envisage rebuilding the state on religious foundations, namely the precepts of Islam. Their purview is all-inclusive, spanning the population as a whole, and their ambition is clearly to take the place of previously functioning forms of state power. The rise of Islamism, so much deplored in other Arab countries, has here taken an unusual turn as a result of a situation, which is confused to say the least. The Washington-based United States Institute of Peace (USIP) has gone so far as to advocate reinforcing Islam in order to strengthen the institutions of civil society![2] In the light of Somalia's extremely instructive experience over the last few years, the usual questions on this subject need reformulating. The question in Somalia is not so much when and how the Islamists will take power but why they have not already done so, as the state no longer exists.

Leaving aside issues linked to charitable work, my aim is to describe the obstacles preventing a take-over by religious forces. After explaining the factors favoring the progression of the Islamists, we shall show the limitations inherent in their rise to power. The seeds of division, which triggered the breakdown of Somali society and are denounced by the cross-clan discourse of the fundamentalists, are also what is preventing an Islamic republic from emerging.[3]

The Rise of Islamism in Somalia

Ideas of holy war and an Islamic state are not new in Somalia. During the years 1899–1920, an insurrection led by Muhammad Abdulle Hassan held off the British colonialist armies in the north of the country, and subsequently assumed mythical status in the nationalist struggle for independence. During a pilgrimage to Mecca in 1893, Muhammad Abdulle Hassan had met and adopted the ideas of Muhammad bin Salah, a Sudanese *shaykh*, who, in 1887, had founded the Salahiya brotherhood.[4] He went on to oppose the laxity of the traditional brotherhoods, especially the Qadiriya, of which a leading member, Shaykh Uways bin Mohamed, was assassinated by a fanatical follower of the Salihiya, at Brava on the South Coast in 1909. Mohammed Abdulle Hassan denounced tobacco consumption, the passion for *qat,* and ancestor worship, and launched a reformist movement, which, growing from a series of raids into a military conquest, held out against the British until 1920.[5] He was given the nickname the 'mad mullah' by the colonial authorities when he returned to Berbera and refused to pay customs duties. The British are said to have let him go free on the grounds that he was mad! The name was also a reference to an insurrection, previously led by another 'mad mullah' in Afghanistan a few years before.

Less well known are the millenarist movements, which started in the south.[6] They were put down more rapidly. In 1924, Shaykh Hassan Barsane led a rising in the Shabelle against the Italian Fascists, who wanted to confiscate weapons from the people. By the end of the year, he had been defeated and he died in prison five years later. Sufi Baraki established a base in the port of Brava and welded together several religious communities or *jama'a* in the Lower Shabelle in 1923. But he was forced to withdraw to the Upper Juba, where he joined forces with Alyow al-Sarmani, the Sharif of Qorile, founded a community at Dai Dai and was killed by the Italians in 1925.

Religious extremism was reined in by the consolidation of the colonial administration and, after independence, by the emergence of a modern elite. The military coup d'état of 1969 imposed a 'socialist' dictatorship headed by Siyad Barre. He created a secular regime, which rescinded Decree no. 3 of 1962. The regime had also incorporated the Islamic *shari'a* into Somali law on the same footing as customary law. The adoption in 1972, of a Latin transcription of Somali, offended not only the other Arab League countries but also the traditional brotherhoods, which had fought against such projects during the colonial period on the grounds that they were attempts to spread Christianity. Protest was ruthlessly suppressed. In 1975, ten *'ulima's* were publicly executed for denouncing a decree granting women equal rights of inheritance.

Paradoxically enough, the communities that had most in common with the government's collectivist experiments were those set up on an Islamic rather than a clan basis, the *jama'a* of al-Berdale in the north, and Bardera, Beled Karim, and Mana Mofa in the south.[7] Repression failed, however, to prevent a radical current from emerging in the late 1970s. The Reform Society (Jama'at al-Islah) and the Islamic Youth Union (Wuhdat al-Shabab al-Islami), were patterned on the Muslim Brotherhood in Egypt (al-Ikhwan al-Muslimun). Somali students in Saudi universities founded the hardline Wahhabite Salafiya group in 1978.[8] Moreover, Shaykh Muhammad Moallin, who had been imprisoned for fifteen years by Siyad Barre, founded the People of Islam Society, known as Ahli or Jama'at Ahl al-Islam.

The removal of the dictator and the ensuing chaos gave free rein to these forces, expressed via a number of so-called *harakat* (movements). The Islamic Union (al-Ittihad al-Islami), a fusion of the smaller Salafiya and Ahli groups, emerged in 1991, when it attempted to gain control of the Adane locality. The Union, founded by 'Ali Warsame, an Isaaq, occupied the northeastern towns of Garoe and Bosaso in June 1992. It was soon driven out by the main armed faction in the area, the Somali Salvation Democratic Front (SSDF), but subsequently established a foothold in the northwest at Las Qoray, Borama, and Burao, where training camps were observed for a time. Under the command of Hassan Daher Aweys, a Hawiye Haber Gidir of Air lineage, the movement spread toward Luuq on the Ethiopian frontier in late 1992, Mogadishu's Wadajir neighbourhood in 1993, the city's northern suburb in August 1994, and Belet Huen in Hiran region in June 1995.[9] Further south, al-Ittihad established itself in Kismayo and pushed toward Merca and Qorioley in late 1999. A similar development occurred in the northwest, which had unilaterally declared its independence under the name of Somaliland. In this region, Muhammad Shaykh Osman's Somali Islamic Union Party was in conflict with the Somali National Movement (SNM), which had fought against the Siyad Barre dictatorship, and which took power in Hargeisa in 1991, while the Salafiya movement received backing from Khartoum in its struggle against 'President' Ibrahim Egal's troops at Borama.

Some of these organizations, with their militias and tribunals, have a real capacity for military action. They have carved out a place for themselves in the political arena by forming opportunistic alliances with the warlords, especially with Muhammad Farah Hassan 'Aideed' and 'Ali Mahdi in Mogadishu. The traditionalist Rally of Traditional 'Ulima's (Majma' al-'Ulima'), received the support of General 'Aideed' in its struggle against al-Ittihad, which had initially found favor with Mahdi and the Saudis. Mahdi, however, soon became wary of competition from the Islamists and eventually expelled them from north of Mogadishu. After the death of general 'Aideed' in 1996, however, his son Hussein moved closer to al-Ittihad in order to counter the Ethiopian army's incursions into Somalia. Because of their divergent interests, there was never any military co-ordination in the field. In 1999, the forces of Hussein 'Aideed' openly clashed with those of al-Ittihad at Merca, Qorioley, and Mogadishu.

Such shifting alliances ultimately raise the question of where the Islamic movements stand. Are they simply armed factions? In theory, the fundamentalists' goal is not a military one but offers a negative answer to this question. Modern fundamentalists owe their political success to three main factors: charitable work, the capacity to maintain order, and a religious-nationalistic message claiming to transcend the clan alignments that have torn Somalia apart.

Support for the Destitute

In many countries, acute deprivation is the trigger for Islamism. This is not specific to Islam: most religions often gain ground in times of war and crisis. In Kenya, for example, the famine of 1897 precipitated conversions to Christianity, since the missions have provided what today would be called humanitarian aid. Similarly, in Somalia, a country with more than 90 percent Muslims the rare inroads of Christianity have only reached the descendants of orphans or delinquents rejected by their clan. Irish and Italian missionaries in Berbera converted many of the latter before 1909. It was the year when the British prohibited Christian missions so as not to provoke the ire of local notables. As a result of the lack of facilities in Somalia, higher education had to be pursued in Christian institutions in Sudan, Uganda, and Aden. This Christian minority was able to play an important political role via people as Michael Mariano, who headed the National Unionist Front at the time of Independence. Several hundred members of the Ethiopian Orthodox Church, Oromo or Somali refugees, who migrated from the Dire Dawa region after the Ogaden war in 1977, joined this handful of Christians.

Islam has also historically made headway in Somalia by recruiting among the excluded. In the south, it enabled the Bantu farmers to cast off the domination of their masters and to rise in the social hierarchy.[10] The jama'a congregations of the Shabelle and the Juba comprised farmers, domestic workers, criminals banished from their clans, and former slaves. Freed or runaway slaves constituted between fifteen and thirty thousand of the faithful according to estimates dating from the 1940s.[11] Italian colonization precipitated the movement by abolishing slavery and exempting the jama'a from payment of 'indigenous' taxes. A number of peasants took refuge with the religious chiefs in order to help forced laborers on local plantations escape, and took part in the revolts of Shaykh Fareg in 1924 and Shaykh Ahmed Nur in 1926.[12] The jama'a also took in the disabled, the sick, and the elderly, a practice akin to that of traditional brotherhoods today.[13]

The same type of multi-clan social composition is found in the displaced persons camps run by Qadiriya *shaykhs* in Mogadishu. These camps are identifiable by the flag they fly showing a verse from the Qur'an and are very different from the other camps that have sprung up in the urban fabric. The largest of them already existed before the collapse of the dictatorship in 1991; at that time, they housed destitute and socially maladjusted people, especially, the mentally ill. Respected as a source of religious immunity, many of them are surrounded by a protective wall and consist of corrugated iron buildings rather than simple nomad huts. Some of them are equipped with a generator and a pump, perhaps even with a vehicle and a telephone. Such a level of sophistication—albeit relative—indicates a real capacity for self-management and initiative regarding public health, education, land use, collective catering, refuse disposal, maintenance of latrines and wells, etc.

Another distinctive feature of these camps is that they function in networks. One type of network is created when a *shaykh's* pupils spread his message by founding their own camps. For instance, there are Yusuf Baal Baal and Shiali Abdille, who followed the teaching of one of Mogadishu's best known *shaykhs*, 'Ali Mumin; and Ahmad Gureh, who was the pupil of a famous healer, Adan Dhere. In some cases, those involved are the direct descendants of *shaykhs*, such as Shiali Abdille or Mahdi Mohamed. Some choose to carry on running a camp in the same place, as Shaykh Mouaïdin did when his father, 'Ali Mumin, died in 1998. Others prefer to set up camp elsewhere as Shaykh Rufa did in Lafoley on the road to Afgoi, whereas his father, Nur Hussein, lived in the center of Mogadishu.

An equally widespread type of network consists of cells, which are developed during a *shaykh's* lifetime and are run under his direct authority. 'Ali Mumin, for example, headed two camps managed by 'lieutenants,' Hussein Naley in Wardigley and Yussuf Hadj in the Yaqshid-Jungle neighborhood. Shiali Abdille, set up annexes on the city limits in the dunes on the way to Isaley airfield. Bur Bishaaro, 'good news hill,' and Araade, 'white sand,' are Qur'anic schools dating from the 1980s. In late 1999, according to their leaders, they respectively housed fifty and forty families of displaced persons. Darkenley and Eebhele Ambar were set up during the war; their names refer respectively to a tree and to an inmate 'who found God.' Each of these two sites is thought to shelter up to seventy destitute families if the information is reliable. Shaykh Adan Dhere presides over what is almost a small empire, simultaneously managing six satellite camps: Sala'as at Huruwai and Hassan 'Ade at Wardigley, each of which bears the name of its chief; Koofi ('a Muslim bonnet'), Kaawo ('the quarry'), and Tendo ('the tent') near to Keysaney Hospital and Isaley; and Wahra 'Ade ('the white kid') on the road to Balad. However, most of these sites contain only a small mosque, with a well, if they are lucky.

A camp's religious emblems provide no guarantee that it is efficiently run. Only the Mogadishu *shaykhs* have managed to keep up with events and cope with new arrivals. Swept along by the flood of migrants, mainly from Baidoa, the *shaykhs* who came with their followers from the provinces have been less successful and their camps are undistinguished. Abdi Shimoye settled in Mogadishu's industrial estate, Hassan Mohamed, had to make do with a piece of waste land, renamed Burdhubo, and Aweys Shaykh Muhammad, pitched his tent on the edge of the city on the road to Afgoi.

Although Shaykh Yusuf Baal was from Mogadishu, he is no exception. He founded his *jama'a* near Bakara market in 1950. As a member of the Abgaal clan, he was forced to retreat before the 1991 thrust of the Haber Gidir combatants and made it to the northern edge of Mogadishu, where he bought a piece of land. This short move explains why his camp is in a kind of intermediate position, neither as poor as those of the *shaykhs* from the countryside, nor as well-organized as those of the other Mogadishu *shaykhs*. The Baal site does not have a surrounding wall or a generator, but it looks like a shantytown rather than a collection of huts.

Most of the traditional brotherhoods lack the resources to meet even the most basic needs of the destitute. Despite their undeniably deep roots in society, most of them are funded solely by the Muslim *zakat* tax. Arab donors have been put off by them, especially Wahabites from the Gulf states, who have little desire to support the development of Sufi Islam. Nor are they suited to the kind of institutionalization, which would enable them to work in partnership with western-type NGOs. There is no co-operation between *shaykhs* of equivalent rank; followers occupy a subordinate position and sometimes do not wait until their master is dead before founding their own school and emancipating themselves from being dominated by a network. Sunna wa-l-Jama'a, the 'Community of the Mosque,' is the only site to have been set up by *shaykhs* from different backgrounds and it is not so much a camp as a place for prayer on the western side of the large building of Isbiga, the former single party. Elsewhere, *shaykhs* provide nothing more than moral protection for existing camps, Adan Dhere at Fohle, Muhammad Mahmud at Kahelmi, and Hussein Shaykh Mahdi Muhammad at al-Naima.[14]

On the other hand, outside support considerably extends the range of the modern Islamists' charitable work. They owe their undeniable financial muscle largely to substantial funding from Saudi Arabia, the Emirates, and to a lesser extent, from Iran and Sudan. Saudi funds for Somaliland is going through the offices of the Islamic Relief Organization and the Muslim World League in Djibouti. Funds also pass through one of the 186 Islamic banks that exist worldwide. With 18,655 local branches, these banks have flourished in recent times. They manage some $80 billion of funds worldwide and have assets worth more than $166 billion. In 1985, these figures were $5.8 and $7.6 billion respectively. The Dubai Islamic Bank, which was founded in 1975, is now the United Arab Emirates' sixth largest bank in terms of assets.[15]

In Somalia, this bounty has provided funding for schools, hospitals, and mosques. The Kuwaitis and the Saudis provided assistance and support to the Mogadishu orphanages. It is associations such as Kuwait's Society for Revival of Islamic Heritage from (Osman Ben 'Afan) and the Abudubai Welfare Organization (Darkenley); the Saudis of Ibrahim al-Ibrahim (Shureye) and al-Haramein (Darkenley); and the Sudanese of African Muslims (Jeysira) and the Muslim World League (Hamar and Wardigley) that showed the greatest support. Opponents of institutions of this type regard them as indoctrination centers, which are allegedly preparing children for a holy war whereas, traditionally, the Muslim system known as *kafala* involves sponsoring or adopting an orphan.

The unrest has made it easier for fundamentalist ideas to be spread by local NGOs, such as al-Hay'at al-'uliya li-Da'wat al-Islam, the 'High Committee for the Preaching of Islam.' The displaced persons camps at Mogadishu are breeding grounds for fundamentalists, who have set up numbers of Qur'anic schools there and distributed quantities of food during the major religious festivals. A similar situation was observed in the early 1960s, when Somali refugees in Kenya asked to be united with Mogadishu. Aid was distributed in centers where insurgents rubbed shoulders with drought victims, namely the Boran, an Oromo group from Kenya. The latter were 'Islamicized' as part of the process whereby religious ideas spread through personal contact; later on, in the 1970s, the Boran and Oromo group from Kenya began to make the pilgrimage to the tomb of Shaykh Nur Hussein in Bale.[16]

The Capacity to Keep Order

A philanthropic mission is seldom without political overtones. In Somalia, the National Charitable Organization, al-Jam'iya al-Khayriya al-Wataniya, which appeared in the 1920s, spawned a political party for the Digil and Mirifle clans, the Hizbia Digil Mirifle in 1947. Similarly, the Patriotic Benefit Union was in 1943, a seedbed for the great nationalist independence party, the Somali Youth League. In 1991, the fundamentalists began efforts to build on the ruins of the state a rudimentary kind of reorganization at local level. They have restored a semblance of order and imposed a certain discipline by means of Islamic law, the shari'a, and by ground patrols in the areas they control.

In these areas, they have won a reputation for cracking down on crime more efficiently than the other armed groups and as a result have acquired funding from business circles. During the negotiations held to discuss setting up a joint administration in Mogadishu in 1998, the Islamic tribunals in the south managed to dismantle most of the roadblocks and to ban the carrying of arms in public. The death penalty has rarely been applied, but delinquents and repeat offenders have been punished by flogging and amputation, and some rudimentary inter-neighborhood co-operation to apprehend troublemakers has taken place.

This coincidence of interests between business circles and the Islamists is, however, unlikely to command real allegiance from a population eager for peace. The problem is that the dislocation of Somali society presents a formidable hurdle for initiatives of this type, especially in Mogadishu. Armed clashes on Bakara market in April 1999, for example, discredited the Islamic tribunals that were supposedly controlling the district, but which proved incapable of settling trade disputes between Haber Gidir, elements close to Hussein 'Aideed' and Murusade brought in by Muhammad Qaniare Afrah.

What is more likely to prove attractive is the ideological profile of the fundamentalist approach. At a time when armed factions have been jostling for control of power and wealth in Somalia, the Islamists have filled a power vacuum. Both traditional and new authorities have been taken aback by denunciations from radical groups such as the *tekfir* (converts). In the south, neither councils of elders nor warlords had any alternative proposals. Only the institutions re-established in the north have proved capable of drawing up a blueprint for social reconstruction on the basis of a fragile peace. In Hargeisa, the Somaliland authorities thought they could forestall fundamentalist influence by taking Islam as a foundation stone of the law. Article 25 of the constitution promulgated in 1997 prohibits for example, alcohol production and consumption and pledges to limit the consumption of *qat*, a plant acting as a stimulant which is very popular in the region. Christians are not allowed to stand for election, and the Catholic Church in Hargeisa, which dates from 1943, has been closed, waiting for the Vatican to recognize Somaliland's independence in order to re-open.

The Seeds of Religious Nationalism

Somali Islamism's greatest strength lies in its cross-clan approach. In this context, religion possesses the virtue of rallying the nation, whilst the prevailing chaos is interpreted as a curse from heaven.[17] Some believe that the current sphere of fundamentalist influence corresponds fairly closely to the regions, where early forms of nationalism came into being, namely Nugal, where the 'mad mullah' rebellion took place in 1899–1920; Gedo, which was Shaykh Abdirahman Mursal's headquarters in 1917–1924; and Benadir, especially the town of Marka, which was the cradle of the Bimal dervish movement in 1902–1908.[18] In the second decade of the twentieth century, the diatribes pronounced against the European invaders by members of the Salahiya brotherhood, including Shaykhs Muhammad Gulayd, Sayyid Muhammad Abdallah Hassan, and 'Ali Nairobi at Jowhar and in the Juba, were fairly typical of their kind.

During this period, religious opposition to the inroads of colonialism also expressed economic grievances arising from the confiscation of land, the abolition of slavery, and the slowdown of agricultural activity that could have ensued. A conjunction of interests of this type united several clans in defense of a common cause. From 1896 onward for example, Shaykh Abokor Asir, 'Saa'amawaayo,' 'he who always co-ordinates his actions in time,' has succeeded in uniting the Bimal and broadening his social footing on military rather than on religious foundations. A detachment of 500 Italian soldiers was needed to crush the two thousand faithful, who fought at Turunley in 1907 and at Jilib and Shalambood in 1908.[19]

In 1992 and 1993, the power of al-Ittihad similarly rose on a wave of nationalism against an 'invasion' by infidels, who were, in this case, the U.S. Marines who had landed in Mogadishu to try to restore order in Somalia.

In response to the fragmentation of the armed factions, al-Ittihad called upon believers to unite, thereby earning itself the sobriquet Tawhid ('Unification'). Rejection of the G.I.s did not, however, lead to an alignment transcending clan divisions. The Islamic tribunals, which today operate south of Mogadishu, still reflect kinship loyalties, and the Islamists' nationalist 'exploits' soon revealed their limitations. The latter are essentially due to the nature of Somali Islam, which is marked by the predominance of customary law and internal divisions within the 'umma.'

A Syncretic Islam

Historically, Somalia came into contact with Islam in the late seventh century, when the ruling Ummayad Dynasty in Damascus sent emissaries to impose a highly symbolic control over the coastal area.[20] However, the difficulty of the terrain checked the penetration of Islamic influence into the hinterland. Even on the coast, Mogadishu soon ceased to pay tribute to the successors of the Ummayads, the Abassids of Baghdad; nor were the Sultans of Oman more successful in formalizing their authority.

In other words, Islam was propagated very gradually in Somalia, particularly by brotherhoods, whose Sufi practices, despite their Shaf'i allegiance, did not conform to the canons of orthodoxy of the *'ulima's* of Cairo and Mecca.[21] The nomads continued to follow their pre-Islamic traditions. Muhammad Haji Mukhtar believes that the nomads of the north, in particular, were not converted to Islam as early as they like to make out in line with their claims to direct descent from the prophet. Although the sea crossing was extremely dangerous, the region was nevertheless insufficiently remote to provide a refuge for the first Muslims to be expelled from Mecca, and it lacked the cities, natural harbors, and economic assets to provide a home for the adherents of a fundamentally urban religion. According to Mukhtar, the Arabs fleeing from the struggles for the prophet's succession and later from the Shiite schism probably landed on the Benadir coast in the south. The Julanda tribe, for example, may originate from Oman and have been pushed inland by a Shiite group known as the Zaidi fleeing from Ummayad persecution. Even today, the Geledi clan, living around Afgoi, claims descent from the Julanda family, a name that has otherwise disappeared.[22]

A number of noble families pride themselves on an often dubious Arab ancestry, fabricated to support their case. Their claims deserve little credence. In fact, the distinctive cultural features of a predominantly pastoral society were not likely to produce a very austere form of Islam. In Rahanweyn country there is a sub-clan called Seka Diid, 'those who refused to pay the Muslim *zakat* tax.' In the Arab world, the Somalis tend to be regarded as 'bad' Muslims. They are particularly criticized for their syncretism and their partiality for *qat*. Use of *qat*, which is prohibited by Islam, is indicative of certain accommodations with local practices. In Mogadishu, the followers of the late Shaykh Omar Rabi are not alone in having the reputation of being great *qat* chewers.

Habitual users justify themselves by saying that *qat* induces divine visions when the Qur'an is being read; rather than being merely trance-inducing, it is said to be a spiritual stimulant, *qut al-awliya'*, 'food of the saints,' Other users argue that the Qur'an makes no explicit reference to the use of qat and that its message is somewhat ambivalent. While verse ninety of the 'Table' *sura* forbids alcohol on the same grounds as gambling and sorcery, verse fifteen of the 'Muhammad' *sura* promises rivers of wine for the faithful in paradise. War and famine also provide excuses for drug abuse: *sura* five, verse three of the Qur'an authorizes the consumption of proscribed foodstuffs in such circumstances, provided there is no intention to commit a sin.

In the same vein, *zar* and *mingi* possession rites retain some influence, especially among women. Rain worship is still fairly widespread among pastoralists. The nomads of Somaliland in the north have incorporated into the *dikr* ceremonies of the brotherhoods the *jenile* dance, celebrating the god Wak during *zar* celebrations. Islam made little headway among the Degodia of the south, who worship a rain god known as the *wobur*. Their syncretism is reminiscent of that of the Kenyan Oromo, whose local *ayaana* spirit worship has been absorbed by Islam.

The pastoral communities are certainly less receptive to sorcery than the Bantu farmers of the Shabelle, who revere *uganga* spirits and whose villages are protected by a crocodile *bahar*, or the Afar livestock farmers of Djibouti, who wear amulets to ward off sickness and consult oracles. The Somali do, however, believe in *baraka*, a mixture of luck and divine blessing. Shaykh Ibrahim Hassan Jeberow, who led a holy war in the 1840s, put heart into his men by invoking magical powers in the name of the Ahmadiya brotherhood, to which he was said to belong.

The Primacy of Custom over Muslim Law

Syncretism of this kind, which reflects the complexity of social life, has little in common with the 'totalitarian' vision of the Islamists. Historically, Islam has been incapable of providing support for a major national project. Over a long period, the Sufi brotherhoods gradually penetrated into the interior of the country, spreading along kinship lines via a hereditary and 'patrilinear' mode of transmission.[23] Since they owed their distinctiveness to their genealogical identity rather than to the content of their teaching, they were not successful in overcoming the *caado* tradition. The *shari'a*, for example, has never taken precedence over *ugub* judicial doctrine or the provisions of *xeer* (customary law), which covered criminal matters *(dhiig)*, the law of war *(dagaal)*, labor law *(shaqo)* and the civil code *(dhaqan)*.[24] Before settling in a place, *jama'a* congregations always had to ask permission from the clans, whose territory they wished to occupy and to whom they owed tribute. They were required to respect customary law and their land rights were not inalienable. However, repeated conflicts would eventually get the better of the land claims of the host clan, especially when the colonial administration supported the religious communities, in the hope of developing agriculture on a more rational basis.

The *jama'a*, which consisted of the descendants of slaves, serfs, and fugitives, never commanded great respect. Although they spread rapidly, they were never integrated into the rest of society. The proud Somali nomads wanted to have nothing to do with them, although Islam had justified slavery under the pretext of conversion. In 1922, leading Darod figures wrote to the British that they would rather die than be treated as par with those inferior tribes, who were sold as slaves, as it was authorized by their religion.[25]

The *jama'a*, established at Bardera by Shaykh Ibrahim Hassan Jeberow, around 1815, exemplified this power relationship with the traditional authorities. Around 1840, Shaykh Ibrahim Hassan Jeberow launched a holy war, forbidding tobacco smoking, condemning customary dances, obliging women to wear the veil, and restricting social relations between the sexes. The elephant was said to be an impure animal, so the ivory trade was also prohibited, to the annoyance of the region's merchants. The sultan of Geledi, Yusuf Mohamed, was particularly reviled for straying from the 'right way,' and the faithful were invited in the crudest terms to leave 'the sect of this greedy asshole'! But the sultan, in alliance with the merchants, soon put a stop to the insolence of the dissenters. In 1843, Ibrahim Hassan Jeberow fell on the field of battle fighting against a numerically superior enemy (some 20,000 against 40,000).[26]

Today, the elders react in a similar way to the reformism of the Islamists, whose opportunism, lowly social extraction and foreign origins they denounce. In Mogadishu, people recall how Shaykh 'Ali Muhammad 'Dhere,' one of the most influential al-Ittihad preachers, was supposedly used by the Siyad Barre dictatorship as a prosecution witness during the trial of the *'ulima's* in 1975. The fundamentalists are often in conflict with local notables. At Burtinle to the south of Garoe, there were even clashes in late 1999 between al-Ittihad and a Muslim sect affiliated to the Qadiriya and known as *timaweyne*, the "long-haired ones." Three years earlier at Las Anod, traditional chiefs chased troublemakers who had overrun the Qur'anic schools away toward Erigavo.

A Divided Islam

Most importantly, the fundamentalists have proved incapable of rising above the divisions that beset Islam and society in Somalia. Early in 1993, Sudan vainly tried to unify the country's main Islamic organizations.[27] These proved incapable of forming a united front against the warlords or of agreeing on a blueprint for an Islamic state. They have to some extent repeated the mistakes made earlier by Muḥammad Abdille Hassan, whose campaign never achieved the stature of a real national liberation movement and is therefore not comparable with Sudanese Mahdism between 1881 and 1892. The 'mad mullah' was unable or unwilling to unite the different components of the Somali population in a holy anti-colonialist war, which could well have taken a nationalist turn. Instead, he fell back on Darod clan affiliations, taking refuge among his people in Dulbahante territory when the British closed his mosque in 1897. At the time of the Jubaland rebellion in 1916, his supporters proved similarly unable to unite the Marehan, and further less capable to rally non-Darod clans.[28]

It is true that the Sufi and brotherhood-based nature of Somali Islam is not propitious to the 'ecumenical' efforts of those who claim to rally the nation. There are many competing 'chapels,' including the Askariya, the Dandariya, and the Marganiya. Some of them have nothing more than a local audience: the Shadhiliya, the Alawite offshoot of a Comoran Shaykh, Marouf, has a modicum of influence in the south, while the Rifa'iya, or Rufaiya, is represented among the Arabs of the Somaliland coast. The main brotherhoods are the Qadiriya and the Ahmadiya. The former was founded in Baghdad by Abdul-Qadir Jilani (1077–1166); the latter at Mecca by Sa'id Ahmad bin Idris al-Fasi (1760–1837). Eternal rivals, they both had to spread widely. The Rashidiya, which was started by Ibrahim al-Rashid, a pupil of Sa'id Ahmad bin Idris al-Fasi, produced an offshoot, the Salahiya. It is a branch of the Ahmadiya. The Andarawiya takes its name from Muhammad bin Ahmad al-Dandarawi (1839–1910) as well. The Qadiriya, with the tacit support of the British, extended its ramifications in the late nineteenth century via the Zayla'iya of

Shaykh Abdul-Raman al-Zayli'i in northern Somalia and the Uwaysiya of Shaykh Uways bin Muhammad at Brava on the south coast.[29] The influence of the latter, who lived from 1847 to 1909, extended as far as Uganda and Tanganyika, where the local Muslims resisted colonial penetration.[30]

At the time, the brotherhoods' transnational vocation alarmed the Europeans, just as the expansionist tendencies of today's Islamist movements alarm Somalia's neighbors. A strategic perspective highlights the full spread of Somali fundamentalism; it may however exaggerate its real influence. The fact remains that Iranian, Sudanese, and Saudi Arabian interference in the Gedo frontier region, especially around Luuq, was sufficient to constitute a threat not only to neighboring countries but also to the western powers. Some observers believe that the rising power of al-Ittihad was a major reason for American humanitarian intervention in December 1992.[31]

Fear of Islamist Expansion

The United States' allies such as Kenya, Ethiopia, Uganda, and even Burundi have grounds for viewing, with some alarm, the recrudescence of Islamic militancy in East Africa, despite its remoteness and their overwhelming Christian majority.[32] To take one example, the guerrilla group, called 'the National Council for the Defense of Democracy' was set up in 1994 by Leonard Nyangoma and has differed from its Palipehutu rival by establishing closer links with Muslim extremists in order to win support from Sudan and the Arab countries. The Uganda of President Museveni, Washington's bridgehead in the region, is not immune either.[33] From 1971 to 1979, the Amin Dada dictatorship oscillated between Libya and Saudi Arabia. In April 1990, the remnants of Amin Dada's soldiery, General Moses 'Ali's Uganda National Rescue Front, attempted a coup d'état in Kampala with Khartoum's support.

Since then, the Islamist movement in Uganda has been disparate and scattered. Known as the *tabliq*, a term which designates 'militant faith' and refers to a movement which originated in Pakistan, it comprises more or less organized groups such as the Liberation Tigers, the Allied Democratic Forces, Shaykh Abdul Kyesa's 'Saved,' and deserters from the Uganda Muslims Salvation Front.[34] Although from 1994 onward, it has had some success in the Halkum Kaira region, it mainly operates from the 'democratic' Congo along the western frontier, where it has joined Hutus formerly involved in the genocide in Rwanda. Khartoum's backing, provided in retaliation for Kampala's aid to the rebellion in the south of Sudan, is one of the few permanent forms of support enjoyed by these guerrillas. In June 1999,

Sudanese missionaries belonging to the Ahmadiya brotherhood were involved in bomb attacks in the Ugandan capital.

Somalia's neighbors, Kenya and Ethiopia, are naturally frontline targets for an upsurge of Islamism. They are both predominantly Christian countries with large Somali minorities, whose irredentism is liable to combine with religious demands. Since the momentous attack on the U.S. embassy in August 1998, Nairobi has every reason to fear the damaging effects of an 'Islamist international.' The Amhara and Tigrean Christians of the Ethiopian highlands are traditionally suspicious of the Somali Muslims of the plains. Today, Addis Abeba's greatest fear is a link-up between Somali fundamentalism and the Somali and Oromo guerrillas, who are active in the east and the south. In June 1996, they began tentative moves toward military cooperation. Islam, the focal point of which is here the cult of Shaykh Nur Husayn in Bale, has been conducive to the unification of the Somali and Oromo opposition movements, which have much in common. It is often hard to distinguish a true Oromo or Humbanu from other Cushitic peoples of the region such as the Somali and the Sidama, known as Sarri.[35]

There have been strong religious overtones in the dissidence of the Somali of the Ethiopian Ogaden and the Haud frontier zone. During the 1960s' disturbances, this led to the foundation of the evocatively named Nasrullahi, or 'Grace of God' guerrilla group. It was later followed up by a more structured non-religious organization, the Western Somali Liberation Front (WSLF), which called for the Ogaden to be annexed to Mogadishu. The WSLF went into terminal decline after it was defeated in 1978, then became involved in a repression under the Siyad Barre's dictatorship and was 'disavowed' by Somalia in the wake of a reconciliation agreement with Ethiopia in 1988. Irredentist claims had in any case lost much of their popularity by being regarded as straightforward frontier disputes at the government level.[36] Since the state has ceased to exist in Somalia, they have now become pointless.

Shaykh Ibrahim Abdallah's Ogaden National Liberation Front (ONLF), which had been founded in the Gulf and was led by a graduate of the Islamic University of Riyadh, then continued the struggle, moving toward a more religious, pro-independence position. The replacement of Shaykh Ibrahim Abdallah in 1998, by a former admiral of the Somali navy, Muhammad Omar Osman, has not prevented the struggle for the independence of the Ogaden from becoming 'Islamicized.' The ONLF is now split between dissidents who have agreed to collaborate with the Ethiopian authorities and a faction that has resumed the armed struggle, thus laying itself open to the same accusations of fragmentation as those leveled at the warlords in Somalia. Its views on Ogadenia's independence are unpopular with the region's minority clans, especially the Isaaq and the Gadabursi, who look askance at the growing power of the numerically predominant Ogadeni. The resulting political fragmentation into a large number of factions has facilitated the task of organizations such as the Islamic Solidarity Party and the Ogaden Islamic Union Party. The former, which is known as Tadamun and largely consists of traditionalist notables, took part in the 1992 regional elections. While al-Ittihad was behind a series of bomb attacks against hotels in the capital and personalities associated with the regime, the latter chose to go underground.

Addis Abeba is also confronted with armed opposition from the Oromo, numerically the country's largest ethnic group. Admittedly, the Oromo, whose language is transcribed in Latin characters, base their identity less on Islam and more on membership of an age group or *gada*. Their conversion to Islam, which began in the eighteenth century and went on as late as the 1930s, was, however, largely a reaction of *gabbar* peasants to Shewa Christianity and to the inroads of the Amhara and Tigrean *neftagnia* colonists.[37] Oromo nationalism, later, incorporated a religious dimension and enjoyed support from Somali Islamists. Led by Adem Muhammad, the Muslim Oromo of Habro, Delo and Wabe, founded an Oromo-Abo Liberation Front, which claims to have 500 combatants in the Bale-Arsi region and which includes populations close to the Somali.

Known as Djihad Oromo, the Islamic Front for the Liberation of Oromia (IFLO) was founded in 1969 by Shaykh Ibrahim Bilissa and taken over in 1986 by Shaykh Jara Aba Gedda, whose real name is Abdulkarim Muhammad Ibrahim Hamed. Siyad Barre's 'socialist' Somalia, where he had been imprisoned between 1969 and 1975, did not, at that time, back the latter. In exile in Saudi Arabia after 1978, he took a harder Islamist line, which then took precedence over nationalist claims. When Mengistu's 'Marxist' dictatorship in Addis Abeba fell in 1991, he launched ground attacks on the Oromo Liberation Front (OLF), a veteran of armed struggle in the region and an organization tending to be dominated by Christians of the so-called *bente* faction, close to Pentecostal movements. The assassination of the IFLO vice-president Shaykh Ahmad Yussuf Ahmad, at Dire Dawa in January 1992, caused the two guerrilla forces to close ranks momentarily against their common enemy, who was probably behind the liquidation of this opponent.

No real reconciliation was, however, attempted with a movement accused of undermining the traditional order and ceasing to respect the authority of the elders. Within the OLF, Yohannes Benti, a leader better known by his nom de guerre Galassa Dilbo, recently had to make way for a Muslim, Dawud Ibsa Avana. A restructuring of regional alliances strengthened this Islamization of the Oromo rebellion. The IFLO has won backing from Khartoum, has an office at Djibouti and has moved closer to al-Ittihad. Meanwhile, confronted with Ethiopian incursions into Somalia, Hussein 'Aideed' gave his backing to the formation of an Oromo, Somali, and Afar liberation army in August 1997. In late 1999, however, he stopped supporting the OLF; it was a way to ease up in order to obtain a break from the Ethiopians since he had sustained serious military reverses.

Islamization of these rebellions, whether authentic or not, has provoked a violent reaction from Kenya and Ethiopia. While Nairobi helped opposing factions to counter al-Ittihad, Addis Abeba did not balk at sending troops into Somalia. In August 1996, its army initially did no more than cross the frontier. In 1998, however, the war with Eritrea encouraged Ethiopia to press home its advantage, each of the two belligerents supporting armed factions on the ground. Interference of this kind is indicative of a real anxiety. It also overestimates the power of al-Ittihad. The western powers have contributed to this flawed analysis since Cold War strategists replaced the communist enemy with Islam.

The Somali are not the only ones to exaggerate the situation and play on the fears aroused by al-Ittihad in the region. In a sense, this is a ploy to capitalize on the latter's nuisance value. The Somaliland government presents itself as a bulwark against the fundamentalist threat and makes no bones about negotiating for support on these grounds, especially, from the Ethiopians. This being the case, the western powers would be well advised to help strengthen the authority of the capital, Hargeisa, so as to prevent the area from becoming a haunt of terrorists of all kinds like in the south, since article 56.3 of the Somaliland constitution forbids extradition procedures. Meanwhile, in Mogadishu, the notables are pleading for a resumption of humanitarian aid. They maintain that the notorious Osama bin Laden probably visited the city in March 1999, looking for a new base to fall back upon in the event of his expulsion from Afghanistan.

Despite the difficulties involved in getting hold of reliable information about a country at war, the question still arises of how long such a shadowy and nebulous Islamist movement will last. Given the divisions and syncretism that characterize Somali Islam, it is by no means certain that fundamentalist influence has any chance of enduring. Irrespective of military defeats and political vicissitudes, the Islamists' totalitarian blueprint does not seem calculated to suit a society where the pastoral tradition is still very strong.

A comparison with the Taliban phenomenon in Afghanistan does not go very far. Some similarities can be found in al-Ittihad's aspirations to promote unity and to cut across clan-based divisions, combined with the exhaustion of a population exasperated by the ideological vacuity and avarice of warlords. However, the parallel stops there. So far, the Somali Islamists have succeeded neither in combining their efforts, nor in rising above lineage cleavages, nor in forming a military front strong enough to tip the balance of power in their favor on a long-term basis.

In this context, the Islamist movement's aspirations to replace the state remain mere intentions. The fundamentalists do not control liberated areas, unlike the guerrillas, who elsewhere in Africa have managed to impose a semblance of administration on the territory under their control. In Somalia, the modern fundamentalists do not possess the advantage of fighting against a government. As a result of the prevailing chaos, they need to provide yet more proof of their capacity to rebuild the country. Here, their charitable non-governmental organizations necessarily play a crucial role. They provide an outreach into civil society, which competes directly with the cronyism of the warlords, the patronage of business circles, and classic forms of assistance from more traditional Muslims.

Notes

*   This article forms part of an IRD research program on armed conflicts, forced population movements, and humanitarian aid in East Africa. More precisely, it is an outcome of two field missions, one to Somaliland in 1997, the other to Mogadishu late in 1999, as well as many interviews with members of the Somali diaspora in the other countries of the region.

1. Raghe 1997: 381.
2. USIP 1999: 3.
3. The Somalis use the adjectives 'fundamentalist,' 'radical,' and 'extremist' indiscriminately when speaking of the Islamists. Indigenous people tend to make a distinction between 'traditionalist' and 'modern' fundamentalists, the latter unlike the former putting forward an ideology that is 'alien' to their customs and is in fact imported from the Arabian peninsula.
4. Sheikh-Abdi 1992.
5. British aircraft in a bombing raid sometimes referred to as the 'African Guernica' since it was the first air attack on the African continent that eventually destroyed Mohammed Abdulle Hassan's fort in the Ethiopian Ogaden. During the First

World War, the British had contemplated bombing the German army in Tanganyika, but the vegetation cover had prevented them.
6. Mukhtar 1996.
7. Lewis 1994: 159.
8. Salafi, is a generic term, which designates a return to salaf, the religion of the ancestors, and to fundamental Islam. In Uganda and Kenya, it also refers to fundamentalist movements, such as the Society for Preaching and Denouncement of Qadianism and Atheism in Kampala.
9. Hashi 1996: 100–106, Luling 1997: 296.
10. Declich 1995.
11. Cassanelli 1988: 324.
12. Cassanelli 1988: 278.
13. Swayne 1985: 101, 260.
14. For the other Mogadishu camps, see Pérouse de Montclos 2000: 65.
15. Wilson 1983. On the political role of these Islamic banks in Sudan, see Jamal 1991: 103–109.
16. Baxter 1987.
17. Samatar 1994.
18. Mohamed-Abdi, M. 1997. "Rétrospective de la crise somalienne et réhabilitation de la société civile," in Mohamed-Abdi, M. and P. Bernard, ed., Pour une culture de la paix en Somalie, Paris, Actes du second congres international des études somaliennes, October 25–27, 1995, 103–50.
19. Cassanelli 1982: 242–45, 251.
20. At the same time, some authors, in view of the maritime trade with Persia, have not excluded a Shiite component more radical than the Sunnism of the Arabs; proof of this can be found in the etymology of the Shanshiya clan name, which may refer to a region of Iran. Cf. Mukhtar 1995: 5.
21. Pouwels 1987: 273.
22. Mukhtar 1995: 8–9.
23. Lewis 1984: 127–68.
24. Mohamed-Abdi 1997: 149.
25. Besteman 1995: 50.
26. Cassanelli 1982: 135–38, 145.
27. La Lettre de l'Océan Indien, February 27, 1993.
28. Turton 1969: 641–57.
29. Martin 1992: 11–32; Samatar 1992: 48–74.
30. Martin 1969: 471–86. On Islam's transcontinental links, see Galaal 1980: 23–30.
31. Gilkes 1994: 52.
32. Chande 2000: 349–69.
33. Kasozi 1986.
34. Kayunga 1993.
35. Lewis 1998: 99–105.
36. Markakis 1997: 497–513.
37. Hassen 1992: 75–101.

Chapter Fourteen

Civil Associations, Social Movements, and Political Participation in Lebanon in the 1990s

Karam Karam

Ever since the beginning of the 1990s, Lebanon has been going through a period of transition between emerging from the war and entering into a sustainable peace, a period that has not yet led to significant changes liable to shed light on the characteristics of a new period. The elements that would allow a final emergence from the state of war (1975–90) have only been partially implemented—this includes the process of reconstruction and reconciliation, the application of constitutional reforms, the war in the southern part of the country, and the regional peace processes. Observing Lebanese society in this period of transformation and mutation reveals new modes of participation in public life, through emerging and developing civil associations and social movements, in addition to more institutionalized modes of participation. Bearing in mind the different forms of mobilization in Lebanon as a whole, I will particularly concentrate in this paper on the study of two social movements: the rally for the municipal elections (RME) and the rally for an optional civil code to govern personal status—civil marriage (RCM).

My research falls within the purview of social change, analyzed through the interactions between advocacy movements, and their interactions with state policies. In studying these movements, I use as a reference the analytical concepts of political opportunities, mobilized structures, and experienced, qualified elements as well as the dynamics of their relations, as elaborated by McAdam, McCarthy, and Zald (1996). This study allows me to submit the following hypotheses: first, civil associations in Lebanon in the 1990s generated a certain type of social movements that reflect many forms of political participation and contestation. Furthermore, these social movements, by taking advantage of political opportunities and mobilized resources, expand access to political space for civil society actors. Finally, the interactions between these movements and political power established an unconventional mode of participation that has acquired an increasingly institutionalized form.

I shall deal with these matters in three parts. I shall first establish a conceptual, analytical framework of the social movements, one that is appropriate and adapted to the Lebanese context, while remaining careful of the contextual similarities and variations of their effect on the dynamics of collective action. I shall then study the relations between the development of civil associations in Lebanon and the emergence of a certain type of social movement, by describing the political structures within which they belong. Finally, I shall analyze the dynamics of those movements through the structures, the resources and the collective elements of experience, showing how their interactions with political power and with other actors contribute to the reshaping of Lebanese political space.

I am presenting here observations and hypotheses based on examples taken from a period I consider as being transitional, rather than on data which is complete and definitive. The idea is to outline certain forms of social movements in Lebanon in order to open a critical debate of this phenomenon in comparison with other movements in different contexts.

Definition and Analytical Framework of Social Movements

In the 1970s, researchers and theoreticians of social movements began to take interest in the rise of social movements outside Europe and America; their attention went hand in hand with an attempt to universalize the concept and to construct a trans-boundary theory applicable to different political and social contexts. Lebanon of the 1990s contained several forms of social movements that have always and continue to accompany the processes of normalization, demobilization of militias, reconciliation, and the reconstruction of society and of state institutions, even while necessarily taking note of the precariousness of constructing an emerging social reality and of the relevance of a conceptualization elaborated elsewhere (McAdam, Tarrow, and Tilly 1998).

My analysis falls within the purview of "the approach to the mobilization of resources" (AMR) (Obershall 1973 and Tilly 1978), and its extension into the approach of "the structure of political opportunities" (SPO) (McAdam 1982 and Tarrow 1989), redefined in the light of recent theoretical and empirical developments (McAdam, McCarty and Zald 1996). The approach to the mobilization of resources deals with the internal aspects (micro) of the social movements and with the factors related to the origins of collective action. Whereas the SPO approach deals with external factors (macro) related to certain elements of the political context, which determine peoples' decision to go into action or not (Duyvendak 1994). The importance of combining the two approaches lies in the fact that it confers rationality to the actors of the social movements and to the normality of their movements just as it does to all political actors.

McAdam, McCarthy, and Zald (1996) proposed a conceptual framework organized around three factors representing the different theoretical currents that are analyzing the emergence and development of social movements. First, the structure of political opportunities and the constraints facing social movements in the national contexts within which they emerge and which last for a certain period of time. Second, the mobilized resources and structures of the organization, whether formal or informal, compose and coordinate the activities of a movement. Third, the collective elements of interpretation, perception, or experience of the individuals regarding their collective action and which, in the interactive dynamics with the other two factors, allow the understanding and analysis of a social movement.

While admitting that any attempt in the direction of McAdam, McCarthy, and Zald's framework is problematic, I shall attempt an intermediary definition that takes into account the latest developments of the phenomenon. The social movement is a form of collective action that takes place by a concrete and concerted mobilization in favor of a cause and through interaction with adversaries, implying a certain degree of organization and continuity outside the institutional channels, with the aim of bringing about change or preventing change. McAdam and Snow (1997) noted some elements common to social movements by deconstructing the different conceptualizations of the phenomenon: an action of contesting; a collective or common action; objectives geared toward change; a minimum of organization; a certain degree of continuity in time; and a mixture of non-institutional or unconventional collective action and of institutional activity. I shall maintain this definition and these elements since they occupy a central position in the conceptualization of social movement.

The Sense of Politics and Political Sense

According to the definition proposed by Touraine (1984, 1978), social movements are a singular and important component of political participation. "They are the texture of society. The study thereof is not confined to sociology, it is not a specialty of the latter; it is rather the flag of all the sociology of action" (Touraine 1978, 45–46). This definition implies a political vision of social movements and a distinction between the 'political sense' of the movements—the search for the main elements of the movements—and the 'sense of politics' of the movements—as well as their response to opportunities in given contexts (Duyvendak 1994). According to Offe, (1997) social movements, particularly "new ones," reflect the existence of a political public space irreducible to the political regime, through the absence of interdependence among the social spheres (economic, political and social), which is opened to citizens' participation. This public space is taken over by the social movements that seek to politicize the organizations of 'civil society' and build a form of action free of state intervention.

This political concept of social movements stresses the political regime and the structure of opportunities that belong to it. Admitting that "the structure of political opportunities" is a vague notion makes this definition systematic with respect to the following four factors: the degree of openness of the political regime; the degree of stability of political alliances; the existence of back-up forces in strategic positions and the existence of divisions of elites; and the capacity of a political regime to develop public policies (Tarrow 1996). These variables as a whole constitute indicators for the degree to which political regimes are open or closed to to social movements. As certain opportunities facilitate collective action, social movements, through their interactive dynamics, also create opportunities (Gamson and Meyer 1996).

The notion of the political sense of a social movement is divided into two definitions. The first comprehends politics in a wider sense and encompasses any movement in favor of collective goods and values, and any collective problem that mobilizes the masses. The second considers that a social movement is only political when it engages in confrontation, or when it addresses itself to the political authorities to bring about, through public intervention, a solution to the problems that led to the mobilization. Conflicts that are settled between private protagonists within civil society, through the media and in the public space, are not enough to confer on them a political nature (Neveu 1996). Based on these characteristics, I consider a social movement to be 'political' when it confronts or addresses itself to the political authorities; when it intervenes regarding public policies; and when it takes part in the public debate with other political actors within the political space—that is with the government, parliamentarian groups, political parties, etc.

The relations between civil associations and social movements in Lebanon in the 1990s

The appearance of a new type of association

The concept of association encompasses a variety of sociological objects that differ historically with respect to their objectives, functions, and composition. The characteristics of associative activity in Lebanon are the result of a history, wherein there is a mixture of family and community strategies, social movements, and political events. Associations in Lebanon, primarily belonging to the charity and community type of groups, took various forms according to the evolution of sociopolitical realities—such as the transition from the Ottoman empire toward a mandate, followed by the creation of a state, the 1958 crisis, the civil war of 1975–1990, and the post-war period since 1990. The 1958 crisis broke out in Lebanon between different progressive movements (i.e., more Arab nationalists than pronationalists, mainly Muslim). They took arms and went down in the streets to protest against the international policy (especially regarding Lebanon's rapprochement with the West and Lebanon's alignment on the Eisenhower Doctrine) and against the domestic policy lead by Camille Chanoun, president at that time. This crisis became a religious conflict within an agitated regional and international context. This crisis not only revealed the frailty of the National Pact of 1943, but also highlighted deep dysfunctions of the Lebanese socioeconomic system. The passage from one moment to the other has brought about a renewal of the overall models of social and collective mobilization. Moreover, the emergence of new types of associations throughout the twentieth century does not exclude the development of previous models of associations. In fact, quite the opposite, for older types of associations developed either by accumulation of new models or by adapting to new realities (through internal reforms, for example). As it has evolved, the field of associations can be said to constitute an accurate reflection, and sometimes even an efficient vector, of social change.

Despite apparent similarities among the different types of associations, their actions and positions in the public space change according to their nature, their characteristics, and their field of activity. Today, we witness an inflation of the number of associations created after the war (an average of 250 to 300 new associations are created each year, according to the registries of the Ministry of Interior), particularly of the family, charity, and community types. However, along the more traditional associations, a new type emerged and developed rapidly (e.g., according to the Ministry of the Environment more than 150 ecological associations were created in the 1990s); their field of activity being of 'general interest' and their functions based on a logic of 'advocating,' which is different from the logic of charity, community, family activities, or providing services. Thus, new associations break away from the older forms in terms of function, management, and membership. The new associations, as will be shown, can be seen to have broken away from the older forms in terms of function, organization, and the characteristics of their membership.

The first characteristic of this new type of associative mobilization appears in their declared activities and objectives. Mobilization extends to fields of activity that had been previously neglected, such as human rights, ecology, public freedoms, and democracy. On the one hand, this type of association, with 'claims,' is in tune with the times since their concerns are also on the agenda of globalization. The study of the relations between the Lebanese associations and their international counterparts, allows us to underline the financing coming from abroad, which encourages the development of certain types of activities over others. This relationship with foreign partners also raises the question of the transfer of technology and 'know-how' from the field of associations to other fields and the adoption of certain models. On the other hand, such concerns do not only belong to the post-war period of state and national reconstruction—to repair the destruction that affected certain domains—but they are also part of the quest for a new political consensus and an attempt to reestablish the social link between the different countries. It should be noted that some associations (of socioeconomic development and women's associations, for example), which were very active toward the end of the war, directed part of their activities toward human rights, ecology, public freedoms, and democracy, taking into account the new policies of international donors and the post-war situation.

The second trait is that this type of association differs from others in terms of organization. Instead of a hierarchical and vertical organization, new horizontal structures that are more flexible are set up. In comparison with socioeconomic development associations and other community and family associations dealing with health and education, the associations dealing with 'claims' work on a modest budget (an average of $20,000 per year, rather than more than $10 million per year for the larger development NGOs). They operate in an ad hoc manner, by reducing the number of paid staff (limited to managing the secretariat). They depend on a group of voluntary workers and specialize in their field of interest. This mode of organization and internal management reinforces the position of these associations in the eyes of both donors and public institutions (such as the ministries). Yet their freedom remains precarious since it depends on voluntary participation, the numbers of which cannot be controlled; their types of activity and the general context in which it takes place also determine these numbers.

Third, these post-war advocacy associations are distinguished by the characteristics of their advocates. Generally, they are formed by two groups: the majority consists of 'youth' between twenty-two and forty years old, with weak political affiliations, even though they may have affinities for one political current or another. A minority are over forty years old and had actually taken part in partisan activities in the past, often within the same political party or tendency; they find in today's action within the associations a form of self-criticism and a substitute for their past. These associations are also characterized by the trans-regional and trans-community affiliation of their members, who declare themselves to belong to no religious or ideological side. The majority belongs to the middle class whereas the minority comes from the upper classes. A large number of university students, teachers, and members of liberal professions (lawyers, engineers, and journalists, for example) are well-represented in these organizations. What is new in such mobilization is that the structure of associations constitutes a non-violent means of achieving change. Moreover, it also takes place within the national and state framework, on Lebanese territory. Since the end of the war, this new type of association, even though in the minority and sometimes elitist, has left its mark on Lebanese public space by its participation in associations or in wider collective action in defense of common interests, and has in some cases ended up as a social movement.

Associative Action, Collective Action and Social Movement in Lebanon

One must make the distinction between the three levels of action, associative, collective, and social movement, the better to understand the passage from one to the other, their links, their mode of functioning, and their development. Observation and empirical research of Lebanese associative circles will help me to provide some precisions. What I mean by 'associative action' are the activities and actions of an association as a group (an organization or an institution) that acts in a unified manner—as a single actor within the public space, that is, as a legal person. Consequently, with regard to its activities within the public space, the association is considered, by the public authorities and by the other actors, as one single actor with the status of a legal person. This is also true from a legal point of view since the law, by conferring the status of a legal person upon the association, grants it the right to stand as civil party, to acquire goods and property, etc. In this sense, I do not consider the action of an association within the public space as being a form of collective action. Even if the internal dynamics of an association can be considered as a form of collective action, they are not so, since they take place in a private space, the space of the association. Thus, for example, when an ecological association achieves a reforestation project or when it defends a protected site, this is an associative and not a collective action. An action is collective when, within the public space, an association presents or achieves a project in common with another association or another actor (a sports club, a municipality, etc.) and not only with its own members. In other words, the association moves to collective action in its external dynamics at the moment when, as a legal person, it associates itself with one or more legal persons or actors to achieve a common objective, interest, or project.

A social movement is a more advanced form of collective action (according to the above-mentioned definition and characteristics); one that implies contestation, particularly unconventional, within a public space or domain, facing other actors (Tarrow 1998, Neveu 1996, Chazel 1992). In that sense, one cannot consider the ephemeral collective actions of associations as a social movement if they do not have such characteristics. The passage from one form of action to the other does not take place in a linear manner and one does not exclude the other: they can be linked, separate, or concomitant. A social movement takes place when, on the one hand, the problems and conflicts (economic, political, social) cannot be settled through conventional channels, and on the other, when the association's views, which are at stake, are too important for it to manage on its own; finally when it cannot stand up to the strength of its opponents and calls upon other organizations or persons to participate in the movement (Giuny and Passy 1997). Sometimes, the national dimension of an issue will facilitate the mobilization of scattered associations. Some post-war social movements constitute, within given limits, the extension into other domains of public life, of demands and claims originally raised by new civil associations that developed during that same period. When these demands become a main problem in particular contexts for a larger part of society, then a social movement is created. This particular type of social movement is the subject of my study: social movements that have civil associations as a basis of organization. In other words, the social movements in the Lebanon of the 1990s constitute the collective expression and contestations of Lebanese civil associations—that is, of civil society.

The Lebanese Political Regime as a Structure of Opportunity

What are the favorable or unfavorable conditions in the Lebanese political regime for the emergence and development of social movements? What kind of relations and interactions do they establish with the state and with the other political and economic actors? The analysis of constitutional frameworks, of the political regimes and the assessment of their degree of openness or lack of openness, constitute a set of indispensable variables for studying the impact of social movements on a given society. As far as the Lebanese system is concerned, I shall dwell on three aspects: political reforms and the post-Taëf constitutional framework, the *troïka* system and the practices of the political authorities.

The constitutional laws form the basic framework for the emergence and development of social movements. Yet, their adoption and application remain determined by the will of the political power and they depend on the degree of the latter's openness to those movements. In certain political regimes, the basic rights of citizenship (such as public freedoms and freedom of elections) are no longer the object of mobilization since they are granted and guaranteed by the law. This leads the movements to orientate themselves toward cultural and specific matters (Rucht 1988).

In Lebanon, we observe both types of mobilization, reflecting the contrast between the liberalism of constitutional texts and between the arbitrary and restrictive application thereof. The constitutional reforms brought about by the Taëf agreement, particularly those that were applied as of 1990, did not change anything in the system of public freedoms (expression, association, meeting, demonstrations, etc.), or in the separation of powers, both being confirmed by constitutional laws. The war was over in 1990, with the implementation of the Taëf agreement (Taëf is the city where the agreement was signed), which was at the initiative of the Arab League and supported by Syria and the United States. The agreement was concluded in 1989 by the deputies elected in 1972. This agreement instituted a new era of rules for the political game, both institutionally and practically. These new rules were peaceful but nonetheless well rooted in the heritage of the national pact of 1943 and of the political denominational system. Where public freedoms are concerned, the change in Lebanon manifests itself in the practices of the political authorities, in their increasingly restrictive degree of openness, as well as in the increasing intolerance—rather than in the laws and texts. The restrictions take the form of imposition by the political authorities of anti-constitutional measures and practices prohibiting demonstrations, public meetings, and the establishment of new associations with pre-political objectives.

The Lebanese political regime cannot be compared to other regimes in the region—which tend to be characterized by one ideology and one person. The Lebanese regime imposed as of 1990, at a given regional and international point in time, is rather open to any actor accepting the rules of the game; that is, accepting the Taëf agreement, the demobilization of the militias (with the exception of the ones carrying out the resistance against Israel in the South), the rejection of violence in the process of participation in public life and, finally, tacit and unconditional allegiance to Syria and to its trusteeship. This system brought to power heterogeneous elites with no common political or ideological project, who easily compete with one another, either seeking profit and interests or to protect certain positions of power. The precariousness of the Lebanese system stems from the fact that these political elites were not able, with the help of stable democratic mechanisms, to overcome the conflicts and the divergences of society. They are always in need of an outside arbiter to permanently fix the rules of the game. One aspect of the Taëf regime is the *troïka,* which calls for the sharing of power by the three presidents (of the Republic, of the Council and of the Assembly).

Paradoxically, the permanent conflicts within the presidential triumvirate widen the structure of opportunities, and allow a margin of maneuvers for political and civil actors outside the circle of power, allowing them to play on the alliances and the oppositions. In other words, the *troïka* regime superimposed on a religious democracy of a liberal and pluralistic aspect, makes it difficult for the system to be closed as long as it represents society in its diversity. There is a relationship of cause and effect, on the one hand, between the pluralism of society and the degree of openness of the system, and on the other, with respect to the margin of participation.

There may have been talk, within certain limits, of a system or systems that were blocked during the period of the war, when the regions/communities closed in upon themselves, which created micro societies that were more 'homogenous' and less 'pluralistic,' as well as structures that were more rigid and less open. The normalization of the Lebanese political scene imposed by the Taëf regime reopened the 'borders' by allowing a greater number of actors to participate, even if some others were excluded. The holding of presidential and parliamentarian elections, as well as the ministerial changes since 1992, even though they had been marked by factional and client-oriented criteria, allowed a rotation of power among different political actors and forces and, by doing so, the redefinition of power relations. This mechanism makes it difficult for one single group to hold or retain power, because it establishes a 'game' between the 'loyalists' and the 'opposition,' which makes the political scene mercurial and without fixed borders. Moreover, the often arbitrary rules that govern political participation and representation—the laws, the ballots, and the breaking up of electoral constituencies—limit the access to power of non-traditional political forces that could constitute political options or allies for social movements.

In this context, it is very easy to only see the weaknesses of the social movements in Lebanon in the 1990s; while they were timely, they were of a limited duration and capacity. Yet, despite the latter obstacles, it is also important, as suggested by Touraine (1999), to understand the social and political innovation they bring, even if they are limited and brief. These sociopolitical mobilizations, by having a large media coverage, were, through the action of their actors, expanding the scope of participation and establishing new practices and new modes of action by dealing with both vast issues (national solidarity, municipal elections) and increasingly specific issues of a cultural and categorical nature (civil marriage, the disabled, political eligibility at age eighteen, and those missing during the war).

In the light of the movements of social and political mobilization in Lebanon as a whole, I shall focus my study on two social movements: 'the Rally for the holding of Municipal Elections' (RME), and 'the Rally for an optional civil code on personal status law—Civil Marriage' (RCM). I have stressed these two movements over others because of their duration (a little more than one year for the first, while the second has been active for more than two), the themes of their claims, and their diversified actions.

The Rally for the Holding of Municipal Elections

On the April 3, 1997, the Lebanese parliament voted as a majority in favor of the prime minister's request to postpone municipal elections, which were to be held between July 1 and July 8, 1997, and to extend the mandate of the municipal councils, and of the mayors to June 30, 1998, the final date for the holding of municipal elections. For several reasons, there had been no municipal elections in Lebanon since 1963. The postponement was decided in spite of the constitutional reforms of 1989, which had insisted on administrative decentralization and on a balanced development among regions. Moreover, the postponement disregarded the citizens' wish to participate in the municipal elections, a wish manifested by the massive mobilization of voters seeking to obtain their voting ballots. Following the prime minister's request to withdraw the draft law submitted to parliament by the government, the president of the republic threatened to resign if elections would not be held on the expected dates. The crisis that was thus set off within the executive power rapidly transcended the issue of municipal elections to touch upon the functions of the two presidents and the application of all the constitutional reforms. The intervention of an outside arbiter (the Syrian power) became necessary to put an end to the crisis by ending the matter on the basis of 'no winner and no loser.'

On April 16, 1997, the Lebanese Association for Democratic Elections (LADE)—established in 1996 to discuss electoral laws and to ensure democratic elections—following the decision adopted by parliament, invited all groups and people interested in the question of municipal elections to a meeting in order to discuss the measures to be adopted and the collective action to be followed in order to prevent the postponement or cancellation of local elections. In the course of the meeting, attended by fifteen associations (working on issues as diverse as ecology, human rights, democracy and public freedoms, development, and rights of the disabled) and by individuals concerned, a preparatory committee was set up to elaborate a plan of action on the basis of the different participants' discussions and proposals.

On April 29, 1997, based on the plan of action prepared by the committee, the organizers decided to launch a national campaign under the name of "Rally for the Municipal Elections,' their main mode of action being a national petition. The RME carried on their movement until the municipal elections were held, and they did so by adopting several modes of organization, and by mobilizing different structures: weekly meetings; meetings in different regions of the country; setting up a support committee, which brought together more than 150 associations, political parties (most Lebanese political parties supported the movement) and private companies; setting up permanent representation in the regions for people to sign the petition; and they mobilized different sectors in support of the campaign (lawyers, engineers, women, students, teachers, workers, etc.). All the above actions were supported by a vast media campaign until the end of the movement.

On September 12, 1997, following a recourse deposited by fourteen deputies encouraged by the RME, the Constitutional Council declared the decisions of parliament and of the cabinet to be null and void as well as unconstitutional, and the council called for the elections to be held. Subsequently, the RME diversified its modes of action, from demonstrations to a sit-in in front of parliament. On December 22, 1997, parliament voted for the holding of the municipal elections as a result of a consensus between the two large parliamentarian groups (the head of parliament's group, and that of the prime minister's). The RME pursued its campaign by stressing the significance and importance of municipalities until it dissolved itself on July 18, 1998, following the last round of municipal elections.

The Rally for an Optional Civil Code on Personal Status— Civil Marriage

Ever since the establishment of the Lebanese state and the adoption of its first constitution in 1926, the political class introduced a religious dimension into civil service and into personal status laws, which are decided by religious courts. Several political parties and parliamentarian groups attempted, in vain, since the 1950s to abolish this religious dimension and, in particular, to establish civil marriage in Lebanon. This was taken into account in the projects for constitutional reforms of 1989 and the president of the republic, Elias Harawi, often expressed his desire to establish civil marriage.

On March 7, 1998, Harakit Huquq al-Nas (Movement for the Rights of Individuals)—established toward the end of the 1980s to struggle against war, violence, injustice, and religion in politics—organized a conference on civil marriage and a civil code on personal status. On March 18, 1998, the president of the republic added to the Council of Ministers' agenda a draft law on civil marriage. The majority on the council adopted the draft law. The prime minister, who had voted against it, refused to sign the draft for submission to parliament. Following its adoption by the council, the Muslim religious authorities held a meeting at Dar al-Fatwa, condemned the draft and demanded its withdrawal. This religious rejection was supported by a strong mobilization by the 'Committees of Islamic Associations,' who had organized demonstrations, particularly in Tripoli and Beirut. Faced with the rapid mobilization of those opposed to the draft law, the minister of the interior called a stop to all demonstrations. Yet, the religious authorities of all sects as well as certain political figures convened meetings and took a stand by setting up an opposition front to prevent the submission to parliament of the draft law.

At that same time, certain student groups took the initiative of launching a petition in favor of civil marriage in the different Lebanese universities. They held a meeting on March 23, 1998, to rally their movement. On the next day, the Harakit Huquq al-Nas association organized a meeting to discuss a national campaign in favor of a civil code on personal status. About fifty associations, political parties, and the representatives of student groups took part in the meeting, which set up a committee entrusted with the preparation of a plan of action. The campaign was launched the following month under the aegis of Harakit Huquq al-Nas, and with the participation of all the groups concerned, including the students and the political parties: 'the Rally for an optional civil code on personal status—Civil Marriage' (RCM) was born. Its organizers adopted the same modes of action and structures of the RME: several committees; periodical meetings; a petition; an information campaign; regional and sectorial mobilization; mobilization of the media; a 'sit-in' in front of the Council of Ministers and parliament; and submission of a draft law. The RCM carried out its plan of action over two years. The first, from April of 1998 to April of 1999, during which they prepared a database on the issue of civil marriage, collected 55,000 signatures and established a support committee of seventy-five associations and political parties. Following a second period of quiet between April and November of 1999, the movement prepared a draft law for submission to parliament before April 2000.

Interactive Dynamics among Structures, Resources, and Experience

I undertake to study these social movements within that vast national configuration, bearing in mind their emergence and development. To do so, I adopt a method of analysis that allows me, from a dynamic and interactive perspective, to correlate political opportunities, the structures mobilized, and the experience accumulated. By applying this analytical method to different stages of the process of a social movement, I can, on the one hand, understand the conditions and factors that contribute to its emergence and, on the other, follow its evolution and the changes that ensued. In other words, the interplay of these three factors throughout the movement's life generates, in itself, new structures, opportunities, and collective experiences. This correlation allows us to understand the complexity of social movements, such as, why does a particular movement manage to achieve its objective while another movement, with efficient structures, is unable to achieve the goals of its mobilization?

Origins, Structures, and Militants

Ever since the 1950s, when the first demands were made for a civil code on personal status, and since 1963, when the last municipal elections were held, no social group thought of mobilizing for collective action to claim those rights. The two movements, RME and RCM, were born in reaction to decisions taken by those in political power. In order to understand the reasons why, at a given movement, certain groups decide to pool their efforts to defend certain rights and to achieve common objectives, we shall have to go back to the development of protest action in the late 1980s in Lebanon.

Without attempting to trace their genealogy, the two movements examined in this paper have their roots in other movements and have benefited from the experience of those who preceded them between 1987 and 1996. The accumulation of experience and know-how throughout that period today allows, for groups to more frequently resort to social movements as a form of action to protest or to advocate. Both the RME and the RCM share a number of actors and a non-violent mode of action with the anti-war movement led by trade unions, the disabled, and women (Slaiby 1993) between 1987 and 1990. Contrary to 'contesting' movements linked to political parties (such as Hezbollah or the Lebanese Forces), who started to question the legitimacy of the ruling power after the implementation of the Taëf agreement—and who ended up in certain cases in bloody confrontations with the armed forces—the RME and the RCM, learned to avoid the infiltration of their demonstrations and of their membership. They also learned how to precisely define the theme and limits of their mobilization. Later on, the solidarity movement in favor of displaced persons—those who fled from Southern Lebanon when their villages had been bombarded in April 1996—revealed the existence of associative structures that had, so far, been neglected and seemed inefficient, in various regions of the country. The mobilization of those structures became a priority for the groups leading social movements on a national scale. RME and RCM therefore benefited from pre-existing associative structures in order to develop themselves. At the start of each mobilization, one association called upon others to rally around so as to create a social movement. The participation of several associations and political parties provided formal networks and structures along which the movements spread out.

Two periods are to be noted in their development: a preparatory period, which could last several months, and a period of mobilization, which ended with the folding up of the movement and which includes moments of decline. The two movements in question had preset a date to put an end to their mobilization. The RME chose the day following the holding of municipal elections to fold up its movement. The RCM made it clear that if by April 2000 they had not yet achieved their objective, they would stop the movement while continuing to pursue the matter by using other means. In both movements, I make a distinction between two categories of actors: members and participants. Among the members, I make a distinction between organizers and militants. The organizers are the professionals of the 'claiming' action, who decide the theme, the forms of organization and the policy of the movement. The militants implement the plan of action decided by the organizers and, together, they carry out the mobilization in the field. The participants are the individuals or groups who rally around the movement while it unfolds in the field; they constitute its publicity. The members form the core and main body of the movement, since they are also the members of the organizations that originally formed the social movement (McCarthy and Zald 1977, Zald, and McCarthy 1987, 1979).

The Political Context in the Late 1990s and the Background of Experience

The context in which RME emerged in April 1997 was characterized by a closed and rigid political regime vis-à-vis public freedoms, particularly freedom of expression and freedom of association. The Ministry of the Interior had, since the early 1990s, imposed practices that went against the constitutional principles concerning freedom of association. For one thing, the ministry had transformed the receipt proving that associations had informed the administration of their establishment into a prior authorization; moreover, the Ministry intervened regarding the statutes and activities of associations. These practices went hand in hand with the government's decision in 1993 to ban demonstrations and public gatherings while tightening censorship of the media and other means of expression. Early in 1997, increasing interference of political authorities in the affairs and functions of other state institutions led the president of the council to tender his resignation. Similarly, interventions in trade union elections broke up the unity of the General Confederation of Workers by creating two groups, with two presidents, each claiming to be the legitimate representative of the confederation. All these crises, including the postponement of municipal elections, underlined the conflicts within the political power between the presidents of the republic, the council and parliament, a conflict over their prerogatives and respective positions and interests. In other words, the problems that erupted in the public space were, largely, a reflection of the problems existing in the political space and power circles.

Depending on their different allegiances, the organizers of the RME had different interpretations of the crises. This made it difficult from the start in April 1997, to define the theme and nature of their movement. One group wanted to denounce all violations of public freedoms by launching a vast campaign for democracy that would extend beyond the municipal elections. Another group called for an elitist action through the publication of a communiqué refusing the postponement of elections and proposing the amendment of the electoral law. A third group opted for a popular movement around the municipal elections that would mobilize the 1.2 million voters who had manifested their will to participate in the elections by withdrawing their ballot cards and who felt cheated by the decision to postpone them. Once the differences had been aired and the situation analyzed by each of the present members, the organizers had to adopt a common interpretation and to seek a consensus in order to launch the movement. By adjusting their respective frames of interpretation (Goffman 1991, Snow et al. 1986), they were able to entrust to a committee composed of ten intellectuals the elaboration of a plan of action to be submitted to all groups at the next meeting. The committee proposed the launching of a social movement, whose aim was the holding of elections and whose ambition was to mobilize all potential voters around one slogan: 'no to postponement, no to appointing, yes to municipal elections.' The organizers as a whole adopted the plan of action and decided that the movement would fold up the day after the elections.

Opportunities and Political Forces

The choice of the theme and nature of the movement as well as the choice of the modes of action reflects the political opportunities available to the organizers. The first opportunity they wished to seize in order to strengthen their movement was the popular consensus regarding the municipal elections and the massive mobilization of the voters who had taken their ballot cards—1.2 million voters or 75 percent of the electorate. The mobilization was seen as an indicator of a sense of civic duty that the organizers hoped to recover for their movement (after few months of mobilization, it turned out to be an overestimation). They confined the theme of their movement to the holding of the elections so as to benefit from this popular surge, rather than scattering it along several fronts. Yet, such a choice was also a strategic choice, since by limiting the scope of its claim, the movement risked inciting the enmity of the political powers to a lesser degree, than if they had fought for all the public freedoms. At another level, the form adopted by the movement, that of a 'rally,' was decided in keeping with the opportunities given by the political regime. The organizers wished to avoid any request for prior authorization, particularly from the Ministry of Interior. Contrary to other forms of organization, a 'rally' does not need prior authorization; it is a free framework that can be formed and folded up by the will of its members. Thus, the organizers of the RME avoided all legal obstacles to their movement, and in such a situation, the organizers could only adopt petitioning as a mode of action that was legal and guaranteed by the law (particularly since the ban on demonstrations and public gatherings was still in force in April 1997). From the legal point of view, petitioning, as a form of action, needs no prior authorization, whereas tracts and brochures must be vetted by security before distribution. Once again, the organizers tried to avoid the constraints of the political regime while remaining within the boundaries and under the protection of the law, particularly constitutional law.

During the preparatory stage of the movement, the organizers of RME had neither set of political alliances nor ties with the power circles that could change the decision concerning the postponement of elections (Tarrow 1998). Moreover, alliances at the level of political power were too vague and unstable for the organizers to join the camp of those who called for the elections (the president of the republic and the thirty-six out of 128 deputies who voted against the postponement). They avoided such a course in order to protect the movement from being manipulated or taken over by one political camp or the other. Yet they had personal relations with some members of parliament through whom they tried to establish a political parliamentary back-up by involving them in the movement.

Mobilization and Development of the Movement

The RME officially launched its movement in August 1997, following five months of preparation, during which the members worked out several plans of action. In terms of organization, RME adopted the form of weekly meetings that were open to all members and participants and at which the management of the movement took place. Another more specialized form was the setting up of sectorial committees (women, students, trade unions, professions, and the disabled) and media committees (spots, communiqués, and press files). The members mobilized two forms of structures, formal and informal (Klandermans 1992). The first ones included the associative structures that existed at the origin of the movement. Through their regional branches, RME organized several meetings once a week for several months in order to mobilize other groups and thus decentralize the movement via regional committees. The second form of structures included the informal networks of social activity, which allowed RME to reach neighborhood committees, family leagues and interpersonal circles. Everywhere, RME tried to set up fixed posts for signing the petition. They regularly published in newspapers a list of new posts for signing, with addresses, or a list of support groups (around two hundred associations, political parties, private societies, sports clubs, etc.). RME wanted to pursue its goal to the end, that of mobilizing the citizens at the local level in support of a theme that was both national and local. They resorted to all possible structures for the petition to reach towns and villages.

It is from this perspective that RME prepared their media campaign. Thanks to a number of militant journalists with the necessary know-how, RME had daily media coverage of all its activities. Then, the media committee prepared publicity spots, which were broadcast for free on the two main television channels (LBC and MTV), as well as radio spots and publicity frames for the newspapers (Champagne 1991, Gamson and Modigliani 1989). Finally, the press played an important role in distributing the petition in all the Lebanese regions (seven newspapers had published the petition before the militants distributed it in the field). This campaign, widespread and free of cost, was a true challenge for the members seeking a vast mobilization in the field, since they, sometimes, have had to face negative effects of media demonstrations. In fact, people first came to know the movement from the media, before the members could reach the field in the different regions. Following that, the militants used public places, cultural events, and cinema houses as locations to publicize the petition, obtain more signatures, and explain the purpose of their movement. They distributed T-shirts and stickers that read *"baladi, baldati, baladiyati"* ('my country, my village, and my municipality') alongside the name of the movement.

Political Back-up and Expansion of the Scope of Interpretation

On more than one occasion, the police hindered the activities of RME; the pretext being that the government had banned demonstrations and public meetings. The members would peacefully explain that their movement was legal (Della Porta 1995). Their meetings were often bolstered by the presence of members of parliament, and political and public figures, who acted as protectors. In fact, RME formalized the implicit alliance between the movement and certain deputies through a parliamentary nucleus in favor of holding the municipal elections. Some of its legitimate members helped a group of fourteen deputies to prepare a protest against the decision to postpone elections and submitted it to the Constitutional Council on August 13, 1997. On September 12, 1997, the council decided that the decisions to postpone elections and extend the mandates of the municipal councils were invalid; the Constitutional Council asked that the elections had to be held in accordance with constitutional laws.

Because of its implications, this decision constituted a turning point for RME. First of all, it gave a renewed energy to the movement and to the militants, who began to feel the impact of their mobilization of public opinion and the importance of capable political support in order to carry out a campaign at the institutional level. Subsequently, this decision renewed the faith of militants in certain public institutions' capacity to control and act as a counter-balance to power. Finally, members of RME came to redefine their frame of interpretation and add a new demand to their claims: to defend the decision of the Constitutional Council. This decision was, for them, an opportunity to show public opinion the efficiency of their movement and the need to pursue mobilization to the very end so that the verdict would be respected and implemented.

The second turning point, on the path of RME, was when parliament came to vote on December 22, 1997, on the decision to hold the municipal elections in June of 1998. As that parliament session was being held, RME invited the citizens to join non-violent sit-ins outside the building of the National Assembly, where the slogans of the movement were repeated. Several political forces (the Socialist Party, the Lebanese Forces, and partisans of General 'Aun, for example) as well as the Confederation of Lebanese

Workers seized the opportunity to demonstrate against police repression and the restrictions barring access to the media. Those demonstrations witnessed rhetorical confrontations of certain political groups as well as mutual accusations of treason and collaboration (between the pro-Syrians and the pro-Israelis), while others were there to defend political freedoms and the holding of the municipal elections. The RME militants had to calm the tension and remind the participants of the goal of the demonstration, thus distancing themselves from certain political groups. Despite these incidents, the RME's call for a demonstration in front of the parliament broke the ban on political demonstrations and expanded the range of its mobilizing action (Tilly 1986, Traugott 1995).

Following parliament's decision, RME was once again called upon to redefine its policy in order to lead its movement in light of the changes in public politics regarding the elections. In the debates preceding the definition of a new consensus on the collective frame of interpretation, some members went so far as to call for the movement to be transformed into a political force so that it may nominate its own candidates in elections. The majority refused, and chose to expand their frame of interpretation (Snow et al. 1986). Simultaneous with the petition, RME insisted in its campaigns, on the importance of municipalities in local development and on the right of voters to uphold the common interest of their communities. In order to attract a new public, who had so far shown little interest in the cause of municipal elections, RME organized several music concerts featuring a popular singer. In the same vein, the members organized lectures, gatherings, and debates in different regions to explain the role of municipalities and encourage candidates to run for them with well-defined projects. They wanted to re-concentrate the debate on the municipalities within each local community, as well as in the public spaces and fora of each town. RME maintained its mobilization pace until its dissolution after the last round of municipal elections on June 18, 1998.

When analyzing the impact of their movement on the holding of municipal elections, the members of RME placed themselves in a wide context. They linked the holding of the elections to factors inherent to the Lebanese regime, to the decision of the Constitutional Council, and to the agreement between the two big groups in parliament (that of the prime minister and of the head of parliament) at the time when the decision was voted. They also included external factors that provided a favorable climate, namely the speech of U.S. Secretary of State Madeleine Albright during her visit to Beirut on the importance of local elections, as well as the consent of the Syrian regime. On the one hand, the importance of RME resides in the fact that for the first time in the post-war period in Lebanon, a movement was mobilized in all the regions, for one cause and with the same slogans. RME always imposed the same slogans in the regional demonstrations so as to maintain the unity of the movement and prove the possibility of organizing a collective action despite political and regional divergences. Moreover, RME allowed some of its militants to occupy the public space at both the national and the local levels; in the media, at conferences, in public meetings and debates, and by having them present in public places to discuss the movement with people and have them sign the petition. The movement proved the possibility of the emergence of 'new actors' specialized in certain sociopolitical matters.

The Social Movement as a 'Generalized' Mode of Participation and Political Claims

Comparing RME to the social movement for civil marriage reveals important elements related to the emergence and development of social movements in general. Encouraged by the RME and the results of its experience, civil groups decided to launch a social movement in defense of the draft law for civil marriage voted by the Council of Ministers. In April 1988, the organizers of RCM had chosen the social movement as their form of political action for claiming rights. Their choice was made in spite of the crisis caused by the vote on the project among the three presidents, within the political regime, and in spite of its categorical rejection by the religious powers. The transmission of experience and knowledge from the RME to the RCM, was remarkable from several aspects: the modes of action, forms of organization, structures mobilized, and even the debate that took place during the meetings that preceded the launching of the movement. The RCM benefited, on the one hand, from the existence of a formal political structure that had for long been working on the question of civil marriage and from the mobilization of students in several universities at a time when the organizers of RME were still at the stage of preparing the movement. Those two groups rallied around the RCM as it was launching its campaign. They agreed on a collective framework of interpretation that consisted of: (1) submitting a draft of an optional civil code of personal status and not only to claim the establishment of a civil marriage; (2) not to consider the movement as an act of opposition to a group (political or religious), but rather as a movement claiming a constitutional right, which is included in public freedoms; (3) consulting other groups who had worked on the question of civil marriage and carried out long term action based on education and information.

The two movements (RME and RCM) stemmed from the same sociopolitical 'milieu'—the 'claiming' associations of the 1990s—and had almost the same actors, particularly at the level of the organizers and members. However, when the RCM launched its movement on the basis of the same structures and with same members as the RME, it did not take into consideration the fact that the militants were tired from one year of mobilization. Moreover, the concomitance of the two movements raised the problem of defending an entirely different cause for the militants of RME.

Subject of Claims and Faced Challenges

The RCM took over some of the formal structures of the previous movement, such as civil associations and certain political parties. Yet, a large part of the structures, particularly at the local level (local associations, sports clubs, and family leagues, for example) did not mobilize themselves over the question of civil marriage. On the one hand, the majority of those structures rallied around their religious institutions to form a social countermovement to the cause of civil marriage (Duyvendak 1994). On the other hand, others preferred to remain neutral, either because they did not want to stand against the religious authorities and certain political figures, or because they were not concerned by the matter. All the advantages brought together for the RCM to carry on its movement did not mitigate the influence of the religious powers. Indeed, the RCM avoided the establishment of its group identity in a negative manner, by standing in opposition to the other. It affirmed its will to establish a new social and cultural identity. Yet, for the Lebanese politico-religious system, a civil, personal status law, even optional, was a major challenge to the power and prerogatives of religious institutions in particular. The RCM demanded recognition of certain civic rights by referring to the freedom of citizens to choose their own way of life. Such a claim prevented it from placing its movement at the center of Lebanese society. In spite of such a difficulty, the RCM counted on parliamentarian support in order to have its draft law adopted. What remains to be seen is whether the weight of the opponents, particularly the religious powers, would succeed in preventing the institutionalization of civil marriage, particularly since the president of the republic promised the religious leaders, in January 2000, that no draft that could be seen to go against religion would be discussed without consulting them in advance. What also remains to be seen is whether parliamentarian groups, who have been working on the question of civil marriage for decades will benefit from the RCM, so as to make their draft law more legitimate and more representative.

Non-violent Social Movement, Independent of Institutional Powers

Several social movements of the type I have described were born in Lebanon in the 1990s. The ecologists are increasingly mobilizing in the form of collective action and through federations, which can constitute permanent structures to carry on social movements. The youth, who were mobilized in the RME, today have their own movement in favor of political coming-of-age at eighteen. The movement for searching for the missing from the civil war, created at the beginning of the war, called upon 'professionals' in the field of 'collective action' to help them better negotiate with political institutions. The same is true of the disabled who are mobilizing different resources and structures of Lebanese society in order to defend their rights.

Such movements do have common traits that call for grouping them within one single category. One can find, in most of them, some characteristics of the 'claims' associations of the 1990s, since they did inherit their organization and their structures.

Such movements are, first of all, pacifist movements, which marks a break from the violence of fifteen years of war and helps them gain support for their mobilization efforts. Violence was the cause of the downfall of several movements that developed during the same period. The Movement of the Starving of Shaykh Tufayli, to give an example, was dismantled and banned following deadly confrontations with the army in 1997. The difference resides in the fact that while the latter acts in opposition to order and legitimacy, the former acts on the basis of implementation of the law and claiming civil rights. The established order is never contested. In other words, I differentiate between two types of movements: those who want to achieve change by bringing down the regime ('the revolutionaries') and those who seek change through a greater participation in the institutions by relying on constitutional rights and obligations (the 'reformists').

If the latter type of movement manages to maintain its formation to the end, it is also because they avoid extreme dependence on external support (whether from the state, the community, or ideological sources). Such a movement invests in and makes use of all possible means to achieve its objectives; it does not cease its comings and goings between public and private space, and between the various institutions belonging to the state, the community, the family, and civil society. They establish contacts with traditional leaders in order to mobilize their followers; they also contact others in order to obtain financial aid and technical support; they negotiate in order to rally public figures for their fame. Yet, the relative independence of such a movement vis-à-vis traditional powers appears in the fact that community or political groups no longer exclusively define common good and the direction of any collective action. Such a movement constitutes both an avant-garde in the public space and an opposition to the 'traditional' forces, forces that neither believe in nor would allow for the possible emergence of new autonomous actors. It is in this middle position that the strength and weakness of such a type of movement resides. The movement, according to Touraine (1999), enters the political space while at the same time, defending its independence vis-à-vis the other actors on the political stage.

These common characteristics however, masks the divergences and dispersion of such a movement that hampers its capacity to unify itself. In that sense, it differs from the movements of the pre-1975 Lebanese left; the latter appeared as a relatively unified social force in spite of their ideological differences, and this allowed them, at least for the first two years, to wage the same battle. Today, a common framework of interpretation and, sometimes, an ideological framework for each movement often hide several orientations and trends in the movement's various components. In most cases, the consensus or compromise within the movement is frequently only achieved with respect to the object of the mobilization, and without including other sociopolitical domains. Behind, it hides the undercurrents of interactions and power conflicts, which the media also help in hiding by presenting only the common stand. Those movements often try to make up for their weakness in mobilizing by resorting to actions, which are sometimes only for the sake of media coverage. The fundamental stake for them is their capacity to transcend media operations and to allow the emergence of new actors and new permanent modes of action by promoting their movement at the national level (from the national to the local). This rediscovery of political action allows them to impose their presence vis-à-vis the state and other dominant forces and to bring about certain changes and transformations in society or in public policies. One can already see the beginnings of institutionalization of collective action, which appears in the attempt to create federations among different associations (working on issues related to ecological and human rights issues, for example) and in the creation of political parties based on those movements.

Chapter Fifteen

Donors, International NGOs, and Palestine NGOs: Funding Issues and Globalized Elite Formation

Sari Hanafi

For the past few decades, an intense debate has periodically emerged in the Palestinian Territories as well as in other Arab countries regarding the relationship between foreign donors, international non-governmental organizations (INGOs), and local NGOs. This issue is usually presented in terms of an opposition between local agendas and that of others, often those of the West. It is in this context that this study seeks to raise questions related to the agenda of donors and local recipients and the relationship between them. It will focus on the emergence of what I call a 'globalized' Palestinian elite composed of the leadership of NGOs and the local leadership of international NGOs. We will examine the decision-making process from the negotiation phase between Palestinian NGOs (PNGOs), INGOs, and foreign donors, to the implementation of projects by PNGOs, which draws on the outlines of the policies and strategies of local development.

This chapter is based on two previous research studies:
1) A survey that I conducted in the summer of 1998. I interviewed donors, who assist Palestinian NGOs, compiling systematic data on projects, policies, priorities, and funding sources. The organizations researched were: governmental (GOVs), inter-governmental (IGOs), and international non-governmental (INGOs).
2) Preliminary investigation concerning a research study that I am currently coordinating with the objective of analyzing and delineating the nature of the relationship between donors, INGOs, and PNGOs with regard to

agenda setting. They will be presented and analyzed in my book co-written by Linda Taber (2005).

Could One Speak of a Global Agenda?

In the context of a municipal and state sector (and, in some respects, private sector) paralyzed by the events of the Intifada, Palestinian NGOs have assumed important responsibilities not only in social affairs but also, in some regards, in the economic survival of Palestinian society. Paradoxically, the number of NGOs did not decrease after the Palestinian National Authority's (PNA) arrival. The Palestinian NGO boom was encouraged by a doubly restrictive political and economic situation; while Israeli occupation continued in many areas, there was evident mismanagement of public affairs on the part of the PNA. This context, however, does not provide a full explanation for what Salamon termed the 'associative revolution' (1993: 1). This phenomenon can be traced to the new international paradigm whose constitutive elements stem from neo-liberal ideological roots.

Stimulated by the World Bank's report on poverty in 1990 (which attempted to correct the side-effects of widespread Structural Adjustment Programs) and the fall of the Berlin Wall that same year, western governments identified a cluster of policy ideas, which are currently held as a model for good economic and political management. This model is known as the 'Washington Consensus' in certain economic circles, while many political scientists have referred to it simply as 'good governance.' The model is based on three elements: a competitive market economy, a well-managed state, and a democratic civil society. While the model can be seen as market-driven and consumer-led, and therefore firmly embedded in neo-liberal thought, Archer sees such a model as signifying an important break with neo-liberalism,[1] in its recognition that the market is not the entire answer (Clayton 1994: 7). Such a model rehabilitates the state, which is given central social and economic responsibilities, and attempts, albeit timidly, to promote human rights and democracy—both seen as requirements of the modern market economy and a well-managed state. While neo-liberalism destroyed the relationship between government, the economy, and society, 'good governance' re-unites society's political, economic, and social dimensions (Clayton 1994: 7–34).

However, it is only recently that the 'good governance' model has addressed the importance of the role of NGOs, and specifically the transformation of their role from executor to a new development actor, working complementarily with the state and not as an alternative to it. This concept of 'good governance' has been mainly articulated along two dimensions, the prescriptive and the normative, since it is concerned with the transition of states to a liberal economic system, while minimizing the negative effects of such a transition on society. However, proponents of 'good governance' also articulate a third analytical dimension, which seeks a conception of political power not in terms of a monolithic actor—the state—but in conjunction with other actors, such as local networks and NGOs. The analytical perspective seeks to supersede an institutional approach toward political action in favor of a study of multiple actors in situations of interaction, conflict, and negotiation.

Influenced by the model of 'good governance,' development policy and aid transfers have, since the end of the Cold War, come to be dominated by what Mark Robinson (1993) calls a 'New Policy Agenda.' The agenda is not monolithic and varies in its specifics from one official aid agency to another, but in most cases it is driven by beliefs revolving around the twin poles of neo-liberal economics and liberal democratic theory (Moore 1993). Firstly, markets and private initiatives are perceived as the most efficient mechanisms for achieving economic growth and providing the greatest amount of services to as many people as possible. Secondly, NGOs are seen as vehicles for democratization and essential components of civil society. This "New Policy Agenda," or as Imco Brouwer (1998) refers to it, the "New Washington Consensus," serves as established parameters among international actors for the methods of promoting political and economic reform in countries undergoing transition.

While there is a broad measure of agreement between various donors on the content of the 'good governance' agenda, there are differences in the emphasis they place on the promotion of human rights. Archer notes that while the British government has a very broad definition of good government, the German government emphasizes the promotion of popular participation in the political process. Canada, Denmark, Norway, and the U.S. all lay particular stress on the promotion of human rights and democratic reform (1994: 12–17). In any case, the new policy agenda has been noticeably promoted in many contexts through the allocation of specific funds for programs related to institutional reform and civic education. In this respect, it has been rather fashionable, in some contexts, to support human rights and democracy through civic education.

Donor Assistance to Palestinian NGOs: An Overview [2]

In the context of the peace process and the transitional national status of the Palestinian territories, international donor contributions to Palestinian NGOs have played a vital role. While the role played by these donors is significant, with over 130 foreign donors assisting Palestinian NGOs today, there are no reliable statistics or other data concerning the scope of their activities and the level of assistance to NGOs, other than a survey (Hanafi 1999)[3] undertaken by the Welfare Association.[4] Furthermore, there is little research investigating donor impact on local NGO agendas in the areas of development and democratization. An intense debate has periodically emerged in the Palestinian territories, as well as in other Arab countries, in the past few decades regarding the issue of agenda setting. It has become clear from this debate that the issue is usually posed in terms of opposition between the 'local' agenda and that of other actors, often western; moreover, socially and politically contentious topics prompt discussion concerning agenda priorities.[5] On many occasions, PNA officials have considered sectors like human rights and democracy, as well as gender, to be over-funded, and responding to donor agenda. This is criticized not only by PNA officials but also by some intellectuals, who consider such an agenda to be politically serving the interest of the 'enemy.' A subsequent crisis between NGOs and the PNA concerning funding erupted in June 1999, leading to the creation of the Ministry of NGO Affairs in that same month.[6] The PNA often regards NGOs with suspicion because of their foreign ties and the fact that their activities sometimes substitute state service provision, thus reducing state control over resources and services.

While the donor role played by the international community has been significant in the case of Palestinian NGOs, there are no reliable statistics or other data about the scope of activities and the level of assistance.[7] Consequently, the Welfare Association initiated a survey of donor organizations assisting the Palestinian NGO sector in order to compile systematic information about policies, projects, and funding sources.

The information collected was compiled in a computer database capable of generating statistical and graphic reports about the distribution of project funding by sector and sub-sector, geographical area (at the level of district, city, or village/hamlet), sources of funding, and direct and indirect beneficiaries. The database can provide cross-tabulated information for thirty different criteria.

The survey gathered information from about one hundred organizations. Despite the reluctance of a few organizations to release detailed information, in general, the data obtained forms a sound basis for a database on PNGO projects funded by international NGOs. Together, these donors contribute more than $60 million annually to the NGO sector, for a total of $248 million in the last four years. This contribution constitutes an estimated 10 to 20 percent of total international donor assistance to the Palestinian territories (See Table 1).

Funding Distribution: Sectoral Profile

The survey attempted to determine the amount of funding allocated to different sectors. Irrespective of the various peaks and falls in funding over the years, an overall image of funding direction for the four-year period 1995–98 can be ascertained (See Table 2):

1) Education and health still remain the most important sectors of interest for NGOs, although formal responsibility for these areas was transferred to the Palestinian National Authority more than four years ago. While education received 23.3 percent of donor funds to Palestinian NGOs (about $56 million) from 1995–98, health received 19.6 percent ($50 million).

2) The other sectors share smaller portions of the remaining 58 percent in donor funds. Although the largest Palestinian economic sector is agriculture, it remains neglected or ignored by donors, with only $18 million (7.4 percent) directed to the sector in the four-year period. The Palestinian Agriculture Relief Committee (PARC) is the primary NGO working in the sector and has received $12 million of this figure in support of agricultural activities.

3) The traditional NGO sectors of culture and social services also have small shares of total funding, with $20 million for each (about 8 percent) for the period 1995–98.

4) Micro-credit activities and the private sector in general lag far behind other sectors, indicating the lack of NGO activity in the economic sphere. Only 3.9 percent of total funding ($10 million) was devoted to these activities. Additionally, tourism, while important in the region, remains very marginal in the activities of the Palestinian NGOs, with only 0.4 percent of total funding ($1 million).

5) It is very clear that there has been a dramatic shift in the orientation of both donors and Palestinian NGOs from relief assistance to development

assistance. There is a very small percentage of relief activities in terms of total funds ($2 million, representing 1 percent) for the period 1995–98.
6) There is a new interest and awareness toward the environment on the part of Palestinian NGOs, which could be encouraged by INGOs in the context of international debate on environmental issues and a decentralization of efforts between state and civil society. These projects involve core development issues for Palestinian society since most environmental projects concern water supply, sewerage, and solid waste treatment. These activities constitute 2.9 percent of total funds ($7 million)
7) With time, human rights and democracy assumed more importance in terms of funding. In 1998, this sector constituted 9.5 percent of funding ($5 million). Over the last four years, however, this area averaged only 4.4 percent of total funding (about $11 million). This percentage may be somewhat, but not substantially, higher since a few donors did not provide full information concerning projects in this sector.
8) According to the survey, the research sector received 1.9 percent of funding ($4.6 million), but since this sector was funded by international foundations, which did not always have a local presence, the percentage of funding it receives is assumed to be somewhat larger than the figures suggest.

Sub-sectoral Profile

We will now view the distribution of funding by sub-sector. Using sub-sectors allows more precision in determining sectoral profiles, although this was not possible to determine for all projects. The most enlightening sub-sectors studied proved to be women's development and the disabled. Projects for women received 7.2 percent of total funding, or $18 million over the last four years, while 11.4 percent of total funding was directed to the needs of the disabled ($28 million). In some sub-sectors, such as early childhood or youth, it was difficult to identify, which portion of a funded project was oriented toward these categories.

Distribution of Funding by District

The location concerned here is the geographic location of the implemented project and not that of the head office of PNGOs or the implementing agencies. When accurate data was not available on the geographical distribution of funds, the funding was considered for distribution over all of Palestine. Due to a lack of more detailed information, implementing agencies or beneficiaries operating only in the West Bank or only in Gaza were considered to implement their projects only in those respective areas.

The distribution of funds for NGO projects was found to be extremely lopsided as regards the Gaza Strip and West Bank, with only $26.4 million for Gaza (19 percent) and $111.5 million for the West Bank (81 percent). The distribution is disproportionate to population and to apparent need: according to the latest census figures, the population of the Gaza Strip is 1,022,207 (35 percent of the Palestinian population) and has a far higher rate of poverty and unemployment than the West Bank (see Tables 3–5). This funding imbalance could be explained by such structural factors as the historical weakness of the PNGO sector in Gaza[8] compared to that of the West Bank. Logistical issues may also play a part as the overwhelming majority of donors are based in the West Bank, and especially in Jerusalem, which could be considered as a kind of 'clientele relationship.' However, some donors held the view that the PNA invests proportionately more in Gaza than in the West Bank (although this has not been verified by statistics on funding) and chose to compensate for this by directing more funding to NGOs in West Bank.

A look at the distribution of funding by district within the West Bank reveals that Jerusalem, contrary to the widespread belief that donors neglect it, enjoys a relatively larger share of total West Bank funding (25 percent) than other districts. While some donors do not support projects in Jerusalem for reasons of 'political sensitivity,' other donors have given the district priority due to religious significance or as a means of supporting the area's endangered Palestinian population. The second most popular location for funded projects is Ramallah (7 percent of funding for the total West Bank) followed by Bethlehem (6 percent), Nablus (4.8 percent), Hebron (4.8 percent), and Jenin (3.8 percent). Bethlehem benefits from a level of funding disproportionate to its population, especially when compared to larger cities such as Hebron and Nablus, probably due to the development efforts and special projects associated with the celebration of Bethlehem 2000. Tulkarm and Qalqilya represent marginalized districts. In the distribution of funding by districts in the Gaza Strip, Gaza City represents 30 percent of the total funding of the region.

In comparing the distribution of funding to population by district (according to the findings of the Palestinian census of 1998), the survey findings are only significant as a percentage and not as an absolute number due to the fact that only a portion of these projects were geographically identifiable. Table 6 demonstrates that the share of funding for Jerusalem is equal to its share of population (11 percent), while Hebron, Tulkarm, Qalqilya, Tubas, and Salfit are under funded compared to the size of their population. In the Gaza Strip, the cities of Deir Balah, Khan Younis, and Rafah are very poorly funded compared to the governorate of Gaza.

Accordingly, we can state that the distribution of funding shows not only an imbalance between center and periphery and between urban and rural, but also with respect to population density. Some districts with a high population density received relatively small shares of funding.

Supply Availability in Relation to Need Assessment

To what extent does foreign funding, which is constrained by administrative, economic, and political factors, promote the priorities of PNGOs? How can donor supply (funding) be correlated with local perceptions of developmental needs? One method of determining such a relationship is to analyze donors' adherence or non-adherence to the priorities presented by local needs assessments. With this objective in mind, the Welfare Association Consortium, which manages the World Bank-supported PNGO Project, conducted a survey to identify local needs in areas of service provision for the poor and marginalized in Jerusalem, the West Bank, and Gaza (Ayed 1998). This study identifies separate priorities for Jerusalem, the West Bank, and Gaza.

Interestingly enough, a focus on sectors reveals that the projects funded by donors (the supply), as recorded in the Welfare Association survey, are not so different from the needs assessment outlining local demand. Does this indicate a consensus between the donors and the local partners about the politics of development? As will be demonstrated below, simply examining sectors is insufficient in this regard; project content is of great importance and may paint a contradictory picture. Below, we compare the Consortium's local needs assessment with the Welfare survey on donor funding patterns:

1) The local needs assessment found that a priority common to the areas is "non-formal and community education." According to the Welfare Association survey, education, both formal and non-formal, receives the greatest portion of funding with 23.3 percent ($58 million).

    Early childhood education was well served, especially in 1998, with 4.5 percent of total funding and 2.4 percent in the period from 1995 to 1998. Vocational training did not receive a significant amount of funding—

about $5 million during the four years, representing 2 percent of total funding. For Gaza, the needs assessment identified community health education as a priority, which was in fact well served, especially in terms of education on family planning and reproductive health.

Some experts have complained that the reproductive health education sub-sector is actually over-funded and has surpassed the absorptive capacity of Palestinian society. While there is a near consensus among social scientists that education and job opportunities for women are the major factors in reducing fertility, donors still tend to focus on culture as the determining factor of a high fertility rate.[9]

2) Health was also listed as a priority for all three geographical areas in Palestine. According to the Welfare Association survey, 19.6 percent of total funding was oriented to this sector ($50 million).

3) Income-generating and micro-credit projects, especially for women and orphans, the disabled and former political prisoners, were another priority in all three geographical areas of Palestine. According to the survey, $8 million was disbursed to this sector, constituting 3.9 percent of total funding, with most of it directed toward projects for women. Apparently, PNGOs adhere to this global trend without necessarily questioning its relevance to the Palestinian context. In any event, the impact of donor-financed NGO credit schemes is now so pervasive that, as some have observed, it appears to be having a transformational effect on society itself: an expectation that NGOs will deliver credit as part of their programs has become endemic among Palestinian village residents. Supply seems to shape demand, and the experience of the Grameen Bank and other institutions has demonstrated that the poor are bankable, i.e., poor people can also respect the rule of this market and of the financial institutions (Hulme and Edwards 1997: 9).

4) Rehabilitation for the disabled was a priority for both the Gaza Strip and West Bank (excluding Jerusalem). Funding for this purpose, either in the field of health, social services, education, or vocational training for the disabled was significant, with $28 million (11.4 percent of total funding), but would appear to be particularly disorganized according to information from primary actors involved. A chief complaint is of an unbalanced distribution of resources by area. The situation is exacerbated, according to other actors, by occupancy rates at some centers that are well below capacity, most probably due to Israeli-imposed movement restrictions and difficulties for the population in entering Jerusalem. A survey conducted

by the Palestinian Planning Center in Gaza reached the same conclusion. However, this survey also indicated that existing vocational training programs for the disabled are insufficient, especially in the West Bank.

5) Housing was listed as a priority in the needs assessment survey, but this area is rarely the focus of projects funded by the donors (0.8 percent). Donors apparently consider this sector to be the responsibility of the Palestinian National Authority or of the private sector.

Based on this analysis, two issues can be raised: the first concerns the relationship between the development sectors donors are willing to fund and local perceptions of needs; the second relates to the assumptions made about NGO service provision and the needs of the society. With regard to the former, it becomes apparent that sectoral priority is not as significant or as revealing as the activities carried out within the sector: that is to say, the issue is not that there is, for example, too much of a focus on women, but whether or not this target group is assisted by the relevant projects. The question of agenda exists at the supra-sectoral level (where general policies, rather than selection of the sectors of intervention of the donor, are determined) and the infra-sectoral level (where project design, methodology, and approaches are determined) much more than at the sectoral level. To further explain this perspective, we will discuss the following issues: project versus program, advocacy versus service provision, and discourse versus actual practices.

Concerning the actor's legitimacy in determining needs assessment, current discourse concerning NGOs recognizes that the social services offered by NGOs respond to heterogeneous trends in the demands formulated by various communities (Salamon 1993: 1). Generally, in this view, such services do not encompass, except in rare cases, the population on a national level. Thus certain areas are (deliberately or not) left without service. Moreover, service provision is generally interpreted as being addressed to target groups chosen in a rational manner (i.e., marginalized groups, the unemployed, etc.). This interpretation, however, neglects the relevance of pragmatic factors such as geographical proximity of beneficiaries, specific group relations, and political affiliations that often influence the selection of the target group to a greater extent than other rational factors. Thus the process of selection of beneficiaries by NGOs, which is often guided by factors other than overarching societal or national interest, has replaced the standardization of services at the national level previously carried out by the state. Therefore, the studies and decisions taken by the NGO sector have replaced state planning.

In the Palestinian case, it becomes problematic to discuss priorities for the NGO sector because the work of NGOs, reflecting a political and social plurality, is so fragmented. The relationship between these organizations can vary from cooperation to rivalry, and indeed competition. These diverse actors select sectors of priority according to a perception that they are responding to the needs formulated by the target groups at the village or city level. But which groups or individuals specifically determine the priority for the NGOs: the state, NGO coalitions, sectoral coordinating bodies, private consultants, or other institutions? If the state assumes this role, then it is possible that the raison d'être of an organization may be called into question, as relative autonomy of NGOs in relation to the state allows them, for instance, to advance a conception of services that can provide an alternative to state policies. Even though the NGO conceives its mission as being complementary to that of the state, the latter should not impose its choice of priorities. Moreover, even though it would appear legitimate that the PNA maintains security strategies (since the Palestinian territories still remain largely under occupation), NGO priorities are certainly guided by a social logic as opposed to a political one. In this sense, to speak of NGO priorities does not mean that a consensus exists in the society or within the sector of the NGO, or between this sector, the state, the private sector and the other institutions of civil society (unions and political parties). This consensus is only possible when mechanisms facilitating cooperation exist between the different actors, which is not the case in the Palestinian territories.

The needs assessment survey of the Welfare Association Consortium was certainly the most reliable survey produced in the Palestinian territories up until 1998 (the study was made in 1999), but it was open to criticism for the insufficient attention focused on the actual amount of funds donors are disbursed in certain sectors. For example, whereas community health education was recommended in Gaza, the investigation conducted in 1998 on awareness programs and research in family planning and reproductive health indicates an excessive proliferation of such activities (Hanafi 1999). The focus of such programs is contraceptive awareness, family planning and the like. In a similar way, the Consortium's needs assessment identifies the rehabilitation of the disabled as a priority without sufficiently considering the volume of assistance directed at this sub-sector. Indeed, the various PNGO and INGO actors interviewed in the Palestinian territories insisted that initiatives were being carried out in some regions while in others there was a lack of rehabilitation centers. In fact, the actors working in this area on the ground are quite fragmented; while the United Nations Relief and Works Agency (UNRWA) manages rehabilitation services in refugee camps, the Union of Palestinian Medical Relief Committees, with its populist political affiliations, the Palestinian Red Crescent Society, a PLO (but not PNA) affiliated organ, and finally a succession of small Christian and Islamic health associations administer the remainder of services. This diversity of actors, enmeshed in power games and political rivalry, makes coordination very difficult.

Donor Community Profile

Historically many INGOs have operated as implementing agencies in Palestine,[10] a role justified by their technical expertise in providing social services to developing countries and their status as foreign organizations with diplomatic support from their respective governments that allow relative freedom of movement under Israeli occupation.

Some of these INGOs have gradually moved from this function to that of donor agencies while aiding in the establishment of a substitute local NGO as implementing agency. This was the case of the Civic Forum, which broke away from the U.S.-based organization, National Democratic Institute (DNA), and became a Palestinian NGO. Similarly, the Ard al-Insan organization began its existence as the Gaza branch of the Swiss INGO, 'Terre des Hommes,' but became independent in 1996. Some Palestinian counterparts have complained that implementing INGOs did not help build Palestinian capacity, but instead replaced it. However, the proportion of INGOs acting as implementing agencies is very small and their function in this capacity appears to remain justified in light of their actual work on the ground in the context of continuing political uncertainty in Palestine.

Coordination between donor agencies and INGOs ranges from the the informal to none at all. As UNESCO coordinator, Francis Dubois commented, "All organizations recommend coordination but do not want to be coordinated." Brynen argues that one factor inhibiting the development of effective mechanisms of donor coordination is the unfair allocation of the financial burden among countries (Brynen, et al. 1999). At the NGO level, there is the Association of International Development Agencies (AIDA), which attempts to coordinate between ten to twenty INGO members. As the president of AIDA declared, however, the meetings have become general discussions of the impediments to work imposed by Israel and, to a lesser extent, the PNA, rather than being focused on coordination.

The U.S. has been the largest donor country to Palestinian NGOs, with $44 million disbursed between 1995–98 (19 percent of total funding to Palestinian NGOs over the three-year period). However, compared to the size of its economy and the period of support to NGOs in Palestine, the U.S. share is quite small. Germany, with $32 million (14 percent of total funding over the same three-year period), has been the second largest donor, followed by Norway with $28 million (12 percent of total funding), Sweden with $22.5 million (9.7 percent), Switzerland with $17 million (7.4 percent), and the Netherlands with $15 million (6.6 percent). In this respect, Norway stands out as the most generous country if we calculate its contribution relative to the size of its economy, or Gross National Product (GNP), which reflects a willingness to complement the state's political initiatives with economic aid to Palestinians.

All these figures concern funding given by the gamut of donors, be they governmental agencies or NGOs from each of those countries. While the former constitute only a quarter of the total number of organizations, this does not necessarily signify marginal funding on their part since the budgets of the INGOs and NGOs are not necessarily collected only from their respective populations (from charitable donations for example) but from governmental sources as well. Generally, NGOs are characterized by closeness between the state and NGOs working in foreign countries, which are funded mainly by the state or by international agencies. In the French model, however, NGOs remain relatively autonomous and do not depend on state funding. But with globalization and the creation of supra-state organizations such as the European Union, even the latter organizations intend to gradually and eventually procure their funding from the French government or the European Union—as is the case of Pharmaciens Sans Frontières (Pharmacies Without Borders) or Vétérinaires sans frontières (Veterinarians Without Borders).

The survey raised issues concerning the functioning of the INGOs and other donor agencies. The following observations can be made:

1) Some donors are badly equipped, ill prepared, and lack first-hand knowledge concerning the socioeconomic environment of Palestinian society and the complicated structure of PNGOs. This has implications for the quality of project follow-up. Many donors do not ask for more than a final report at the end of the project.
2) donors reserve a large proportion of their budget for operating costs; in one case, an organization used approximately 60 percent of its budget for

the expenses of two expatriate employees: one, the director, and the other, an accountant. Clearly, the latter could be replaced with a local employee.

3) Western donors channel their aid either directly to the PNGOs or indirectly through INGOs. It was noted, however, that donors sometimes direct aid through INGOs unnecessarily, even for such purchases as hospital equipment, and that the organizations then deduct a percentage of the funds to cover their own operating costs. This was the case when the European Union's European Commission for Humanitarian Operations (ECHO) disbursed funding for the Palestinian Red Crescent via Italian NGOs.

Some Elements of Local NGO Agenda-Setting

This part seeks to raise questions on the practices of agenda setting by donors and local recipients and the relationship between them. As noted above, the sectors funded by donors do not vary considerably from the needs assessment conducted by the Welfare Consortium survey, considered by the consortium to be the expression of the 'national NGO agenda.' Does this indicate that the donor-driven agenda and the constituency agenda are the same and that the global is effectively inspired by the local—that there is sufficient coordination, interaction, and negotiation between INGO, local NGO, and donor? It may instead be more informative to view the relationship as one of osmosis between donor and INGO elites on the one hand, and a local NGO elite on the other hand. This raises the issue of the emergence of a 'globalized' Palestinian leadership elite. Thus, the question is no longer whether the NGO agenda is donor-driven or constituency-driven; instead we should ask if an oppositional relationship really exists between donors and the membership of this 'globalized elite.' Before examining the characteristics of this 'globalized elite,' we will briefly study the decision-making processes, which take place at the donor level.

Some Elements of the Donor Decision-Making Process

Agenda setting by local NGOs is obviously a much more complicated process than a simple imposition of the donor community's agenda over that of the local actor. Certainly, donors have their own agendas, which reflect their economic and political interests. USAID, for example, defines itself in its website as "an independent federal government agency that conducts foreign assistance and humanitarian aid to advance the political and economic interests of the United States" (see *www.usaid.gov*). In the case of donor contributions to the Palestinian National Authority, a donor's policy can be made quite clear, for example, when it provides technical assistance through a foreign actor who will, in one way or another, return the expenditure to the donor country (See Brynen et al. 1999). However, the question is more complicated regarding NGO agendas. Donors tend to have either a broad framework for sectoral priorities, allowing for flexibility and leaving room for general interpretation or, in the case of a specific sector, have no clearly defined programs or projects.

In some cases, we noticed the absence of any real agenda, and in other cases existing agendas did not necessarily reflect rational choices. As Brynen et al., argue, these decisions are driven, in large part, by institutional and idiosyncratic factors, as well as a substantial degree of serendipity. The counterparts, while conducting the survey, expressed problems of priority identification and of effective program formation. In these cases, the donors are likely to leave the allocation of funds open and encourage PNGOs to submit proposals, instead of choosing the more effective option of working with a qualified, competent, and transparent partner on a permanent basis.

While donor agencies are traditionally studied in the context of institutions, I will instead approach them as organizations in order to better examine the subjectivity of the various actors. In the view of Crozier and Friedberg (1977), an organization is a social construct aiming to solve problems of collective action. The existence of the organization itself suggests a minimum of integration regarding the behavior of the concerned social actors who, nevertheless, pursue divergent objectives. The organization constructs a structuring game, whose nature and rules are based on a series of possible 'winning strategies.' Thus, no action is produced nor any decision made arbitrarily by members of the organization and there remains room for uncertainty of outcome and maneuver by its various actors. The concept of organization preserves the autonomy of the actors while its rules influence collective decisions by limiting differences with regard to the fundamental objectives of the organization. These rules are the product of human activity and constitute an external constraint on individual decisions in a system of legitimization. The rules must also be in harmony with the 'philosophy' of the organization and its members, and must work as a process of regulation rather than of fixed constraints. Thus, through collective action, this process of regulation allows for not only the creation but also the transformation of the rules (Carré and Zaoual 1998: 328). This approach proves useful in grasping the diversity of the actors within the organizations themselves. The decision-making process of donor and PNGO actors does not represent fixed and immutable rules but instead reflects negotiation and even contradictions within the organization.

Based on observations from fieldwork, the administrative staff is responsible for selecting local partners and suitable proposals and has decision-making power to modify and negotiate with the directing office and with superiors. These technocrats are certainly more than mere executors since they play a major role in decision-making. Substantive interaction exists between the donor's primary orientation and feedback from the administrative staff's 'on the ground' experience. Therefore, I observed an actual process of *governability* operating in the decision-making involved in donor assistance.[11] While the general directive of the British foreign ministry for 1998–99 was to focus funding on poverty issues, for example, a British cooperation officer in Jerusalem who had criticized this directive as one-dimensional, explained to me how he succeeded in convincing his superiors that poverty in Palestine is not concentrated in specific areas as in comparable countries, but is, in fact, dispersed over the entire area. Rather than relief for poor people, he suggested, the donation could be part of a development strategy for Palestinian society, which could, in turn, benefit poor people.

Examining the influence of research funding agencies on the local agenda of research centers is also a very complicated issue. When funding agencies support a specific research topic, they do so at the expense of other topics. Thus, though research topics are indirectly manipulated, donors rarely exert control over the actual research process. Moreover, there is a tendency among funded researchers to project the official political positions of the donors' governments or the donors themselves. This influence should not be exaggerated, however, as it is demonstrated in the case of the German foundation which supported a conference organized by the Economic and Social Commission for West Asia (ESCWA) on the impact of the peace process on some industrial sectors in the Middle East. Although it was clear that the foundation sought to emphasize the positive impact of the peace process on the industrial economies of the countries in question, most of the studies presented at the conference indicated the opposite—at least in the transitional period imposed by the fitful progress of the peace process. Finally, it must be emphasized that the global agenda is not monolithic. Here we must distinguish clearly between development agencies, the solidarity groups (such organizations as American Near East Refugee Agency,

ANERA, and Association France Palestine Solidarity) and other organizations with a humanitarian ideology that emphasizes universality.

An Emerging Globalized Palestinian Elite

As mentioned above, the similarities in the agendas of those allocating supply and those articulating demand in NGO projects suggest the emergence of a new elite composed of NGO leadership members susceptible to the influence of a kind of global agenda. This elite is new in the sense that in a more competitive funding acquisition process, the 'old' elite, composed of such actors as voluntary charitable societies and, in some cases, the traditional elite of rural areas, has been effectively supplanted. The new Palestinian globalized NGO elite reflects the broader process out of which it has emerged, including the pervasive national context of the peace process and the foreign assistance provided to support the transition to a post-conflict order. Before characterizing this elite, a few observations are in order.

A comparison of PNGO discourse, including that within its leadership, with actual practices is quite revealing in that the former emerges as a kind of dogma or 'profession of faith.' This 'profession of faith' is usually framed in dichotomous terms: black versus white or, more importantly, 'global' versus 'local.' As will be briefly discussed here, these dichotomies do not necessarily reflect NGO actors' own beliefs, but rather the fact that the actors operate within these categorizations and manipulate them according to context. PNGO actors, for example, often speak of a 'national agenda,' which guides their developmental approach, yet they rarely address the legitimacy of those speaking in the name of national interests nor do they examine the agenda from a pluralistic perspective. In a revealing example, many NGOs have demonized one donor in particular in local discourses, suggesting that donors are selected according to the interests of the national agenda. Our interlocutors often portrayed USAID as an institutional Satan and as the enemy of the Palestinian people. It is quite likely that USAID was singled out for such critique because it is associated with the U.S. government and, due to the supportive positions of that government toward the state of Israel, with Israel itself. However, we were surprised to find that, contrary to their own declarations, five of these actors had actually applied for funding from USAID. Some had received grants and others did not. Finally, while Palestinian NGOs often talk about local agenda, they are, in fact, much closer to the global agenda, especially concerning the importance of certain issues such as gender awareness policies, capacity building, participatory approaches, integrated projects, and community-based projects.

Three major characteristics of this Palestinian globalized elite can be observed.

1) It is supportive of the peace process: the globalized NGO elite supports the current negotiated peace process or, at the minimum, believes in the necessity of giving this process and the PNA sufficient time to accomplish goals in the absence of armed struggle or violence. Thus, this elite differs considerably from the nationalist-Islamic elite.

2) It is urban-based: donor funding has been focused in Jerusalem and other large Palestinian cities, thus ensuring the emergence of an urban elite.

3) It consists of a professionalized class: the Palestinian elite is no longer associated with pure activism or activists, but is composed of the technically trained, university-educated activists and technocrats, who did not previously have any connection with militant Palestinian activism. The absorption of donor ideas and norms also has implications not only for methods but also in the area of human resources. In this respect, it is clear that a predominance of English-speaking university graduates with financial skills becomes increasingly important. Although the skills of professionals are no doubt necessary, Arabic-speaking field managers and specialists have seen their importance waning in organizations.[12]

It is clear that the emergence of a new elite within the context of national liberalization in a specific cultural milieu creates some paradoxes that the actors should be aware of. The new elite is not the sole construct of donor influences, owing much to a national context in which the shift to the peace process has replaced an armed and populist struggle against Israeli occupation with a civic and state opposition to the same occupation. Political and social actors have also changed in response to a different social agenda.

We must also consider the question as to whether the elite is necessarily democratic and if promotion of civil society by donors is necessarily analogous to the promotion of democracy. A glance at the literature concerning development agencies and international NGOs reveals that often the distinction between these two objectives, the promotion of civil society and the promotion of democracy, become confused. Theoretically, the concept of civil society is analogous to Habermas's public sphere: it is a context in which a plurality of trends and different social and political actors debate their ideas. In this sense, while the existence of civil society is an indispensable tool for developing democracy, it is not democracy itself. This confusion cannot be simply reduced to the problem of the projection of a 'western' concept in the Third World, for even in many western contexts, civil society does not always produce democratic behavior among the dominant elite but instead creates intolerance, racism, and xenophobia. Civil society construction and democracy building are not coterminous objectives. Democracy building extends well beyond civil society, requiring broader structures and some sort of redistribution of power among social actors. The confusion between these two goals has an impact on NGO projects and activities and also on the character of the new elite.

More importantly, the second factor in forging a democratic elite concerns the internal practices of NGO actors. As will be argued in the conclusion, broader power structures in Palestinian society are reflected in the NGO sector. Moreover, as this paper suggests, donors do not pay sufficient attention to internal governance of local NGOs, often satisfied with no more than a certified audit. There is insufficient focus on the functions of the board of directors or the general operation of the NGOs. Subsequently, little consideration is given to the 'personalization' of NGOs, many of which are referred to and better known by the name of their directors. If there is a change in the directorship of an NGO, it can almost be referred to as a sort of coup d'etat. Therefore, and in this respect, donors do not promote a democratic elite.

Finally, one can ask if the proximity of an NGO to donors necessarily signifies a distancing from its constituency. The idea of a globalized NGO elite does not logically dictate that the local organizations in question will undergo a process of separation from their roots. If donors require local NGOs to be accountable to them through a different reporting mechanism, there is no cause-effect relationship that dictates that the NGOs become less accountable to their own constituency and to their 'grass roots.' There are many complex factors that affect the relationship between the NGO and the community. Beyond any external influences, in the Palestinian case, it is evident that there is a trend among many Palestinian NGOs toward elitism, which is related to factors within the local context more than to their relationship to donors. Local NGOs, for example, often pay insufficient attention to the types of linkage, which bind them to the public, and many often put too great an emphasis on the dissemination of English-language information. Two donors related a similar anecdote along these lines: when they requested that their partner NGO translate various materials into English, they were simply told, "It's not necessary!"

Conclusion: A Globalized Elite in the National Landscape

As Hassan Asfour, the minister of NGO affairs, stated, Palestinian NGOs receiving funding from western donors make up only about 20 percent of the total, suggesting that the globalized elite discussed here does not include the entire leadership of PNGOs. Islamic PNGOs tend to use local and diaspora charity networks to collect funds, while some popular organizations and pro-Fatah organizations often have PNA support in addition to a small level of western funding. However, the 20 percent of PNGOs that do receive western donor funds are clearly the largest, and therefore the most significant. For sure, the Union of Palestinian Medical Relief Committees, which provides about 30 percent of health services in the West Bank, and the *zakat* committee of Anabta, which receive no western donor funds, are not in the same league. Part of the 20 percent constitutes the globalized elite, which generally has leftist roots, and is connected, in particular, to the Palestinian People's Party (ex-Communist Party).

The policies of the largest donors have created huge PNGOs, which exert virtual monopolies in certain fields: PARC in agriculture, UPMRC in health, and Bisan in training, for example. The advent of these organizations and of the globalized elite, in fact, corresponds to the huge funding disbursements, which appeared quite suddenly following the PNA's installation in Palestine. This created an environment characterized by smaller NGOs without the absorption capacity to receive these funds and donors lacking adequate executive administration. Consequently, larger NGO structures, with the administrative capacity to receive such large disbursements, flourished in this new environment. This, of course, is but one factor in an intricate process and other factors will rise following further empirical research.[13] Moreover, this study considers the globalized elite in bipolar terms and not as an all-encompassing categorization—by tilting toward a globalized agenda or resisting it, PNGO leadership members will find themselves positioned somewhere between the two.

The emergence of this globalized elite is an ongoing process and is dependent on two factors: an ideological conviction and an imbalance of power. Some local NGOs perceive and internalize the donor agenda not only as global but also as universal and self-evident. It is perceived as appropriate to international changes and national transitions brought about by the peace process and the construction of the Palestinian national state. Thus, the recipient NGOs adopt this agenda in good faith and will also defend it. However, the conviction, real or apparent, cannot hide the imbalance in the power relationship between both donors and NGOs, which translates into weak negotiations in constructing the agenda of the development project.

Table 1: Donors Assistance to the Palestinian National Authority and PNGOs ($ million)

Total Contribution	1996	1997
Donor aid to the PNA and NGOs from government agencies	549.414	432.259
MOPIC's Report: donor aid to NGOs from government agencies	58.069	45.995
MOPIC's Report: percentage	10%	11%
Welfare Survey: donor aid to PNGOs from government agencies and INGOs	54.804	76.897
Welfare Survey: percentage	10%	18%

Table 2: Distribution of Funding By Sector ($1000 and percentage)

Sector	Funding in 1995	Percentage 1995	Funding in 1996	Percentage 1996	Funding in 1997	Percentage 1997	Funding in 1998	Percentage 1998	Total	Total Percentage
Agriculture	3936.2	6.5%	5717.8	10.5%	4603.8	5.9%	3843.7	6.7%	18101.5	7.4%
Culture	2899.4	4.8%	3074.4	5.7%	7054.3	9.0%	7579.9	13.2%	20608.0	8.2%
Democracy	331.0	0.5%	146.0	0.3%	1741.0	2.2%	1800.0	3.1%	4018.0	1.5%
Education	12206.2	20.2%	14321.0	26.4%	16771.4	21.5%	14340.8	25.0%	57639.5	23.3%
Environment	653.9	1.1%	2035.6	3.8%	2367.6	3.0%	2138.4	3.7%	7195.5	2.9%
Health	9710.6	16.1%	10621.6	19.6%	18230.2	23.4%	11202.1	19.5%	49764.5	19.6%
Human Rights	301.9	0.5%	537.4	1.0%	2891.9	3.7%	3682.8	6.4%	7414.0	2.9%
Infrastructure (except water)	2000.0	3.3%	2106.0	3.9%	2937.0	3.8%	193.3	0.3%	7236.3	2.8%
Institution Building	6527.5	10.8%	3343.5	6.2%	1796.5	2.3%	1838.0	3.2%	13505.5	5.6%
Micro Credit	3389.2	5.6%	1960.5	3.6%	2402.5	3.1%	1817.0	3.2%	9569.2	3.9%
Multi-sectoral	12446.9	20.6%	533.9	1.0%	567.7	0.7%	1156.0	2.0%	14704.5	6.1%
Relief	352.3	0.6%	352.3	0.6%	1066.0	1.4%	699.0	1.2%	2469.7	1.0%
Research	661.5	1.1%	923.8	1.7%	1338.6	1.7%	1685.1	2.9%	4609.0	1.9%
Social Services	2324.8	3.8%	4826.4	8.9%	8390.9	10.7%	3700.4	6.4%	19242.5	7.5%
Tourism	33.0	0.1%	60.0	0.1%	67.0	0.1%	880.0	1.5%	1040.0	0.4%
Trade and Industry	1813.0	3.0%	1820.0	3.4%	4197.0	5.4%	235.4	0.4%	8065.4	3.0%
Vocational/Technical Training	868.8	1.4%	1898.8	3.5%	1634.5	2.1%	656.8	1.1%	5059.0	2.0%
Grand Total	60456.3	100%	54279.1	100%.	78057.9	100%	57448.7	100.0%	250242.0	100

Table 3: Distribution of Funding By District ($1000 and Percentage)

District	Funding in 1995	Percentage 1995	Funding in 1996	Percentage 1996	Funding in 1997	Percentage 1997	Funding in 1998	Percentage 1998	Total	Total (percentage)
Jenin	217.0	0.4%	1310.0	2.5%	2157.0	2.8%	776.0	1.4%	4460.0	1.8%
Tobas	100.0	0.2%	100.0	0.2%	300.0	0.4%	100.0	0.2%	600.0	0.2%
Tulkarem	304.4	0.5%	438.0	0.8%	446.5	0.6%	497.2	0.9%	1686.1	0.7%
Nablus	783.7	1.3%	1746.7	3.3%	1894.7	2.5%	989.0	1.8%	5414.1	2.2%
Qalqilya			70.0	0.1%	66.0	0.1%	49.3	0.1%	185.3	0.1%
Salfit	100.0	0.2%	114.0	0.2%	131.0	0.2%	100.0	0.2%	445.0	0.2%
Ramallah	1246.2	2.1%	725.3	1.4%	3636.8	4.7%	2357.8	4.2%	7966.1	3.1%
Jericho	75.0	0.1%	80.0	0.2%	500.5	0.6%	147.4	0.3%	802.9	0.3%
Jerusalem	5508.3	9.2%	5849.0	11.0%	10088.5	13.1%	6046.6	10.8%	274924	11.0%
Bethlehem	796.8	1.3%	1079.3	2.0%	2251.3	2.9%	2571.6	4.6%	6699.0	2.7%
Hebron	1418.0	2.4%	1436.2	2.7%	1621.0	2.1%	458.6	0.8%	4933.8	2.0%
North Gaza	450.0	0.8%	450.0	0.8%	464.0	0.6%	756.1	1.4%	2120.1	0.9%
Gaza	1345.9	2.3%	1110.1	2.1%	3098.8	4.0%	4212.8	7.6%	9767.5	4.0%
Deir Balah					17.0	0.0%	7.0	0.0%	24.0	0.0%
Khan Yunis	100.0	0.2%	205.0	0.4%	262.5	0.3%	129.0	0.2%	696.5	0.3%
Rafah					137.0	0.2%	148.0	0.3%	285.0	0.1%
Gaza Strip	3538.2	5.9%	2556.5	4.8%	4930.6	6.4%	3108.6	5.6%	14133.9	5.7%
West Bank	7163.9	12.0%	12342.9	23.3%	16654.3	21.6%	10785.4	19.3%	46946.5	19.1%
Palestine	35986.7	60.3%	22777.9	43.0%	27094.6	35.1%	21119.1	37.9%	106978.3	44.1%
Israel	127.5	0.2%	163.5	0.3%	733.8	1.0%	416.5	0.7%	1441.2	0.6%
Lebanon	393.6	0.7%	393.6	0.7%	693.0	0.9%	1019.1	1.8%	2499.3	1.0%
Grand Total	59655.2	100.0%	52947.9	100.0%	77178.8	100.0%	55795.1	100.0%	245577.0	100.0%

Table 4: Distribution of Funding By District For the West Bank ($1000 and Percentage)

District	Funding in 1995	Percentage 1995	Funding in 1996	Percentage 1996	Funding in 1997	Percentage 1997	Funding in 1998	Percentage 1998	Total	Total (percentage)
Jenin	217.0	1.2%	1310.0	5.2%	2157.0	5.4%	776.0	3.1%	4460.0	3.7%
Tobas	100.0	0.6%	100.0	0.4%	300.0	0.8%	100.0	0.4%	600.0	0.5%
Tulkarem	304.4	1.7%	438.0	1.7%	446.5	1.1%	497.2	2.0%	1686.1	1.6%
Nablus	783.7	4.4%	1746.7	6.9%	1894.7	4.8%	989.0	4.0%	5414.1	5.0%
Qalqilya			70.0	0.3%	66.0	0.2%	49.3	0.2%	185.3	0.2%
Salfit	100.0	0.6%	114.0	0.5%	131.0	0.3%	100.0	0.4%	445.0	0.4%
Ramallah	1246.2	7.0%	725.3	2.9%	3636.8	9.1%	2357.8	9.5%	7966.1	7.1%
Jericho	75.0	0.4%	80.0	0.3%	500.5	1.3%	147.4	0.6%	802.9	0.6%
Jerusalem	5508.3	31.1%	5849.0	23.1%	10088.5	25.4%	6046.6	24.3%	27492.4	26.0%
Bethlehem	796.8	4.5%	1079.3	4.3%	2251.3	5.7%	2571.6	10.3%	6699.0	6.2%
Hebron	1418.0	8.0%	1436.2	5.7%	1621.0	4.1%	458.6	1.8%	4933.8	4.9%
West Bank	7163.9	40.4%	12342.9	48.8%	16654.3	41.9%	10785.4	43.4%	46946.5	43.6%
Grand Total	17713.3	100.0%	25291.4	100.0%	39747.6	100.0%	24878.9	100.0%	107631.2	100.0%

Table 5: Distribution of Funding By District For Gaza Strip ($1000 and Percentage)

District	Funding in 1995	Percentage 1995	Funding in 1996	Percentage 1996	Funding in 1997	Percentage 1997	Funding in 1998	Percentage 1998	Total	Total (percentage)
North Gaza	450.0	8.3%	450.0	10.4%	464.0	5.2%	756.1	9.0%	2120.1	8.2%
Gaza	1345.9	24.8%	1110.1	25.7%	3098.8	34.8%	4212.8	50.4%	9767.5	33.9%
Deir Balah					17.0	0.2%	7.0	0.1%	24.0	0.1%
Khan Yunis	100.0	1.8%	205.0	4.7%	262.5	2.9%	129.0	1.5%	696.5	2.8%
Rafah					137.0	1.5%	148.0	1.8%	285.0	0.8%
Gaza Strip	3538.2	65.1%	2556.5	59.2%	4930.6	55.3%	3108.6	37.2%	14133.9	54.2%
Grand Total	5434.1	100.0%	4321.6	100.0%	8909.9	100.0%	8361.4	100.0%	27027.0	100.0%

Table 6: Distribution of Funding for 1995–98 Compared to the Population ($1000 and Percentage)

District	Population	Population Percentage of Palestinian territories	Funding for 1995–98 ($)	Percentage of Funding
Jenin	203,026	7.0%	4460.0	1.8%
Tobas	36,609	1.0%	600.0	0.2%
Tulkarem	134,110	5.0%	1686.1	0.7%
Qalqilya	72,007	2.0%	185.3	0.1%
Salfit	48,538	2.0%	445.0	0.2%
Nablus	261,340	9.0%	5414.1	2.2%
Ramallah	213,582	7.0%	7966.1	3.1%
Jerusalem	328,601	11.0%	27492.4	11.0%
Jericho	32,713	1.0%	802.9	0.3%
Bethlehem	137,286	5.0%	6699.0	2.7%
Hebron	405,664	14.0%	4933.8	2.0%
North Gaza	183,373	6.0%	2120.1	0.9%
Gaza	367,388	13.0%	9767.5	4.0%
Deir Balah	147,877	5.0%	24.0	0.0%
Khan Yunis	200,704	7.0%	696.5	0.3%
Rafah	122,865	4.0%	285.0	0.1%
Total	2,895,683	99%	73577.8	30%

Notes

1. For more on this point of view, see Wood's (1997) relevant criticism of 'good governance.' Wood considers the term as representative of a revival of ethnocentric, modernizing ideology, attempting to make one society's myths another's reality.
2. This section was published in Sari Hanafi, Pouvoirs et Associations dans le Monde Arabe (Paris: CNRS Editions, 2002), 125–47.

3. The Welfare Association sponsored a survey of donor organizations that assist the Palestinian NGO sector, in order to compile systematic information about policies, projects, and funding sources. Data was collected in accordance with the following themes: a) organization profile; b) strategies and policies for development assistance; c) current and future areas and sectors of interest; d) projects funded in Palestine since 1995: nature of projects, local NGO counterpart(s), target groups, volume of funding or co-funding; e) contact information: local and/or head offices of these organizations. Also, other informal questions were raised concerning the setting of the agenda.
4. The Welfare Association is a privately funded non-profit organization registered in Switzerland and established in 1983 by a group of prominent Palestinian business and intellectual figures.
5. For example, at a regional conference organized by the Ibn Khaldoun Development and Research Center in Cairo in 1990, the categorization of Copts in Egypt as a 'minority' quickly turned the discussion toward research agendas and whether the organization was submitting to the interests of foreign 'neo-colonial' donors.
6. This debate is not confined only to Palestine. In 1998, another polemic arose concerning the funding provided by the British Consulate for a center for Human Rights to carry out research on violence in an Egyptian village. The Egyptian state expressed its anger over the 'abuse' of freedom of speech as well as the increasing role of NGOs in social and political development by arresting the director of this center. Meanwhile, a debate appeared within the Egyptian scientific community in terms of a crisis in research priorities and the need to discuss local and foreign agendas (Hanafi 1999).
7. Except for Ministry of Planning and International Cooperation's (MPOIC) Donor Assistance Monitoring Report which represents primarily bilateral assistance between governments or government-sourced assistance.
8. Palestinian NGOs were established legally in Gaza only after 1967. Previously, Egyptian military authorities simply banned the formation and registration of local organizations and professional unions, with the sole exception of the Lawyers' Union.
9. For an extensive analysis of the productive health, see chapter 3 in Hanafi and Taber 2002.
10. For a discussion of the history and structure of donor coordination, please refer to Brynen et al. (1998).
11. In Michel Foucault's analysis of the concept of governability, the power of technocrats and bureaucrats in western societies lies in their responsibility for preparing the reports and studies that enable politicians to make decisions. In this sense, they share the decision-making process with politicians.
12. Similarly, Khalil Nakhleh (1998) leveled strong criticisms regarding the impact of what he called 'development brokers' on the national linguistic landscape—"They succeeded in inserting certain aspects, or expressions, of the English language in daily local parlance that pertain to development issues. However, the aspects of the English language which have been introduced through this process tend to be segmented, not part of a coherent whole, often void of content, unconnected to a basic thought process ... merely icing on the cake! As a result, our 'national linguistic landscape' is evolving in a lopsided manner, by giving prominence, fre-

quency and preference to a certain category of English words. It is not an exaggeration to make the claim that no day passes without hearing, in one context or another, words such as 'workshop,' 'infrastructure,' 'training of trainers,' 'feedback,' 'donor countries.' Yet there is a resounding silence on certain conceptual categories, such as 'training for what,' 'economic development to what end,' 'the nature of national landscape,' 'labor market needs,' etc." (1998).

13. Which will be a focus in a forthcoming publication co-written with Linda Taber (2005).

Chapter Sixteen

Conclusion
Arab NGOs: Advocacy and the 'Globalized' Debate on Democracy in the Arab World

Nabil Abdel Fettah and Sarah Ben Néfissa

The papers gathered together in this book were introduced during an international conference that took place in March 2000; substantial changes have occurred in the world and in the Arab region since. The introduction not only highlighted the administrative and political obstacles weighing heavily on Arab NGOs, but also stressed the need for a thorough reform of the Arab political system as a prerequisite for the development of these organizations. Once developed, they can fulfill their role as mediators and valuable interlocutors for their respective states, their societies, and other international actors. Today, political reform is high on these countries' agendas, a phenomenon directly related to the disruptive international events that took place in the aftermath of September 11, 2001, particularly the American invasion of Afghanistan, the goal of which was to capture the United States' most wanted public enemy, the Saudi Arabian, Osama Bin Laden. However, it was the invasion of Iraq by American armed forces that effected the most dramatic changes in the region. This attack was accompanied by a series of American and European[1] initiatives designed to foster political reform in the Arab region on the one hand, and implement reforms of economic, educational, communication, and religious systems on the other. The underlying idea behind these reforms was to tackle the roots of terrorism in the region, such as the deprivation of several generations of citizens from political participation in the Arab world, and the diffusion of both formal and informal obscurantist religious discourse.

What are the consequences of this new parameter on the attitude of regional public authorities and on the NGOs and Arab civil society?

The attitude of Arab public authorities varies from one country to another depending on the country's political position in the region, its domestic situation, the main features of its political system, and on the status of its civil society. While some regimes settled for admitting the need for reform, without taking genuine measures to carry reforms out, others agreed to make more or less important changes, even if this has often bolstered their authoritarianism in the name of the war against terrorism and Islamist extremism. However, it is important to highlight that the Arab League, for the first time in the history of its summits of Arab leaders, dedicated one meeting to democratic reform and human rights.[2]

However, for civil societies and mainly advocacy Arab NGOs, the new situation has unquestionably reinforced their influence and their critical discourse vis à vis Arab political regimes and the highly ambiguous position of the American administration to the so-called Arab democratic question.

This resurgence of the roles played by Arab advocacy NGOs and by civil society actors has taken place almost everywhere in the Arab world, particularly in Egypt. It is possible to say that Egyptian advocacy NGOs initiated an important dynamic on that issue in order to coordinate the actions and the positions of the NGOs in the other countries of the region. The reactivation of the role played by the Arab advocacy NGOs highlighted their eminently political functions, which were more relevant than those fulfilled by political parties and other civil society actors and organizations. This phenomenon is rooted in several factors: the social and educational background of the leaders of these NGOs, who are from the upper elite; their knowledge of the current prevalent jargon of international organization and governance; their methods, experience, and ability to establish contacts with international actors; their networks; their knowledge of the financial sources, and so on. All these factors prepared Arab advocacy NGOs to face and actively participate in the so-called globalized debate on democracy in the Arab world. It is important to stress their flexibility with respect to the new international order as well as their ability to harmonize their approaches and discourses.

The same is not true of Arab political parties, who should be the foremost partners in any discussion on democracy. Their activism is not only blocked by the regimes, which are authoritarian to larger or greater degree, but is also stalled by their internal political affairs and by the calendar and terms of the elections. Involved to some extent with the ruling elite and paralyzed by internal political wrangles, the political organizations of the Arab world have consequently cleared the way for NGOs to take their place and respond to democratic demands. The activation of Arab advocacy NGOs took place in different ways: the organization of meetings, seminars, and conferences; the writing of new releases and manifestos; the signing of petitions addressed to Arab regimes, international and regional organizations, and, more widely, to the international community as a whole.

In all of this, it is important to highlight the meeting organized in Cairo in July 2004,[3] which gathered together close to forty NGOs engaged in the field of human rights, and about one hundred intellectuals from fifteen different countries in the region. The organization set up by the Cairo-based Center for Human Rights Studies and by the Egyptian Organization for Human Rights was concluded with a powerful report which was published in three languages: Arabic, French, and English. This report denounces, on the one hand, the opposition of Arab political regimes to reform, and requests a genuine democratization of political systems on the other. Besides demanding freedom of speech and of political, unionistic, and civil actions, the participants noted the lack of regard accorded by Arab peoples to the principle of democratically elected and alternating government. According to the participants, this principle is a prerequisite to a true democracy. They not only raised the need to establish a time limit to the presidential mandate but also gave their backing to the idea of transforming monarchical regimes into constitutional ones.

At the national level, the public arena has also been shaken up by the impact of civil society actors, be they NGOs, intellectuals, or cultural and political personalities. In 2003, in Saudi Arabia, a petition signed by 104 intellectuals was addressed to the royal family. This petition demanded a reform of the institutions of government and the establishment of a true constitutional monarchy. These intellectuals also requested the introduction of universal suffrage at both the local and the national levels; the independence of the judiciary; respect for primary public freedoms; and, more especially, the right to form associations and, finally, to respect human rights. The petition also requested economic and women's rights reforms. Although the response from the royal authorities was insufficient, it is important to note the attitude of Prince Abdallah Ben Abdel Aziz, heir to the throne, who agreed to meet with the petition's signatories. Similar phenomena took place in other Gulf countries and in Syria where political and intellectual factions called for reform. In 2004, seven hundred Syrian intellectuals approached the authorities with a petition demanding political reform and the release of political prisoners in Syria. This petition also called for the revoking of the emergency law enacted in 1963. The signatories stressed the need to suspend "'exceptional tribunals,' to stop arbitrary arrests and to free all political prisoners." Finally, the petition called for political reforms and "the right to create political parties."

Domestically, Egypt is currently witnessing a revival of the debate over democracy. It would nevertheless be misleading to believe that such a phenomenon is merely the result of external pressures and a new international and regional political landscape. The phenomenon is also and most certainly connected to the upcoming domestic elections in 2005 and to the sensitive issue of the successor to the president. This revival of the democratic debate presents new characteristics. The debate is now raised by both the political forces of the opposition, which used to be the only instigators, and by the leading elite, the National Democratic Party (NDP) in particular. The NDP finally admitted the democratic failings of the political system, which have been the focus of the demands made by the civil and political opposition. Moreover, certain measures show how the public authorities make the effort, if limited, to listen to the claims made by Egyptian civil society. This is how the oldest organization for Human Rights in the Arab world, the Egyptian organization, was finally recognized as a legal entity. This decision was followed by the creation of a National Committee for Human Rights, based on the same model as the other consultative High Councils, such as those for women or culture, which gathered administrative officials and some personalities from civil organizations. Similarly, the regime agreed to implement some reforms that these NGOs and particularly feminist NGOs,[4] demanded. Although, the Egyptian regime refuses to abrogate the emergency law, which has been frequently reenacted since the assassination of President Anwar Sadat in 1981, the government has recently cancelled seven military orders, which Sadat had promulgated in his favor. In March 2004, the regime cancelled jail sentences for press offenses. Although these measures do not meet all demands made, it is important to note that the Egyptian government has finally admitted the need to reform legislation related to unions and political parties. While the Egyptian political parties manifested a partial change in their stance on the debate on democracy in Egypt, it is also important to remark on the substantial mobilization of the main Egyptian advocacy NGOs, and of a large sector of the intelligentsia, and of journalists and politicians. As of now, Egyptian advocacy NGOs no longer hold back from expressing their opinion and taking a stand as political actors on the national scene. The main Egyptian advocacyv NGOs formed part of the Committee for the Defense of Democracy, which wrote a plea for political, constitutional, and democratic reform in October 2003. Similarly, it is important to underline the creation of the Egyptian Movement for Change, which in 2004 distributed a petition signed by 590 politicians, intellectuals, artists, and academics.

These two mobilizations of the Egyptian NGOs do not disregard Egyptian Islamist movements and other marginalized groups from the political and official intellectual elite, as political parties usually do during their meetings.

The intensity of the democratic debate also changed. It indeed changed by crossing certain certain lines, so that these actors no longer hesitate in demanding constitutional reform in order to reduce the presidential role, to modify its investiture and the length of its mandate.

Since the investiture of Mohamed VI as king of Morocco, a certain political liberalism has prevailed, especially with wider freedoms of speech and press, and by a revival of civil society action and partisan activities. In January 2004 a new family code was passed as law, which met long-held demands of the feminist and human rights movements. The attacks of May 16, 2003 in Casablanca, and of Madrid in March 2004, directly involving Moroccans, led to a setback to a more authoritarian regime with the adoption, in particular, of an anti-terrorist law and a more aggressive stance on the regime's part to all trends of Islamicists, the independent press, and human rights organizations.

The Moroccan experience demonstrates that the Islamist issue remains, for the current regimes, the main excuse for slow political reform. The American administration associates Islam with terrorism and extremism and consequently regards such an argument as acceptable. This was also the excuse set forth by the new NDP leadership to justify the policy of fostering democracy 'in steps.'

Although some changes occurred in the Arab world, this new regional dimension did not foster any alleviation of the control exercised on political and civil society organizations; on the contrary it encouraged regimes such as that in Tunisia to take authoritarian measures with respect to the Islamic question. Nonetheless, some progress was made when an independent candidate campaigned during the 2005 presidential elections in Tunisia, representing a breakthrough in a political landscape characterized almost unrelievedly by monolithism.

Notes

1. The G8 summit, the European Union Summit, the NATO summit, and so on.
2. Two Arab states organized conferences dedicated to the reform: Egypt and Yemen.
3. This conference followed another one, which took place in Beirut in March 2004, and which was organized by the Center for Human Rights Studies in Cairo. It brought together fifty-two organizations from thirteen countries.
4. The creation of a tribunal for the family, where Egyptian women, can, for instance, plea for their right to award their nationality to their children, when they are married to foreigners. This tribunal also gives them access to a quicker divorce.
5. The Egyptian Organization for Human Rights, the Nadim Center for Victims of Violence, the Hisham Mubarak Law Center, the House for Union Services, the Center for Prisoner's Support, and the Nida' al-Jadid Association.

Bibliography

Abdul Hadi, I. 1992. *al-Intifada wa ba'd qadaya al-tanmiya al-sha'biya*. Ramallah: Bisan Center for Research and Development.

———. 1994. "Ishkaliyat al-intikhabat fi-l-mu'assasat al-wataniya wa mutatallabat al-taghyir," in G. Giacaman, ed. *al-Mu'assasat al-wataniya, al-intikhabat, wa-l-sulta*. Ramallah: Muwatin, The Palestinian Institute for the Study of Democracy, 11–37.

———. 1995. "Palestinian Non-governmental Organizations: Crowded Agenda," Draft Paper, Canadian-Palestinian Partnership Workshop, March 1995, Jerusalem.

'Abd al-Fadil, M. et al. 1996. *al-Mujtama' wa-l-dawla fi-l-watan al-'arabi fi zil al-siyasat al-ra's maliya al-jadida*. Cairo: Madbuli.

'Abdallah, T.F. 1999. "Qanun al-jam'iyat al-ahliya al-jadid wa-l-masar al-dimuqrati fi Misr," *al-Mustaqbal al-arabi*, 247.

Abdallah, A. 1985. *The Student Movement and National Politics in Egypt*. London: Al Saqi Books.

Abers, R. 1996. "Learning Democratic Practices: Distributing Government Resources Through Popular Participation in Porto Alegre, Brazil," Technical Paper, UCLA Conference, "Planning and the Rise of Civil Society: A Symposium Celebrating the Planning Career of John Friedmann," April 11–13, Los Angeles.

Abu Sido, H.F. and Mona Ghali. 1995. "Aid and International Organizations in Palestine: Instruments of Development or of Foreign Policy?" *Middle East International* 499 (April): 16–17.

Abu-Amr, Z. 1995. *al-Mujtama' wa-l-tahawul al-dimuqrati fi Filastin*. Ramallah: Muwatin.

Adams, D.W. and J.D.Von Pischke. 1992. "Micro-enterprise Credit Programs: I," *World Development* 20 (October 10): 1463–70.

Al-Ali, N. 2000. *Secularism, Gender and the State in the Middle East: The Egyptian Women's Movement*. Cambridge: Cambridge University Press.

Arab Human Rights Movement. 1999. *The Casablanca Declaration*, adopted by the First International Conference of the Arab Human Rights Movement, April 23–25, Casablanca. Cairo: Cairo Institute for Human Rights Studies.

Ardier, Robert. 1994. "Markets and Good Government," in A. Clayton, ed., *Governance, Democracy, and Conditionality: What role for NGOs?* Oxford: Intrac.

Aron, R. 1962. *Paix et guerre entre les nations*. Paris: Calmann-Levy.

Ayed, N. 1998. "Needs Assessment for Services to the Poor and Marginalized in Jerusalem, the West Bank and Gaza," Draft report, Jerusalem.

Al-Ayyubi, N.N. 1989. *al-Dawla al-markaziya fi Misr*. Cairo: Markaz Dirasat al-Wihda al-'Arabiya.

Badie, B. 1993. *L'État importe*. Paris: Fayard.
———. 1995. *La fin des territoires—essai sur le désordre international et sur l'utilité sociale du respect.* Paris: Fayard, Collection L'Espace du Politique.
Barber, B. *Jihad vs. McWorld: How Globalism and Tribalism are Reshaping the World.* New York: Ballantine Books.
Barghouthi, M. 1993. *Palestinian Health: Toward a Healthy Development Strategy in the West Bank and Gaza Strip.* Jerusalem: Union of Palestinian Medical Relief Committees (UPMRC).
———. 1994. "Munazzamat al-mujtama' al-madani wa dawraha fi-l-marhala al-muqbila," in *al-Mujtama' al-madani wa-l-sulta*. Birzeit: Birzeit University.
Barghouthi, M. and R. Giacaman. 1990. "The Emergence of an Infrastructure of Resistance: The Case of Health," in Jamal R. Nassar and Roger Heacock, eds., *Intifada: Palestine at the Crossroads*. New York: Praeger, 73–87.
Barsky, Y. 1995. *The Struggle is Now Worldwide: Hizballah and Iranian Sponsored Terrorism.* New York: Anti-Defamation League.
Baumgarten, H. 1991. *'Palaestina: Befreiung in den Staat': Die palaestinensische Nationalbewegung seit 1948.* Frankfurt: Suhrkamp.
Baxter, Paul T.W. 1987. "Some Observations on the Short Hymns Sung in Praise of Sheikh Nur Hussein of Bale," in A. Al-Shahi, ed., *The Diversity of the Muslim Community: Anthropological Essays in Memory of Peter Lienhardt.* London: Ithaca Press, 139–52.
Bayat, A. 2001. "Social Movements, Activism and Social Development in the Middle East," *Transnational Associations* 2: 74–98.
el-Baz, Shahida et al. 1995. Technical Paper, NGOs committee preparing International Conference on Women, September 4–15, Beijing.
Beatty, S., A.N. Al-Madhaji, and R. Detalle. 1996. "Yemeni NGOs and Quasi-NGOs, Analysis and Directory," Part 1: Analysis. Unpublished.
Beaud, M. 1997. *Le basculement du monde*. Paris: La découverte.
Bellion Jourdan, J. 2004. "Réseaux transnationaux de l'aide humanitaire islamique: les ONGs islamiques," in *ONG et gouvernance dans le monde arabe*. Paris: Karthala et CEDEJ, 113–42.
Ben Néfissa, S. 2000. *ONG, Gouvernance et développement dans le monde arabe.* UNESCO/MOST (Management of Social Transformation), Discussion Paper 46.
Ben Néfissa, S. and A. Qandil. 1995. *Les associations en Égypte (al-Jam'iyat al-ahliya fi Misr)* Cairo: Al-Ahram Center for Political and Strategic Studies.
Berg, Robert J. 1987. *Non-governmental Organizations: New Force in Third World Development and Politics.* East Lansing, MI: Center for Advanced Study of International Development, Michigan State University.
Berman, S. 1997. "Civil Society and the Collapse of the Weimar Republic," *World Politics* 49 (April): 401–29.
Bernard, A., Helmich, H., and Lehning P.B., eds. 1998. *La Société civile et le développement international.* Paris: Center de Développement de l'OCDE.

Besley, T., and R. Kanbur. 1988. "The Principles in Targeting," Preliminary version presented to the World Bank Symposium on Poverty and Adjustment, July.

Besteman, Catherine. 1995. "The Invention of Gosha: Slavery, Colonialism and Stigma in Somali History," in Ali Jimale Ahmed, ed., *The Invention of Somalia*. Lawrenceville, NJ: Red Sea Press.

Bibars, I.M.D. 1987. "Women's Political Interest Groups in Egypt: An Analysis of Women's Political Interest Groups in Egypt and an Evaluation of their Effectiveness in the Establishment of Personal Status Law no. 100 of 1985," M.A. thesis, American University in Cairo.

Biggs, S. and A. Neame. 1995. "Negotiating Room for Maneuver: Reflections Concerning NGO Autonomy and Accountability within the New Policy Agenda," in M. Edwards and D. Hulme, eds. *Beyond the Magic Bullet: Non-governmental Organizations—Performance and Accountability*. London: Earthscan.

Bishara, A. 1994. "Interview," *Middle East Report* 186 (January–February): 5–7.

———. 1995. "Munaqashat," in *al-Mujtama' al-madani wa-l-tahawul al-dimuqrati fi Filastin*. Ramallah: Muwatin.

———. 1996. *Musahama fi naqd al-mujtama' al-madani*. Ramallah: Muwatin.

Bishara, R. 1996. "NGOs Up Against Public Suspicion" (interview), *Palestine Report* (December 6): 8–9.

Blair, H. 1997. "Donors, Democratization and Civil Society: Relating Theory to Practice," in D. Hulme and M. Edwards, eds., *NGOs, States and Donors*. Hampshire, London: Macmillan Press: 23–42.

Boltanski, L. 1993. *La souffrance a distance*. Paris: Métailié.

Bourdieu, P. 1977. *Outline of A Theory of Practice*. Cambridge, UK: Cambridge University Press.

Bourgey, A. 1985. "La Guerre et ses Conséquences Géographiques au Liban," *Annales de Géographie* 521, XCIV: 1–37.

Bratton, M. 1988. "The politics of NGO-Government relations in Africa," *World Development* 17: 567–87.

———. 1994. *Civil Society and Political Transition in Africa*. Boston: Institute for Development Research.

Brouwer, I. 1998. "US and European Democracy Assistance to Promote Democracy in Palestine and Egypt," Draft Paper for Discussion, in Sari Hanafi, "Donors, International NGOs and Palestinian NGOs: funding issues and globalized elite formation," presented during UNESCO conference, March 29–30, 2000, Cairo.

Brown, L.D. and D.C. Korten. 1989. *The Role of Voluntary Organizations in Development*. Boston: Institute for Development Research.

Bryant, C.G.A. 1993. "Social Self-Organization, Civility and Sociology: A Comment on Kumar's 'Civil Society,'" *British Journal of Sociology*, 44, 3 (September).

Brynen, R. 1996. "Buying Peace? A Critical Assessment of International Aid to the West Bank and Gaza," *Journal of Palestine Studies*, 25, 3 (Spring): 79–92.

Brynen, R., A. Hisham, and C. Woodcraft. 1999. *Donor Assistance in Palestine*. Prepared for the Center for International Cooperation, New York University/Pledges of Aid, Social Science Research Council.

Brynen, R., B. Korany, and P. Noble, eds. 1995. *Political Liberalization and Democratization in the Arab World: Volume 1—Theoretical Perspectives*. Boulder, CO: Lynne Rienner Publishers.

———. 1998. "Conclusion: Liberalization, Democratization and Arab Experiences," *Political Liberalization and Democratization in the Arab World: Volume 2—Comparative Experiences*. Boulder, CO: Lynne Rienner Publishers: 267–78.

BTUTP, 1993. "The Redevelopment of the Area of Sabra." Unpublished report. Beirut: Bureau Technique d'Urbanisme et des Travaux Publics.

Byrne, A. 1996. "'Manufacturing Consent' in Post-Oslo Palestine," *News from Within* 12, 11 (December): 21–24.

Cairo Times. 2000. "Easier Said Than Written," February 24–March 1, vol. 3: 30.

Cairo Times. 2000. "No Cash, No Explanation," March 2–8, vol. 4: 1.

Calhoun, C. 1994. "Social Theory and the Politics of Identity," in Craig Calhoun, ed., *Social Theory and the Politics of Identity*. Oxford: Blackwell: 9–36.

Calhoun, C., E. LiPuma, and M. Postone, eds. 1993. *Bourdieu: Critical Perspectives*. Cambridge: Polity Press.

Caramel, L. 2001. "Les réseaux de l'antimondialisation," *Critique internationale*, October 13: 153–61.

Carapico, S. 1998. "Pluralism, Polarization, and Popular Politics in Yemen," in R. Brynen, B. Korani, and P. Noble, eds., *Political Liberalization and Democratization in the Arab World: Volume 2—Comparative Experiences*. Boulder, CO: Lynne Rienner Publishers: 241–66.

Carapico, S. 1998. *Civil Society in Yemen: The Political Economy of Activism in Modern Arabia*. Cambridge, MA: Cambridge University Press, 1998.

Carothers, T. 1999a. *Aiding Democracy Abroad: The Learning Curve*. Washington, D.C.: Carnegie Endowment for International Peace.

———. 1999b. "Civil Society." *Foreign Policy* (Winter): 18–31.

Carré, H. and H. Zaoual. 1998. "La dynamique des ONG: une approche interactionniste," in J.P. Deler, Y.A. Fauré, and P.J. Roca, eds., *ONG et développement*. Paris: Karthala.

Cassanelli, Lee V. 1982. *The Shaping of Somali Society. Reconstructing the History of a Pastoral People, 1600–1900*. Philadelphia: University of Pennsylvania Press.

———. 1988. "The Ending of Slavery in Italian Somalia: Liberty and the Control of Labor, 1890–1935," in S. Miers and R. Roberts, ed., *The End of Slavery in Africa*. Madison, WI: University of Wisconsin Press.

Castoriadis, C. 1975. *L'institution imaginaire de la société*. Paris: Éditions du Seuil.

Champagne, Parick. 1991. "La construction médiatique des malaises sociaux," *Acte de la recherche en sciences sociales* 90: 64–75.

Chande, Abdin. 2000. "Radicalism and Reform in East Africa," in Nehemia Levtzion and Randall Pouwels, eds., *The History of Islam in Africa*. Oxford: James Currey, 349–69.

Chatterjee, P. 1993. *The Nation and its Fragments: Colonial and Postcolonial Histories.* Princeton, NJ: Princeton University Press.

Chaudhry, K.A. 1997. *The Price of Wealth. Economies and Institutions in the Middle East.* Ithaca: Cornell University Press.

Chazel, F. 1992. "Mouvements Sociaux," in R. Boudon, *Traité de Sociologie.* Paris: Presse Universitaire de France: 263–312.

———, ed. 1993. *Action collective et mouvements sociaux.* Paris: Presse Universitaire de France.

CIHRS. 2001. The Fourth International Conference of the Human Rights Movement in the Arab World, July 19–22, Preparatory Papers, Cairo.

Clark, J. 1991. *Democratizing Development: The Role of Voluntary Organizations.* West Hartford: Kumarian Press.

———. 1995. "The State, Popular Participation, and the Voluntary Sector," *World Development* 23: 593–601.

Clark, J. and B. Balaj. 1996. "NGOs in the West Bank and Gaza," Draft report, February. Washington, D.C: World Bank.

Clayton, A. 1994. *Governance, Democracy and Conditionality: What Role for NGOs?* Oxford: INTRAC.

———, ed. 1996. *NGOs, Civil Society, and the State: Building Democracy in Transitional Societies.* Oxford: International NGO Training and Research Centre (INTRAC).

Cohen, J. 1985. "Strategy or Identity: New Theoretical Paradigms and Contemporary Social Movements," *Social Research* 52, 4 (Winter): 663–716.

Cohen, J. and A. Arato. 1992. *Civil Society and Political Theory.* Cambridge, MA: The Massachusetts Institute of Technology Press.

Consulting Center for Studies and Documentation. 1993. *Survey of Actual Servicing and Developing Realities in the Southern Suburb of Beirut.* Beirut: The Consulting Center for Studies and Documentation.

———. 1995. *Hizballah in the Press: With Data Analysis.* Beirut: The Consulting Center for Studies and Documentation.

———. 1995. *The Information Wing of Hizballah and the Operation Room of the Resistance 1994: Pages of Glory in the Book of the Nation.* Beirut: The Consulting Center for Studies and Documentation.

———. 1996. *The Information Wing of Hizballah and the Operation Room of the Resistance 1995: Pages of Glory in the Book of the Nation.* Beirut: The Consulting Center for Studies and Documentation.

Cordellier S., ed. 1999. *Les 80 idées-forces pour entrer dans le 21 ème siècle.* Paris: La Découverte.

Courrier de la Planète. 1995. "UN monde de citoyens," 31, November–December.

Craissati, D. 1998. "Social Movements and Democracy in Palestine: A Future for Radical Politics in the Arab World?" Ph.D. diss., Department of Political Science, Universitaet Hamburg.

Crozier, Michel and Erhard Friedberg. 1977. *L'acteur et le système.* Paris: Seuil.

Dakkak, I. 1983. "Back to Square One: A Study in the Re-Emergence of the

Palestinian Identity in the West Bank 1967–1980," in A. Schoelch, ed., *Palestinians Over the Green Line*. London: Ithaca, 64–101.

———. 1988. "Development from Within: A Strategy for Survival," in G. T. Abed, ed., *The Palestinian Economy: Studies in Development Under Prolonged Occupation*. London: Routledge, 287–310.

——— 1992. "Towards a Protected Palestinian Development Space," in A. Brown, R. Heacock, and F. La Torre, eds. "Palestine: Development for Peace," Conference Proceedings. Brussels: The European Coordinating Committee of NGOs on the Question of Palestine (ECCP), 195–202.

Danzon, M. and P. Poitrinal. 1996. "A l'Est, l'économisme contre la santé," *Manière de voir: Scénarios de la mondialisation* 32 (November): 20–22.

Declich, Francesca. 1995. "Identity, Dance and Islam among People with Bantu Origins in Riverine Areas of Somalia," in Ali Ahmed Jimale, ed., *The Invention of Somalia*, Lawrenceville: Red Sea Press, 191–222.

Deegan, H. 1993. *The Middle East and Problems of Democracy*. Philadelphia: Open University Press.

Deler, J. P., Y. A. Faure, and P. J. Roca. 1998. *ONG et développement*. Paris: Karthala.

Della Porta, D. 1995. *Social Movement, Political Violence and the State*. Cambridge, UK: Cambridge University Press.

Detalle, R. and E. Volpi. 1999. "Social Assessment of the Social Fund for Development of the Republic of Yemen." Unpublished.

Devine, J. 1996. *NGOs: Changing Fashion or Fashioning Change?* Bath, UK: Center for Development Studies, University of Bath.

Dia, M. 1993. "A Governance Approach to Civil Society Reform in Sub-Saharan Africa," Technical Paper, No. 255, Africa Technical Department Series. Washington D.C.: World Bank.

Dubet, F. 1994. *Sociologie de l'expérience*. Paris: Seuil.

Durand, M. F., Levy J. and Retaille D. 1992. *Le monde: Espace et Systèmes*. Paris: Presses de la Fondation nationale des sciences politiques and Dalloz.

Duyvendak, J. W. 1994. *Le Poids du Politique. Nouveaux mouvements sociaux en France*. Paris: L'Harmattan.

Easton, David. 1965. *A System Analysis of Political Life*. Chicago: University of Chicago Press.

Edwards, M. and D. Hulme, eds. 1994. *Making a Difference: NGOs and Development in a Changing World*. London: Earthscan.

Edwards, M. and D. Hulme. 1995. *Beyond the Magic Bullet: Non-governmental Organizations—Performance and Accountability*. London: Earthscan.

Egyptian Organization for Human Rights. 2000. "Press Release," January 19.

European Commission. 1999. "Country Strategic Paper. Republic of Yemen. 1998—2000." Unpublished.

Eyerman, R. and A. Jamison. 1991. *Social Movements: A Cognitive Approach*. Cambridge: Polity.

Fadl Allah, H. 1994. *Hizballah: The Other Choice*. Beirut: Dar al-Hadi.

Fadl Allah, H. 1979. *al-Islam wa mantiq al-quwa*. Beirut: al-Dar al-Islamiya.
———. 1990. *al-Haraka al-islamiya: humum wa qadaya*. Beirut: Dar al-Malak.
Fanon, F. 1990. *The Wretched of the Earth*. Harmondsworth: Penguin: 171.
Faure, Y., A. Piveteau, and P.J. Roca. 1996. "ONG/ÉTAT: penser le lien," *Histoires de développement* 34–35 (December).
Fisher, J. 1998. *Nongovernments: NGOs and the Political Development of the Third World*. West Hartford: Kumarian Press.
Foley, M.W. and B. Edwards. 1996. "The Paradox of Civil Society," *Journal of Democracy* 7, 3 (July): 38–52.
Forum du développement de l'action civile. 1998. *Masirat tatwir al-amal al-ahli wa qanun al-jam'iyat al-ahliya al-jadid*, August, Cairo.
Fowler, A. 1993. "Non-governmental organizations as agents of democratization: An African Perspective," *Journal of International Development* 5: 325–39.
———. 1996. "Strengthening Civil Society in Transition Economies—From Concept to Strategy: Mapping an Exit in a Maze of Mirrors," in A. Clayton, ed., *NGOs, Civil Society, and the State: Building Democracy in Transitional Societies*. Oxford: International NGO Training and Research Centre (INTRAC).
Galaal, Musa H.I. 1980. "Historical Relations between the Horn of Africa and the Persian Gulf and the Indian Ocean Islands through Islam," in C. Mehaud, ed., *Historical Relations across the Indian Ocean*. Paris: UNESCO: 23–30.
Galtung, Johan. 1971. "Feudal systems, structural violence, and the structural theory of revolutions," Proceedings of the IPRA Third Conference, Assen, Van Gorcum.
Gamson, W., and A. Modiliagni. 1989. "Media Discourse and Public Opinion on Nuclear Power," *American Journal of Sociology* 95: 1–38.
Gamson, W., and D. Meyer. 1996. "Framing political opportunity," in D. McAdam, J. McCarthy, and M. Zald, eds., *Comparative Perspectives on Social Movements: Political Opportunities, Mobilizing Structures, and Cultural Framings*. Cambridge: Cambridge University Press: 273–290.
al-Genhani, al-Habeeb. 1999. "Civil Society between Theory and Practice," *'Alam al-fikr*, No. 27 January–March, No. 28 October–December. Kuwait: al-Majlis al-Watani li-l-Thaqafa wa-l-Funun wa-l-Adab.
Ghalyun, B., A. Bishara, G. Giacaman, and S. Zeidani, eds. 1993. *Hawl al-khiyar al-dimoqrati: dirasat naqdiya*. Ramallah: Muwatin.
Ghalyun, B. et al. 1992. *Bina' al-mujtama' al-madani al-'arabi: dur al-'awamil al-dakhiliya wa-l-khayriya fi buhuth wa munaqashat nadwat al-mujtama' al madani fi-l-'arabi wa dawrihi fi tahqiq al dimuqratiya*. Cairo: Markaz Dirasat al-Wihda al-'arabiya.
Ghandi, L. 1998. *Postcolonial Theory*. New York: Columbia University Press.
Ghils, P. 1995. "Le Concept et les notions de société civile," *Associations Transnationales* 3 (May–June): 136–55.
Giacaman, G. 1993. "al-Dimuqratiya fi nihayat al-qarn al-'ashrin: nahwa kharta fikriya," in B. Ghalyun, A. Bishara, G. Giacaman and S. Zaydany, eds., *Hawl al-khayar al-dimuqrati: dirasat naqdiya*. Ramallah: Muwatin, The Palestinian Institute for the Study of Democracy: 7–56.

Giacaman, R. 1989. "Health as a Social Construction: The Debate in the Occupied Territories," *Middle East Report* 161 (November–December): 16–19.

Giacaman, R., I. Jad, and P. Johnson. 1995. "For the Public Good? Gender and Social Policy in Palestine," in Women's Studies Program, ed., *Gender and Society Working Papers* 2. Birzeit: Birzeit University: 7–35.

Giddens, A. 1994. *Beyond Left and Right: The Future of Radical Politics.* Cambridge: Polity.

Gilkes, P. 1994. "Descent into Chaos: Somalia, January 1991–December 1992," in Charles Gurdon, ed., *The Horn of Africa Today.* London: University College Press.

Gilliam, A. 1991. "Women's Equality and National Liberation," in C.T. Mohanty, A. Russo and L. Torres, eds., *Third World Women and the Politics of Feminism.* Bloomington and Indianapolis: Indiana University Press.

Giugni Marco, P.F. 1997. *Histoire de Mobilisation Politique en Suisse De la contestation à l'intégration.* Paris: L'Harmattan.

Giuny, Marco and Florence Passy. 1997. *Histoire de la Mobilisation Politique en Suisse. De la contestation à l'intégration.* Paris: l'Harmattan.

Goffman, E. 1991. *Les cadres de l'expérience.* Paris: Minuit.

Government of Yemen and UNDP (Yemen country office). 1997. "Poverty Eradication and Employment Generation Program of the Government of the Republic of Yemen," UNDP Programme Support Document, Draft Paper.

Gramsci, A. 1971. *Selections from Prison Notebooks*, ed. and trans. Q. Hoare and G.N. Smith. London: Lawrence and Wishart.

Gresh, A. 1988. *The PLO: The Struggle Within: Towards an Independent Palestinian State.* London: Zed.

Halliday, F. 2000. "Global governance: prospects and problems," *Citizenship Studies* 4, 1 (February): 19–33.

Hammami, R. 1995. "NGOs: The Professionalization of Politics," *Race and Class* 37, 2: 51–63.

———. 2000. "Palestinian NGOs Since Oslo. From NGO Politics to Social Movements?" *Middle East Report* 214 (January–March): 16–19, 27.

Hammami, R. and S. Tamari. 2000. "Anatomy of Another Rebellion," *Middle East Report* 217, October–December.

Hanafi, S. 2002. "Les ONG palestiniennes et les bailleurs de fonds: Quelques éléments sur la formation d'un agenda," in S. Ben Néfissa in collaboration with S. Hanafi, eds., *ONG dans le monde arabe.* Paris: Edition CNRS.

———. 1999. "Research Profile on Population Issues in Palestine," Technical Paper, "International Population Agendas and Regional Responses," Middle East Awards program, Population Council, December 15, Cairo.

———. 1999. "Profile of Donors Assistance to Palestinian NGOs: Survey and Databases," Report Submitted to the Welfare Association, Jerusalem.

Hanafi, Sari. 1999. "Between Arab and French Agendas. Defining the Palestinian Diaspora and the Image of the Other," in Seteney Shami, ed., *Social Science in Egypt: Emerging Voices.* Cairo: The American University in Cairo Press.

Hanafi, Sari and Linda Tabar. 2005. "The Emergence of the Palestinian Globalized Elite: Donors, International Organizations and Local NGOs." Beirut: Institute of Palestine Studies (English); Ramallah: Muwatin (Arabic).

Hann, C. and E. Dunn, eds. 1996. *Civil Society, Challenging Western Models*. London and New York: Routledge.

Hansen, G. 1996. *Constituencies for Reform: Strategic Approaches for Donor—Supported Civic Advocacy Programs*. Center for Development Information and Evaluation, U.S. Agency for International Development.

Al-Haraza, M.M. 1998. "The popular associations" in Yemeni Center for Strategic Studies. *Annual Report, Yemen 1998*. Sana'a: Yemeni Center for Strategic Studies, 89–117.

Harb El Kak, M. 1996. *Politiques Urbaines dans la Banlieue–Sud de Beyrouth*, Beirut: Center d'Etudes et de Recherches sur le Moyen Orient Contemporain.

Harik, I. 1994. "Pluralism in the Arab World," *Journal of Democracy* 5, 3: 43–56, July.

Hashi, Abdinur Nur. 1996. *Weapons and Clan Politics in Somalia*. Mogadishu, Somalia: Horn of Africa, 100–106

Hassan, B.D. 1999. "Ways of Strengthening Cooperation with International Human Rights NGOs," Working Paper, First Conference of the Arab Human Rights Movement, April 23–25, Casablanca.

Hassan, M. 1992. "Islam as Resistance Ideology among the Oromo of Ethiopia: The Wallo Case, 1700–1900," in Said Samatar, ed., *In the Shadow of Conquest: Islam in Colonial Northeast Africa*. Trenton, Red Sea, 75–101.

Hawkins, J. 1997. "The Palestinian NGO Trust Fund: An Alliance between NGOs and the World Bank." *Middle East International* 543 (February): 18–19.

Held, D. 1987. *Models of Democracy*. Stanford: Stanford University Press.

Hetata, S. 1997. "Mutilation, Identity, and Aid." Unpublished.

Hilal, J. 1998. *The Palestinian Political System After Oslo*. Ramallah: Muwatin, Institute for the Study of Democracy.

———. 1995. "The PLO: Crisis in Legitimacy," *Race and Class* 37, 2: 1–18.

Hiltermann, J. R. 1991. *Behind the Intifada: Labor and Women's Movements in the Occupied Territories*. Princeton: Princeton University Press.

Hirshman, A.O. 1971. "Underdevelopment, Obstacles to the Perception of Change, and Leadership," in *A Bias for Hope: Essays in Development and Latin America*. New Haven and London: Yale University Press, 342–360.

Hoodfar, H. 1999. *Between Marriage and the Market*. Cairo: The American University in Cairo Press.

Hulilat, S. 1991. "Dinamiyat al-tanmiya al-badila: nushu' al-munazzamat al-jamahiriya fi-l-aradi al-muhtalla wa tatawwurha," *Afaq filastiniya* 6 (Summer): 33–88.

Hulme, D. and M. Edwards, eds. 1997. *NGOs, States and Donors. Too close for comfort?* New York. Macmillan Press: 168–90.

Husscin, M.H. 1996. *And the Resistance Won*. Cairo: Yafa Center for Studies and Research.

Ianni, Octavio. 1995. Teorias da Globalização, Rio de Janeiro: Civilização Brasileira.

Ibn Khaldoun Center for Development, ed. 1995. *Civil Society in the Arab World Project*. Cairo: Dar al-Amin.

Ibrahim, F. 1995. "Die arabische Debatte ueber Zivilgesellschaft," in Ferhad Ibrahin and Heidi Wedel, eds., *Probleme der Zivilgesellschaft im Vorderen Orient*. Opladen: Leske and Budrich: 23–48.

Ibrahim, Saad Eddin. 1993. *al-Mujta' al-madani*. Cairo: Ibn Khaldoun Center.

———. 1995. "Civil Society and Prospects of Democratization in the Arab World," in A. R. Norton, ed., *Civil Society in the Middle East*, vol. 1. Leiden: E.J. Brill: 27–54.

Al-Ilwi, Said Ben Said. 1996. *Hal ta'ni al-dimuqratiya mahd al-tadawul 'ala al-sulta*. Conference on Ishkaliyyat ta'aththur al-tahawwul al-dimuqrati fi-l-watan al-'arabi. February 29–March 3, Cairo.

Information Center of al-Imdad Organization. 1992. *"Al Imdad" Organization in Lebanon: Giving Hands in Five Years*. Beirut: The Information Center of al-Imdad Organization.

Information Center of Jihad al-Bina'. 1990. *Jihad al-Bina' Development Association*. Beirut: The Information Center of Jihad al-Bina'.

———. 1995. *Faithfulness to the Resistance Society: Together We Resist, Together we Build*. Beirut: The Information Center of Jihad al-Bina'.

———. 1995. *The Giving Hand: Six Years of Jihad Al Bina': 1988–1994*. Beirut: The Information Center of Jihad al-Bina'.

Izraelwicz, E. 2000. "Demain, quel gouvernement pour le monde?" *Revue des deux mondes*, February: 42–49.

Al-Jabiri, A. 1997. "Ay dawr li-l-munazamat al-ahliya fi zaman al-khaskhasa wa-l-'awlama," Draft Paper, al-Mu'tamar al-thani li-l-munazamat al-ahliya al-'arabiya, Cairo.

Al-Jabri, M.A. 1993. "Ishkaliyat al-dimuqratiya wa-l-mujtama' al-madani fi-l-watan al-'arabi," *al-Mustaqbal al-'arabi* 167 (January). Beirut: Markaz Dirasat al-Wihda al-'Arabiya.

Jain, P.S. 1996. "Managing Credit for the Rural Poor: Lessons from the Grameen Bank." *World Development* 24, 1: 79–89.

Jamal, A. 1991. "Funding Fundamentalism: Sudan," *Review of African Political Economy*, no. 52, November, 103–109.

Jarbawi, A. 1995. "Munaqashat," in *al-Mujtama' al-madani wa-l-tahawul al-dimuqrati fi Filastin*. Ramallah: Muwatin.

Jessop, B. 1998. "The Rise of Governance and the Risks of Failure: The Case of Economic Development," *International Social Science Journal*, no. 155, 29–46.

Kandil, Amani. 1992. "al-Mujtama' al-madani fi Misr," in B. Ghalyun, ed., *al-Mujtama' al-madani fi-l-watan al-'arabi wa dawrihi fi tahqiq al-dimuqratiya*. Cairo: Markaz Dirasat al-Wihda al-'Arabiya.

Kandil, A. 1994. *al-Mujtam' al-madani fi-l-'alam al-'arabi: dirasat li-l-jam'iat al-ahliya al-'arabiya*. Washington: CIVICUS.

———. 1995a. *Civil Society in the Arab World*. Washington, D.C.: CIVICUS.

———. 1995b. *Dawr al-munazzamat al-ghayr hukumiya fi misr*. Cairo: Rasa'il al-Nida' al-Jadid.

Kasozi, A.B.K. 1986. *The Spread of Islam in Uganda*. Nairobi: Oxford University Press.

Kayunga, A. 1993. "Islamic Fundamentalism in Uganda: the Tabligh Youth Movement," in M. Mamdani and J. Oloka-Onyaango, eds., *Uganda: Studies in Living Conditions, Popular Movements and Constitutionalism*. Vienna: Journal für Entwicklungspolitik.

Keane, J. 1988. *Democracy and Civil Society*. New York: Verso.

Keohane, R.O. and E. Ostrom, eds. 1995. *Local Commons and Global Interdependance: Heterogeneity and Cooperation in Two Domains*. London: Sage Publications.

Al-Khafaji, I. 1993. "Beyond the Ultra-Nationalist State," *Middle East Report* 187/188 (March–April/May–June): 34–39.

Khalil, A.A. 1993. *al-Qawanin al-muqayida li-l-huquq al-madaniya wa-l-siyasiya fi-l-tashri al-misri*. Cairo: Egyptian Human Rights Organization.

El-Khawaga, D. 1997. "Les droits de l'homme en Egypte: Dynamiques de relocalisation d'une référence occidentale," *Egypte/Monde arabe* 30–31, 2-3: 233–34.

Kinely, R. 1995. *Sociology and Development: The Impasse and Beyond*. London: University of London College Press.

Klandermans, B. 1992. "The Social Construction of Protest and Multiorganizational Fields," in M.C. McClurg and A. Morris, eds., *Frontiers in Social Movements Theory*. New Haven and London: Yale University Press.

Koivusalo, M. and E. Ollila. 1997. *Making a Healthy World: Agencies, Actors and Politics in International Health*. London: Zed Books.

Kooiman, J. 1993. "Social-political governance," in *Modern Governance*. London: Sage Publications: 35–50.

Korani, B. and P. Noble. 1998. "Introduction: Arab Liberalization and Democratization—The Dialectics of the General and the Specific," in R. Brynen, B. Korani, and P. Noble, eds., *Political Liberalization and Democratization in the Arab World (vol. 2, Comparative Experiences)*. Boulder, CO: Lynne Riener Publishers: 1–10.

Korten, D. 1990. *Getting to the 21st Century: Voluntary Action and the Global Agenda*. West Hartford: Kumarian.

Kuechler, M. and R.J. Dalton. 1990. "New Social Movements and the Political Order: Inducing Change for Long-term Stability?" in R.J. Dalton and M. Kuechler, eds., *Challenging the Political Order: New Social and Political Movements in Western Democracies*. Cambridge: Polity, 277–300.

Laidi, Z. 1994. *Un monde prive de sens*. Paris: Fayard.

———. 1998. "Les imaginaires de la mondialisation," *Esprit* (October).

———. 1999. "Pourquoi vivons–nous dans l'urgence," *Études* (June).

Lamchichi, A. 1994. *Islam, Islamisme et Modernite*. Paris: L'Harmattan.

Leca, J. 1996. "Gouvernance et institutions publiques. L'Etat entre sociétés nationales et globalisation," in De Foucauld J.B and Fraissier, ed., *La France en prospectives*. Paris: Odile Jacob: 317–50.

Leftwich, A. 1993. "Governance, democracy and development," *Third World Quarterly* 14: 605–24.

Lesh, A.M. 1996. "The Destruction of Civil Society in the Sudan," in R. Norton, ed., *Civil Society in the Middle East*, vol. 2. New York: E.J. Brill.

Lewis, I.M. 1984. "Sufism in Somaliland: A Study in Tribal Islam," in A.S. Ahmed, and D.M. Hart, eds., *Islam in Tribal Societies, From the Atlas to the Indus.* London: Routledge and Kegan Paul, 127–68.

———. 1994, *Blood and Bone: The Call of Kinship in Somalian Society.* Lawrenceville, NJ, Red Sea Press.

———. 1998. *Saints and Somalis. Popular Islam in a Clan-Based Society.* London: Haan.

Lipton, M. 1988. *Successes in Anti-Poverty.* Issues in Development, Discussion Paper 8. Geneva: International Labour Office.

Lorrain, D. 1998. "Administrer, gouverner, réguler," *Annales de la recherche urbaine* 80/81: 85–92.

Luling, V. 1997. "Come back Somalia? Questioning a Collapsed State," *Third World Quarterly*, 18(2).

Lustiger-Thaler, H. 1989. "State and Civil Society Counterpoints: Variations on a Theme," *Canadian Journal of Political and Social Theory* 13, 3 (Autumn): 121–31.

Lustiger-Thaler, H. and L. Maheu. 1995. "Social Movements and the Challenge of Urban Politics," in L. Maheu, ed., *Social Movements and Social Classes: The Future of Collective Action.* London: Sage: 151–68.

MacDonald, L. 1994. "Globalizing Civil Society: Interpreting International NGOs in Central America," *Millennium: Journal of International Studies* 23: 267–85.

Madani, A. 1997. "Tashriat wa qawanin al-munazzamat al-ahliya al-'arabiya," al-Mu'tamar al-thani li-l-munazzamat al-ahliya al-'arabiya, Technical Paper, Conference on Legislation and Laws of NGOs, May 17–19, Cairo.

Maheu, L. 1991. "Les nouveaux mouvements sociaux entre les voies de l'identité et les enjeux du politique," in L. Maheu and A. Sales, eds., *La recomposition du politique.* Montreal: Presses de l'Université de Montréal (PUM): 163–92.

———. 1992. "Mouvements sociaux et politiques. Les enjeux d'une articulation entre grandes problématiques du politique," in G. Boismenu, P. Hamel and G. Labica, eds., *Les formes modernes de la démocratie.* Montreal: Presses de l'Université de Montréal (PUM): 210–24.

——— (with the collaboration of H. Lustiger-Thaler). 1995. "Les mouvements sociaux: Plaidoyer pour une sociologie de l'ambivalence," in F. Dubet and M. Wieviorka, eds., *Penser le sujet autour d'Alain Touraine.* Paris: Fayard, 313–34.

———, ed. 1995. *Social Movements and Social Classes: The Future of Collective Action.* London: Sage.

March, J.G. and J.P. Olsen. 1995. *Democratic Governance.* New York: The Free Press, 2–5.

Markakis, John. 1997. "The Somali in the New Political Order of Ethiopia," in Hussein Mohamed Adam and Richard Ford, eds., *Mending Rips in the Sky. Options for Somali Communities in the 21st Century.* Lawrenceville, NJ: Red Sea Press, 497–513.

Markaz al-Buhuth al-'arabiya, ed. 1992. "Qadaya al-mujtama' al-madani fi daw' utruhat gramshi." Proceedings of a conference. Cairo: Markaz al-Buhuth al-'Arabiya.

Markaz Dirasat al-Wahda al-'arabiya, ed. 1992. "al-Mujtama' al-madani fi-l-watan al-'arabi wa dawrahu fi tahqiq al-dimuqratiya," Proceedings of a conference. Beirut: Markaz Dirasat al-Wihda al-'Arabiya.

Martin, B.G. 1969. "Muslim Politics and Resistance to Colonial Rule: Sheikh Uways B. Muhammad Al-Barawi and the Qadiriya Brotherhood in East Africa," *African Journal of History* 10(3): 471–86.

———. 1992. "Sheikh Zaylai and the Nineteenth-Century Somali Qadiriya," in Said Samatar, ed., *In the Shadow of Conquest: Islam in Colonial Northeast Africa*. Trenton: Red Sea: 11–32.

———. 1996. *Muslim Politics and Resistance to Colonial Rule: Shaykh Uways B. Muḥammad al-Barawi and the Qhadariya Brotherhood in East Africa*. Trenton, NJ: Red Sea.

Marzouk, M. 1997. "The Associative Phenomenon in the Arab World: Engine of Democratisation or Witness to the Crisis," in D. Hulme and M. Edwards, eds., *Too Close for Comfort? NGOs, States and Donors*. London: Macmillan Press: 191–201.

Al-Masri, S. 1998 and 1999. *Tatbia' wa tamwil: qissat al-jam'iyat ghayr al-hukumiya*, vols. 1 and 2. Cairo: Markaz al-Nadim li-l-Abhath wa-l-Ma'lumat.

Al-Maytami, M.A.W. 1999. "La réforme économique au Yémen: résultats et implications," in R. Leveau, F. Mermier, and U. Steinbach, eds., *Le Yémen Contemporain*. Paris: Karthala: 339–64.

McAdam, D. 1982. *Political Process and the Development of Black Insurgency, 1930–1970*. Chicago: University of Chicago Press.

McAdam, D. and A.D. Snow, eds. 1997. *Social Movements: Readings on their Emergence, Mobilization, and Dynamics*. Los Angeles: Roxbury Publishing.

McAdam, D., J.D. McCarthy, and M. Zald, eds. 1996. *Comparative Perspectives on Social Movements: Political Opportunities, Mobilizing Structures, and Cultural Framings*. Cambridge, UK: Cambridge University Press.

McAdam, D., S. Tarrow, and C. Tilly. 1998. "Pour une cartographie de la politique contestataire," *Politix* "Les Sciences du Politique aux Etats—Unis. II—Domaines et actualités," 41: 7–32.

McCarthy, J. and M. Zald. 1977. "Resource Mobilization and Social Movement A Partial Theory," *American Journal of Sociology* 82, 6: 1212–41.

Meister, A. 1969. *Participation, animation et développement*, Paris: Anthropos.

Melucci, A. 1988. "Social Movements and the Democratization of Everyday Life," in J. Keane, ed., *Civil Society and the State: New European Perspectives*. London: Verso: 245–260.

Meyer, J.W., and W.R. Scott, eds. 1992. *Organizational Environments: Ritual and Rationality*. Newbury Park, London, New Delhi: Sage Publications.

Milani, C. 1999. "La globalisation, les organisations internationales, le débat sur la gouvernance," Gemdev, Groupement d'intérêt scientifique pour l'étude de la Mondialisation et du Développement, *Mondialisation, les mots et les choses*. Paris: Khartala.

———. 2001. "Les différentes dimensions de la globalisation et l'essai d'une régulation par le marché," *Cahiers du Brésil Contemporain* Ecole des Hautes Etudes de Sciences Sociales (EHESS) No. 41/42. Centre de recherches sur le Brésil contemporain, Paris.

Ministry of Planning and Development, Yemen, and UNDP. 1998: *Yemen: Human Development Report 1998*. Sana'a: Ministry of Planning and Development and UNDP.

Mohamed-Abdi, Mohamed. 1997. "Somalia: Kinship and Relationships Derived from It," in Hussein Mohamed Adam and Richard Ford, eds., *Mending Rips in the Sky: Options for Somali Communities in the 21st Century.* Lawrenceville, NJ: Red Sea Press.

Mohamedou, M.M. 1998. "Transformation et démocratisation politiques: nouveaux schémas d'interaction entre l'administration publique et la société civile en Afrique du Nord," *Revue internationale des sciences administratives* 64, 1: 85–96.

Moore, M. 1993. "Good government? Introduction," *IDS Bulletin* 24, 1: 1–6.

MOPIC. 1998. *MOPIC's 1998 First Quarterly Monitoring Report of Donors' Assistance.* Ramallah: Ministry of Planning and International Cooperation (MOPIC).

Moussali, A. 1995. "Modern Islamic Fundamentalist Discourses on Civil Society, Pluralism and Democracy," in R. Norton, ed., *Civil Society in the Middle East.* New York: E.J. Brill.

Muhamad A.M. 1997. "Somalia: Kinship and Relationships derived from it," in H.M. Adam and R. Ford, eds., *Mending Rips in the Sky: Options for Somali Communities in the 21st century.* Lawrenceville, NJ: Red Sea Press.

———. 1997. "Retrospective de la crise somalienne et rehabilitation de la societe civile," in A.M. Muhamad and P. Bernard, eds., *Pour une culture de la paix en Somalie, Paris, Actes du second congrès international des études somaliennes,* October 25–27, 1995, Paris.

Mukhtar, Mohamed Haji. 1995. "Islam in Somalia in History: Fact and Fiction," in A.A. Jimal, ed., *The Invention of Somalia.* Lawrenceville, NJ: Red Sea Press

———. 1996. "The Plight of the Agro–Pastoral Society in Somalia," *Review of African Political Economy* 23(70), December, 543–53.

Nakhleh, Khalil. 1998. "A critical look at foreign funding to Palestine: Where is it heading?" in Nader Izzat, ed., *Funding Palestinian Development.* Birzeit: Birzeit University, Planning for Development Series.

———. 1998. "A critical look at foreign funding to Palestine: Where is it heading?" in N.I. Said, ed., *Funding Palestinian Development.* Planning for Development Series. Birzeit: Birzeit University.

Nasr, S. 1985. "La Transition des Chiites vers Beyrouth: Mutations sociales et Mobilisation Communautaire à la veille de 1975," in *Mouvements Communautaires et Espaces Urbains dans le Mashreq,* Beirut: Center d'Etudes et de Recherches sur le Moyen Orient Contemporain.

Neveu, E. 1996. *Sociologie des mouvements sociaux.* Paris: La Découverte.

New Woman Research and Study Center. 1996. *The Feminist Movement in the Arab World: Intervention and Studies from Four Countries.* Cairo: Dar al-Mustaqbal al-'Arabi.

———, ed. 1998. *al-Mara'a wa-l-qanun wa-l-tanmiya.* Cairo: New Woman Research Center.

———. 1999. "Misr: al-mar'a fi-l-munazzamat al-ahliya," in Arab NGO Network, al-*Mar'a fi-l-munazzamat al-ahliya al-'arabiya.* Cairo: Dar al-Mustaqbal al-'Arabi.

Nicholson, M. 1994. "L'influence de l'individu sur le système international. Considération sur les structures," in M. Girard, ed., *Les Individus dans la politique internationale.* Paris: Economica.

Norton, A. R. 1995–96. *Civil Society in the Middle East*, vols. 1 and 2. Leiden; New York: E.J. Brill.
———. 1987. *Amal and the Shi'a*. Austin: University of Texas Press.
Nunnenkamp, P. 1995. "What donors mean by good governance," *IDS Bulletin* 26, 2: 9–16.
Oberschall, A. 1973. *Social Conflict and Social Movements*. Englewood Cliffs: Prentice Hall.
———. 1993. *Social Movements: Ideologies, Interests and Identities*. New Brunswick, NJ: Transaction Publishers.
Offe, C. 1990. "Reflections on the Institutional Self-transformation of Movement Politics: A Tentative Model," in R.J. Dalton and M. Kuechler, eds., *Challenging the Political Order. New Social and Political Movements in Western Democracies*. Cambridge: Polity: 232–50.
———. 1997. *Les démocraties Modernes à l'Epreuve*. Paris: L'Harmattan.
Osmont, A. 1998. "La Governance—concept mou, politique ferm," *Annales de la recherche urbaine* 80/81.
Ottaway, M. and T. Chung. 1999. "Debating Democracy Assistance: Toward a New Paradigm," *Journal of Democracy* 10, 4 (October): 99–113.
Organization for Economic Cooperation and Development (OCDE), Development Co-operation Directorate (DAC). 1993. *Orientations on Participatory Development and Good Governance*. Paris: OCDE/GD, 191.
Palecon, 1998. "Project Profile: Palestinian NGO Project," http://www.palecon.org/update/dec98/profile.html.
Palestinian NGO Network. 1994. "Risala ikhbariya." Jerusalem: Palestinian NGO Network.
Pérouse de Montclos, Marc-Antoine. 2000. "Villes en guerre en Somalie, Mogadiscio et Hargesia," *Les dossiers du Cesped* 9.
PNGO. 1995. "A Suggested Framework for Relations between Palestinian NGOs and the Palestinian Authority," in *Perspective on the PNGO Network* (PNGO Newsletter). Jerusalem: Palestinian NGO Network.
PNGO. 1997. "More on Legislation concerning Charitable Societies, Social Bodies and Private Associations," in *Perspective on the PNGO Network*, PNGO Newsletter. Jerusalem: Palestinian NGO Network.
Pouligny, B. 2001. "Acteurs et enjeux d'un processus equivoque," *Critique internationale* 13 (October): 163–76.
Pouwels, Randall L. 1987. *Horn and Crescent: Cultural Change and Traditional Islam on the East African Coast, 800–1900*. London: Cambridge University Press.
Powell, W.W. and P.J. DiMaggio. 1991. *The New Institutionalism in Organizational Analysis*. Chicago: University of Chicago Press.
Pratt, N. 2000. "Labor, State, and Economic Liberalization: Hegemony and Counter hegemony," *Arab Studies Journal* VIII: 2.
Putnam, R.D. 1993. *Making Democracy Work: Civic Traditions in Modern Italy*. Princeton, NJ: Princeton University Press.
———. 1995. "Bowling Alone: America's Declining Social Capital," *Journal of Democracy* 6, 1 (January): 65–78.

Qandil, A., and Ben Néfissa, S. 1995. *al-Jam'iyat al-ahliya fi Misr*. Cairo: Al-Ahram Center for Political and Strategic Studies.

Quandt, W. 1998. *Between Ballots and Bullets: Algeria's Transition from Authoritarianism*. Washington, D.C.: Brookings Institution Press.

Raghe, Abdirahman Osman. 1997. "Somali NGOs: A Product of Crisis," in Hussein Mohamed Adam and Richard Ford, ed., *Mending Rips in the Sky, Options for Somali Communities in the 21st Century*. Laurenceville, NJ: Red Sea Press.

Rhodes, R.A.W. 1996. "The New Governance: Governing Without Government." *Political Studies* 44, 4: 652–67.

Richards, A. 1995. "Economic Pressures for Accountable Governance in the Middle East and North Africa," in A. R. Norton, ed., *Civil Society in the Middle East*, vol. 1. Leiden: E.J. Brill: 55–78.

Rieff, D. 1999. "The False Dawn of Civil Society," *The Nation*. February 22: 11–16.

Robinson, G.E. 1993. "The Role of the Professional Middle Class in the Mobilization of Palestinian Society: The Medical and Agricultural Committees," *International Journal of Middle East Studies* 25, 2 (May): 301–26.

Robinson, M. 1993. "Governance, Democracy and Conditionality: NGOs and the New Policy Agenda," in A. Clayton, ed., *Governance, Democracy and Conditionality: What Role for NGOs?* Oxford: INTRAC.

———. 1994. "Governance, Democracy and Conditionality: NGOs and the New Policy Agenda," in A. Clayton, ed., *Governance, Democracy and Conditionality: What Role for NGOs?* Oxford: INTRAC Publication, 35–53.

———. 1995. "Strengthening Civil Society in Africa: The Role of Foreign Political Aid," *Ids Bulletin* 26: 70–81.

———. 1997. *Building a Palestinian State: 'The Incomplete Revolution.'* Bloomington: Indiana University Press.

Roca, P.J. 1996. "Moins d'État et plus d'ONG?" in S. Cordellier, ed., *La fin du tiers–monde?* Paris: La Découverte.

———. 1995. "Le masque de l'urgence," *Courrier de la Planète* 27.

Roche, M. 1995. "Rethinking Citizenship and Social Movements: Themes in Contemporary Sociology and Neoconservative Ideology," in L. Maheu, ed., *Social Movements and Social Classes. The Future of Collective Action*. London: Sage: 186–219.

Roman, S. 2000. "La 'bonne gouvernance' pierre philosophale du développement économique?" *L 'Economie Politique* 6: 39–51.

Rose, Richard and Guy Peters. 1978. *Can Government Go Bankrupt?* New York: Basic Books.

Rosenau, J.N. 1992. "Governance, order, and change in world politics," in J. Rosenau and E.O. Czempiel, eds., *Governance Without Government: Order and Change in World Politics*. Cambridge, UK: Cambridge University Press: 1–29.

———. 1995. "Governance in the Twenty-first Century," *Global Governance* 1: 13–43.

———. 1997. *Along the Domestic–Foreign Frontier, Exploring Governance in a Turbulent World*. Cambridge, UK: Cambridge University Press.

Rougier, B. 1999. "Yémen 1990–1994: la logique du pacte politique mise en échec," in Leveau, R., F. Mermier, and U. Steinbach, eds., *Le Yémen Contemporain*. Paris: Karthala: 101–60.

Roy, S. 1996. "Civil Society in the Gaza Strip: Obstacles to Social Reconstruction," in A. R. Norton, ed., *Civil Society in the Middle East*. Leiden: E.J. Brill.

Rubin, B. 1999. *The Transformation of Palestinian Politics: From Revolution to State–Building*. Cambridge, MA: Harvard University Press.

Rucht, D. 1988. "Themes, Logics, and Arenas of Social Movements. A Structural Approach," *International Social Movement Research* 1: 305–29.

El-Saadawi, N. 1980. *The Hidden Face of Eve: Women in the Muslim World*. London: Zed Books.

———. 1997. *The Nawal El-Saadawi Reader*. London: Zed Books.

Sadowski, Y. 1993. "The New Orientalism and the Democracy Debate," *Middle East Report* 183 (July–August): 14–21, 40.

Salamé, G. 1991. "Sur la causalité d'un _otali: Pourquoi le monde arabe n'est–il pas démocratique?" *Revue française de Science politique*, 41, 3 (June): 307–41.

Salamon, L. M. 1987. "Of Market Failure, Voluntary Failure, and Third-Party Government: Toward a Theory of Government Non-profit Relations in the Welfare State," in: S.A. Ostrander and S. Langton, eds., *Shifting the Debate: Public/Private Sector Relations in the Modern Welfare State*. New Brunswick, NJ: Transaction Books, 29–49.

———. 1993. *The Global Associational Revolution: the Rise of the Third Sector on the World Scene*. Occasional Papers 15. Baltimore: Institute for Policy Studies, Johns Hopkins University.

Salamon, L.M., H.K. Anheier, R. List, S. Toepler, S.W. Sokolowski and Associates. 1999. *Global Civil Society: Dimensions of the Nonprofit Sector*. Baltimore, MD: The Johns Hopkins Center for Civil Society Studies.

Salem, A. 1991. *In Defense of the Freedom of Association*. Cairo: Legal Research and Resource Center.

Samatar, Ahmed I. 1994. "The Curse of Allah: Civic Disembowelment and the Collapse of the State in Somalia," in Ahmed I. Samatar, ed., *The Somali Challenge. From Catastrophe to Renewal*. Boulder, CO: Lynne Rienner, 95–146.

Samatar, Said. 1992. "Sheikh Uways Muhammad of Baraawe, 1847–1909: Mystic and Reformer in East Africa," in Said Samator, ed., *In the Shadow of Conquest: Islam in Colonial Northeast Africa*. Trenton: Red Sea, 48–74.

Al-Saqour, M. 1999a: "Poverty Policy Framework for Yemen; Strategy Paper." Sana'a: Unpublished

———. 1999b. "Operational Plan for the Preparation, Formulation and Implementation of NAPPE." Unpublished final draft. Sana'a: National Action Plan for Poverty Eradication in Yemen (NAPPE).

———. 1999c. "Capacity building of SSN (Social Safety Nets)." Unpublished final draft. Sana'a: National Poverty Alleviation and Employment Generation Programme of Yemen.

Al-Saqqaf, A. B. 1999. "La Constitution du Yémen réunifié," in R. Leveau, F. Mermier, and U. Steinbach, eds., *Le Yémen Contemporain*. Paris: Karthala: 161–68.

Al-Sayyid, M.K. 1995. "The Concept of Civil Society and the Arab World," in R. Brynen, B. Korany, and P. Noble, eds., *Political Liberalization and Democratization in the Arab World: Volume 1—Theoretical Perspectives*. Boulder, CO: Lynne Rienner Publishers.

———. 1999. "Helping Out is Hard to Do," *Foreign Policy* (Winter): 25.

Schein, E. 1992. *Organizational Culture and Leadership*. San Francisco: Jossey-Bass Publishers.

Schiddler, G. 1997. "al-Mujtama' al-madani wa dirasat al-siyasa fi-l-Sharq al-Awsat," *Al-mujtama' al-madani wa-l-hayat al-siyasiya al-urduniya*. Amman: Markaz al-Urdun al-Jadid li-l-Dirasat.

Schneider, H. 1999. "Gouvernance participative: le chaînon manquant dans la lutte contre la pauvreté?" Paris: Cahier de politique économique, 17.

Scott, A. 1990. *Ideology and the New Social Movements*. London: Unwin Hyman.

Scott, W.R. 1992. "The Organization of Environments: Network, Cultural, and Historical Elements," in J. W. Meyer and W.R. Scott, eds., *Organizational Environments: Ritual and Rationality*. Newbury Park, London, New Delhi: Sage Publications, 155–75.

Sen, A. 1994. "Food and Freedom." Text of Third Sir John Crawford Lecture given at the Eugene Black Auditorium of the World Bank. Washington D.C.: The World Bank.

———. 1996. "The Political Economy of Targeting," in Bominique van de Walle and Kimberley Nead, eds., *Public Spending and the Poor*. Washington D.C.: World Bank, 11–24.

Sha'aban, A.H. 1999. "Economic Sanctions and Human Rights," Working Paper, First Conference of the Arab Human Rights Movement, April 23–25, Casablanca.

Shalan, Thaira. 1999. "Les organisations non gouvernementales et la société civile au Yémen," in Leveau, R., F. Mermier, and U. Steinbach, eds., *Le Yémen Contemporain*. Paris: Karthala: 285–300.

Shammas, C. 1994. "The Scenarios I Prefer Were Not Possible," *Middle East Report* 186 (January–February): 15–17.

Sharara, W. 1997. *The Hizballah Nation: Lebanon as an Islamic Society*. Beirut: Dar al-Nahar.

Sheikh-Abdi, Abdi. 1992. *Divine Madness: Mohammed Abdulle Hassan, 1856–1920*. London: Zed Books.

Shukr, Abd al-Gaffar. 1996. "Min al-istibdad ila-l-dimuqratiya fi-l-watan al-'arabi," *al-Nahj* 44, 12 (Summer–Autumn): 9–26.

———, ed. 1997. *al-Jam'iyat al-ahliya wa azmat al-tanmiya al-iqtisadiya wa-l-ijtima'iya fi Misr*, 1st ed. Cairo: Markaz al-Buhuth al-'Arabiya.

Skocpol, T. 1991. "Targeting within Universalism: Politically Viable Policies to Combat Poverty in the United States," in C. Jencks and P.E. Peterson, eds., *The Urban Underclass*. Washington D.C.: The Brookings Institute.

Slaiby, G. 1993. "Les Actions collectives de résistance civile à la guerre," in F. Kiwan, ed., *Le Liban aujourd'hui*. Beirut and Paris: Centre d'Etudes et de Recherches sur le

Moyent Orient (CERMOC) and Centre National de Recherche Scientifique (CNRS).

Smilie, I. and H. Helmich, eds. 1999. *Stakeholders: Government–NGO Partnerships for International Development.* London: Earthscan.

Smouts, M.C. 1995. *Les organisations internationales.* Paris: Armand Colin.

———. 1999. "Démocratie et Gouvernance Mondiale," Technical Paper, United Nation Educational, Scientific and Cultural Organization (UNESCO) General Conference, Paris.

Snow, D. et al. 1986. "Frame Alignment Processes, Micromobilization and Movement participation," *American Sociological Review* 51, 4: 464–81.

Stewart, S. 1997. "Happy Ever After in the Marketplace: Non-government Organisations and Uncivil Society," *Review of African Political Economy* 71: 11–34.

Stinchcombe, A. 1965. "Social Structures and Organizations," in J. March, ed. *Handbook of Organizations.* Chicago: Rand McNally.

Stork, J. and B. Doumani. 1994. "After Oslo." *Middle East Report* 186 (January–February): 2–4.

Stocker G. 1998. "Cinq propositions pour une theorie de la gouvernance," *Revue Internationale des sciences sociales*, No. 155 Paris: UNESCO.

Sullivan, D.J. 1993. *Private Voluntary Organizations in Egypt. Islamic Development, Private Initiative and State Control.* Gainesville, FL: University Press of Florida.

Sullivan, D.J. 1995. *Non–governmental organizations and freedom of association: Palestine and Egypt, a comparative analysis.* Jerusalem: PASSIA.

Swayne, H.G.C. 1985. *Seventeen Trips through Somaliland: A Record of Exploration and Big Game Shooting, 1885–1893.* London: Rowland Ward.

Tamari, Salim. 1991. "The Palestinian Movement in Transition: Historical Reversals and the Uprising," *Journal of Palestine Studies* 20, 2 (Winter): 57–70.

———. 1992. "Left in Limbo. Leninist Heritage and Islamist Challenge," *Middle East Report* 179 (November–December): 16–21.

———. 1995. "Fading Flags. The Crises of Palestinian Legitimacy," *Middle East Report* 194/195 (May–June/July–August): 10–12.

Taraki, L. 1989. "Mass Organizations in the West Bank," in N. Aruri, ed., *Occupation: Israel Over Palestine*, 2nd ed. Belmont: Association of Arab-American University Graduates (AAUG): 431–63.

———. 1990. "The Development of Political Consciousness Among Palestinians in the Occupied Territories, 1967–1987," in J.R. Nassar and R. Heacock, eds., *Intifada: Palestine at the Crossroads.* New York: Praeger: 53–71.

Tarrow, S. 1989. *Democracy and Disorder. Protest and Politics in Italy, 1965 1975.* Oxford: Oxford University Press.

———. 1996. "States and opportunities, the political structuring of social movements," in D. McAdam, M.J. McCarthy, and M. Zald, eds., *Comparative Perspectives on Social Movements: Political Opportunities, Mobilizing Structures, and Cultural Framings.* Cambridge, UK: Cambridge University Press: 41–61.

———. 1998. *Power in Movement. Social Movements and Contentious Politics*, 2nd ed. Cambridge, UK: Cambridge University Press.

Tendler, J. 1982. *Turning Private Voluntary Organizations into Development Agencies: Questions for Evaluation.* A.I.D. Program Evaluation Discussion Paper 12. United States Agency for International Development, PN-AAJ-612, April.

———. 1997. *Good Government in the Tropics.* London: John Hopkins University Press.

Thabit, A. 1996. *al-Mujtama' wa-l-dawla fi-l-watan al-'arabi fi zil al-siyasat al ra's maliya al-jadida.* Cairo: Madbuli.

Tilly, C. 1978. *From mobilization to revolution,* Reading, MA: Addison-Wesley.

———. 1986. *La France conteste de 1600 à nos jours.* Paris: Fayard.

Touraine, A. 1978. *La voix et le regard.* Paris: Seuil.

———. 1984. *Le Retour de l'Acteur.* Paris; Fayard.

———. 1984. *Le retour de l'acteur. Essai de sociologie.* Paris: Fayard.

———. 1995. "Democracy: From a Politics of Citizenship to a Politics of Recognition," in L. Maheu, ed., *Social Movements and Social Classes: The Future of Collective Action.* London: Sage: 258–75.

———. 1999. *Comment sortir du libéralisme?* Paris: Fayard.

Traugott, M., ed. 1995. *Repertoires and Cycles of Collective Action.* Durham, London: Duke University Press.

Turton, E.R. 1969. "The impact of Muhamad Abdil Hassan on the East of African Protectorate," *Journal of African History* 10, 7: 641–57.

UNDP. 1996. *Governance for Sustainable Human Development, a UNDP Policy Document.* September (published online at www.undp.org). UNDP: Management Development and Governance Division.

UNDP. 1998. *Yemen—Development Cooperation 1998 Report.* Published online, www.undp.org.

UNDP. 1999. *Human Development Report 1999.* New York, Oxford: Oxford University Press for UNDP.

UNESCO. 1998. "Governance." *International Social Science Journal* 155 (March).

UNICEF. 1994. *Strategy Paper on the Strengthening and Promotion of Egyptian NGOs.* Cairo: UNICEF.

United States Institute of Peace. 1999. *Removing Barricades in Somalia.* Washington D.C.: United States Institute of Peace.

USAID. 1994a. *Final Evaluation of the US–Egypt Cooperative Health Program.* Cairo: USAID.

———. 1994b. "NGO Participation in Municipal Decision Making: Limitations and Potential in Tunisia" (report prepared by R. Payne). Washington, D.C.: USAID, Global Bureau, Center for Governance and Democracy.

———, Mission For West Bank and Gaza. 1999a. "Annual Program Statement: Civil Society Program," http://www.usaid–wbg.org/.

———, Mission For West Bank and Gaza. 1999b. "Annual Program Statement: Community Services Program," http://www.usaid–wbg.org/.

———. 1995. "Strengthening NGOs for Democratization and Sustainable Development in Morocco: an NGO Assessment." Unpublished report by R. Payne. Washington, DC: USAID.

———. 1995. *PVO Development Project. Evaluation Report.* Cairo: USAID.

———. 1998. "USAID Announcement," in *al-Ayam*, February 7, Yemen.

———. 2000. "Report on the final evaluation of the USAID-supported Private and Voluntary Organization Development Project." Cairo: USAID Office of Human Development and Democracy, Democracy and Participation Division.

Usher, G. 1995. *Palestine in Crisis: The Struggle for Peace and Political Independence after Oslo.* London: Pluto.

———. 1997. "Fatah and the PA's Crisis of Legitimacy," *News from Within* 13, 5 (May): 13–15.

Van Wicklin III, W. 1987. "Challenging the Conventional Wisdom About Private Voluntary Organizations as Agents of Grassroots Development," Draft Paper, 28th Annual Convention, International Studies Association, April 16, 1987, Washington D.C.

Van Rooy, A., ed. 1998. *Civil Society and the Aid Industry: The Politics and Promise.* London: Earthscan.

Vivian, J. and Gladys Maseko. 1994. "NGOs, Participation, and Rural Development: Testing the Assumptions with Evidence from Zimbabwe," United Nations Research Institute for Social Development Discussion Paper DP 49, January.

Wallerstein, Emmanuel, et al. 1991. *al-Idtirab al-kabir*, 1st ed. Beirut: Dar al-Farabi.

Waltz, S. 1995. *Human Rights and Reform.* Berkeley: University of California Press, 220–25.

Weiner, M. 1998. *The Clash of Norms: Dilemmas in Refugee Policies.* Cambridge: Massachusetts Institute of Technology, The Rosemarie Rogers Working Paper Series.

Whaites, A. 2000. "Let's Get Civil Society Straight: NGOs, the State, and Political Theory," in D. Eade, ed., *Development, NGOs, and Civil Society.* Oxford: Oxfam: 124–41.

White, S. 2000. "Depoliticising Development: The Uses and Abuses of Participation," in D. Eade, ed., *Development, NGOs, and Civil Society.* Oxford: Oxfam: 142–55.

Wiktorowicz, Q. 1999. "The Limits of Democracy in the Middle East: The Case of Jordan," *Middle East Journal* 53, 4 (Autumn): 606–20

Wilson, D. 1998. "From Local Government to Local Governance: Re–casting British Local Democracy," *Democratization* 5, 1 (Spring): 90–115.

Wilson, J. 1989. *Bureaucracy: What Government Agencies Do and Why They Do It.* New York: Basic Books, HarperCollins Publishers.

Wilson, R. 1983. *Banking and Finance in the Arab Middle East.* London: St Martin's Press.

Wood, E.M. 1990. "The Uses and Abuses of 'Civil Society,'" *Socialist Register* 26: 60–84.

Wood, G. 1997. "States Without Citizens: The Problem of the Franchise States," in D. Hulme and M. Edwards, ed., *NGOs, States and Donors: Too close for comfort?* New York and London: Macmillan Press, 79–92.

World Bank. 1999. *What is Social Capital?* Washington D.C.: The World Bank.

———. 1987. *Financing Health Services in Developing Countries—An Agenda for Reform.* Washington D.C.: World Bank.

———. 1993. *World Development Report. Investing in Health.* Washington D.C.: World Bank.

———. 1994. *Egypt PVO Sector Study. Financial Profile of Egypt's PVO Sector.* Washington D.C.: World Bank

———. 1994. *Governance and Development* (November). Washington D.C.: World Bank.

———. 1995, "Egypt PVO Sector Study. PVO Social Assistance: Direct Aid to the Poor," Washington D.C.: World Bank.

———. 1997. *Country Report: Lebanon.* Washington, D.C.: World Bank.

———. 1998. "Partnership for Development: Proposed actions for the World Bank— A Discussion Paper: Partnerships Group-Strategy and Resource Management."

———. 1999. *Country Assistance Strategy of the World Bank Group for the Republic of Yemen: report 19073–YEM.* Washington, D.C.: World Bank.

Yahya, M. 1994. "Forbidden Spaces, Invisible Barriers: Housing in Beirut," Ph.D. diss., Open University, The Architecture Association.

Yemeni Center for Strategic Studies. 1998. *Annual Report, Yemen 1998.* Sana'a: Yemeni Center for Strategic Studies.

Yunan, Y.L. 1975. *Tarikh al-wizarat al-misriya.* Cairo: Al-Ahram Center for Strategic and Political Studies.

Zald, M.N. and J.D. McCarthy, eds. 1979. *The Dynamic of Social Movements.* Cambridge, MA: Winthrop Publishers.

———. 1987. *Social Movements in an organizational society.* New Brunswick, NJ: Transaction Books.

Zimmerman, R.F. 1998. *Dollars, Diplomacy and Development: Dilemmas of US Economic Aid.*